"*The WealthTech Book* gives in depth and valuable insights about the transformation of the wealth management industry. By showcasing several examples of new digital solutions and technology driven changes the book and its renowned authors deep dive into the subject."

Marc P. Bernegger, Fintech- and Crypto-Entrepreneur and Investor

"Like most other industries, the banking industry has had to deal with digitization, disruptive innovations and regulatory changes during the last years. New players entered the market, which facilitated the simplification of products and processes in this customer centric business field. In this constantly changing environment it's easy to lose track of the current trends of state-of-the-art, cutting-edge technology.

Asset management has not been exempted from these disruptive ongoing trends. Robo-advisory even though still unclear in which ways it will add-value to customers will undoubtedly garner much attention. *The WealthTech Book* provides a great insight on the ongoing changes in the financial industry, especially on the topics of Wealth Management, Digital Platforms, Ecosystems, Blockchain and many more."

Dr Peter Bosek, Chief Retail Officer, Erste Group AG

"FinTech has the potential to significantly alter the financial landscape, enabling financial inclusion and lifting wealth management to a new level. This book provides an in-depth overview of the multiple facets how FinTech will change wealth management – a valuable guide to professionals, regulators, and everyone interested in the future of finance."

Prof. Dr Markus Brunnermeier, Director Bendheim Center for Finance, Princeton University

"The wealth management industry has reached a turning point fuelled by new technologies and greater access to information for both traditional and new investors. The industry is now challenged with searching far and wide for alpha in an increasingly regulated world – while also managing the complexities that come with better informed and empowered investors. This convergence has led to some of the most innovative investment solutions and services seen in decades. It has also set the stage for the next turning point: the gradual transference of wealth from baby boomers to digital-savvy millennials."

David Craig, President, Financial and Risk, Thomson Reuters

"Everybody talks about Block[...] few people know how to impl[...] *The WealthTech Book* is the u[...] technologies can be applied [...] institutional clients worldwide. [...] 'black book' of the leading FinTech and WealthTech thought-leaders globally. Every investor should have it on his/her bedside table."

John Davies, CEO, Just Loans Group PLC and Chairman, Kompli-Global Ltd

"Wealth management is at the dawn of a huge revolution: digitization is changing the customer journey value chain and business models of modern wealth management. The crowdsourced book tells you why and how the change will happen."

Prof. Dr Oliver Gassmann, Director, Institute of Technology Management, University of St. Gallen

"This book is the first of its kind to give a comprehensive overview on the future developments in this evolving field. WealthTech is of highest relevance for SIX which combines expertise at the intersection of financial services and technology by providing securities trading, clearing and settlement, as well as financial information and payment transactions. Our owners which consist of financial institutions rely on us to provide them with innovative solutions in the field of WealthTech as well as FinTech and RegTech."

Dr Romeo Lacher, Chairman of the Board of Directors, SIX Group

"Investing globally provides huge opportunities. *The WealthTech Book* shows investors how to use big data and AI to achieve alpha. It provides deep insights on how technology will impact the global asset management and private banking sector. I would like to thank Susanne Chishti for her insightful initiative. The post digital revolution world will be formed by decisions made today. As a robotics and blockchain friendly investor, I know that the first thing before investing is to have an extensive knowledge of the ecosystem. *The WealthTech Book* could be an invaluable guide to access these new and upcoming investment opportunities."

Alice Lhabouz, President, Trecento Asset Management

"In the first book, the authors provided a broad view of FinTech to provide readers with an in-depth study of the interplay between finance and technology, as well as the trends across the FinTech spectrum. In this follow-up book, the authors have built on that firm foundation taken a deeper dive into the wealth sector of the FinTech spectrum. In doing so, the authors have once again provided new and returning readers a pragmatic and insightful look into how AI, Blockchain and other key technologies will lower the barrier of investment and make wealth generation much more accessible to a wider pool of consumers globally. Definitely a relevant read for both experienced and novice FinTech practitioners!"

Robin Loh, Chief Digital Officer, Allianz Asia Pacific

"Following vast disruption in the retail and ecommerce space, the wealth/asset management and private banking industry is facing its own 'Uber moment'. Staying abreast of new trends and technologies – which span well beyond the use of artificial intelligence in 'robo-advice' – is going to be a challenge. *The WealthTech Book*, crowd-sourced from industry experts and thought leaders in digital disruption, is a valuable tool for industry players looking to stay relevant in this fast-changing environment."

Joy Macknight, Deputy Editor, The Banker

"What if? The single, repetitive question every innovator, every entrepreneur, every policy maker asks themselves. What if there was another way, a better way, a new way? Well, what if this book not only opened your mind, but it also helped expanded and accelerated your potential? I believe it will. Whether you work in the sector, consume from it, supply to it, aspire to be part of it, I encourage you to invest in yourself, digest the book, and join the conversation. Make your mark. Ask yourself what if?"

Simon Paris, Deputy CEO, FINASTRA

"You've done it again! On the heels of *The FinTech Book*, a global best seller across 107 countries, *The WealthTech Book* is another outstanding compilation of excellent and actionable content. It provides a very useful and detailed summary of important issues impacting the wealth management industry.

Whether you are a start-up or an incumbent leveraging new technology to create new and/or better wealth management products, services and delivery, this book is a must read. I recommend it with alacrity."

R. Todd Ruppert, retired CEO, T. Rowe Price Global Investment Services; venture partner, Greenspring Associates; senior advisor SenaHill Partners and Motive Partners; serial FinTech investor and advisor

"Following the success of Susanne's previous curated works in *The FinTech Book* comes *The WealthTech Book*. This is an important development as it demonstrates the granularity of how technology is attacking all of the structures of finance from retail banking and payments to commercial, investment and private banking to insurance and wealth management. *The WealthTech Book* is a timely arrival to show the specifics of how technology is changing the world of big money and high-net-worth people. About time, as the new generation of technology billionaires don't really want some sharp-suited person calling them all the time. Leave it to the apps!"

Chris Skinner, CEO, The Finanser Ltd

"I am very impressed by the way Susanne Chishti again collects all stakeholders of the industry and motivates them to share their thoughts on the future development of the industry. I like the structure of the book – cover all relevant topics and each exactly to the point. For a traditional banker it offers a fast track to a new world."

Dr Johann Strobl, CEO Raiffeisen Bank International

"*The WealthTech Book* is a must read as it provides an excellent overview of the trends, new technologies and reasons why the sector is transforming. Wealth Management will always fulfil a crucial role in consumers as it helps them give peace of mind on their financial future. Technology is creating a win–win for consumers and the sector allowing better net returns for investors and better RoE for those institutions timely adopting technology. Finding the balance between Tech and Human relationship and trust is what the next decade is about! Exciting times and an exciting read!"

Radboud Vlaar, Partner, Finch Capital (OGC)

The WealthTech Book

Library of Congress Cataloging-in-Publication Data

Names: Chishti, Susanne, editor. | Puschmann, Thomas, editor.
Title: The wealthtech book : the fintech handbook for investors, entrepreneurs and finance visionaries / edited by Susanne Chishti, Thomas Puschmann.
Description: Hoboken : Wiley, 2018. | Includes index. |
Identifiers: LCCN 2017056769 (print) | LCCN 2018006547 (ebook) | ISBN 9781119362180 (pdf) | ISBN 9781119362227 (epub) | ISBN 9781119362159 (paperback)
Subjects: LCSH: Investment analysis—Handbooks, manuals, etc. | BISAC: BUSINESS & ECONOMICS / Finance.
Classification: LCC HG4529 (ebook) | LCC HG4529 .W427 2018 (print) | DDC 332.63/2042—dc23
LC record available at https://lccn.loc.gov/2017056769

A catalogue record for this book is available from the British Library.

ISBN 978-1-119-36215-9 (paperback)   ISBN 978-1-119-36218-0 (ePDF)

ISBN 978-1-119-36222-7 (ePub)   ISBN 978-1-119-44451-0 (Obook)

10 9 8 7 6 5 4 3 2 1

Cover design: Wiley
Cover image: pkproject/Shutterstock

Set in 10/13pt Helvetica Lt Std by Aptara, New Delhi, India
Printed in Great Britain by TJ International Ltd, Padstow, Cornwall, UK

The WealthTech Book

The FinTech Handbook for Investors, Entrepreneurs and Finance Visionaries

Edited by
Susanne Chishti
Thomas Puschmann

Contents

5. Blockchain Applications in Asset and Wealth Management

6. Founders' Success Stories

7. Enterprise Innovation

8. Global Overview of WealthTech

9. What is the Future of WealthTech?

Preface

With the development of digital wealth management ("WealthTech"), including robo-advisory platforms and virtual advice, the global investment management industry is facing huge disruption. In addition to successful digital wealth management solutions, customer preferences are changing and the millennial generation often prefers a "do it yourself" approach via apps instead of meeting a financial advisor in person. Considering that trillions of pounds will be inherited by this tech-inspired generation from their wealthy baby boomer parents, and the general trend that consumers are used to a great digital experience, most asset managers and private banks will need to closely review their product, distribution and marketing strategies over the next decade to stay in business.

In addition, the pressure to lower fees and achieve higher returns has allowed WealthTech solutions to shine, helping to generate higher alpha, reduce risk and significantly lower the costs of money management, financial planning and advice, while at the same time delighting their customers with a superior user experience.

Some emerging business models – such as robo-advisors – were initially focused on servicing customer segments which could not be serviced profitably by traditional players, before moving upstream and competing with incumbents. Other propositions are focused on empowering existing financial advisors and private bankers with the latest digital innovation and technologies, or supporting portfolio managers to fight information overload through solutions leveraging the latest artificial intelligence and big data analytics intelligence.

Overall, the WealthTech sector is booming globally, with FinTech entrepreneurs and investors across the world working on the most cutting-edge solutions. In order to share with our readers the best content globally, we have followed the same approach as with *The FinTech Book* – the first globally crowdsourced book on the financial technology revolution, which was published by Wiley in 2016 and has become a global bestseller.

The FinTech Book exceeded all our expectations: the book is available in five languages across 107 countries, as a paperback, e-book and audiobook. More than 160 authors from 27 countries submitted 189 abstracts to be part of the book. About 50% of all contributors were chosen to write for the final book. When we launched *The FinTech Book* across the world during 2016, our authors and readers had many opportunities to meet us in person, get their books signed at global book launch events and deepen their FinTech friendships worldwide.

In 2017 we decided to extend our FinTech book series by writing three new books on how new business models and technology innovation will change the global asset management and private banking sector ("WealthTech"), the insurance sector ("InsurTech") and regulatory compliance ("RegTech"). We followed our approach of crowdsourcing the best experts, to give the most cutting-edge insight into the changes unfolding in our industry.

The WealthTech Book is the first global book on this subject – a book that provides food for thought to FinTech newbies, pioneers and well-seasoned experts alike. The reason that we decided to reach out to the global FinTech community in sourcing the book's contributors lies in the inherently fragmented nature of the field of financial technology applied to investment management, financial advisors and private banks globally. There was no single author, group of authors or indeed region in the world that could cover all the facets and nuances of WealthTech in an exhaustive manner. What is more, with a truly global contributor base, we not only stayed true to the spirit of FinTech and WealthTech, making use of technological channels of communication in reaching out to, selecting and reviewing our would-be contributors, but also made sure that every corner of the globe had the chance to have its say. Thus, we aimed to fulfil one of the most important purposes of *The WealthTech Book*, namely – to give a voice to those who would remain unheard, those who did not belong to a true FinTech community in their local areas, and spread that voice to an international audience. We have immensely enjoyed the journey of editing *The WealthTech Book* and sincerely hope that you will enjoy the journey of reading it at least as much.

More than 240 authors from 25 countries submitted 236 abstracts to be part of the book. We asked our global FinTech community for their views regarding which abstracts they would like to have fully expanded. Out of all the contributions, we selected the best and asked our selected authors to write the 71 chapters in this book. We conducted a questionnaire among all our selected authors to further understand their background and expertise. 80% of our authors have postgraduate university degrees and strong domain expertise across many fields; 74% of our final authors had had their articles published before. See Tables 1 and 2.

Table 1: **What is the highest educational qualification of our authors?**

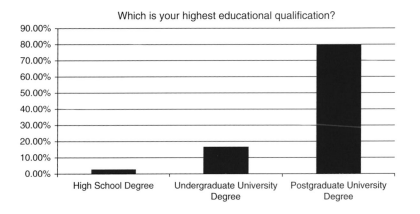

Which is your highest educational qualification?

Table 2: **List of all areas our authors have domain expertise in (multiple choices possible)**

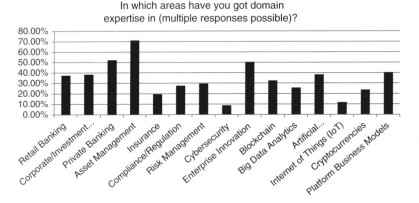

In which areas have you got domain expertise in (multiple responses possible)?

Tables 3 and 4 show that more than 35% of our authors are entrepreneurs working for FinTech start-ups (many of them part of the founding team), 40% come from established financial and technology companies and another quarter from service providers such as consulting firms or law firms servicing the FinTech sector.

More than 25% of our authors work for start-ups with up to 5 people and another 28% for start-ups/SMEs (small and medium-sized enterprises) with up to 50 people. More than a quarter of our authors are employed by a large organization, with more than 1000 employees.

In summary, we are very proud of our highly qualified authors, their strong expertise and passion for FinTech, either being entrepreneurs or often "intrapreneurs" in large established organizations committed to playing a significant role in the global FinTech and WealthTech revolution. These remarkable people are willing to share their insights with all of us over the following pages.

This project would not have been possible without the dedication and efforts of all contributors to *The WealthTech Book* (both those who submitted their initial abstracts for consideration by the global FinTech community, and the final authors whose insights you will

Table 3: The types of company our authors are working in

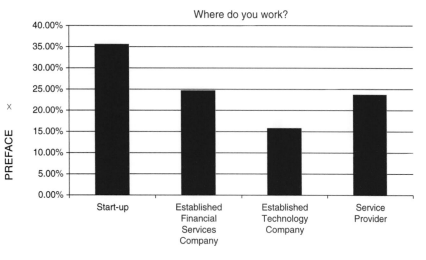

Where do you work?

Table 4: The size of companies our authors work for

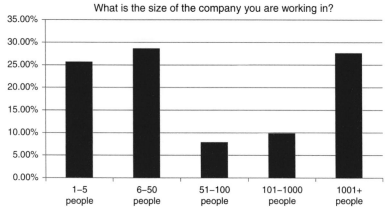

What is the size of the company you are working in?

be reading shortly). In addition, we would like to thank our editors at Wiley, whose guidance and help made sure that what started off as an idea, became the book you are now holding in your hands.

Finally, I would like to thank my fantastic co-editor Thomas Puschmann, Head of the Swiss FinTech Innovation Lab. Editing a crowdsourced book naturally takes several months, and Thomas was always a pleasure to work with, given his strong domain expertise and vision for the future of WealthTech!

Susanne Chishti
Co-Founder, The FINTECH Book Series

CEO & Founder FINTECH Circle & the FINTECH Circle Institute
www.FINTECHCircle.com

About the Editors

Susanne Chishti

(Twitter: www.twitter.com/SusanneChishti)

Susanne Chishti is the CEO of FINTECH Circle, Europe's first Angel Network focused on FinTech opportunities and the founder of the FINTECH Circle Institute, the first global peer-to-peer FinTech learning platform to acquire FinTech and digital skills. She is co-editor of the bestselling title *The FinTech Book*, which has been translated into five languages and is sold across 107 countries. Susanne is recognized in the European Digital Financial Services "Power 50" 2015, an independent ranking of the most influential people in digital financial services in Europe. She has been selected as top 15 FINTECH UK Twitter influencer and as the UK's "City Innovator – Inspirational Woman" 2016. Susanne is a FinTech TV commentator on CNBC and a guest lecturer on financial technology at the University of Cambridge.

After completing her MBA, she started her career working for a FinTech company (before the term "FinTech" was invented) in Silicon Valley, 20 years ago. She then worked for more than 15 years across Deutsche Bank, Lloyds Banking Group, Morgan Stanley and Accenture in London and Hong Kong. Susanne is an award-winning entrepreneur and investor, with strong FinTech expertise. She is a mentor, judge and coach at FinTech events and competitions such as SWIFT Innotribe and FinTech & InsurTech Startup Bootcamp. She is also a conference speaker at leading FinTech events globally.

FINTECH Circle is a global community of more than 100,000 FinTech entrepreneurs, investors and financial services professionals globally. FINTECH Circle's advisory practice services clients including leading financial institutions such as BNP Paribas and the UK's innovation agency NESTA, which appointed FINTECH Circle as partner for the £5 million Challenge Prize to work on Open Banking initiatives for SME banking in 2017.

Susanne is also a non-executive director of the Just Loans Group plc, Kompli-Global and Lenderwize Ltd.

About FINTECH Circle

FINTECH Circle (www.FINTECHCircle.com) is a global community of 100,000 FinTech entrepreneurs, angel and VC investors, financial services professionals and FinTech thought leaders, focusing on FinTech seed investing, education and enterprise innovation. FINTECH Circle's CEO, Susanne Chishti, co-edited *The FinTech Book* published by Wiley, which became the first globally crowdsourced book on financial technology and a global bestseller across 107 countries in five languages.

Twitter: @FINTECHCircle

Instagram: @FINTECHCircle

About the FINTECH Circle Institute

The FINTECH Circle Institute (www.FINTECHCircleInstitute.com) is a peer-to-peer online learning platform, designed to empower finance professionals with the necessary digital skills to adapt to the rapidly changing industry. With board members ranging from traditional banks and FinTech experts through to academics from leading universities, the platform offers practical bitesize courses on topics including WealthTech/ robo-banking, InsurTech, RegTech, blockchain, artificial intelligence, enterprise innovation and start-ups. Every quarter, new bitesize classes are released online to ensure that members have access to the latest FinTech insights and industry experts working on the most cutting-edge FinTech innovations globally.

Twitter: @FTC_Institute

Join our LinkedIn Group to share your FinTech knowledge and learn from others:

www.linkedin.com/groups/8184397

Thomas Puschmann

(Twitter: www.twitter.com/PuschmannThomas)

Thomas Puschmann has spent more than a decade at the nexus of technology and business. Currently, he is founder and director of the Swiss FinTech Innovation Lab at the University of Zurich and a member of the Swiss Innovation Council Innosuisse. In addition, Thomas is a senior advisor for many public and professional initiatives and projects. He is a founder of Swiss FinTech Innovations, an independent association of major Swiss financial institutions, a founder of the consulting firm FinTech Innovations and an advisory board member of the Center on Global Internet Finance. Lastly, he is a judge and mentor for several start-up competitions in Europe and Asia and a conference speaker.

Thomas holds a PhD in business administration with a specific focus on information systems from the University of St. Gallen and a master in management and information sciences. Before his current position he was heading a large international financial services research project from the Universities of St. Gallen and Leipzig where he was working on his postdoctoral lecture qualification. In addition, Thomas was a visiting scholar at the MIT Sloan School of Management and a member of the board at ESPRiT Consulting and The Information Management Group where he was responsible for business technology.

About the Swiss FinTech Innovation Lab

The Swiss FinTech Innovation Lab is a cross-disciplinary platform for education, research and entrepreneurship that involves researchers and practitioners from banking and finance, business informatics, innovation management, social sciences, economics, law and many other disciplines. The lab researches and teaches on the topic of the digitization in the financial services industry together with participants from the whole value chain, including banks, insurers, start-ups, service providers, regulators, and various other organizations and associations from the financial services ecosystem. It aims to create knowledge in this emerging field to improve and foster intra- and entrepreneurship. Hosted at the University of Zurich, the Swiss FinTech Innovation Lab cooperates with a broad international network of researchers and universities.

Web: www.swissfintechinnovationlab.ch

Twitter: www.twitter.com/PuschmannThomas

LinkedIn: www.linkedin.com/in/thomaspuschmann

Acknowledgements

After the global launch of *The FinTech Book* in 2016, we met thousands of FinTech entrepreneurs, investors and financial services professionals who all loved the book and wanted to learn more about how financial technology will change the global investment/wealth management sector and private banking.

We came up with the idea for *The WealthTech Book*, spoke to our FinTech friends globally and everybody supported the idea. FinTech entrepreneurs across all continents were eager to share their powerful insights. They wanted to explain the new business models and technologies they were working on to change the world of finance. FinTech investors, "intrapreneurs", innovation leaders at leading financial institutions and thought leaders were keen to describe their embrace of the FinTech revolution across investment management and private banking. Finally, our WealthTech visionaries wanted to share their vision for the future.

The global effort of crowdsourcing such insights was born with *The FinTech Book*, which became a global bestseller across 107 countries in five languages. We built on this success with *The WealthTech Book*. We are aware that this would not have been possible without the FINTECH Circle global community, the Swiss FinTech Innovation Lab community and our own personal networks. We are very grateful to the almost 100,000 members of FINTECH Circle for joining us daily across our websites (www.FINTECHCircle.com, www.swissfintechinnovationlab.ch), our Twitter accounts and our LinkedIn groups. Without public support and the engagement of our global FinTech community, this book would not have been possible.

The authors you will read about have been chosen by our global FinTech community purely on merit – no matter how big or small their organization, no matter which country they work in, no matter if they are well known or still undiscovered, everybody had the same chance to apply and be part of *The WealthTech Book*. We are proud of that, as we believe that FinTech and WealthTech will fundamentally change the world of finance and asset management. The global FinTech and WealthTech community is made up of the smartest, most innovative and nicest people we know. Thank you for being part of our journey. It is difficult to name you all here, but you are all listed in the directory at the end of this book.

Our publisher, Wiley, has been a great partner for *The FinTech Book* and we are delighted that Wiley will again publish *The WealthTech Book* in paperback and e-book formats globally. Special thanks go to our fantastic editor, Gemma Valler. Thank you to you and your team – we could not have done it without your amazing support!

We look forward to hearing from you. Please visit our website www.WealthTECHBook.com for additional bonus content from our global WealthTech community! Please send us your comments on *The WealthTech Book* and let us know how you wish to be engaged by dropping us a line at learn@FINTECHCircle.com or thomas.puschmann@uzh.ch.

Susanne Chishti

Twitter: @SusanneChishti

Thomas Puschmann

Twitter: @PuschmannThomas

ACKNOWLEDGEMENTS

xiv

Introduction

2

Hybrid Advice Model

▶ **ROBO-ADVICE**
Value prepositions
for **all** generations

▶ **PERSONALIZED**
Client service and
social selling

▶ **JOBS**
Jobs replaced
by robots?

▶ **NEW CLIENT SEGMENTS**
- Digitals
- Hybrid clients
- Digital deniers

▶ **GAMIFICATION**
- Reward beneficial long-term
  behaviour
- Core principles: autonomy,
  mastery and purpose

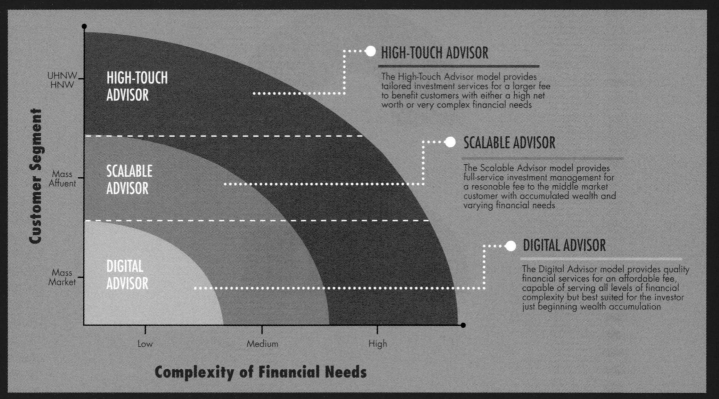

Customer Segment

UHNW
HNW — HIGH-TOUCH ADVISOR

Mass
Affluent — SCALABLE ADVISOR

Mass
Market — DIGITAL ADVISOR

Low   Medium   High

Complexity of Financial Needs

HIGH-TOUCH ADVISOR

The High-Touch Advisor model provides
tailored investment services for a larger fee
to benefit customers with either a high net
worth or very complex financial needs

SCALABLE ADVISOR

The Scalable Advisor model provides
full-service investment management for
a resonable fee to the middle market
customer with accumulated wealth and
varying financial needs

DIGITAL ADVISOR

The Digital Advisor model provides quality
financial services for an affordable fee,
capable of serving all levels of financial
complexity but best suited for the investor
just beginning wealth accumulation

Source: Chapter 12

Powered by **Artificial Intelligence**
- It will be everywhere, yet invisible to use
- Intelligent services that anticipate our needs, organize
  work and perform time-consuming repetitive tasks

Executive Summary

A recent study on the jobs that are most likely to be replaced by robots in the future predicts that personal financial advisors have a 58% risk of becoming obsolete and ranking first place compared with all others.[1] Interestingly, from a historical point of view, the banking industry has been among the first adopters of online advisory services. For example, Citibank and Chase Manhattan provided the first home banking systems for their customers already in 1981, and the Norwegian Focus Bank offered mobile transactions in 1999, long before the Apple iPhone was launched in 2007. The digital development of banking can generally be split into three phases, each focusing on a different area of digitization:[2]

- **Internal digitization (phase 1).** The first phase of digitization concentrated on internal processes, such as advisory, payment transactions, or portfolio management. Here, banks focused on the automation of financial services processes like, for example, cash transactions with ATMs.

- **Provider-oriented digitization (phase 2).** In the second phase financial service providers focused on the integration of core banking systems. For this, they had to standardize processes and application functions which were delivered from standard core banking solution providers such as SAP or Temenos.

- **Customer-oriented digitization (phase 3).** This third phase of digitization is centred around customers and their processes, redefining today's inside-out, product-centred to an outside-in logic. This phase is characterized by the application of new IT developments like social media, robo-advisors, cloud computing, etc.

However, instead of continuing this forward-looking tradition, banks remained very passive in automating customer advisory until now and instead, in recent years, such solutions merely emerged from non-banks like Betterment or Wealthfront. Currently, banks quickly follow-up in developing or integrating robo-advisor solutions into their existing environment. The reasons are the technological advancements that come from artificial intelligence, blockchain and big data, etc., combined with changing customer behaviour, which lead to a fundamental change in client interaction. One prominent example is the robo-advisor. Although robo-advisors still only account for a very small part of the total assets managed by human advisors, the potential seems huge, be it in established markets or in emerging ones like China. But do clients really prefer digital-only over human-only solutions? The answer depends on the technological affinity and the complexity of clients' needs and very often leads to hybrid models which involve both personal and robo-advisory: there is no one-size-fits all approach. And it's not only the millennials that use them, their adoption may be beyond demographic factors. One reason for using them is the rich customer experience provided by robo-advisors, which also applies for other digital client-facing solutions (e.g. chatbots, gamification tools, etc.), which allow for improved personalized services. With increasingly open application programming interfaces (APIs), it becomes easier to link to banks' existing systems – like Lego bricks, even across company boundaries – and thus enhance a "seamless" customer and service experience for clients.

Summarized, this part focuses on how client advisory might change in the future, driven by technological advancements.

---

[1] Frey, C. B. and Osborne, M. A. (2017). "The Future of Employment: How susceptible are jobs to computerisation?", *Technological Forecasting and Social Change*, 114(C), 254–280.

[2] Puschmann, T. (2017). "Fintech", *Business & Information Systems Engineering*, 59(1), 69–76.

Ten Reasons Why Digital Wealth Management Will Become a Worldwide Market Standard

By Michael Mellinghof
Managing Director, TechFluence UK

Currently, digital wealth managers worldwide manage an estimated $130bn, approximately 70% of it in the USA and almost half of it by just one market participant: Vanguard. Compared with the $60trn of assets under management in the wealth management industry globally (estimates by TechFluence), this 2017 figure is incredibly small, almost negligible – so far, at least!

However, the growth picture is strong, with realized annual growth rates of +50% in some cases and an expected market size of robo-advice providers between $489bn in assets under management by end 2020 (estimate by Cerulli[1]) or $2.2trn by 2020 (by A. T. Kearney[2]).

TechFluence expects the number of robo-advice product offerings to rise significantly to around 500 in five years' time – in Europe alone. As of May 2017, there are 73 robo-advice providers in the market in Europe;[3] if you include automated product offerings from incumbents, this number exceeds 120.

---

[1] Cerulli Report, "Retail Direct Firms and Digital Advice Providers 2015: Addressing Millennials, the Mass Market, and Robo Advice", published 2015.

[2] A. T. Kearney Study, "Hype vs. Reality: The Coming Waves of 'Robo' Adoption", published June 2015.

[3] Please find updates at www.techfluence.eu/investtech.html.

What are the drivers for these market expectations and this significant change to an industry that has been going on almost without significant structural change for decades? The following reasons are all relevant and their combined impact is fuelling the change in the worldwide asset and wealth management industry:

1. Low interest rate environment. With an almost zero interest rate environment in the majority of global capital markets, the historically high management fees of mutual funds or wealth management mandates become more visible than in the past, when a government yield of 5% – realized on the bond allocation of a portfolio – easily earned the management fee on the whole portfolio. If coupons – as of spring 2017 – are close to zero, then equity performance must do the job, which is much more difficult to obtain for portfolio managers. As a result, clients tend to notice a high level of management fees more nowadays, as they are also more cost sensitive in the absence of a "risk-free" income from government bonds.

2. The internet has brought an incredible transparency into this sector. After 20+ years of internet and comparison portals, clients of all age groups use these tools for investments: comparison of fund performances or wealth management performances, or performances and ratings of client advisors on social media portals. The inherent complexity of the capital markets and investments has shielded the industry for a number of years, until now the margin compression kicks in via exchange traded funds (ETFs) and robo-advice.

3. The technical progress in general in the past 10 years is an enabler of change in the wealth management industry too. The development of cloud technology and the technologies enabling a mobile lifestyle (3G, 4G, 5G networks) is making it rather unattractive for clients to sit down in a bank branch with an investment advisor for two hours and wait until he has been told by his computer what is the "best" product to offer. On a modern smartphone, users have access to the same in-depth information as the advisor, but in an independent form.

4. Technology leads and has led to social changes. If a user has access to information from a neutral source (i.e. independent from a product provider), he will use this information to challenge institutions, their data quality, their recommendations, etc. While in the past what a banker or wealth manager said was taken for granted, it is now being questioned. The old world has lost its information headstart. In some digital tools, users can simulate backtests themselves, whereas the client advisor usually has to request this from another unit. Clients suddenly can be in control, if they want to.

5. The offers of the incumbents do not fit into the zeitgeist any more. Brick-and-mortar branches in reality always were cost factors, but were seen as revenue generators by many. This was true as long as there were no other access points for clients to their individual and general financial information. In the 1980s, people would walk into a bank branch in order to inquire about current stock prices or collect their financial statements. Now it is one click on a smartphone and if too many clicks are necessary, the user/client will avoid using it.

6. Regulation has also helped to kickstart the robo-advice movement. Nowadays an initial meeting with a client advisor is bound to be a lot longer than 10, 20 or 30 years ago due to regulatory obligations. By complying with current regulations, market participants have a long compulsory journey to reach execution. This makes any digital solution with only a few clicks or a few sentences with a chatbot – like Amazon's Alexa – a lot more attractive.

7. Regulation is also responsible for a phenomenon coined the "advice gap". As the time required for a regular investment advice conversation is very high, banks and asset managers have started to increase the minimum assets under management often above $100,000. This turns clients with liquid assets of $100,000 or less into an attractive target group for digital players.

8. The existence of a competitive market of ETFs was one of the key drivers of robo-advice. Only a widely accessible low-cost product alternative to mutual funds enables digital players to add their automated solutions and still be significantly lower in price than actively managed funds or mandates. As most digital wealth managers use ETFs for their solution design, they now act as a powerful distributor for ETF providers.

9. Data is the oil of the future. Wealth data by nature is of particular interest, but so far was only used by banks, etc. for cross-selling of other lucrative financial products. However, such data is also very interesting for other market participants, for example retailers, the luxury industry, car manufacturers, etc. In the past, data was not available – nowadays, it becomes available more and more due to regulation (Payment Services Directive 2 (PSD2) as a start) and changes in society: data sharing becomes the new norm and banking cannot stay behind such a powerful social trend.

10. Accessing the right kind of data for these non-financial players has been proven difficult and expensive in the past. By offering access to wealth management products, such luxury producers gain direct access to wealth data. If, for example, a luxury watch producer from Switzerland learns about a big in-flow in its robo-advisor, it might be a good time to send the client some marketing material on watches, too. So far there have been many barriers to prevent non-financial firms entering the financial advisory business, especially as the advisory process was not feasible for them. In the digital world this becomes a lot easier, as all items of the value chain are available from various providers.

11. Brands are even more important. They become more relevant in the digital than in the offline world, as the next competitor is only one browser window away. Price comparison tools are used to filter out providers by the buyers, who are price sensitive. For users who favour quality, prime brands give the highest safety net when buying online. The risk of fraud is simply too big. Once a product is physically delivered and the payment made, it can be quite bothersome and costly to return the unwanted item and ideally receive the money back. Users must then either choose a prime brand or a prime online shop in order to avoid trouble. In many cases, both.

12. Translated into the financial world – where trust is of even higher importance – this means that either the provider of the financial product (i.e. the ETF) or the cooperating bank should be a well-known firm, as this creates trust. If the sponsor of a robo-advice tool, on the other hand, is a prime brand itself (like a luxury brand or a global retail or product brand), then no-one will question the functioning and seriousness of the offer. The initiator can then even use second-tier banks and products without brand and thus offer very competitive prices, or even offer the service for free. This strategy would make sense for such non-financial players, as their main interest is access to the wealth data – and margins in their core business are likely to be higher than in digital wealth. Robo-advice becomes a cross-selling or client acquisition channel.

So, how will the market structure in the asset and wealth management industry look in 10 years' time? TechFluence expects the following three developments: (1) Incumbents that are able to digitize their DNA quickest will continue to grow, even more dynamically than today, but with lower profit margins. (2) Those incumbents who are not able to adapt to the new digital competitors fast enough will either acquire a digital competitor relatively late in the cycle or disappear, merge, etc. The digital competitor landscape of today consists of start-ups and traditional FinTech firms, who have built tech for financial institutions in the past already. (3) The FinTech "traditionalists" have very good chances to use their competitive advantage to grow via international horizontal and vertical integration. Within the start-up category, those start-ups that acquire enough clients fast enough before incumbents manage to digitize their DNA will become mainstream players. Whether they are able to build global brands remains to be seen. In the digital world this is, generally speaking, possible (for example Uber), but more complex in a heavily regulated environment like wealth management. The pure existence of robo-advisors leads to high pressure on margins within the traditional asset and wealth management world. As this sector did not have a lot of pressure in the past to modernize its structures, the speed the digital competitors have will most likely lead to some casualties and will force traditional players to change quickly. Geographically, North America is the most developed market in robo-advice so far, while Europe and Asia are lagging behind: both regions are more fragmented, and this means growth will happen later and probably less dynamically in the European case and at lower margins in the Asian case.

However, one figure is similar globally: the percentage of equity funds underperforming their benchmark over the years is constantly very high. Analysis by Standard & Poor's shows that in Europe, 86% of actively managed funds over the last 10 years (after costs) underperformed their benchmark,[4] which means they should not be in the market. In the USA the situation is even worse, with 98.9% of actively managed equity funds underperforming, according to the same study. This asset pool is still vast and forms the carrot for many more digital "rabbits" that need a lot less assets under management to break even. The future of wealth management in the digital world looks bright – especially for clients, as their total expense ratios will decrease. The competitor landscape in asset and wealth management will be a lot more fragmented than now.

Maybe the new market leader in the digital wealth management space has not been founded yet. The digital world enables financial education at a high scale. Those players who are able to include tools in their offering that address financial illiteracy efficiently in developed and less developed markets will have the best chance of winning the crown in the long term.

---

[4] *Financial Times*, "86% of active equity funds underperform", by Madison Marriage, 20 March 2016.

What Do Wealthy Clients Think About Digital Wealth Management?

By Prof. Dr Teodoro D. Cocca

Professor for Wealth and Asset Management, Johannes Kepler University Linz

The rise of FinTech is forcing banks to rethink the way they interact with their customers. The ongoing discussion about the revolutionary potential of technological innovation in wealth management and other areas of banking is mostly dominated by the view of industry experts and consultants. Unfortunately, more often than not, the client perspective is neglected. This chapter aims to close this gap, based on in-depth survey results completed by wealth management clients in Switzerland, Germany and Austria. In contrast to other chapters, which examine data from general customer surveys, this study only considers customers in the segment of high-net-worth individuals (HNWIs), defined as having liquid financial assets of at least EUR 500,000. The average sum in financial assets of the people surveyed is EUR 2.5 million, and the average age is 59 years. Thus, the data basis corresponds to an average client book of a private bank offering wealth management services. The surveys were carried out in 2012, 2014 and 2016, which allows for historical comparison.[1] The focus on wealth management in these three countries promotes the discussion of adapting digital financial services in an environment where mostly older wealth management clients are typically serviced personally by private bankers, with a strong client–advisor relationship.

Today's Client Preferences

The surveyed people are divided into three segments, based on the individual degree of digitization (see also Cocca, 2016[2]):

[1] LGT Private Banking Report 2016, 2016.

[2] https://www.researchgate.net/publication/311740686_Potential_and_Limitations_of_Virtual_Advice_in_Wealth_Management

- **Digital deniers.** The client has a personal advisor and does not use any virtual banking channels.

- **Hybrid client.** The client has a personal advisor, but also uses virtual banking channels for services related to wealth management.

- **Digitals.** The client has no personal advisor and more than half of his/her wealth is with an online bank.

Figure 1 shows how these segments have developed proportionally between 2012 and 2016. The values refer to the distribution of the assets among the three customer segments (not the number of customers). It is easy to recognize that the hybrid customers make up by far the largest proportion (around 80%). Furthermore, it is clear that the proportion of digital deniers has decreased continuously, whereas the proportion of digitals

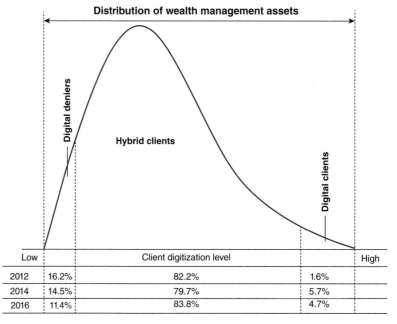

	Distribution of wealth management assets	
Low	Client digitization level	High

	Digital deniers	Hybrid clients	Digital clients
2012	16.2%	82.2%	1.6%
2014	14.5%	79.7%	5.7%
2016	11.4%	83.8%	4.7%

Figure 1: Distribution of wealth management assets across client segment

has increased significantly, albeit non-linearly, since 2012. This variation can be explained by the fact that the increase in digitals has dropped off again between 2014 and 2016, especially in higher-wealth segments, and a small reduction of the growth rates can be observed.

Tomorrow's Client Preferences

Respondents were also surveyed about their future use of virtual wealth management services. In this case, Cocca (2016[2]) shows that 28% of respondents foresee themselves primarily interacting directly with their client advisor, 43% will likely not use a client advisor at all and, instead, will mainly interact with the bank online, and 35% show a willingness to make use of completely virtual offers by a third party not linked to a traditional bank (e.g. FinTech). These three central aspects of the current discussion about the disruptive potential of digitization for wealth management are now analysed in depth. This makes it easier to identify the sociodemographic and behavioural features of customers who show a high tendency for disruptive behaviour. We consider it disruptive behaviour when the customer demonstrates expressed willingness to: (1) consider virtual consultation through its client advisor; (2) bank without a client advisor; or (3) obtain truly virtual advice provided by a third party, whereby we assume an increasing level of disruptive behaviour from (1) to (3). Figure 2 describes some sociodemographic and investment-specific variables of these three customer types. For example, the figure shows that the proportion of under-50-year-olds in the sample is 25.2% for those surveyed who consider a virtual consultation through their client advisor. On the other hand, this percentage is 30.7% among the respondents who show a willingness for truly virtual advice provided by a third party.

As Figure 2 illustrates, the potential for disruption is highest among younger, male, well-informed clients with higher net worth and a more venturesome risk appetite. This profile thus corresponds to the description of the early adopters for future virtual wealth management services.

		Client Level of Disruptive Behaviour →		
		Readiness for virtual interaction with my/a client advisor	Readiness for banking mostly online with my bank without client advisor	Readiness for truly virtual advice not from my bank
Age	< 50	25.2%	28.8%	30.7%
	> 60	46.7%	41.9%	39.4%
Gender	Female	18.7%	17.5%	15.7%
	Male	81.3%	82.5%	84.3%
Net worth	< EUR 1.5 million	70.1%	62.5%	63.0%
	EUR 1.5 - 5 million	26.2%	31.9%	32.3%
	> EUR 5 million	3.7%	5.6%	4.7%
Knowledge about investment matters	Very good knowledge	22.4%	24.4%	30.7%
Willingness to take risks	Venturesome	31.8%	35.0%	37.8%

Figure 2: Client readiness for disruptive behaviour

Technological Affinity

The fact that using digital services for information and communication in everyday life has spread dramatically does not automatically mean that online services related to wealth management and investment advisory will experience the same kind of demand. This is a false conclusion, which unfortunately has been stated in many recent publications. Based on this new data, the specific correlation between general technological affinity in everyday life and the current use of virtual wealth management services can finally be investigated. Moreover, the degree of readiness for disruptive behaviour is also taken into account.

Table 1 shows that there is a medium correlation between the overall technological affinity and the use of online banking services. However, there is a high correlation between general technological affinity and the affinity to future disruptive customer behaviour. There is a low correlation between social media and mobile usage and the other variables, which suggests that social media and mobile banking use do not provide a particularly good indication of the current or future use of virtual wealth management services. In general, there is a low correlation

Table 1: Correlation between technological affinity, effective usage and digital disruption (2016)

	General technological affinity	Social media use	Online banking use	Mobile banking use
Social media use	0.347			
Online banking use	0.533	0.287		
Mobile banking use	0.386	0.298	0.279	
Digital disruption readiness	0.858	0.329	0.502	0.354

Notes: *n* = 369, significance level 0.01 (two-sided).

between the variables that measure the current use and those that relate to a willingness to use virtual banking services in the future, which may indicate that the questions about the willingness to use online services in the future should be taken with a grain of salt, as they could overestimate the actual behaviour.

Projections

For the reasons stated above, the projection of future proportions of customer segments is not based on questions relating to potential future use but on the historical, already observed, real figures, which have been derived from the surveys in 2012/2014/2016. The development of the digital deniers and digitals, as shown in Figure 3, will be extrapolated using three different calculation methods based on the average observed growth rate of these segments in the years 2012 to 2016: (1) continued use of historical growth rates between 2012 and 2016 (base scenario); (2) proportions of hybrids assumed to be constant and the decline in digital deniers directly assumed as an increase in digitals; (3) historical growth rates between 2012/2014 and 2014/2016 alternately used for the following years (oscillating scenario). The resulting estimate of the proportion of digital clients for 2020 is between 8% and 10% of the total number of customers.

Conclusions

The following conclusions can be drawn from this analysis.

- From today's point of view, the majority of wealthy customers favour a hybrid advisory model. At least, this is the general conclusion about all customers, based on their preferences expressed today. However, the data also proves that even from today's point of view, there is quite a relevant customer group, which could be approached for a purely virtual solution. With an approximate share of 5%, this niche represents a considerable business opportunity. However, at the same time it should also be mentioned that a business model that completely abstains from virtual elements would be met with a positive response by the customer group of the digital deniers, and thus also represents a business opportunity from today's point of view. This data supports a multi-channel approach for banks that aspire to represent the full range of customer preferences.

- A particularly high willingness for future virtual wealth management services, which have a disruptive character, can be seen in younger, male, well-informed clients with higher net worth and risk appetite. This corresponds to the profile of the typical customer, who should have a particularly high adoption rate for virtual wealth management services. This also points

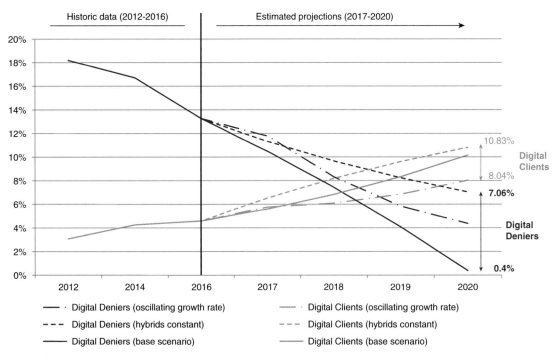

Figure 3: Distribution of wealth management assets across client segments

to possible obstacles that need to be overcome when it comes to getting additional customer groups excited about virtual solutions. Particular attention should be paid to the fact that a relatively high sophistication level in investment themes is directly connected to adaptation. A noteworthy fact is that the gender difference is striking. This factor has so far hardly been mentioned in publications, but it is likely to be important for the implementation of a virtual solution since a high adaptation for female customers will also be very important for the broad adaptation of virtual solutions.

- With the same growth rates as observed in the last four years, the proportion of wealthy customers using virtual wealth management services exclusively would increase to around 8–10% by 2020. Having said that, it should be noted that these projections are all based on extrapolation and thus a

more or less linear continuation of observed past growth rates. Exogenous factors can, however, exacerbate or even diminish such a development in the near future. The decisive factors will be the benefits and associated costs for such virtual solutions, possible changes in the regulatory framework conditions, and the general development of customer preferences.

- An observable general technology affinity does not necessarily mean a high penetration of virtual wealth management services. The wide-ranging connection between the widely observed distribution and adaptation of virtual channels in the consumer market and the expected demand for virtual consulting for financial services and wealth management services in particular is a possible scenario. However, the data seen here calls for caution, since wealth management services could contain specific characteristics, which could at least suggest a much less rapid adaptation. Notably, current preferences (see the first item in this section) suggest that human counselling in wealth management could be more difficult to substitute than previously thought.

- A particularly striking characteristic in the dataset is the fact that the tendency to use virtual wealth management services is lower in higher-wealth segments. The complexity level of wealth management advisory services should be an important parameter regarding the suitability for virtualization. It is easily conceivable that standardized services can be provided more efficiently by an algorithm, whereby comparative cost advantages can be achieved in contrast to the service provided by people. It is not readily apparent, though, how the solely technical provision of consulting services can be sufficient in a trust-based business such as wealth management, in order to capture a large market share. Especially in the higher-wealth customer segments, wealth management consulting exhibits a high degree of complexity. The combination of legal, tax and financial issues, for example, is hardly suitable for mapping by algorithms, since each case has so many degrees of freedom and requires such case-specific solutions that standardization can hardly be achieved efficiently. An additional layer of complexity is also created by the frequently encountered relevance of various jurisdictions, leading to more complex asset structuring and wealth management.

Challenges of Digitizing Wealth Management Advisory

By Jasper Humphrey
Ex-Head Technology, Systems, Modules, swissQuant Group AG

It is not simple being a wealth manager in 2018. Regulatory overheads, pressure on margins, the implicit complexity of keeping up to date with the latest technology while still needing to run complex change programs, all add to the headaches of the modern bank executive.

Here, I present some techniques that we have used to help banks to diagnose and treat the migraine. A modern wealth advisory process is commonly broken down into logical stages:

- **Understanding the client's situation.** Here the advisor performs a process to measure the risk tolerance of the client (how much risk the client prefers to take) and the risk capacity of the client (how much risk the client's circumstances allow them to take).

- **Defining a suitable investment strategy.** The advisor may recommend that the client's wealth tracks a portfolio with certain risk or reward characteristics, or follows a certain structured product strategy.

- **Recommending suitable investments.** The client is presented with a portfolio that meets the investment strategy.

- **Controlling and monitoring the client's wealth portfolio.** The advisor shall periodically monitor the wealth portfolio to ensure that it continues to meet the investment strategy and the client's situation.

Regulations such as MiFID 2 (the Markets in Financial Instruments Directive) are designed to ensure that the wealth manager proves that investments recommended are suitable for the client; therefore, firms have no choice but to implement repeatable processes and record evidence.

Digital internet-based technologies allow these processes to be implemented reliably and flexibly, which thus enables other value-added services such as online capability, mobile usage, increased customization or alternative interfaces such as video or chat.

Let's go through the advisory process stages in more detail, and see how a systematic quantitative approach can help to bring coherence as clients move through the process.

First the client profiling: the problem is to describe the client's risk preference and client circumstances as one or more numbers. Two approaches are commonly used – ask the client "Where are you on this risk scale?" or give the client a questionnaire and infer the risk preference from the answers using a model. The problem with the former is that often the client cannot easily answer the question, and the problem with the latter is that the data required to validate the model is not available, and therefore it is based on heuristics. Estimating risk capacity is also problematic, as the advisor may not have all the data in the case of held-away investments. Could secure application programming interface (API) integration with custody institutions hold the solution?

Whatever the approach taken, digital technologies help to differentiate this stage – immersive design, playing an economic game to measure risk appetite, or mining client profiles or transaction data can all be considered.

Now we have the client risk preference, is it possible to automate the selection of an investment strategy? In the past, this would have involved a discussion with the advisor: what is the right account type – advisory account, execution only or investment mandate, or a combination of all three? This decision can easily be captured over a digital channel. For execution-only, the client demands information, research and crisp execution, which has been available in digital form for decades. With investment mandates, the client is looking for a hands-off solution but may still specify preferences and restrictions, for example ethical investments only. The business model is about efficiency, so only clients with high assets under management were offered restrictions, as this required specialist investment management. Now quantitative software solutions are available that allow the efficient implementation of restrictions for the mass market, thus there is a convergence of advisory and investment mandate management.

For standard advisory, the client risk preference would be described on a discrete scale, for example 1 (low risk) to 7 (high risk); it was trivial, therefore, to map clients to a set of seven matching portfolios selected by the CIO of the bank. The issue with this implementation is that neither is client customization taken into account, nor is it easy to make an argument that the entire variety of client circumstances, tolerance and aspirations can easily be mapped to the fixed set of portfolios. For such implementations, it is harder and harder for institutions to justify the fee premium over competing solutions such as exchange-traded funds. Is it possible to create a model that is flexible enough to describe client customizations and variety, but also systematic enough to be implemented cost effectively? We believe that it is, by using techniques such as portfolio optimization and goal-based investing. The (lack of) performance of some CIO strategies can also be mitigated by allowing the client to specify which benchmark portfolio they would like to track (perhaps from other investment managers).

For other advisory clients that are not interested in a portfolio-based approach, the bank needs to provide a way to generate, propose and implement ideas. Traditional approaches to idea generation (such as macro or thematic investment) can be combined with more fashionable approaches such as using big data management techniques in combination with machine learning models. Time will tell on the feasibility and future returns. Any ideas proposed need to be suitable with respect to the client's profile; therefore, the advisor needs to also measure the risk of the strategy/idea. This requires a sophisticated risk management approach – see Figure 1.

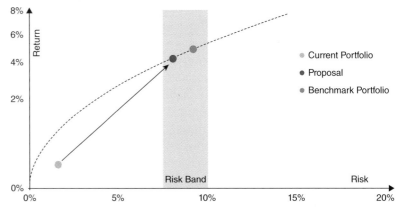

Figure 1: A portfolio optimizer can propose a target portfolio that is closer to a benchmark portfolio

Once a strategy is chosen, is it possible to automate the process of selecting investments? This depends on the exact strategy, but in general, yes.

For a benchmark tracking strategy with customizations or restrictions, portfolio optimizers can be used to generate a new portfolio. The optimizer can take the benchmark portfolio as an input and minimize the tracking error to it, yet still be faithful to the restrictions. For idea generation strategies, it is possible to create solutions that search the available universe of products for the best match to the strategy. Additionally, it is possible to search the universe of products that can best be added to a source portfolio for hedging or other reasons.

Digital technologies allow easy large-scale monitoring of client portfolios. Some monitoring checks are simple and data-driven, for example portfolio concentration risk, but some checks require sophisticated risk management techniques, for example calculating a risk measure of the portfolio is within defined bounds.

The cloud enables the scaling up of monitoring to hundreds of thousands of portfolios, by providing almost limitless and elastic compute, yet the choice of algorithm is also hugely important for an efficient risk management solution. Consider a typical wealth manager's investment offering of 100,000 products. In order to calculate the risk of the portfolio in aggregate, the bank must analyse which products have diversification effects with others. This presents a problem with high dimensionality – 10 billion combinations need to be analysed! Our recommendation is to instead model the investment world using risk factors – a set of asset classes/markets/regions/industries that describe the majority of the investment risk. The 100,000 products are then mapped to the risk factors and only the diversification effects of the risk factors need to be modelled. This enables the portfolio risk to be calculated quickly, which is especially important if the risk management needs to be exposed over a digital channel or if what-if analyses are taking place during an advisory meeting.

So, it is possible to automate the process from the beginning to the end and provide robust and reproducible advisory processes!

This capacity for automation then enables either fully automated or hybrid advisor business models.

Even though the business model can be automated, digital solutions present wealth managers with many management challenges.

A common approach is for the four functions to be abstracted behind robust and secure APIs, which enable the bank delivery channels to innovate without changing the business engineering and processes behind them. These APIs have essential complexity in terms of data security, access control, API management and versioning, self-hosting vs cloud. The mastering of this complexity is often jurisdiction and institution specific, so general guidelines cannot be given other than to say that solving these details requires expert advice and should not be underestimated.

In summary, the intersection of increased automation and adoption of digital technologies leads to many challenges that can be successfully (but not easily) solved using quantitative techniques, innovation and investment in technology, and capable change management.

The Hybrid Advice Model

By Tobias Henry
Digital Wealth Lead – Managing Principal, Capco

In its simplest form, the hybrid approach combines the best components of human-based financial advice and digital advice, offering a flexible and tailored wealth management solution to clients of all demographics.

The hybrid advice solution is underpinned by a flexible business model that can support customers throughout their financial lives, from mass market to ultra-high net worth. The hybrid approach, as shown in Figure 1, has three models to offer customers, depending on their customer segment (defined by investable assets) and the complexity of their financial needs.

The level of human interaction, product complexity, fees and accounts offered change between business models. The business models shown in Figure 2 indicate the optionality of the solution and illustrate the flexibility of the hybrid approach to meet the needs of all customer segments and financial needs.

The hybrid model has many inherent benefits to the financial advisor, the business and the client that make it an attractive and mutually beneficial proposition.

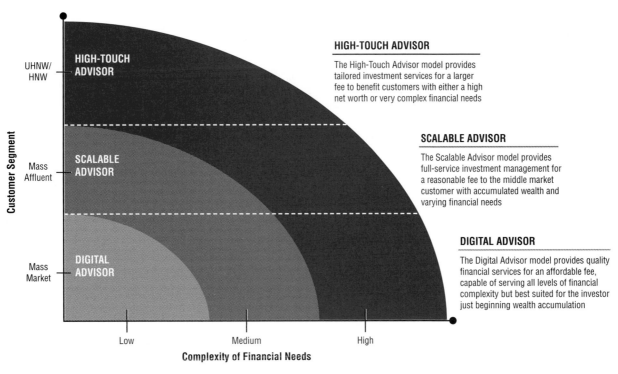

HIGH-TOUCH ADVISOR
The High-Touch Advisor model provides tailored investment services for a larger fee to benefit customers with either a high net worth or very complex financial needs

SCALABLE ADVISOR
The Scalable Advisor model provides full-service investment management for a reasonable fee to the middle market customer with accumulated wealth and varying financial needs

DIGITAL ADVISOR
The Digital Advisor model provides quality financial services for an affordable fee, capable of serving all levels of financial complexity but best suited for the investor just beginning wealth accumulation

Customer Segment: UHNW/HNW, Mass Affluent, Mass Market
Complexity of Financial Needs: Low, Medium, High

Figure 1: The hybrid advice model

HYBRID ADVISOR BUSINESS

	DIGITAL ADVISOR	SCALABLE ADVISOR	HIGH-TOUCH ADVISOR
	Provides mass market investors access to affordable, quality financial services	**Enables advisors to offer mass affluent investors financial services akin to their needs**	**Offers investors with complex financial needs a dedicated and tailored advisory experience**
ADVISOR ROLE	Ongoing access to call centre support model	Advisor guidance during account opening, Ongoing access to advisor guidance as needed	Dedicated human advisor guidance from account opening to ongoing portfolio management and reporting
DIGITAL FEATURES	Onboarding, Omni-channel access, Account Funding, Model Generation, Investment Management, Rebalancing, Tax-loss Harvesting, Reporting	Onboarding, Omni-channel access, Account Funding, Model Generation, Investment Management, Rebalancing, Tax-loss Harvesting, Reporting	Onboarding, Omni-channel access, Account Funding, Reporting
ACCOUNT MINIMUM	$0 - $100,000	$100,000–$500,000	$500,000+
COST TO CUSTOMER	Low e.g. 0-30bps	Medium e.g. 30-150bps	High e.g. 150bps+
ACCOUNT TYPES	IRAs, Retirement, Goal-saving	IRAs, Retirement, Goal-saving, Financial planning, 529s	IRAs, Retirement, Goal-saving, Financial planning, 529s, Estate Planning, Insurance, Lending, Healthcare
PRODUCT OFFERING	ETFs, Equities	ETFs, Equities, Mutual Funds, Fixed Income	ETFs, Equities, Mutual Funds, Fixed Income, Real Estate, Insurance, Annuities, Alternative Investments

Business rules determine the ability for customers to move between hybrid models. Rules can be based on investor goals, AUM, investment complexity, account types, level of human interaction required. Preferences can be captured during client onboarding, and monitored on a regular basis to determine which customer could be moved up/down models

Figure 2: Optionality and flexibility of the hybrid model

Notes: BPS = basis points; IRA = individual retirement account; ETF = exchange traded fund

The greatest benefit of the hybrid approach is that it increases scalability to the financial advisor, allowing the advisor to attract and serve more clients while maintaining high-quality service. This is mainly because the implementation of a digital platform helps automate manual and time-consuming processes for the client and financial advisor.

Digital advice firms are not held back by complex legacy systems; as such, digital advice firms have focused their platform functionality on addressing important problems facing traditional wealth management. Client onboarding, performance reporting and client profiling have been optimized and digitized, and in the main are provided as out-of-the-box solutions by digital advice platforms. In addition, services such as portfolio construction, rebalancing and tax harvesting can all be automated. Digital services increase advisor efficiency and improve client experience through the customization and collaboration inherent in the hybrid approach.

The digital platform also acts as a catalyst for driving business growth through acquisition of new customers and, subsequently, new assets. A digital offering provides a low-cost feeder channel to attract millennial customers, who have huge earning potential over time.

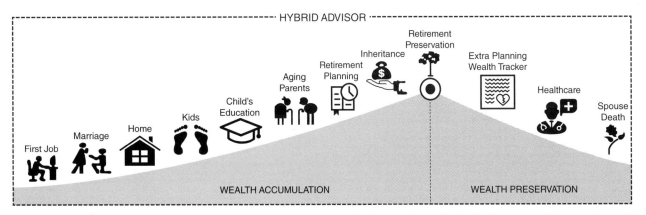

Figure 3: The hybrid model allows advisors to service customers independent of their demographic and available assets

The hybrid model enables advisors to attract new assets from new and existing customers and, equally as important, it allows the advisor to retain assets currently managed. This is because of a fundamental principal of the hybrid approach's flexible business model: allowing advisors to service customers independent of their demographic and available assets, and throughout their financial lives (see Figure 3). As a client accumulates more wealth, and their financial needs become more complex, the hybrid model allows advisors to efficiently transition clients from a digital-only experience to one with more human interaction and enhanced services.

As advisors realize efficiencies of scale, implementing a digital platform provides the parent business with enhanced transparency and control across the value chain. Supervisory regulation within financial services requires firms to ensure products and services meet the needs of their clients. Digital platforms provide automated guidelines to enhance monitoring, supervision and risk scoring.

Providing a solution that appeals to, attracts and helps retain clients ultimately drives change and validates business transformation. The transition to a hybrid approach provides immediate benefit to the end customer.

The hybrid approach provides a unified platform accessible by the financial advisor and the client, providing a consistent experience. In addition, the hybrid approach enables channel flexibility across desktop, mobile and tablet. Furthermore, solutions that use cloud-based technologies allow customers to seamlessly move between platforms with no impact to the user experience. In the future, this platform unification will provide the client with a holistic view of their wealth, across multiple providers and products.

The hybrid approach's most material benefit to clients is that they can choose the level of human and digital interaction. The solution provides flexibility, allowing the client to choose their level of advice, product access, fee structure and digital experience. Hybrid enables a personalized solution that is cost-efficient to the business and provides material growth opportunities for the financial advisor.

The Future is Now for Digital Advice

Independent of the form, digital advice and technology are the future of wealth management. Providing a digital experience has become mandatory. Customer and financial advisors expect better digital tools and the flexibility of human interaction to suit their specific needs.

Embracing the FinTech ecosystem and using digital advice platforms to provide a hybrid approach empowers wealth management firms to evolve their business, attract a new generation of customers and serve them in a flexible and cost-effective way.

Moving to a hybrid approach also helps firms future-proof against further changes to the wealth management model, providing greater agility to meet the ever-changing regulatory and customer environment.

Although the future is bright for wealth managers who successfully complete this shift, pressure remains for continued innovation, as non-financial service companies such as Uber, Alibaba and Facebook recognize the opportunity at hand, start offering their own form of financial services and begin a new battle.

No "One Size Fits All" – Personalized Client Service and Social Selling in Wealth Management

By Frank Bertele
Founder and CEO, NETZ

The Era of Wealth Management/ Private Client Disconnect

We have entered an era of increasing disconnect between wealth managers and private clients. A survey[1] shows that the most important element for a private client in a wealth management relationship is a "client-focused service", or in other words a personalized customer experience (65% of responses). However, today's wealth managers do not seem up to the task, as the vast majority of clients complain that their adviser is not able to deliver a client-centric experience throughout the relationship cycle and that they feel misunderstood in terms of product and risk preferences.

In a world where digitization and more competition is constantly increasing the competitive pressure, and time spent on regulation and administration is eating up time spent with clients, wealth managers need to adopt quickly. The flaws within the private banking industry have been exposed and can no longer be masked by strong investment returns.

Starting a New Approach

At first glance, you are probably wondering how it's possible to become more client-centric with less time available for clients. The historically prevailing mindset of "more time spent with clients =

more revenues" fails to deliver. Today the equation is "**the right amount of time spent with the right client providing the right advice = higher revenues**". A higher level of "personalization" during each step in the sales process, as shown in Figure 1, is crucial for today's wealth management clients to foster long-term, sustainable client relationships, increase customer satisfaction and loyalty, and thereby drive higher revenues and higher sales productivity. At NETZ we have built services optimizing and automating personalization and social selling techniques around the sales process. By embracing social selling, leading studies show that you can achieve:

- +16% increase in revenues per year;[2]
- +45% increase in sales opportunities;[3]
- +20–25% increase in sales productivity.[4]

Step 1. More Targeted Prospecting

The foundation of a personalized customer experience is identifying and targeting the right audience. The marketing term is "persona". By targeting individuals or businesses with narrow characteristics such as age, job title or wealth, wealth managers can be much more specific in engaging with the audience. A targeted prospect would be, for example, "individuals based in London, working in financial services with a wealth of £1–5 million" or an "individual based in London who has recently sold his company and therefore acquired wealth". The more narrow your list of prospects and audience, the more personalized your approach can be.

---

[1] Source: http://www.bankersumbrella.com/blog/-what-wealthy-clients-want.

[2] Source: https://www.slideshare.net/linkedin-sales-solutions/social-selling-impact-aberdeen-report-2013.

[3] Source: https://business.linkedin.com/sales-solutions/cx/16/01/social-selling-demo-sem.

[4] Source: http://www.mckinsey.com/mgi/overview/in-the-news/social-media-productivity-payoff.

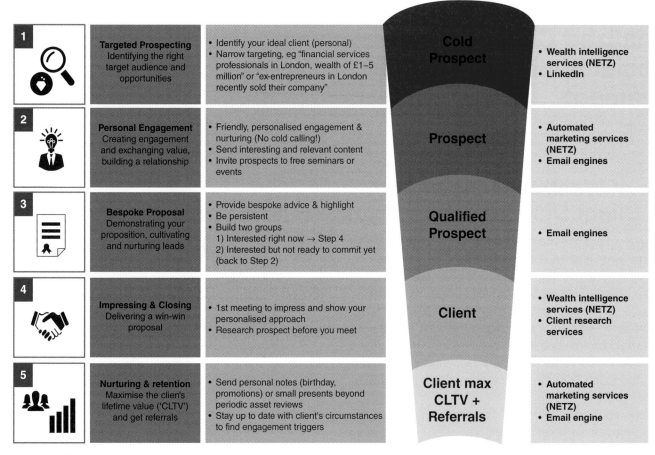

Figure 1: Social selling

Source: NETZ CMS Limited

While there are a lot of tools available such as pay-per-click advertising, social media, email marketing and external lead providers, only very few tools allow for a very targeted campaign for wealth management purposes, where the affluence or level of wealth is important.

Step 2. More Personal Engagement and Awareness

Having defined the target prospect, attention now shifts to creating awareness and engagement with your audience. For us at NETZ, it is surprising to see how many wealth managers still rely on cold calling. Only 28% of cold-called leads engage in conversation, and only 1% of cold calls lead to appointments.[5] Further, the quality of leads is poor, as a cold call feels intrusive and aggressive. Cold calling is obsolete; the best leads are those that make a conscious decision to engage with you.

How can you create engagement?

Best practice marketing dictates a so-called "value exchange" with your prospects. You should aim to provide value to your prospects before pitching to them. Value can be provided by sharing interesting and relevant content (so-called "content marketing"), invitations to free events or webinars. By developing a sequence of personalized, valuable messages, you are able to build trust and ensure you are at the forefront of their mind when it comes to making a decision.

At NETZ we are big advocates of email marketing (through our Dynamic Email Playbook service), because it can be highly targeted, highly personalized, very friendly and non-intrusive. Those prospects responding are genuinely interested in engaging and finding out more. Moreover, email marketing is the most cost-effective tool as it can be highly automated.

Step 3. Offering a Bespoke Value Proposition

Based on your value exchange you should have built a list of qualified prospects who have engaged with you. The objective now is to introduce your value proposition in the most personalized way possible. Highlight how you can help the prospect, provide fact sheets or case studies to underline the value you can generate. And, most importantly, be fully transparent on your fees.

Awards and testimonials are good, but only once the prospect asks for more details.

Based on the response of your qualified prospect, we recommend splitting the qualified prospects into two groups: (1) interested right now and (2) interested but not ready to commit yet. Group 1 has indicated that they are looking for advice right now and are able to act soon; therefore jump to step 4 of the sales process. Group 2 should go through a nurturing campaign and keep receiving more value (see step 2) by sending them interesting articles, news and invitations to events.

The most common mistake of wealth managers is thinking too short-term, discarding any qualified prospects which are not ready to commit yet. They made the effort of engaging and qualifying prospects but because the time might not be right for a prospect, they stop engaging altogether. Based on NETZ market research we had introductory meetings with 30 wealth managers from small and large firms, and six months later only 2(!) wealth managers are still touching base at regular intervals. In other words, more than 90% of wealth managers stop engaging if a prospect is not ready to commit right now in the moment! A study shows that persistence is key in winning clients.[6] On average, 12 touch points (6 phone calls, 3 voicemails, 3 emails), including social interaction, are necessary to convert a qualified prospect into a client.

One important element in building relationships with prospects is the response time once a prospect has reached out to you. Very often, wealth managers do not respond to a lead quick enough and wait for a day or more. A study[7] shows that the time for a first response is directly linked to the success of converting a prospect into a client.

---

[5] Source: https://blog.hubspot.com/sales/cold-calling-statistics and Keller Center Research Report by Baylor University, http://www.baylor.edu/business/kellercenter/doc.php/194525.pdf.

[6] Source: https://uk.insidesales.com/research-paper/autumn-2016-responseaudit-report/.

[7] Source: https://uk.insidesales.com/research-paper/autumn-2016-responseaudit-report/.

The study further shows that the odds of the lead becoming qualified are 21 times greater when contacted within five minutes versus 30 minutes after the lead was submitted. Now, we know that wealth managers are generally very busy and a five-minute response time might not be realistic; however, the key message is that the faster you can respond to a prospect the more likely you will be to turn the prospect into a client. Best practice would be to hire a marketing assistant to respond to emails or calls quickly on your behalf, or use automated email platforms which can be set up in no time.

Step 4. Impressing in Meetings and Closing Deals

Once your qualified prospects are interested in your service, the next step is to impress them in a meeting. As with the other steps of the sales process, personalization is key! At NETZ, we always argue that the first meeting is a unique chance to start connecting with your future client and building rapport. In order to impress, it is invaluable to conduct research and refer to personal circumstances or news about the individual, the individual's company, the industry, or any personal news such as promotions or achievements. In the meeting you might want to invite them to an event they care about, for example a seminar on tax-efficient investments, to sports matches or to the opera.

From our market research with 30 wealth managers, only four impressed in the first meeting and were able to build rapport by knowing details about me and the company NETZ, such as when we started, recent industry news and press articles we were mentioned in. These four wealth managers cared. The other 26 wealth managers were simply running through their services, awards, investment performance and trying to extract information for a fact-find. It is clear which wealth managers are more likely to successfully win our business!

While LinkedIn is a good way to get an understanding of a prospect's professional experience, there is much more insightful information available on the web and going the extra mile will pay off. There are several automated research services such as NETZ which do not cost much.

Step 5. Optimizing Client Retention to Drive Organic Growth

Once your prospect has turned into a client, the key objectives are delivering an excellent service and retaining the client, in order to maximize the client's lifetime value (CLTV) and get referrals.

Many new clients start a wealth management relationship by investing a relatively small amount compared with their total amount of assets. The drivers for maximizing the amount your client invests with you are: (1) the quality of your service; (2) personalized and bespoke advice; and (3) personal relationship.

While points 1 and 2 are at the forefront of the minds of most wealth managers, point 3 is often forgotten. Also, clients have to be nurtured and managed. Alongside the usual asset reviews, clients will appreciate personalized notes from you (for example for birthdays or a promotion). Depending on the value of the client, we recommend small presents and invitations to events they enjoy (for example, sports matches or the opera). Furthermore, by staying up to date with clients' circumstances and news, wealth managers can find valuable engagement triggers.

Beyond keeping a fact-find on your client in a customer relationship management (CRM) tool, today's technology allows for tracking clients' personal circumstances, such as news, achievements and shareholdings. These technologies are essential in staying up to date on your clients and finding engagement triggers.

Ultimately, a happy client will automatically bring more assets onboard and will be more likely to refer a wealth manager to his colleagues or wealthy friends.

There is More to Be Done in a Slowly Changing Landscape

Historically, a lot of innovation has happened in back and middle-office functions, and in financial services for retail customers. An area which has seen virtually no innovation is front-office/business development for private clients. A growing number of wealth managers have recognized that a light-touch, one-size-fits-all approach might do the trick for retail clients but it does not work for affluent and high-net-worth individuals.[8] Some financial institutions have even changed their staff training and compensation structures to put more emphasis on client satisfaction and personalization. Much more has to be done. While US institutions are embracing technology and social selling techniques to foster long-term, sustainable client relationships, the UK and European markets as a whole are lagging behind.

By applying technology and best practice techniques to foster personalization and social selling, wealth managers increase lead conversion, grow customer satisfaction, and thereby drive higher revenues and sales productivity. Today's wealth managers do not have to become experts in the sales process but they have to become aware of what is necessary to win, and that there are technologies and tools to help. Now that is how you can become more productive: "Spend the right amount of time with the right client providing the right advice!"

---

[8] Definitions for affluent and high-net-worth individuals vary. The most common definition for an affluent client is a net worth of at least £100,000, and for a high-net-worth individual it is a net worth of at least £500,000.

How to Give "Sleep-Tight" Robo-Advice

By Paul Resnik
Director Marketing, PanPlus and Co-Founder, FinaMetrica

No investor should ever be surprised by the ups and downs of their portfolio. After paying for financial advice, investors are entitled to "sleep tight". They should never lie awake worrying about changes in the value of their investments.

Regrettably, sleepless nights will be the norm for many investors. Their mistake? They trusted a robo-advisor – an automated advice process that made an investment recommendation. Unfortunately, many of these automated advisors are badly built and recommend investments that are not suitable for the customer.

So, what is wrong with most robo brains? And why do they recommend unsuitable investments? A key problem is that many robos are simply replicating the poor examples set for them by the human advice process!

The investment industry happily "talks the talk" about making recommendations that are suitable for their customers when it helps win clients while avoiding regulatory intent, but it has a very poor record when it comes to "walking the walk" down the path of investment suitability – the matching of investment products to investors, using tools including risk profiling.

Today, it is the investor's unrevealed problem. However, after the next major market correction, this will spread the pain. First, it will be the robo's problem. Soon afterwards, it will become the problem of the sales and marketing departments of the robo, followed by the robo's lawyer. And then the robo's parent firm's professional negligence insurer's problem. And then the jury's problem. Soon, there will be no "sleep tight" for anyone.

When investment suitability is done poorly, everyone is a loser. The client is exposed to assets and asset mixes they are not emotionally prepared to own. So they often sell and buy at the worst possible moments. The robo is exposed to all the risks of an unhappy, complaining client, including reputational damage, eventually leading to fines and class-action settlements.

Conversely, "sleep tight" is a two-way street. Investors/clients sleep tight when they have investments that suit their personality and needs. Owners and operators of robos sleep tight when they have a proper and defensible process for recommending investments to ensure they are suitable. When investment suitability is done well, everybody comes out a winner.

Investment suitability needs to be a process that accurately and scientifically takes into account an investor's financial and psychological needs, but commonly this process is kidnapped by sales opportunism. Instead of rigour and science, there is a race to make a quick sale. "Suitability" might, at best, be cursory or superficial – at worst, it could be an outright lie.

Usually, these suitability mismatches go unnoticed, unrecognized or simply are not considered cause for concern. But then, a sharp drop in asset prices occurs, such as in 2008. In an instant, those mismatches can transform into unhappy clients seeking support, more advice and finally redress. In the current (opposing) practice and regulatory settings, they will win both retribution and compensation.

We have been warned – suitability is the major area of consumer complaints in many countries, pressuring governments and regulators to react. Courts have a history of severely punishing investment professionals who exploit their less-knowledgeable clients by foisting upon them unsuitable financial products. Regulation, however, is struggling to keep up. Prescriptive regulation – where rules must be followed and boxes must be ticked – proved to be a failure. It was simply too hard and costly to enforce, but the new standards-based regulation is just as big a failure. It says "here is a desirable outcome – now meet it however you see fit". But without guidance or rules to be enforced, just about anything can be argued to be meeting the "standard".

Now, robo-advice has arrived into a market where there has been little growth in funds under management for almost a decade, and packs of competitors fight like piranhas over every investable dollar.

Public trust and confidence in financial advice has never fully recovered from the horror and dismay of 2008. A significant portion of the blame is at the industry's feet, because it has not displayed the integrity and consistency of customer experience necessary to earn – or regain – client trust.

However, there is a simple pathway to restoring that lost trust – be trustworthy! That means acting with integrity by putting the needs of the client first and delivering consistent client experiences.

The foundation of trust is to prove that investments are suitable.

First, advice givers must meet five "proofs" of suitability:

- **Know and understand the investor.** To truly understand their client, the advisor must consider three distinct factors which many advisors and advice processes fail to recognize individually:

  - Risk tolerance. The investor's psychological disposition and ability to comfortably deal with rises and falls in the value of their investments.

  - Risk capacity. The investor's ability to realize their goals in the event of a substantial fall in the value of investments.

  - Risk required. The amount of investment risk needed to achieve the returns necessary in order to satisfy the investor's goals.

- **Identify mismatches and examine alternative strategies.** Financial products are not "one-size-fits-all". The system should identify people who have a mismatch between their risk tolerances and the risks they may want, or need, to take on and consider alternative ways that might achieve their goals.

- **Know the products.** Can you explain what is "in" the product, how it works and how it will behave in a downturn? Are investors' needs mapped and framed to portfolios consistent with the person's risk tolerance, needs and goals?

- **Explain the risks.** This step is vital but commonly overlooked, or done poorly. It is, to be fair, a complex and difficult task. It brings together what is known about the investor's risk tolerance and the risk of the recommended products. This allows for all risks to be fully disclosed in ways that the client will be able to understand and comprehend.

- **Obtain informed consent.** A client who understands the details and risks of a financial proposal and how it relates to their individual risk tolerance can give "informed consent". Borrowed from medicine, this term means that the person has had all risks and possible outcomes explained to them and agrees to proceed.

Meeting these proofs requires a complex, multi-dimensional process that uses a wide range of factors to determine an investor's risk profile – that is, the most appropriate level of risk for that person. Risk tolerance is balanced with the "risk required" to achieve the goals given current resources and the "risk capacity" – the ability to still achieve goals even if the investments fail to grow as expected.

Robos that are "direct-to-public" have, for the most part, failed to earn their keep.

The robos making it in the market are, with just a few exceptions, attached to larger financial organizations. Often the robo is augmented by the involvement of a human advisor in a "cyborg" process that is part person and part machine.

Robos pose particular risks to their enterprise owners, because what the robo is doing must integrate with their existing investment advice ecosystem. The first reason is reputational – a brand does not want to diminish itself through a lesser service. The second reason is logistical. Over a lifetime, a client may move through many of the brand's different business arms and the same approach needs to be standardized and practised across all of these different potential contact points.

Financial enterprises who are parents and keepers of robos require four critical consistencies across all arms of their business:

1. **Risk profiling methodology.** The robo, retail bank and private client department must all measure and apply the risk profile consistently.

2. **Mapping of risk tolerance to portfolios.** Mapping is a nuanced process that takes into account any mismatches between risk required, risk capacity and risk tolerance.

3. **Consistent language of risk.** When FinaMetrica published a global book on risk terminology,[1] we found more than 25 terms that describe risk in the setting of financial planning and investments – not one has an agreed definition in the wider world! But within an enterprise, all terms about risk must mean the same thing in every advice channel.

4. **Explanations of risk.** As people absorb and process information in different ways, the explanations of risk must be presented in different formats such as words, visually and numerically. Like language, explanations must also be consistent across all channels.

Robos are proliferating. Most banks, major investment houses, large pension funds and life offices have at least one, while some have a range of robos – each aimed at a different target market.

Many of these robos are not getting investment suitability right. They are getting the risk profiling wrong, which makes it impossible to accurately map the investor to a portfolio and to frame the expectations around that portfolio.

Regrettably, regulators have not mandated that a psychometric risk tolerance assessment should be the first step of the investment suitability process. But regulators have fallen behind, and enterprises that want to stay ahead in a competitive marketplace are doing more than just the "minimum possible requirement" as a point of differentiation.

In our experience, a growing number of enterprises are turning to "best of breed" components, so that they can integrate their chosen tools into their own offerings to clients. We see an increasing trend towards specialist businesses using open architecture APIs, which allow outsiders to access the inner engines of other people's software – for example, using Facebook logins for another company's website.

These enterprises are seeking out "best of breed" providers of algorithms and intellectual property to help them stay ahead of the competition, which grows by the day. By properly risk profiling and understanding clients, they are building a protection against being stomped on by a new entrant like Facebook, Apple or Google, who have an incredibly detailed knowledge of their billions of users.

[1] https://www.riskprofiling.com/Miscellaneous/risklexicon.

How Gamification Can Attract Consumers to Sign Up

By Kris Grgurevic
Chief Commercial Officer, Niiio Finance Group

and Dr John Stroughair
ex-Partner, Goetzpartners

While humans are very good at solving intellectual problems, we are very bad at dealing with issues that require us to trade off short-term pain for long-term gain: we eat too much; we exercise too infrequently; we save too little. When we do save, we tend to make emotionally based decisions that leave us with portfolios that bear no rational relationship to our genuine economic needs. The consequences are dramatic: median net wealth in the USA is only $44,900 and even in Germany, a country with a reputation for thrift, median net wealth is €60,000. Needless to say, people below the median level of net wealth are unable to deal with extended periods of unemployment and are likely facing relative poverty in old age, dependent on state support. The situation is even worse for millennials. This generation is the first since the 19th century to earn less in real terms than their parents, and face the prospect of being taxed to support the retirement of much richer baby boomers while dealing with the highest levels of economic disruption since World War II. The long-term demographic trends in the West make it unlikely that any Western state will be able to finance welfare payments at current levels throughout the working lifetimes and retirement of the millennials; their only chance for sustainable economic well-being is an active, intelligent engagement with the financial markets.

This ought to be an interesting problem for FinTechs to address; the sums involved are enormous and the societal benefits are obvious – here is a chance for FinTechs to demonstrate that they can actually be a force for good in society. Yet what do we see: apps for splitting bills (Splitwise, Billr); apps that use the Tinder model to trivialize stock trading (Robinhood); and apps like Nutmeg and Wealthfront that purport to supply investing advice, if you already have some

money, but leave many clients with portfolios poorly aligned to their actual financial needs. How might FinTechs address the genuine problem and assist millennials to manage their financial affairs in a sustainable manner? It is clear that what might have worked for previous generations will not fly with millennials, they will not blindly follow advice from authority figures and they will expect any solution to be easy and ideally fun. Here the FinTech community can usefully learn from other sectors that have faced similar problems. A good example is the health insurance sector: firms like Vitality in the UK, which clearly have an interest in keeping their clients healthy, encourage their clients to exercise by using trackers like Fitbit and rewarding clients with free Starbucks coffee and movie tickets if they hit weekly targets. Vitality also offers discounted gym membership and cashback rewards for frequent gym visits.

The essence of all these ideas is that of gamification: beneficial long-term behaviour is rewarded with small short-term rewards that are viewed as fun. All of Vitality's customers can afford to buy their own coffee at Starbucks, but the sense of having "won" something gives the reward a psychological worth out of all proportion to its economic value. There are anecdotal reports of Vitality customers running around the block at the end of a long working week to hit their targets.

In a completely different area, the Duolingo app encourages users to practise foreign language skills on a daily basis by awarding game points ("Lingots") that can only be used for in-app purchases. Yet this essentially meaningless reward is enough to keep many users conscientiously honing their language skills. Even when we realize how the app or the company is manipulating our behaviour we play along, our competitive impulses are strong enough that the drive to win even meaningless game points overcomes our laziness and inertia when our own genuine long-term interest would not. Mihaly Csikszentmihalyi described this behavioural pattern in his psychological concept of flow,[1] a state we enter when the challenge and our own skill set are matched and we enter "the zone".

---

[1] Csikszentmihalyi, M. (1990). *Flow: The Psychology of Optimal Experience*. HarperCollins, New York.

Gamification and Financial Management

What is "gamification"? Gamification can be seen as an effective tool for influence in order to drive certain actions.[2] On the one hand, it provides "gamers" with points and achievements to motivate their behaviours ("game mechanics"). On the other hand, it governs how and when these rewards are unlocked over time, as well as the precise reward schedule.

Daniel H. Pink, author of best-selling books and chief speechwriter for former US Vice President Al Gore, described in one of his most popular books[3] the building blocks of motivation which serve as one of the core principles of gamification:

- **Autonomy** – controlling one's own pace and path through the game.

- **Mastery** – getting better over time through practicing and applied learning.

- **Purpose** – aiming at a well-defined goal.

These characteristics are also those identified by Csikszentmihalyi as likely to lead to flow experiences. There is now a significant research effort directed at how to predict and manipulate the gamer's decision processes in order to direct them to goals external to the game. So, how do we begin to apply gamification ideas to finance? There are two apparently contradictory ideas that need to be addressed. Gamification tends to work best when it is applied to one simple, small aspect of behaviour (e.g. persuading the health insurance client to go for a walk rather than sitting down with a beer; or nudging the language learner to practise Polish verbs rather than watching the next episode of *Game of*

Thrones). Yet, if financial advice is to be genuinely useful, it needs to be based on the user's complete financial picture; for example, encouraging people to invest more is generally good, but not if they are carrying large levels of credit card debt.

The solution is to create incentives for individuals to upload their complete personal balance sheet. Normally this would be a tedious exercise that would take up to an hour, if not longer, and cause many potential clients to give up. To be successful this onboarding process has to be itself turned into a game, with users rewarded for completing sections and encouraged to drop the process and return later using any device. The idea is that people will go through fairly complicated setup processes to play games like Minecraft or World of Warcraft because they are confident that the game that follows will justify the time investment and because it is a process that can easily be interrupted and restarted. We have to make the onboarding process for any financial app as painless as that for a gaming app.

A simple example of how a gamification approach can be useful during the onboarding process is to look at the standard assessment of risk tolerance used by almost all robo-advisor wealth managers. This consists of asking people hypothetical questions such as: "Would you prefer a certain return of 6% or a return with a 50% chance of 14% and a 50% chance of 0%?" The response of most people to this question is generally bafflement if they have had limited exposure to finance; or they see what the question is getting at and game the answer. Instead of asking hypothetical questions – which most people do badly at answering – we can use a game-like environment to see what people actually do when faced with risk within the game. Behaviour is a much more accurate guide to preferences than the answers to hypothetical questions.

Once the user's complete financial picture is uploaded, the site can analyse the situation and start nudging the user to make minor modifications – successful modifications in the financial picture lead to rewards. The specific change that is suggested is determined both by the user's individual position and also by his or her goals, which have been determined during the onboarding

[2] http:// community.lithium.com/t5/Science-of-Social-Blog/Gamification-from-a-Company-of-Pro-Gamers/ba-p/19258.

[3] Pink, D. H. (2009). *Drive: The Surprising Truth About What Motivates Us.* Riverhead Books, New York.

process. As the situation changes, the particular challenge presented to the user is changed to reflect the new situation, in a similar way that players move through levels in games.

The user can set up a group of friends and family which will support both cooperation and competition, just as in a classic MMORPG.[4] We can build in simulated shocks that will let users stress their own and their friends' financial situation, which can be done both for fun within the game context but also supplies useful risk management insight.

Conclusion

We believe that gamification can effectively both support the targeting of specific desired customer segments as well as providing the motivation to make financial management approachable and fun for rookies.

If people will spend time running a virtual farm, we should be able to encourage them to play a similar game where in actuality they are managing their own financial situation.

---

[4] Massively multiplayer online role-playing game.

The Counter-intuitive Reality of Robo-Advice Demographics

By Sarah Stewart
Analyst, Strategic Insight

and Brett McDonald, CFA
Associate Consultant, Strategic Insight

Like many emergent technology-based consumer products and services, adoption is often assumed to lean towards younger generations. In the case of the delivery of online financial advice – which often falls under the robo-advice moniker – similar observations can be made about assumptions concerning generational product adoption rates and, in parallel, the budding reality of actual consumer adoption. While many emergent wealth management services have targeted accumulators and the millennial generation, robo-advice and the broader delivery of financial services online is certainly more than a millennial story.

Millennials as a Robo-Advice Target Client Segment

On paper, the millennial age cohort reflects many attractive attributes to be a target for emerging online advice services. From a timing perspective, the first-born of the generation are beginning to reach the age typical of entering the accumulation phase of the financial life cycle. This is the phase where incomes stabilize, families are started, homes are purchased and wealth begins to accumulate as human capital is transformed into financial wealth. This is also the phase where financial advice relationships form, as potential clients accumulate enough assets to garner the attention of, and meet the minimum asset thresholds for, more traditional wealth management practices.

The millennial generation also presents an eye-catching opportunity from a household market size perspective. Differing on a country-by-country basis, the sheer size of the millennial generation rivals the baby boomer cohort as the largest living generation in developed markets.

In addition, and perhaps the most attractive quality of them all, millennials have developed a reputation for being tech-savvy and relatively early adopters of emergent consumer technologies. These combined factors have made this age segment a key target for various robo-advice services, and in many cases these firms have succeeded in onboarding a relatively young customer base.

Unfortunately, younger generations lack a major ingredient which is fundamental to being an attractive wealth management client: the time required to accumulate assets. While younger age segments may be more open to adopting new technology-based services and represent a large market when measured from a population or lifetime value perspective, in the wealth management arena the cohort represents a relatively small opportunity in the short term when measured in terms of their total investable assets.

Early Adopters and Baby Boomers: Certainly Not Mutually Exclusive

While the millennial generation has early adopter tendencies when it comes to digital services, market realities show that other generations have also demonstrated similar tendencies. So much so that, through a North American lens, despite making up a large portion of the client base, millennials represent a minority of robo-advice assets under administration. Generation-Xers, baby boomers and beyond make up a significant portion of the present-day online advice asset base and represent a relatively lucrative target going forward. In fact, looking at the Canadian experience, the average age of an investor using robo-advice services is in their mid-40s, ranging from teenagers to people in their 90s.

For wealth management distributors whose revenues are linked to assets under administration, it is these generations that have had more time to accumulate assets that offer a larger potential market. This is especially true in the near term, as gen-Xers and baby boomers stand to benefit from an intergenerational transfer of wealth more so than their millennial counterparts.

Outside of segmenting the market by age, client preferences offer some hints as to where online advice efforts may potentially bear the most fruit. The preference for digital interaction (as opposed to face-to-face meetings) is not exclusive to one generation, and not all consumers align with their demographic stereotypes. As time passes, older demographic segments are becoming increasingly comfortable in their use of technology. There are retired individuals who prefer completely digital financial advice delivery, just as there are some millennials who would prefer to deal with someone strictly face-to-face. The preference for mode of delivery exists on a continuum, one that is dynamic and subject to shift over time. Proxies from other digitizing industries, however, would suggest that the scale is tipping towards the digital end of the spectrum.

Another client preference continuum to consider when assessing the market potential for online advice offerings is the degree of autonomy a client prefers in dealing with their financial matters, ranging from completely self-directed to delegating all decision making to a professional advisor.

It is the combination of reaching the accumulation life cycle stage, a preference for digital interaction and the inclination to delegate that represents a potential sweet spot for online advice firms.

Online Advice Has a Value Proposition Relevant for Older Generations

Beyond the generations who are approaching the traditional age of retirement, the extension of online advice adoption up the demographic age spectrum holds potential with the retiree market as well. Although many households in this cohort have long-entrenched financial advice relationships, delivering advice through an online interface offers certain advantages that align with the needs of older client segments.

A significant theme behind the broad expansion of FinTech has been the proliferation of services based on the idea of simplifying the complex, and making navigation easy and straightforward. Accordingly, online advice does not require a high degree of tech-savviness, but rather requires a certain degree of digital literacy and comfort operating online. Simple user interfaces that have considered ease of navigability in their design can be comprehended by those with basic levels of digital literacy.

In addition, service accessibility has been a common element and advertised differentiator of many robo-advice offerings to date. The ease of access, whether that is access to a remote financial advisor, customer support, educational resources or even simple account information, has value to clients where physical mobility is a limitation.

Online services also provide an interface and environment that is potentially collaborative, supporting collaboration not just between the robo-advice firm and the client, but between the client and their family members where permissioned access or household account linkages can be facilitated digitally.

There have also been examples of robo-advice firms building products specifically aimed at the retiree market. These product features range from income-oriented portfolios targeting specific monthly income levels to extending access to dedicated financial advisors with specific expertise in retirement considerations.

Of course, servicing older age segments with an online advice offering comes with its challenges. The complexity of a typical client's financial considerations tends to increase as they age, which may be difficult to address through a purely digital offering. As well, many clients may have existing advice relationships, exhibiting a degree of inertia with their existing providers which is difficult to break. Generating a broader awareness of robo-advice among the public, and a sense of trust in what is still a relatively nascent service offering, also presents a more expansive set of challenges.

The Road Ahead Provides Services Across the Demographic Spectrum

From a product development perspective, building on what is already available in online advice delivery channels allows for potential new avenues of value creation specific to older generational age segments.

Advancements in related healthcare technologies offer some potential integration opportunities, an example of which would include the ability to test for cognitive decline in aging clients using an integrated technology-based solution. Elements of estate planning are also gravitating online, allowing those planning for the future to create, file and store materials in a digital vault with familiar elements of accessibility and simplicity built into the value

proposition. Several firms are also working on solutions to take on the problem of financial exploitation of older clients by monitoring bank and investment accounts for suspicious activity and alerting designated family members or friends when triggered.

Most of the activity and innovation on this front has taken place in the start-up community, where it is a safe bet that entrepreneurs will continue to seek out problems to solve, online advice models will continue to evolve and robo-advice's relevance to the retiree cohort will continue to grow.

While many emergent wealth management services have targeted millennials and have developed valuable solutions for savers and accumulators, robo-advice and WealthTech certainly have broader applications across the demographic spectrum.

How Emerging Technologies Will Change Emerging Markets – Welcome Robo-Advisor X.0!

By **Katarina Prozorova**
Founder and CEO, Robo-Advisor IIWOII

Prologue:[1]

> "Why did you title your article that way?" my millennial[2]-age sister exclaimed.
>
> "What do you mean?" I replied.
>
> "Robo-Advisor X.0!"
>
> "You know", I started. "X.0 relates to the mathematical optimization… I mean the selection of a best element from some set of available alternatives."
>
> "No, no, no", she interrupted. "Robo-Advisor X.0 sounds like Robo-Advisor Hugs and Kisses" she laughed.
>
> "Really?" I said. "I didn't consider it that way, wait but why?"[3]

Robo-Advisor X.0 – Hugs and Kisses

Robo-advisors are a class of financial advisers that provide financial advice or portfolio management online with minimal human intervention. Robo-advisors provide digital financial advice based on mathematical rules or algorithms. Robo-Advisors X.0 will provide digital advice using artificial intelligence applications, or rather artificial intelligence applications under Robo-Advisors X.0 control will make decisions instead of us. Robo-Advisors X.0 will offer a future of financial advice and portfolio management substantially different from the current analogue implementation of sophisticated applications as tools and realizing more ambiguous goals.

Digitization becomes the mainstream trend for all industries providing the following social and business functions:

- business processes automation
- artificial intelligence implementation.

For wealth management, as a human capital and intelligence-intensive industry, digitization plays an exceptional role.

Nowadays, quantum computing offers the possibility of technology millions of times more powerful than current systems. For example, the first project of one of the leading players in the quantum computing industry has solved the problem of designing investment portfolios. The goal was to generate the maximum return for a given risk profile to help fund managers not only choose among the thousands of available securities, but also minimize transaction costs by achieving the most optimal portfolio in the minimum number of trades. The speed of technological advancement is growing so fast.

Another example is a robot that has solved a Rubik's cube in less than a second, while the officially recognized Rubik's cube world record belonging to a human is about 5 seconds. Should we be concerned that robots will take over human jobs? Digital disruption is coming to change existing business models and financial ecosystems.

This will lead to two consequences:

- personal and corporate income generation paradigm
- universal basic income proposal.

---

[1] Prolog is also a high-level computer programming language first devised for artificial intelligence applications.

[2] Millennials are considered to be the target audience for disruptive technologies at the earliest stage of implementation.

[3] Reference to the title of the blog, covering the most interesting topics, including artificial intelligence, outer space and others.

The first consequence of digital disruption will be the change of personal and corporate income generation. Intellectual capital (human), information asymmetry and trust are the main drivers of income generation at the moment. Implying that intellectual capital is in line with forecasts and existing growth potential in a rapidly changing environment, information asymmetry will dramatically decrease in coming years. Most business activities could be transformed into algorithms and be automated – business processes transparency.

Trust, honest and ethical behaviour in all areas, especially in finance, will become the main driver of personal and corporate income generation ability. The emergent technology of blockchain will revolutionize the financial services industry and has the potential to reduce systemic risk and financial fraud by empowering millions across the globe to authenticate and transact immediately and without costly intermediaries. Thus, ethics and new technology will lead to the independence of future robo-advisor business models from financial institutions. That will effectively manage agency problems as well as any conflicts of interest in any relationship where one party is expected to act in another's best interests.

To sum up, the most logical business model construction for future Robo-Advisors X.0 is as independent financial advisors.

The second consequence of digital disruption is the universal basic income proposal, or a form of social security in which all citizens or residents of a country regularly receive an unconditional sum of money, either from a government or some other public institution, in addition to any income received from elsewhere. And that is not in such a distant future as it might seem.

The universal basic income proposal has appeared due to the hypothesis that artificial intelligence and robots will replace people's jobs in the majority of human activities. The transformational process has already started – some countries are already planning their "universal basic income" trials.

Owing to the changing and challenging environment, there should be a solution that provides people with advice, including financial advice, and tools to go through this transformation in a more favourable way. Robo-Advisors X.0 are expected to be such a solution. Independent Robo-Advisors X.0 will look after the best interests of each person and help smooth the way to self-actualization, creating the optimal situation for everyone. That will cause a significant impact on society. Robo-Advisors X.0 will change the focus from the current financial status of a person or a portfolio to the drivers of the current financial status, including health, value systems, human capital and randomness. In other words, Robo-Advisors X.0 will help optimize our lives beyond finance to make us wealthier and happier, and will support us like our family and friends do.

Can we title Robo-Advisors X.0 as "Robo-Advisors Hugs and Kisses" after all?

Robo-Advisor X.0 – Mathematical Programming Problem and Optimal Solution

For Robo-Advisors X.0, a person herself/himself becomes an object of optimization. There are different tools to solve this problem, including methods of linear and non-linear programming. In this case, such constraints as personal beliefs (which determine our lifestyle) and financial discipline and health status (which determines medical expenditures) appear in mathematical equations to drive the optimization process. Robo-Advisors X.0 will use disruptive innovations such as:

- data science, bid-data analytics
- advanced algorithms, machine learning, deep learning, artificial intelligence, robotics (including self-learning robots)

- augmented reality, virtual reality (holoportation)
- blockchain
- quantum computing
- 3D printing, including organs printing, artificial womb, etc.
- mind–machine interfaces and more.

Having determined the concept of Robo-Advisors X.0 and indicated the tools to solve optimization problems, we can now move to the implementation algorithm.

Robo-Advisor X.0 – Executive Officer

First, Robo-Advisors X.0 will analyse a person, identifying all strengths and weaknesses, opportunities and threats, which characterize the income/expenditure profile of that person, including the following areas:

- health
- system of values or beliefs, including risk profile
- randomness (life events that have significant impact on personal finance)
- current financial status.

Then, modern tools for analysis and optimization will be implemented to give financial advice and offer personalized financial plans. At this stage, Robo-Advisors X.0 will improve the financial literacy of the customer and clarify risk-management approaches. After a personalized financial plan is developed and confirmed by the customer, a portfolio of appropriate steps can be executed. Thus, Robo-Advisors X.0 use an innovative approach to portfolio management and transform themselves into planners, financial advisors, executive officers or application portfolio managers.

Summary

Disruptive digitization and tools in emerging market economies give enormous opportunities to develop brand-new business models in the digital wealth management industry. Such inefficiencies as limited financial infrastructure, lack of adequate regulation and transparency, low levels of financial literacy, unethical market participant's behaviour and the overall problem of income inequality are considered to be constraints in the process of searching for the optimal robo-advisory solution.

Business process automation and artificial intelligence will drive change. The speed of technological advancement is accelerating; robots could replace people's jobs in the near or mid-term. This will change personal and corporate income generation paradigms and will cause the launch of universal basic income. There should be a solution that provides people with advice and tools to go through this transformation in a favourable way.

Robo-Advisors X.0 are expected to be such a solution. Robo-Advisors X.0 will change the object of optimization from the current financial status of a person or a portfolio to the person him or herself, considering such factors as health, value system, human capital and randomness. Portfolio management is an innovative approach for Robo-Advisors X.0, where Robo-Advisors X.0 are planners, financial advisors, executive officers or portfolio managers. Using the latest technologies, new science and disciplines – like big data analytics, advanced algorithms, deep learning, blockchain, quantum computing, augmented reality, virtual reality, holoportation, mind–machine interfaces, implementing personalized decision making, goal-based investing, gamification, IT-harnessing of economics of scale – robo-advisors will make it possible to realize the best for each person (self-actualization).

Robo-Advisors X.0 will boost emerging markets. So, we're waiting for you, Robo-Advisors X.0…

Presentation Technology – Enriching the Client Experience in a Physical and Virtual World

By Colin Bennett
Head of Digital Distribution, Global, GAM Investments

A significant part of delivering a factual, advisory or educational client experience in financial services is the delivery of content through regulated channels. As financial health, advice and guidance become increasingly digital, the data that underpins the experience comes into sharp focus to facilitate the digital transition. As technology moves the digital world towards a connected Internet of Things (IoT), automated voice control, augmented and mixed reality experiences, our clients will demand content to fill those experiences both in person and online. It is, however, getting increasingly difficult to deliver regulatory-compliant personalized content (e.g. text, video, audio, images, visualizations and charts) without the content metadata being efficiently classified for the audience. Recent regulations, such as the Payment Services Directive 2 (PSD2), may further compound this by driving the need of third parties to provide compliance-approved content to new aggregated services and products.

To present content to any financial audience, it has to be both accurate and legally compliant for the audience. As digital experiences quickly become more personal, the quality of the client experience will be directly affected because content is not efficiently compliant or tagged with reference metadata to drive the content interactions with the audience. In order to deliver a first-class digital experience at scale, be it through automated advice or enriched client interaction, the industry needs to get the metadata layer right first and then from that point onwards the client experience potential is unlocked, production processes can be built and digital content distributed to meet the real-time expectations of the future.

Facilitating Client Experience at Scale

For financial services to play an active part in digitizing their services for the emerging user experience platforms, there needs to be a far better understanding and standardization of the key underlying processes that support the delivery of regulated content at scale. The incumbent organizations have dealt with these challenges well in the physical world of offices, branches, conferences and events, where the delivery of content is slow, controlled, manageable and less dynamic. However, as we digitally transform the end-to-end processes, there is an increased need to be real-time, scale fast and cross international borders to deliver digital services, material and experiences. The legacy methods do not fit with this and are not widely standardized across the industry.

Personalized Financial Content

As the financial market and products are regulated, no matter what the delivery mechanism may be, the data and content has to be delivered with context and has to be suitable for the specific interaction with the specific person. This means that financial information providers are strictly controlled in how they can market or sell a fund, often with different rules per region, country and investor type (professional/non-professional).

To deliver the personalized content, and supporting material such as product-related video, audio, charts or text, there is a growing matrix of content metadata to manage for each person/audience:

- language/content translation
- investor types (professional/non-professional, etc.)
- investor type certification (self-certified or certified, validation conditions)
- regulatory jurisdiction (country, region)

- data rules and visibility logic (show/hide)
- legal disclaimers.

It is becoming increasingly costly and complex to manufacture, approve and manage content due to all the audience delivery variables and metadata options.

The issue that needs to be solved is about regulation, and what can and cannot be done for the investor type that the online service is interacting with. For most observers it seems simple, the classic question posed is: "Why can't we have a Netflix for fund management?" Well we could, the algorithms could personalize and present the universe of product information for someone really easily, but look a little deeper and financial services is a very controlled and regulated market. In order to replicate what Netflix does, financial services would also need to try to replicate the entire supply chain/global film industry standards and their underpinning publishing and certification processes, too.

To support various business lines and clients, a B2B relationship generally requires content that is compliant for professional audiences, B2C communication requires retail approved material, and B2B2C requires both professional and retail content. Currently, content is awkwardly restricted to what an advisor or client can download from websites, email, spreadsheets or fund platforms. As the process becomes more digital, the complexity of content delivery becomes more challenging. Currently, online advice via robo-advisors tends to focus on one or two countries only, and therefore the underlying complexity of managing compliant content at scale has not yet been encountered.

Increasing Demand for Compliant Content

In the future, the production workflows and delivery of financial products supported by digital content have to be fast and hyperconnected. The complexity can be harsh, and inefficiently

dealing with this could severely limit the scalability and compliance of any advanced online financial service provider or big tech platform. It is a problem as only the larger financial service providers of globally accessible content achieve this at scale, as they need to distribute at volume internationally to many types of investors, through many different channels. Even then, the categorization and automation of content is disjointed, highly inefficient and does not cover all digital media content types required to support a rich digital client experience. It is ripe for disruption. Every single financial advisor, be they robo or live, needs to choose how they wish to deliver their content effectively while also being legally compliant with local regulation. This is a huge blind spot for scaling content internationally and therefore digitally (which by its nature has no borders).

Like with Netflix, international and local regulations govern these complex content distribution, registration and suitability rules. The marketing and servicing challenge for any provider of product, financial marketing or educational collateral is to deliver the right content to the right person without being in breach of local regulations. In effect, you need a form of digital rights management, ultimately with a personal and certified digital identity or account to control the suitable delivery of the highly regulated promotional or supporting material for financial products.

A Solution

In order to deliver content to adequately support the whole client experience, the data needs to be consistent right across all contributing and subscribing parties. It's analogous to delivering straight-through processing (STP). End-to-end processes were identified, analysed and fully understood, the process inputs and outputs were mapped, optimized and automation standards agreed and set to allow universal processing of the information. The automation principles still stand and remain solid, even when applied to the customer journeys of today. To unlock this digital transformation blocker, the global finance industry and regulators need to agree, form and sign up to:

- An open standard for classifying financial marketing and regulatory content types.
- A central rules engine representing the latest local content regulation.
- A common transmission "platform" for global distribution and regulatory submissions.
- Multimedia-enablement – applicable to all content types and formats.
- Open API access based on product entitlements.

Until this is resolved, there will always be duplication and inefficiencies; there will be a block to delivering content freely and appropriately to investors through accessible channels, and the customer will suffer. But once this is resolved, content can be manufactured and delivered appropriately online to serve innovative services in innovative ways, increasing the quality of the client experiences we can offer.

Looking at other industries, there may be an answer to power this transformation. In the second quarter of 2017, Spotify purchased Mediachain to resolve their issue with attribution of music to artists utilizing blockchain. Online financial services have in effect the same problem in reverse, for publications, digital assets and content. This content distribution challenge is a perfect use case for a distributed ledger to resolve.

The Future

There is a future where controlled documents and content would be federated from all product providers, collectively stored and managed, rather than a disparate financial service landscape where every single provider builds and maintains a content entitlements engine. There could be an online international entitlements broker that can recognize an individual by their digital identity and auto filter the information they should be receiving depending on their profile. Utilizing advances in digital identity, distributed ledger technologies and smart contracts, each personalized delivery channel could have content tagged for accountability, appropriate delivery and authenticity.

In only a few years' time our clients could be augmenting their reality with financial data; they could be asking Amazon's Alexa about their financial health and the alternative financial options and products available to meet their life goals. But unless the content is classified and the metadata assigned to drive what she says, might she become the first robot to not comply, give unsuitable advice at scale and have to be shut down by the regulator?

Digital Super Powers – The Role of Artificial Intelligence in Wealth Management

By Richard Peers

Industry Lead Retail, Private, Wealth Banking, Microsoft

According to the 2016 Capgemini WorldWealth report, 56% of net income is at risk due to client attrition from lack of digital capabilities, with over two-thirds of high-net-worth individuals (HNWIs) now looking for automated advisory services. When bots and wealth managers work together, they better serve clients' needs, improve the experience and increase loyalty. And because AI scales to meet demand virtually without limit, employees can spend more of their time on higher-priority client interactions, resulting in both cost savings and service quality benefits.[1]

While popular culture has defined AI as artificial intelligence, we believe the term "augmented intelligence" is far more accurate. The combination of machine learning, deep learning technology, bots and intelligent agents on a powerful cloud computing platform has ushered in a new era of computing. This is defined not so much by what machines can do independently or as human substitutes, but rather by how they can amplify human will and action as tireless auxiliaries in countless arenas.

We must recognize this new kind of computing both for what it is and what it is not.

- AI is not merely a new tool. It's a radical shift that makes technology what it always should have been – ubiquitous yet invisible and intuitive to use.
- AI is not about replacing humans. It's about harnessing humanity's collective knowledge and experiences to make better decisions and enrich how we understand and relate to each other and our shared world.
- AI is not about robots. It's about making life easier with intelligent services that anticipate our needs, organize our working environment and perform time-consuming repetitive tasks, freeing humans to be more creative and productive.

Financial services organizations have been tangling with data since the very beginning, but as we look ahead, the most impactful data-driven solutions will go well beyond analytics and include built-in intelligence based on deep learning technology that augments an organization's capabilities in compelling new ways. Solutions that see, hear, speak and understand our needs and emotions – using natural methods of communication, enhanced by vast amounts of data from sources as varied as search engines, news, videos and more – will transform every aspect of the business.

- **See.** Identify faces, text and objects to empower machines to continuously survey their surroundings – for example, facial pattern recognition for security.
- **Hear.** Recognize voices, languages, key phrases and topics to rapidly convert speech to text – for example, voice to text for real-time translation services.
- **Speak.** Seamlessly convert text to speech to enable a natural two-way dialogue with technology – for example, turn lists of FAQs into a voice-based service.
- **Understand.** Contextually infer intent and sentiment to personalize interactions and recommendations – for example, know when to do a warm handoff from chat to a live agent on sensing client frustration.

Private and wealth management clients have come to expect highly personalized experiences, which are hard to support with disconnected channels and systems. With the rising bar of client expectations, the need for quick, secure and highly personalized solutions is paramount. Contextual insights can be delivered at scale to wealth managers to help them prioritize their day,

---

[1] www.worldhealthreport.com.

engage clients, identify opportunities and remain compliant. This empowers them to do what they do best: build long-term rapport and trust by confidently helping clients solve their most important financial challenges. Despite the increasing speed, complexity and scale of the financial services industry, solutions are at hand to bring it under control, making every interaction personal, relevant, compliant and at scale.

Consider the following scenarios:

- Obtaining a 360-degree view of the client's portfolio and using automatic suggestions to improve or advance engagement. The next best action capabilities that make this possible leverage advanced machine learning algorithms to consume client data from customer relationship management (CRM) systems, understand client sentiment and generate relevant and targeted conversations with full orchestration across all the channels a client chooses to use.

- Accessing immediate status of client relationships, preferences and needs. Solutions for real-time insights incorporate tools such as sentiment analysis and business network alerts. These help you assess the likelihood of a meaningful event occurring that might require a timely call from a wealth manager. Personally tailored encounters can engage and delight clients with information and invitations that are relevant to them.

- Managing regulatory changes and compliance. Automate legal and disclosure communications, documentation and record keeping – for example, when an advisor calls this can be monitored and key words can prompt the advisor that certain documentation needs to be signed before further advice can be given.

- Mitigating false alarms with AI-enabled fraud prevention. When a positive fraud event is triggered via an AI model, bots send alerts to clients that corrective measures are being taken.

- Develop new business models, create new products and services, and make data-driven decisions faster than ever before. For example, new wealth advisory services that incorporate AI – which enables quality advice at a much lower cost – as an adjunct to human advisors promise an optimal mix of technology and human intelligence.

- Omni-lingual, instantaneous localization, which can radically simplify how existing services expand into new geographies globally or into previously underserved communities domestically. Such services will dramatically shorten the time to market for new capabilities, providing even more capital to invest in innovation.

The financial services industry is already realizing how bot applications can bring value to several aspects of client engagement and can increase client engagement without increasing costs, such as those listed below:

- Internal knowledge base bots that help employees search documents, policies and locate client information.

- Self-service chatbots that answer clients' questions and direct them to the best resources for further assistance in scenarios such as portfolio status, appointment booking, update on process status, new reports and events.

- Transactional bots that answer simple questions and send alerts for flagged events, such as when a tax event is due or when a trading order closes.

- Secure authentication bots that handle automated authentication through secure channels to complete transactions.

More and more investors are turning to advisory services augmented with robo-advisors for essential investment needs because of their convenience, ease of use, affordability and transparency. They can provide a range of advisory services, from personalized, automated, algorithm-based portfolio management to sophisticated tax strategies and risk management, all at a markedly lower cost than the traditional advisory model. And while they won't replace the traditional advisor any time soon, they will give human experts far greater reach, enable them to better harness relevant information sources and provide them with much-needed support for entry-level investment needs. In this way, wealth management services become much more accessible to mass markets, giving those of more modest means the tools they need to build wealth for the long run. Meanwhile, more sophisticated needs can be served by wealth managers who have better insight served through to their fingertips, ears and eyes.

For those of you curious to know how this will be delivered, the following four ingredients are key:

- **Agents.** As an example, Cortana, Microsoft's digital agent, makes interacting with technology as easy as having a conversation. It works across devices – including iOS and Android-based – and surfaces information about your daily tasks in work and life, often before you know you need it. And, the more you use it, the more personalized your experience will be. To date, there have been 12 billion queries or questions asked of Cortana, and over 145 million active users.
- **Applications.** Intelligence must be infused into every application with which we interact, on any device, at any point in time. We are building applications core to your productivity and communication, as well as business processes, to empower employees to focus their attention on what matters most. When all applications are powered by shared intelligence, entire organizations can act in an integrated, harmonious way, using a rich data model that can infer intelligence from everywhere.
- **Services.** We'll make these same intelligent capabilities that are built into our own apps available to every application developer in the world. Every interface that humans use to interact with technology and the world around them matters. As we build intelligence into everything, whether it's your keyboard, your camera, or your business applications, we are teaching applications to see, hear, predict, learn and act. The fruits of years of pioneering R&D work on speech and vision can be found in Skype Translator, Cortana, our cognitive services application programming interfaces (APIs) and the Bot Framework.

- **Infrastructure.** We're building the world's most powerful AI supercomputer and making it available to anyone. AI requires a complete transformation of underlying infrastructure, from the silicon all the way up to the cloud. As we improve the performance, scale and sophistication of our global, hyper-scale, cloud infrastructure, we're enabling scenarios that were simply not possible before.

Although not a wealth management example, it's worth considering how Microsoft recently migrated its entire treasury suite to the cloud. Today, Microsoft's $100 billion-worth of assets are managed via the Azure cloud, including treasury apps, analytics tools and trading ledgers, and AI is used to support decision-making:

- Operations in 191 countries and more than 30 currencies.
- More than US$300 billion annual cash movement.
- Approximately 2000 bank and custody accounts and relationships with 95 banks.
- 18,000 annual portfolio trades per year, totalling approximately US$600 billion.
- More than 10,000 wire transfers processed per year.

It is an unprecedented time for the industry, with extremely high regulatory scrutiny. As the financial services sector seeks ways to drive product, service and business model innovation and address the cost-reduction imperative, the cloud clearly offers a compelling opportunity for a new era of agility, especially given its potential to scale on demand. But at the same time, trust is a critical concern. Cloud solutions must meet the sector's high standards for data security, privacy and regulatory compliance, just as the frequency and sophistication of cyber attacks grow and become the "new normal". While clients are increasingly global and mobile, they expect transparent, intuitive and consistent service anytime, anywhere. This means today's leading financial institutions must find ways to better understand their clients and efficiently expand services if they want to be industry leaders tomorrow.

Using Artificial Intelligence in Wealth Management

By Holger Boschke
Chairman, TME AG

Like blockchain, artificial intelligence (AI) is one of the biggest buzzwords in banking and very likely will reshape the way financial services are rendered today. But what exactly is AI and how can it be used in wealth management (WM)? What about its risks and can it replace human intelligence?

What is AI?

The term AI was coined in 1955 by the American computer scientist John McCarthy, based on the idea that "every aspect of learning or any other feature of intelligence can in principle be so precisely described that a machine can be made to simulate it".[1]

Other terms – like machine learning, smart automation, cognitive computing, self-service analytics – are all closely related to AI.

What all these terms have in common is that they imply a certain capacity to digest large volumes of complex, unstructured (real-time) data, which enables computers to read, write, speak, listen to, see and interpret that data.

To leverage this capacity, AI platforms need access to high-quality data in huge volumes and regular transactions.

The main drivers for the big data revolution we have already witnessed are volume, velocity and variety of data. Meanwhile, the value and validity of data still seem to be an issue across the WM industry as a whole.

---

[1] McCarthy, J., Minsky, M., Rochester, N. and Shannon, C. (1955). A Proposal for the Dartmouth Summer Research Project on Artificial Intelligence.

Technology giants like Amazon, Apple, Facebook and Google have been using AI technologies for quite some time. In contrast, banks have been rather slow in adopting them, although there are more and more areas where AI is starting to generate real benefits:

- Marketing is a big thing already and a lot of firms – like BlackRock, Deutsche Bank, UBS or Wells Fargo – are using AI engines to analyse people's digital footprints and behaviour, to predict which products and services they are most likely to want to buy.

- There is also a compelling case for RegTech solutions to improve risk management, helping banks to deal with know-your-customer (KYC), regulatory reporting (e.g. under the Markets in Financial Instruments Directive 2 (MiFID2)), risk scoring, churning, etc. and using that information for marketing purposes.

- In addition, AI can help to reduce operational risks by improving (client) security and preventing fraud using biometric processes, like TouchID, face and iris recognition, or even heartbeats from wearables.

How Can AI Be Used in WM?

While these examples are about more efficient and effective processes, from a client's perspective it is about better (i.e. faster, more objective and individual), cheaper (with lower costs resulting from automation) and convenient (anytime and anywhere) advice.

Robo-advisors are a good example of how digitization can help to enhance financial services. But looking at the main components of managing wealth, there are many more opportunities to make use of AI.

Onboarding and Profiling

- Profiling systems can use behavioural analytics to undertake specific personality analysis, asking clients simple and visually supported questions, or use speech recognition software to assess clients' risk preferences.

- In order to help advisors to better understand their clients, some banks use AI systems – for example, IBM's Watson (the supercomputer that won at Jeopardy) – and chatbots to create financial profiles providing users with individual trade ideas.
- BlackRock, the world's largest asset manager, has built its own AI engine called Aladdin, which is used by a few other financial service providers as well; (among others) it can run certain "what-if" analyses.

Such tools will get more and more powerful and eventually be able to simulate these scenarios for a wide range of individual portfolios to facilitate better client interaction.

Portfolio Construction and Management

- Portfolio management is an area where AI has been used for quite some time already and will play an even bigger role going forward.
- High-frequency trading, sentiment analysis, network analysis for portfolio optimization, etc. – there are a lot of examples for its application, despite earlier limitations like struggling to distinguish news between the actress Anne Hathaway and Warren Buffet's Berkshire Hathaway.
- A lot of work currently done by economists and analysts will be replaced by AI-driven research platforms like Kensho, which (among others) is used by Goldman Sachs to analyse historical data, market patterns and market dependencies.
- Eventually this might even change the way we look at portfolio management generally. While there have been debates like fundamental vs macro and passive vs active investing in the past, this time it's about AI replacing modern portfolio theory with something completely new.

Communication and Reporting

- Financial firms have great teams of research analysts, strategists and portfolio managers, yet they all struggle to get their output to clients in relevant and convenient ways. Using speech or vision processing, AI will play a major role in changing the way financial information is communicated.
- Chatbots will be used not only to automate major elements of the customer interaction, for example providing clients with the latest insights and performance reports, but also to come up with alerts for individual portfolios and holdings.
- Providing aggregated wealth views, financial services firms will be able to provide holistic advice, while at the same time obtaining valuable marketing insights about funds held elsewhere.
- It might take a few more years before we are able to witness what we can see in the payment sector with Payment Services Directive 2 (PSD2) right now, but open (enforced) application programming interfaces (APIs) for portfolios will have a similar potential to disrupt existing market structures.

What About the Risks of Using AI?

Talking about AI and automated processes, there are genuine concerns about their systematic risks and over-reliance on computer models: algorithmic trading programs have caused serious volatility and flash crashes in the past, and the risk and pricing models invented by the quants in Wall Street in the early 2000s turned out to be based on subprime.

In order to prevent outcomes like this from happening, validating machine thinking by running endless tests and validation scenarios – as well as putting restrictions and stops in place – should be a top priority. However, this sometimes seems to mirror the debate about self-driving cars, in that the technology used in a number of driving-assist systems (and that is already helping to prevent accidents) is viewed as problematic, as long as automated cars are not 100% safe (which they will never be).

In order to address this, firms need to decide how and to what extent AI will be used, depending on the work in question: whether they simply use it to make better, faster and more informed decisions, use it to supervise work done by humans (or vice versa), or actually delegate decision-making to it.

Can AI Replace Human Intelligence?

Money, and what we do with it, is a highly emotional affair and sometimes completely irrational. In providing emotional support and dealing with feelings, advisors still have an advantage over machines.

At the same time, a lot of advisors are struggling to stay on top of the information needed to provide clients with good advice, or they spend too much time trying to obtain it. Using AI will actually allow them to reinvest some of that time and to focus on other aspects of their client relationships.

Another aspect of AI and automation is that they can be perceived as rather impersonal. But this is an argument one can easily turn on its head: using AI, individual investment proposals will be far more personal than many of the standardized solutions offered so far.

Hence, only those companies that can use the new technology in ways that resonate with the human desire for individuality and empathy, or use it to work alongside their client advisors, will be able to capture its full potential.

Conclusion

- AI will play a huge role in helping wealth managers to better communicate and articulate their value proposition, combining the best of customer relationship management (CRM), portfolio and risk management tools, in order to provide clients with better services and more substantiated advice.

- The capability to integrate and use AI will become a crucial factor in staying competitive over the next five years. At the same time, the new technology will attract new market participants and make some banks look more like IT providers, while others will use AI to become product innovators.

- Being part and parcel of a new service model, AI requires an extensive redesign of existing processes and needs to fit within the overall digitization and business strategy. It also requires a clear understanding of the product and design features and how it can be sourced.

If there is one thing to learn from what we are experiencing right now, it is that enhancing financial services technology is unlikely to be the limiting factor. Even in banking, data is the new currency.

Digital Asset Management in 2020 – Seven Theses

By Ralf Heim
Co-CEO, Fincite GmbH

"Financial products are sold, not bought." This fundamental belief is widespread within the financial industry. Many surveys support this fact. They show that the average customer, if asked on the street, neither knows the performance nor the costs of his investments. Do we believe that new digital applications (so-called robo-advisors), low-cost financial products (such as exchange-traded funds (ETFs)) and upcoming regulatory requirements will change the way we invest? If so, how will these applications look and how will this change the market structure of the asset management industry? We will explore these questions with seven theses.

Speaking on stage three years ago, we often received one question: "How many robo-advisors (by banks or start-ups) will enter the market?" We often wondered about the surprise of the audience as we answered: "We believe everyone who sells financial products offline, might offer them online. It's like websites in the 1990s." Today, many announcements indicate that most banks will provide a robo-advisor soon. For the sake of simplicity, we will use the term robo-advisor for any digital application that supports the customer in their investment journey – no matter if provided by a start-up or a bank, and disregarding whether it matches the regulatory term "investment advice". Furthermore, when we speak of banks, the same might apply for insurers, asset managers or advisors.

Robo-Advice Goes "Hybrid"

How will robo-advice affect offline advice? In "offline advice", it's hard to tell what's being said behind the glass door. A standard protocol is the only, often poorly read, evidence of the advice. After buying a fund, the average customer can only see her current investment value in paper reports or online banking. Important information on performance, costs or risks are rarely provided. This differs in an online process. The customer answers public questions and receives an asset allocation and a selection of investment products based on their profile. Everything that has been "said" can be traced via the internet.

How will these two approaches coexist? As we began our journey together with banks, online advice was often considered a "side experiment". This changed in 2017, driven by regulations such as the Markets in Financial Instruments Directive 2 (MiFID2). Differing from the offline world, robo-advisors can adopt new regulatory requirements without intense training of the workforce or replacement of material. They can implement requirements like suitability checks or product governance before the regulation is in place (or even 100% defined). By doing so, robo-advisors collect early feedback on managing the intersection of conversions and compliance.

We expect these learnings to shape "the general concept of advice" within banks. Today, many want to take the best of both worlds. This means combining the anytime, anywhere, simple and fast digital processes (online) with the social interaction and contextual information (offline) in so-called "hybrid advice".

The Third Generation of Robo-Advice Gets Smarter

So far, we have seen two generations of robo-advisors: the first generation were simple onboarding tools. Deriving a risk score from 5–10 questions, one out of up to 10 model portfolios got suggested. The second generation offered discretionary portfolio management, covering regular rebalancings and dashboards to monitor the portfolio.

In 2017, we see a third generation coming. Applications that take all kinds of values of customers into account. This might look as follows: within their online dialogue, the customer connects their cash and portfolio accounts from all their banks automatically. In the background, application programming interface (API) calls to all their banks are triggered to request this information. Manually, the customer adds up their real estate, pensions, insurances, etc. The application matches this information with financial market data (such as the performance of investment products, real estate prices) to provide a solid base for the online financial advice.

How will this technology impact the market? Banks can offer portfolio checks that help the customer detect bad performance, insufficient diversification, high risks and costs within their portfolio. Very simplified, Bank A says: "Look, your Bank B sold you overpriced products with a cost rate of X, its performance was worse than our product Y and is not diversified enough for your risk profile. I can offer you something better. Interested?" The accessibility of accounts empowers the customer to get "a second opinion" without much effort. This might impact the market. As it's no longer important which bank holds the customers' accounts, market barriers are shrinking.

Robo-Advice Moves All-Finance

Analogous to the evolution in the offline world, we expect robo-advice to go "all-finance".

In the first step, we already see robo-advisors that offer access to alternative investments. Those are, for example, asset classes created by other FinTech companies, which can be executed online – such as investments in loan portfolios from peer-to-peer credit platforms, financing of real-estate projects or loans for trade finance. In the second step, we see robo advisors increasing that focus on products with an asset management component, such as life insurances or corporate pensions. In the third step, robo-advisors might move cross-product. Rebundling is expected to gain relevance in robo-advice. Imagine you connect all your assets and accounts to one application. As the underlying data is there and financial questions are interconnected, the same application can advise you on your asset allocation while also suggesting the right mix for financing your real-estate venture.

Specialized Robo-Advisors Will Rise

At the beginning, most robo-advisors targeted young digital natives. We soon learned two lessons. First: we almost always underestimated the average customer age by more than 10 years. Second: it's hard to get the young digital native "excited for finance". Today, robo-advisors first target the wealthy and/or senior customers.

We expect to see more specialized applications for professions or life stages soon. Take retirement planning for example. While the 25-year-old wants to see the effects of his savings or a pension forecast, a 60-year-old who owns a variety of assets – like houses, insurance policies and pensions – might pose different questions, like: How long will my wealth carry me? Should we sell our house and move to a nicer place? How much can I leave for inheritance? Those questions are still underserved.

Another underserved group are institutional investors. Here, robo-advice is more complex. Institutional investors want to understand whether the offered asset management strategy suits their complex portfolio. They have additional requirements on regulatory reporting, sustainability scores or features such as blacklisting sectors by fundamentals, stocks or regions.

Financial Education is Increasing

We once made a joke at a fund conference. With help from our design team, we took a screenshot from Google Shopping. We "googled" a specific shoe. Google showed us some pictures with prices and a link to a shop. Our design team replaced the search field with the name of a prominent mutual fund and the shoe picture with an efficiency curve showing risk and returns. We replaced the price by cost ratios (like operating cash flow (OCF) or total expense ratio (TER)). Then, we showed on the right-hand side: "Other people purchased instead", featuring a list of funds with better positioning on the efficiency curve plus lower costs. We immediately lost the attention of the audience. Most directly grabbed their phones and searched. Why? Because, from a user experience, it could work exactly like this.

We have already seen that the popularity of ETFs was fuelled by the internet. Simple ideas, such as "no one can beat the market" or "Warren Buffet recommends Index funds" spread fast. Financial portals grew, educating on products and strategies. Financial education gets more present, and "googling" for something we do not know becomes a habit.

Being Compliant Will Make or Break Robo-Advisor

Regulation plays a central role in robo-advice. On the one hand, regulation builds a barrier to entry. Executives of robo-advisors need to know what requirements will meet their business model, no matter whether it is self-execution or discretionary portfolio management. By the nature of online business, failing to comply immediately receives public attention. Thus, knowing if suitability checks match MiFID2 criteria, or requirements on product governance, and documentation – but also data protection documentation – requirements as well as data protection are met, is crucial. For those that do, regulation offers a chance. Some regulation opens up possibilities to build new services (such as Access to Account (XS2A) within PSD2). Whoever complies early might have a head start.

Mass Retail Asset Management Strives for Zero Marginal Costs

Today's asset management industry is complex. The value chain covers research, product manufacture, several steps of bundling and distribution, which itself contains multiple players such as brokers, advisors, insurers and banks. This complexity has its cost, which the customer needs to carry.

Last decade, futurists like Jeremy Rifkin formed the idea of zero marginal cost societies, stating that value creation processes without scarce resources might become fully automated. Robo-advice, often combined with passive ETFs, is following this idea. They lower the marginal costs for the customer's benefit. Still, one cost block remains challenging: customer acquisition costs (CAC). The average robo-advisor pays between $100 and $400 to win one client. This creates a fear that companies with low CACs will enter the market, such as Google, Amazon, Facebook and Apple, or strong product brands like Vanguard.

A company with low CACs plus enough customer touchpoints might outperform large offline salesforces in terms of reach and conversion, without having to carry the fixed costs. It comes down to reach and scale to drive retail asset management towards zero marginal costs, leading to a shift that "financial products might be bought, not mainly sold".

To sum it up: We believe we have only completed 1% of a digital evolution. The best way to "predict the future" is to create it.

Making Digital Advice Personal is as Important as Making Personal Advice Digital

By Shashidhar Bhat
Ex-Head Digital Banking, EMEA, Citi

and Kunal Goklany[1]
Director, Operations and Technology, Citi Bank

Wealth management customers are individuals whose needs go far beyond basic financial products. Attracting these customers and retaining them is very challenging, but is also likely to result in the biggest payoff among all client segments. The world has never seen so much wealth so widely dispersed in so many households globally. Propelled by high earnings and robust investment returns, this growth is projected to continue.

According to the Economist Intelligence Unit (EIU research – Spotlight on the New Wealth Builders, 2015, sponsored by Citi), as shown in Figure 1, since 2010 the number of households in the new wealth builders (NWB) and high-net-worth (HNW) segments has grown faster than the mass market (households with financial assets <$100K) segment. This strong wealth creation looks set to continue, with average growth in NWB wealth matching the strong growth seen in the much smaller HNW segment over the 2014–2020 forecast period. Conversely, the mass market population (<$100K investable assets) is contracting.

Historically, wealth management thrived on personal advice, since the rich could afford this exactly as they obtained personal services for all their other needs. Someone said: "if you want to see the future, it is already here and the rich are enjoying it". As technology has taken hold, and communication has become cheaper, different forms of automated tools have taken precedence in managing wealth too. Also, the expansion of the millennial group of consumers – who are more comfortable with technology – means that opportunities for technology-based investment options have increased. This opportunity has ensured that venture capital (VC) investment in wealth management FinTech is growing at a fast pace (see Figure 2).

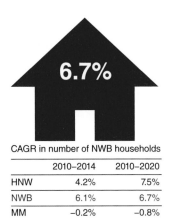

CAGR in number of NWB households

	2010–2014	2010–2020
HNW	4.2%	7.5%
NWB	6.1%	6.7%
MM	−0.2%	−0.8%

Figure 1: The New Wealth Builders (2015)

Source: Economist Intelligence Unit (sponsored by Citi)

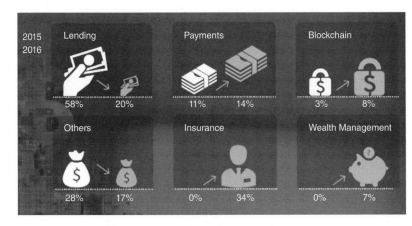

Figure 2: US VC investment in FinTech

Source: CB Insights, Citi Research Global Perspectives & Solutions, January 2017

---

[1] Disclaimer: The authors are writing this in their personal capacity, and this may not necessarily reflect the official views of Citi.

Professional advice received

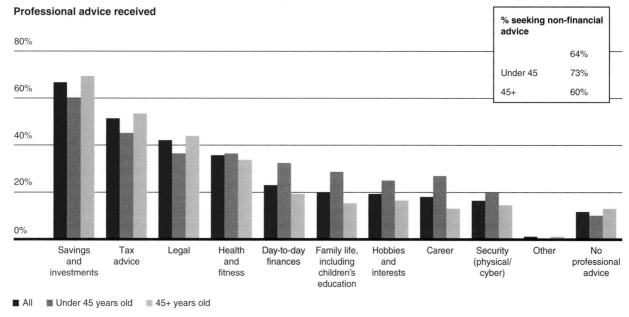

% seeking non-financial advice	
	64%
Under 45	73%
45+	60%

■ All   ■ Under 45 years old   ■ 45+ years old

Figure 3: Professional advice received

Source: PwC Strategy & Global Wealth Management Survey 2016. This article is reprinted with permission from "Sink or swim: Why wealth management can't afford to miss the digital wave", Strategy&, PwC's strategy consulting group. © 2016 PwC. All rights reserved. PwC refers to the PwC network and/ or one or more of its member firms, each of which is a separate legal entity. Please see www.pwc.com/structure for further details. Translation from the original English text as published by Strategy& arranged by Wiley.

Citi Research estimates that wealth management venture investment is tracking pace with investments in blockchain, which is a far more hyped area. Certainly, this is a sign of the opportunity for returns.

Banks need to continue to secure these customers in the face of this challenge, and to do so we recognize that the future of WealthTech lies in some sense in the basics. We recognize the following:

1. Firstly, that customers value relationships and trust in this business far more than in any other financial relationship (see Figure 3). This enables banks to have a major advantage

vis-à-vis other entrants. One of the reasons major disruption in financial services is slow to come is certainly the trust factor. In wealth management, this extends to trust in the wealth advisor too, and this trust – both at the institutional level and at the level of the individual – is earned over a substantial period of time.

2. A customer-centric wealth strategy must focus on first protecting and then growing wealth. Deloitte defines the new investing class as the rewired investor[2] who has come to view risk through

_____

[2] 10 Disruptive Trends in Wealth Management (Deloitte, 2015).

a different lens: she perceives risk as downside, rather than volatility. As a result, advisors have had to emphasize capital markets and hedging strategies that seek downside protection more than traditional portfolio allocations that seek to manage risk through diversification. This amplifies the first point too, in that the returns on investment and other factors are relatively less important and that customers value trust and relationships significantly.

Let's additionally discuss the various elements of the current wealth management landscape:

1. **Low financial advisor productivity.** We find that a significant proportion of advisor time is going on training and meeting compliance requirements. The need of the hour is to invest in improving advisory effectiveness, with an understanding of customers' financial goals and appropriate products. The implication of this is to ensure higher automation of various service and administrative tasks, and to use various technical aids to improve productivity.

2. **Trust.** Post-financial crisis, public distrust in banks overall is extending to lack of confidence with financial advisors. The various mis-selling scandals and consequent large fines that have made the headlines, compliance failures and similarly large fines there have all contributed to a failing sense of trust in banks and their employees. Being a banker is not a popular job description. Banks and their employees are doing a lot to bring that back, and the process continues.

3. **Regulation and its impact on processes.** The financial crisis brought about a large amount of regulation, and that has not abated. The additional challenge of regulation is its increasing divergence, in the sense that each regulator has looked at regulating banks locally as much as the common standards that continue to be required. This is a challenge for global banks especially. Regulation brings technical and process challenges and impacts advisor productivity.

4. **Profitability of various customer segments.** While the wealth space has huge opportunity, not all segments are equally profitable and this changes from time to time. The challenge is in ensuring a long-term relationship view in a constantly changing product offering. Servicing models should be diversified according to the different segments' cost to serve, suitability and risk profile.

5. **Technology and the drag of legacy systems.** The ability of systems to respond proactively to opportunities rather than be tied down reactively in complying with regulation is a competitive differentiator.

6. **Data.** Providing a consolidated view of information, processes and people from various systems and real-time data sources. There is a profusion of available data from both bank and external sources, and to stitch this together for the use of advisors is critical.

7. **Global incomes and taxation.** Governments are looking to implement common reporting standards (CRS, FATCA) and clamp down on tax avoidance, which has specific relevance in the wealth management space given global incomes. This has implications for reporting, KYC/AML and tax advisory software.

In the above context, future technology trends will include:

- Continued **focus on advisor productivity,** including virtualized meetings, paper-free processes and other digital capabilities. Side screen functionality will improve advisor productivity in giving advisors and customers the same view of information and capabilities. Given the increasing complexity of regulatory requirements, including global taxation, the right enabling tools (e.g. KYC, risk profiling) will be even more crucial.

- **Advanced data visualization products** will enable advisors to communicate with customers better and make financial planning sessions faster, thereby again improving advisor productivity and differentiating advisor–client interactions from self-managed investing. Data will play a huge role in understanding customers' needs to create better propensity models.

- Significant **digitization/automation of service** and administrative tasks. Making these available to customers to manage themselves with minimal challenges is the ideal way to focus advisor–client interactions on value-added planning conversations. Services like notifications and the ability for customers to self-manage some asset classes on an execution basis, and the availability of news and market data information, are examples where digitization helps enhance trust, and bring transparency into the relationship with customers.

- **API-enabled platform distribution.** The future of technology is in crowd sourcing innovation. Citi already has over a third of its API list focused around its wealth products, and is signing up partners to provide innovative experiences to wealth customers. These include portfolio performance, rates, transaction details and investing.

- **Robo-advisory products,** which will capture increasing shares of customers' wallets. Robo-advisors are like index funds, which have captured a large share of funds flows. However, exactly like index funds, there are advantages and limitations to robo-advisors. The advantages include low cost, self-service and simplicity. The limitations are the converse – that the model does not work in difficult times and where a detailed assessment is needed of financial objectives. Not surprisingly, a survey (see Figure 4) of financial advisors suggests that they are not hugely concerned about displacement by robo-advisors.

ADVISORS SEE SOME LIMITATIONS WITH AUTOMATED ADVICE

83%
point to the lack of personal support during volatile times as a significant drawback for robo-advisors

72%
agree that automated advice cannot deliver the tactical asset allocation needed, especially during down markets

Figure 4: Automated device limitations

Source: Global Survey of Financial Advisors – reaches out to 2,400 advisors, consultants and decision-makers in 14 countries, Natixis Global Asset Management, 2015

We believe therefore that monoline robo-advisors will plateau and the best outcome for customers is a hybrid advisory model which combines the low cost of robo-advising for certain objectives with the availability of a digitally empowered financial advisor for other objectives.

Conclusion

In conclusion, making the digital personal is going to be as important as making the personal digital. The management of wealth requires a higher level of personal interaction, both initially and ongoing, given the complex nature of the product, customer needs and the various investment choices available. Therefore, the future of WealthTech lies in technology-enabled customer centricity that powers both advised and self-service products and services.

Digitizing Wealth Management Operations

3

Digital Architecture is a precondition for tangible business results

- -

Legacy Mindsets holding firms back

- -

Digitization is much **more than** a cool **app**

- -

Managing whole **customer life cycle**

- -

4 Pillars of Digitization
- Holistic data integration
- Open architecture digital warehousing
- Flexible data visualization
- Hyper-personalization

- -

Financial algorithms based on AI and automated execution

- -

Cyber Security as competitive edge

Omnichannel

Branch

Phone

PC/Tablets

Social

Mobile

Third Party

All channels available to the consumer...
...and are connected

Executive Summary

Wealth management operations is an area which touches all customer- and provider-related processes. In general, an "operating model" is an abstract representation of how an organization operates across process, organization and technology domains in order to accomplish its function. In contrast to a bank's operating model, a bank's business model describes how an organization creates, delivers and captures value for its clients and sustains itself in the process.[1] While business models consider revenues, costs and resulting profitability, operating models concentrate on costs as a primary objective that focuses on efficiency. In the cost category, personnel expenses represent the lion's share and reflect the different situations regarding cost–income ratios, with approximately 80% in Switzerland, 70% in Germany, 60% in the USA, 50% in Sweden and Luxemburg, 40% in Singapore and Hong Kong, as well as 30% in China.[2] Besides employee costs that account for almost 60% of banks' costs, IT costs are the second largest cost block at approximately 20%.[3] In general, banks have the highest IT costs among all industries in relation to their revenue. Three trends characterize the developments towards new operating models for banks:[4]

- **Increasing regulation.** Many banks' project portfolios are loaded with more than 50% of regulatory project costs. Examples are know-your-client (KYC), customer onboarding and automated execution of services.

- **Increasing decentralization.** Many banks have still not transformed their operating models from vertically integrated value chains to more flexible, disintegrated models that are present, for example, in the automotive industry. Thus, banks still have a high degree of in-house "production", which can reach up to 90% in Swiss private banks.

- **Increasing industrialization.** The four principles of industrialization are the cornerstones of future wealth management operations, and technology is a strong enabler for all of them. Omni-channel management, for example, is only possible if services are standardized across all channels.

While industrialization and outsourcing are well-known principles for the three areas mentioned before, digital currencies and blockchain applications are not yet. They require additional elements like network services, wallets and many others. We still do not have a full picture of how digital wealth management operations will look in 20 years from now, but it seems that digital currencies, assets and their corresponding distributed ledger infrastructure will play an important role for future infrastructures. They spur the development of decentralized and industrialized IT infrastructures and thus enable more efficient, automated implementations of regulatory requirements.

Summarized, this part focuses on how wealth management may be better operated through the use of WealthTech.

---

[1] Osterwalder, A. and Pigneur, Y. (2011). *Business Model Generation*. Hoboken, NJ: John Wiley & Sons.

[2] Hintermann, C., Christe, A. and Laarmanen, T. (2014). *Performance of Swiss Private Banks*. Zürich: KPMG.

[3] Gopalan, S., Jain, G., Kalani, G. and Tan, J. (2012). Breakthrough IT banking. *McKinsey Quarterly*, 26(2), 30–35.

[4] Gasser, U. (Harvard University), Gassmann, O. (University of St. Gallen), Hens, T. (University of Zürich), Leifer, L. (Stanford University), Puschmann, T. (University of Zurich), Zhao, L. (City University of Hong Kong) (2017). *Digital Banking 2025*. Available online at: http://xupery.com/wp-content/uploads/2017/08/Digital-Banking-2025.pdf.

Digital Business Model for Wealth Management Operations as Matchmaker of Generations

By Laura Irmler
Senior Consultant, ARKADIA Management Consultants GmbH

The wealth management sector is under increasing pressure. While their traditional and highly conservative approach has satisfied customers for quite some time, a growing number of customers feel attracted by more innovative solutions for their investment needs. Numerous so-called WealthTech start-ups attack incumbent players in different areas. WealthTech activity can be divided into six categories: automated investments and robo-advice; social and copy trading; crowd-investing; analytics and information; and deposits and pensions; as well as platforms. The most advanced solutions can be found in the category of robo-advice. A current market analysis shows that the global investment volume in the "robo-advisors" segment of 2017 will rise by roughly €203 billion to €958 billion in 2021 – with the USA in the lead.[1] Sounds huge, however, compared with the overall market for global assets under management it can almost be neglected (as of today). Further rapid growth can be expected to come from incumbents that start to offer robo-advice as well, as seen in the USA.

Low Cost/High Value?

Robo-advisors work much more cost-efficiently, faster and without emotional influence – just some of the key advantages for customers. However, robo-advice solutions are also advantageous for wealth managers as well. They enable incumbents to serve new customer segments at lower cost levels (e.g. Goldman Sachs has recently announced that it will not only serve the super-rich, but also affluent customers – based on new robo technology). In order to attract younger generations (including the famous millennials), wealth managers are testing digital investment solutions as well. Across the entire market and all age groups it can be observed that an increasing number of customers embrace this more innovative approach – however, at varying momentum across the globe.

But What Does This Mean for Wealth Management Operations in General?

Wealth management providers should inevitably establish digital technologies in their performance spectrum. In doing so, the key to success is to address customers across multiple channels (i.e. to offer a real omni-channel service). Imagine, the grandson would rather buy Asian stocks on an online platform over his iPad, whereas his traditional grandfather gives his advisor a call to buy some Dow Jones stocks. This is one of the biggest challenges wealth management operations are faced with: they must be able to serve different generations with different needs and also be able to serve heterogeneous needs within a generation. On the one hand there are the millennials, who are connected to technology and digitization in general. On the other hand there is a growing percentage of older people, who have worked and saved money for retirement. In particular, in this age group the proportion of those accustomed to traditional human advisory cannot be overestimated. And many high-net-worth individual (HNWI) customers continue to rely on a high level of "human" support, with an advisor whom they can fully trust. There are also aspects that customers pay attention to regardless of their age: costs, returns, personal support and using a selection of different channels.

---

[1] https://de.statista.com/outlook/337/100/robo-advisors/weltweit#market-users.

Omni-channel as the New Mantra

At the same time, not every millennial requires robo-advice and innovative ideas. In general, the wealth management sector has to change from a supplier to a consumer market. Whereas even today banks specify what they want to offer to their customers, a time will come when the customer tells the bank what to offer. For that, a range of communication channels are needed, that can be used in a flexible way depending on changing customer needs. Therefore, an omni-channel approach needs to be integrated into the digital wealth management business model. This means one business logic across all channels: no matter how many front-ends are offered, they need to be based on the same set of information and logic. Thus, all front-ends should be seamlessly managed in one single automated back-end process – that requires one single data hub, ideally even across national borders.

In this setup the customer journey can be completely tracked, 24/7. This means that not only is the wealth manager informed about any transaction in any channel at any time, but the customer can also switch between the channels at any time. Referring to the example above: as soon as the grandson also wants to speak to the advisor when in the process of buying stocks, he needs to be able to switch channels seamlessly.

Beyond Systems and IT – The "Big Picture"!

However, the solution is not to offer all possible channels, but to find the perfect fit between the company's business model and its digital strategy. The challenge lies in defining a framework by asking several questions.

- **Customer segments:** Who is my customer and what is the value added I want to provide?

- **Products and pricing:** What is my product and service offering across channels and customer segments? How can I operate profitably?

- **Business processes and IT:** How can I build optimal processes? Which channels should be offered to satisfy the relevant customer segments?

The requirements from each individual triangle must be aligned with each other in order to provide a consistent business model, as shown in Figure 1:

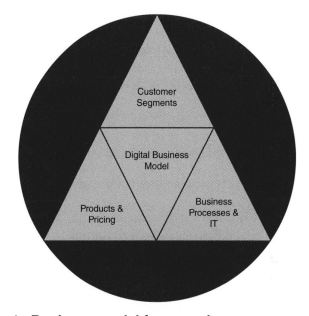

Figure 1: Business model framework

Alignment of Business Perspectives

A segmentation of the customer base seems to be crucial for every wealth management provider. While designing processes and IT architectures, providers need to be aware of their current state of infrastructure. Different systems and system generations, as well as the size and age of a wealth management company, determine the effort required for the digital transformation process as well as the speed of implementation. In addition to that, operational complexity is driven by a wide variety of devices used by customers, as well as by the number of brands and subsidiaries operated by the bank.

Balancing Complexity and Profitability

Customers will be segmented based on their willingness to pay – ensuring that customers with a low willingness to pay are provided with services based on processes with low cost of provision (fully automated, online-based). Based on the willingness to pay and the respective operational costs, price categories can be established. This is a necessary condition for ensuring profitability.

In order to provide maximum flexibility to switch channels, service modules need to be created, representing individually bookable service packages (e.g. an online robo-advisory module including one hour of personal advisory per given period of time). The switch between channels needs to be seamless for the customer. It is furthermore essential that an advisor can track the complete customer journey. That degree of flexibility should also be reflected in the pricing schemes; for example, the individual price point could be determined by the range of booked advisory service modules. For the grandson in our example above, this would mean – depending on the pricing scheme – that he may have to pay an extra charge for switching to an advisor during an online process.

There is No One-Size-Fits-All Approach

There is no perfect blueprint for digital business models, so one could rather speak of critical success factors for a digital transformation process. Wealth management operations need to define a clear focus, determining the procedural stages for the implementation of the business model. Hereby the entire process will be more evolution than revolution, since in the fewest cases a complete change is possible. But it can be a rapid evolution. Based on our experience, the following aspects should be considered in order to ensure a successful transformation process:

- **Customer centricity.** The transformation process is geared to the needs of the customer segments which are to be served.

- **Leadership.** Digital transformation requires full senior management backing.

- **Culture/employees.** Wealth management providers need to establish an innovation culture, as well as foster change in the mindsets of employees.

- **Strategy.** Digitization needs to be the core element of a wealth management provider's corporate strategy, rather than simply being seen as an additional sales channel.

- **Processes.** The process landscape needs to be fully flexible and consistent across communication channels.

- **Technology.** A flexible IT infrastructure as well as agile development methods are key to any digitization initiative.

- **Products/prices.** Products/services, as well as respective pricing schemes, need to reflect individual customers' consumption behaviour.

It seems obvious that an optimal digital business model is, of course, not just IT: it consists of leadership, cooperation, processes, offerings, customer groups, technologies and much more! The goal must be to create a completely flexible organization (in the sense of a holistic system). And even if there is not a one-size-fits-all approach, it's a fact: all wealth management operations need an individual digital business model based on customer-oriented channels to match generations.

How a Digital Architecture Can Lead to Tangible Business Results

By Angelique Schouten
CCO and Global Board Member, Ohpen

The financial services industry is rapidly becoming a customer-centric industry. Unfortunately, not in the right place. Billions are poured into the front end: fancy websites, apps and elegant-looking access to investment portfolios. In the long term, customers, financial companies themselves and regulators would be better served by a comprehensive digital architecture.

Legacy Mindset Holding Us Back

There is no denying it, with (core) systems installed in the 1970s, 1980s and 1990s, banks, wealth and asset managers are ill-equipped to support today's customers and the range of functions, flexibility and scalability they need. IT spending is up to billions, but mainly focused on delivering online capabilities like access to investment portfolios. So, it is no surprise that banks are not able to lower costs and their customers still receive the same standardized direct emails, see the same online (marketing) content and get the same robotic scripted customer service – for example, experiencing slow processing of address changes.

And Digitization is Much More Than a Cool App

Most of today's digitization projects aim to improve the front end and the customer experience: nice-looking websites, mobile applications and robo-investor tools. Very often these digitization projects lack a true "digital proposition". They fail to address the topic of a true and comprehensive digital architecture with at least a high degree of straight-through-processing (STP), accessible data and an audit trail. An audit trail will not result in valuable data for (regulatory) authorities or compliance departments only; applying even basic analytics can help you create new and improved services and lower costs.

Achieving Quantifiable Business Results

A true digital architecture and digital engagement tools can be used to manage client expectations, reduce attrition and realize efficiency. In short, it can provide tangible business returns. Wealth managers can reduce costs by 40%+ across the entire business line, increase conversion rates, lower the average customer age and manage the wealth proposition with only a fraction of the staff after implementing a true digital architecture.

Managing the Customer Life Cycle

The key to achieving quantifiable business results is to capture the entire life cycle of a retail customer, from the orientation phase, client onboarding, servicing and client maintenance to offboarding in one single digitized process.

Onboarding is Part of the Game

Onboarding is important, as your actual relationship starts here. Improving the customer journey can be easy and often starts with asking the right information at the right time.

Digitization Benefits All Types of Customer

A couple of years ago, most marketers in the financial services industry assumed that only the newer generations would be open to digital propositions.

The older generations were, and increasingly are, very active online, but the industry just didn't know it. It is true that a digital proposition attracts a younger client base. But a well-tailored online proposition retains the older generations as they have also adapted to the digital world.

Recommendation: Did you know that by asking for the email address first when a visitor opens an online account, you are making your digital proposition more successful? If this simple field is supported by an automated workflow that frequently triggers the visitor, then you can have a retention rate of 25% of the visitors that aborted the onboarding process initially.

Ease for the Customer is Usually Easy for You

Aligning interests starts with not only knowing the customer, but also knowing what is happening in their lives and finding out whether life events can become touchpoints. Everywhere in mature markets, governments are receding from social security and pensions. This results in more financial responsibility for individuals, and this responsibility stretches throughout the lifespan. From saving for schooling and education, to saving to buy a house.

Most people know this rationally, but fail to anticipate it. Why? Partly because we live in a consumption and credit-driven economy, but also because it is just too much hassle to do something about it.

Client Service/Maintenance

How many people in the UK were logging into their investment portfolios the day after the Brexit vote? A true digital architecture would have predicted this behaviour based on a few simple business rules and pro-actively informed and reassured them.

Now is the age of data. Customers expect to be supported with alerts and nudged into taking charge of their own financial wellbeing. By empowering customers to take care of themselves, financial companies can raise client satisfaction, meet duty-of-care obligations and experience a reduction in operational workload and complaints.

A 30% reduction year on year in inbound telephone calls was realized by a wealth manager as customers felt more in charge with a digital proposition, and this went hand in hand with a significant increase in the net promotor score.

Compliance and Regulators are Also Part of the Fan Base

If the systems handle most operational compliance aspects (controls), banks can start thinking about a fundamental change in the role of compliance. In a truly digital world, compliance officers are sparring partners and business enablers who look ahead to provide robo-investor solutions and answer questions like: How many possible investment portfolios do I need to show in order to offer a value proposition for an execution-only service? Or: In which phase of the sales cycle should I ask what information of prospects and customers?

Digitization leads to a digital audit trail. An increased audit trail leads to more data for analytics, prediction and explanation.

Did you know that having a true digital architecture and using automated workflows and the power of data, compliance departments of 50 people can be reduced to approximately 15 when using digital and operational compliance to the max?

In a digitized environment, compliance officers and regulators can never be blamed for frustrating product development and innovation or being unclear. In this sense, digitization leads to innovation.

Our experience shows that having a true digital architecture and using automated workflows and the power of data, compliance departments of 50 people can be reduced to approximately 15 when using digital and operational compliance to the max.

IT as a Foundation

A true digital architecture means that there is a modern, application programming interface-based (API-based) infrastructure in place. An architecture that has digitized STP core applications for administrating investment accounts, reporting modules, customer relationship management, portfolio builders and workflow managers.

Attention should be centred on an integrated flexible architecture that has a high degree of digitized STP that connects all data. Having accessible and integrated data is the foundation of an audit trail that captures the behaviour of the customer, his or her portfolio, the actions of the technology and the employees. For a multitude of reasons this is more important than ever, but with legacy systems still in place for most parties, harder to achieve. Data analytics will help manage client expectations, again reducing attrition and realizing efficiency and improved results.

Identify the Utility Part of Your Business

Most wealth managers, bank or asset managers will say that their operational processes are unique and differ very much from other financial companies. This belief has led to an industry-wide "spaghetti" of custom-made (legacy) software solutions running on old hardware. One could argue whether a reconciliation process or interest calculation process is really that different from one financial institution to another. After all, in most cases "a savings account is a savings account" and "an investment account is an investment account".

Instead of finding arguments for why their institution really is different and has different operational processes, financial companies should better look for ways to answer three questions:

- Where do we want to add value for our customers?

- What is our core function as a business?

- Which processes are generic, do not add any value and are not a core function?

Financial companies can learn from the great retail brands of the world how to focus on a specific value discipline and build a brand around it: Apple, Nike and Zappos have done this and become leaders in their respective fields.

Just like the above-mentioned companies, financial companies should go back to their core and answer these three relatively simple questions. It would make a difference if they see the need to think differently, and not necessarily try to be different on every single aspect of their business. Defining the added value and core competences on the one hand, and assessing what processes are merely a utility and should be outsourced on the other hand, are the first steps in designing a digital backbone and finding the partner that can help to build it.

"Backboning" Your Financial Proposition

Innovation and technology are necessities to move forward. And increasingly, financial service providers have digital propositions and include some form of robo-investing, whether it is an execution-only, advised or discretionary asset management proposition. Online onboarding is quite normal, and these process flows have been optimized to achieve high conversion rates.

These initiatives have a strong focus on delivering digital propositions to an existing client base, targeting new clients and using a unique brand to reach a certain set of customers (more marketing machines than financial service companies). But a digital architecture goes further and should be the backbone of every financial proposition, as it will lead to happier customers, regulators, employees and shareholders.

A house without a strong foundation is like a digital proposition without a digital backbone. So all those apps and flashy portfolio tools should not be the start of digitization, but a logical consequence of it.

The Personalization Pillar

By John Wise
Co-Founder and CEO, InvestCloud LLC

Digitization is drastically changing wealth management. It is creating opportunities that were not possible just a few years ago. At the forefront of this is "hyper-personalization".

Just as retail marketing has made leaps by leveraging advancements in digital content and data analysis techniques, hyper-personalization is the next value-add step in communication with wealth clients. Hyper-personalization promises to deliver higher client satisfaction at lower cost.

The State of the Industry

The threat to wealth managers who resist digital cannot be overstated, because clients increasingly expect more from their wealth managers, even while revenues evaporate. In addition, wealth management is in general behind the curve in digitizing. Wealth managers must evolve to survive.

High-net-worth individuals (HNWIs) are generally underwhelmed by their wealth managers' digital offerings – including advisors' ability to leverage their data to deliver better advice. Around two-thirds of clients would not recommend their current wealth manager and feel data is not being used to tailor advice.[1]

HNWIs are digitally savvy. They already use digital financial service channels heavily – 69% use online and/or mobile banking and 40% use investment portfolio reviews. Some 47%, a surprisingly high proportion, would consider using a robo-advisor in future – although only 14% of HNWIs use robos today.[2] These trends are even more pronounced among younger HNWIs and those in Asia. All this evidence points to growing digital expectations among HNWIs.[3]

Yet wealth managers tend to be digitally immature and underestimate its importance.[4] Many advisors insist that digital engagement is not crucial for the business of wealth management, and that HNWI clients do not want digital tools.[5] It is therefore no surprise that three-quarters of wealth managers offer no digital communication beyond phone and email.[6]

It is not getting any cheaper to serve clients in the traditional manner. Fee models are being compressed massively, meaning margins are going down. The decline in commission fees is well known, but this is also being seen with fee-based financial advice.[7] While gross and net margins are still quite good among fee-based advisors, this is not sustainable – especially as traditional advisors are increasingly compared with robos – and will eventually lead to unprofitable operations.[8]

The Four Pillars of Digitization

Digitization is the answer to an increasingly tech-savvy clientele and a contracting fee base. But what does that mean in practice?

---

[1] "Sink or swim: Why wealth management can't afford to miss the digital wave", PwC, 2016. www.pwc.com/sg/en/publications/assets/wealth-20-sink-or-swim-gx.pdf.

[2] ibid.

[3] ibid.

[4] ibid.

[5] ibid.

[6] ibid.

[7] Tiburon Research & Analysis, presented at Tiburon CEO Summit, New York, 4 April 2017.

[8] ibid.

There are four leading-practice pillars that reliably define and enable digitization:

- holistic data integration

- open-architecture digital warehousing

- flexible data visualization

- hyper-personalization.

Holistic data integration means consolidating information from internal systems, private data sources and third-party financial institutions to create a comprehensive financial view. This is "real" aggregation. Most companies leverage "screen-scraping" and "HTTP-Post" technology to capture data. The result is incomplete, unreliable, limited-availability data. By contrast, taking a holistic approach to integrating data means directly accessing a financial institution's data through both application programming interfaces (APIs) and open financial exchange (OFX) technologies – the most reliable and trusted formats in the industry.

An open-architecture digital warehouse enables advisors to track and report on an evolving universe of financial instruments and vehicles managed by a diverse stable of money managers. It uses tailored and affordable technology solutions to handle large and complex data sets. It frees firms from being tied to a single accounting system, custodian or money manager, and instead provides reliable safekeeping of all integrated data sources.

Open-architecture digital warehousing also means managing both structured (trades, holdings) and unstructured data (videos, PDFs, social media). It manages the time dimension of data to support real-time business analysis as well as robust historical data review.

Holistic data integration and open-architecture digital warehousing collectively comprise what InvestCloud calls digital aggregation.

Flexible data visualization means harnessing the power of digitally aggregated data to support thousands of views of this powerful and rich data set. HNWIs increasingly expect the ability to customize their views and then store and recall those views, for everything from simply adding or subtracting data columns to detaching views into separate apps. This also includes allowing users to assemble personalized dashboards. The more freedom clients have over their digital experience, the lower the cost to serve them, and the happier they are.

These first three pillars are crucial to support digitization. But what clients experience is based on the degree of empathy their advisors offer them. This comes in the form of hyper-personalization. There are two elements that comprise hyper-personalization in the digital wealth context:

- making the digital experience warm and personable;

- respecting clients' individuality.

It may seem counter-intuitive, but a digital experience can indeed be human. Artificial intelligence fantasies aside, leaders in digital wealth like JPMorgan Chase Asset Management CEO Mary Erdoes are increasingly advocating a hybrid solution. Ms. Erdoes was quoted in the *Financial Times* as saying, "Human beings need human beings to explain the world to them", but also confirmed that their digital wealth offering will cover all wealth management segments they serve – even up to the "ultra" tier of the HNWI segment.[9]

At the end of the day, it's about delivering the best digital experience possible to empower investing while at the same time having human expertise available when it's needed. That may be for episodic meetings (e.g. to review portfolio construction) or to deliver special services (e.g. trust setup). But advisors are

[9] Ben McLannahan, "JPMorgan wealth management head casts doubt on robo advisers", *Financial Times*, 28 February 2017. www.ft.com/content/2cfc2524-fe0b-11e6-96f8-3700c5664d30.

not needed to deliver reports to HNWIs – this can and should be automated.

We are living in an ironic time, during which advisors often critique the digital experience because it is insufficiently personal, while in the same fell swoop delivering reports that are "one size fits all" to their HNWI clients. If you ask any advisor whether his or her clients are all the same, the response will be a resounding "no". So clients should not be treated as if they are all the same.

With the right technology enabler, the digital experience can and should be highly personalized: intuitive, involved and individual.

Intuitive design means the person knows how to use the portal and its tools instinctively – no manual required. Simple, straightforward, honest designs force concentration on the essential aspects of the data presented.

Involved portals engage clients digitally – such as curated content, news and chat – which enhances the value of the portal to clients and therefore the frequency of using the portal. The client portal should become part of clients' regular daily routines.

Individual means tailoring persona-driven digital experiences to clients so that the portal and apps "speak" directly to clients' needs and wants.

While wealth managers know that each client is unique, their experiences are currently all the same. Digital provides the opportunity to differentiate each client experience and therefore appeals to modern HNWIs. Even for those who still value the human touch, a digital experience is still a complement. For many HNWIs, human advisors will continue to be a very important part of the equation, with hyper-personalization as the glue or unique selling point for the advisor.

Technologically, there are many opportunities available for wealth managers to unleash clients' data potential.

Harnessing Hyper-Personalization

Digitization is easy with the right partner and approach. It is crucial to identify and develop personas within the HNWI client base (i.e. gauging how digitally savvy clients are, as well as how "high touch" they are). These personas should be matched to groups of users to ensure maximum respect of individuality.

The digital experiences need to be matched to these personas. The result is large-scale personalization at low cost. Examples of this technology at work include:

- Dynamic client portals representing distinct branding, apps and functionality based on user groups.

- HNWI client reports customized by user group informational needs and wealth manager "service level" (e.g. gold, platinum, etc.).

- Flexible reporting canvases, allowing advisors and even HNWI clients to create and publish custom reports on the fly.

- Tailored mobile apps to HNWI demographic – even more than one per wealth manager.

Truly Personal Service

When hyper-personalization is deployed, wealth managers can truly modernize their operations, becoming forward-thinking service providers who can demonstrate that they understand the individuality and needs of their HNWI clients. This promotes massive loyalty and satisfaction. Human interactions are still a part of this, reserved for when they are needed. This enables businesses to increase the number of clients serviced per advisor, driving down unit and total costs.

HNWI clients are not the same, and their requirements have changed. The wealth management industry is beginning to recognize this, but still has a way to go. Traditional standards of care in wealth management will always be important, but they are expensive to deliver and HNWI clients today want more. A traditional service model must be married to the digital experience, using hyper-personalization, if the industry is to truly address clients' needs and survive as a business model.

Digitization is drastically changing wealth management. It's creating opportunities that were not possible just a few years ago. At the forefront of this is "hyper-personalization".

Just as retail marketing has made leaps by leveraging advancements in digital content and data analysis techniques, hyper-personalization is the next value-add step in communication with wealth clients. Hyper-personalization promises to deliver higher client satisfaction at lower cost.

Digitizing Wealth Management

By Harald Helnwein
CEO, NOVOFINA

At the Blink of an Eye

Imagine yourself in your car on that country road. You are a bit late for your business appointment. Have you brought everything? It is an important presentation! Trees are flying by while you recite to yourself the opening of the speech you are going to give… or not going to give, as round that next corner – out of nowhere and right on your lane – this ridiculous tractor suddenly blocks you! Somehow, in a reflex action, you miss the tractor. But now you are heading exactly towards that massive alley tree. An instant later, you are dead.

Or you aren't. At the blink of an eye, the airbag has saved your life!

Now that you are not dead, lean back, relax and blink your eyes. Doesn't take long, does it? It takes us only 100 milliseconds (1/10th of a second) to blink an eye, the airbag to save our life, or modern stock markets to grow or wipe out all our money.

At the blink of any eye, millions of trades are made at the stock exchange, over and over again. No longer by loud-shouting floor brokers or erratically gesticulating floor traders, but by machines.

Wealth Management is Already Digital

Digital wealth management is not the future; it is the present. Advisors, fund managers, bankers who still think of clients' money as just being "OPM" – other people's money – and have not implemented financial technology for the benefit of the customer, will soon be a thing of the past. For the financial industry, the driver to implement such technology is shifting from increasing their own net returns with things like high-frequency trading (HFT) to confident and savvy clients who now demand better investment solutions for themselves. After all, it is their money that is at risk. And that risk can finally be managed not just by so-called experience (or gut feel), but by modern risk analysis, backtesting, artificial intelligence (AI) and many more FinTech tools that are available now.

Nowadays we do not buy cars without ABS, seat belts, head rests or airbags. We even opt for more electronic safety features that are possible today: blind-spot detection, adaptive headlights, collision warning. Why should we risk our lives by ignoring modern high-tech in transportation? And why should we risk our hard-earned savings in wealth management by ignoring what next-level robo-advice has to offer:

a. Fact-based algorithms, replacing emotion-triggered discretionary trading, avoiding also influences from greed, fear and panic.

b. Precise, more efficient, automated execution of (ideally algorithm-based) trading and investment strategies.

Before we look more at (a) and (b), the top level of WealthTech solutions, let us quickly summarize the different stages digital wealth management has offered so far. This view is similar to what Deloitte concluded in their 2016 report "The expansion of robo-advisory in wealth management".[1]

Clients could enter an online form and then be presented with a so-called risk or investment profile, and could pick recommended products accordingly. This was the first level of robo-advice, while the second level selects the products for the client. The third level, basically what most popular robo-advisors now offer, is a more dynamic form of bundling the products.

---

[1] https://www2.deloitte.com/de/de/pages/financial-services/articles/the-expansion-of-robo-advisory-in-wealth-management.html.

Is level-three robo-advice better or worse than human advice? In reality, it is pretty much the same, as the computer simply matches the profile to a portfolio predefined by humans, so no rocket science there. Also, the fact that mainly exchange traded funds (ETFs) are bundled and no active, direct investment or portfolio management in equities is being provided is often criticized. ETFs also come with external and internal costs, which clients are often not aware of.

The fourth level of robo-advice and digital wealth management goes way beyond bundling off-the-shelf products. Algorithms, from robust and simple to highly complex cutting-edge technologies, build – or are – the investment product or solution. The algos create the portfolio, react to terabytes of historical and/or live data, and ideally execute the orders at better fill-prices and lower costs for the client. Let's take a closer look.

Financial Algorithms – Pillar One of Next-Level Digital Wealth Management

Building wealth is easy. We buy something – stocks, funds, real estate, gold, oil, etc. – at a certain time and we sell it later at a higher price, and then repeat. Losing wealth is even easier. Often we have to sell at a lower price and/or at a much later point in time.

Top-level digital wealth management should replace discretionary decisions (speculation, hope) with fact-based, reproducible rules (algos). The goal is to end up with more realistic expectations in terms of performance and, even more important, risk. Be aware, bad algos can lose all your money as fast as bad human advisors can.

In stock trading, the never-ending discussion is how we (humans) could predict better which stock will go up. We base such guesses on things like trading experience, fundamental analysis, value investing, portfolio theories, efficient market ideologies, sentiment analysis or technical analysis. One, some or all of these approaches can be part of WealthTech, not just technical analysis (a big misconception). The important part is to use the facts (science) in combination with practical experience. Machines are crucial, especially for AI, but after all they are not much more than tools to prove which investment approach (mostly ideas from experienced traders, portfolio managers and quants) is going to work and which one isn't!

Backtesting is one element which helps to dig deeper and quantify any idea or rationale behind a certain idea by testing it against real historical data. The most important goal is not to find the holy grail (which you won't), but to see what wouldn't have worked; what would have led you to lose money? Once you see that 99 out of 100 investment approaches fail at a certain time or market condition, even those that sound logical or that one can find in dozens of investment books, you really understand the power of backtesting and stop risking your own and your clients' money until you can quantify risk realistically.

In modern times, we use internet search and GPS navigation to find a restaurant and not a printed street map from the 1980s. Those GPS devices are very high-tech without us even noticing it – GPS requires quite a lot of satellites in space and calculates locations using Einstein's gravitational deflection of light theories – and we have all of this on our smartphones. Many discretionary investment approaches are like the street map from the 1980s or earlier (like the so-called "modern" portfolio theory from 1952). It may or may not work; 99 out of 100 times it simply doesn't.

Automated Execution – Pillar Two of Next-Level Digital Wealth Management

If the right strategy (or algorithm) is key, how important is a flawless, quick and efficient execution of that strategy (i.e. the actual entries and exits at the stock exchange)? What would you say: does 95% depend on the strategy itself and 5% on the execution, or is the execution's relevance greater or less?

Let us crash into that alley tree again, with our car on our way to the appointment. What did the airbag electronic in our car need to do to save our life? The first part was like the strategy or algo part, if we want to compare it with our trading analogy: a couple of sensors reported some data which the onboard computer interpreted correctly as a crash. In trading, we would have received a buy or sell signal for a stock, but in our car we got a "release that gas immediately" signal for the valve that shot the gas into the airbag.

If the opening of that valve, in other words the execution of that crash signal, had not worked or we had been delayed by just another 100 ms, we would not have survived that crash despite the correct decision to activate the airbag. The same is true for our money; it is lost too, if we do not enter and exit exactly and as efficiently as planned, due to the lack of precise, reliable execution.

HFT is not only a buzzword, it negatively affects every single stock position being entered or exited "normally" these days, no matter whether you are buying 10 shares for yourself or you want to accumulate a million shares for a pension fund. Front running, one example of HFT, can mean that a good strategy ends up with a loss of −5% that year rather than the profit of +5% fair fills would have produced (no matter whether based on a discretionary or algorithm-based strategy).

The real-world outcome of modern investment and trading strategies can depend 25% to 75% (or more) on its execution part alone, so it is not enough just to know what to do, but to do it precisely and efficiently. Times of ad-hoc orders in the heat of the moment on a trading floor – or giving your broker a casual telephone call after lunch – are over.

Digitizing Wealth Management Progresses Rapidly

Robo-advisors that match online-entered personal risk profiles to a set of bundled ETFs were just the beginning of digital wealth management. Financial super algos and smart, precise order executions are the future, a future that some WealthTech companies already provide today.

Survival of the Fittest – Cyber Resilience

By Clyve Lo-A-Njoe, CISSP
CEO, Blue Arca Cyber Security

and Richard Beetz
at the time of writing: Consultant, Blue Arca Cyber Security and Project Manager, Exicon Mobile

The Asian-Pacific region (APAC) is the global leader in having both the largest population of high-net-worth individuals (HNWIs) and the highest amount of HNWI wealth, according to the World Wealth Report.[1] Although the demand for digital capabilities is high globally, the region has the largest share. Our views on digitizing wealth management operations are therefore influenced by the attention on this region, but we believe that they are applicable to the industry as a whole. In APAC, tech-savvy new-rich millennials demand a multi-channel delivery model from wealth management firms. Clients are more willing to use low-cost, high-end digital product propositions such as robo-advisory wealth management services. This is a serious wake-up call for wealth management (WM) firms that are still depending on a traditional servicing model. WM firms will need to embrace digital technologies or accept the potentially detrimental consequences to their business. At the same time, changing delivery models create new opportunities for wealth managers to differentiate themselves from the competition. Incumbents with long-term established client relationships have a head start. Maintaining the client's trust that comes with this relationship, while digitizing a wealth management business, requires strong cyber security controls to be put in place.

Cyber Security as a Competitive Edge for Wealth Managers

Wealth managers must come to terms with the importance of cyber security on their digital operations, and the possible impact on their brand and reputation. To become forward-thinking business leaders, they must educate themselves on how the digital landscape impacts their operations. This includes potential pitfalls and complexities of digital threats. The ongoing digitization process has made data breaches by malicious hackers "the new norm". Therefore, cyber security is no longer an IT risk. It is an operational risk. In case of a data breach, the board is accountable for proper security arrangements.

Digitizing wealth management operations translates into offering superior services and rich experiences. This includes ensuring the confidentiality, integrity and availability of personal data and information. The challenge for WM firms is to deal with cyber security in a faster-changing environment than ever before. Unfortunately, cyber security is often seen as an impedance to business innovation. However, we observe that clients are becoming more aware of cyber risks. Wealth managers must implement stricter cyber security controls. They are now judged on their technologies, policies and procedures to respond to cyber attacks. Although there seems to be a general understanding that the threat cannot be eliminated, only focusing on protective measures is not enough. WM firms that are well prepared before, during and after a data breach earn the trust of their most important clients, giving them a competitive edge.

Adopt a Strategy that Offers Cyber Resilience

A cyber resilience strategy allows open and connected digital wealth management operations. This strategy ensures that cyber security controls support business outcomes. It

---

[1] Bloomberg, "Asia-Pacific wealth exceeds North America's for first time" by Giles Broom. www.bloomberg.com/news/articles/2016-06-23/asia-pacific-region-wealth-exceeds-north-america-for-first-time.

combines the strengths of information security, business continuity and organizational resilience. If a WM firm applies a cyber-resilient framework to their digital operations, then it aligns security from a risk-based approach. This approach is unique and tailored to the digital WM firm, its operations and business objectives. In this cyber resilience strategy the firm takes into consideration that:

1. a data breach is not a matter of "if" but a matter of "when", and
2. people (i.e. "the human element") are the weakest link in the cyber security chain.

It differs from the traditional and outdated cyber security strategy of only focusing on protection (i.e. building a wall between the business and the outside world). Cyber resilience allows the WM firm to accept potential failure in order for its operations to thrive. Operational risks would be mitigated to a predefined acceptable minimum. In this context, wealth managers move to the implementation of building capabilities that ensure better prevention, detection and recovery from cyber attacks. Sophisticated access controls with two-factor authentication and advanced persistent threat (APT) solutions are deployed to prevent malicious hackers and traffic from entering the firm's network. These solutions are monitored 24/7 in second-generation security operation centres (SOC) to ensure timely detection of attacks. Together with the implementation of integrated IT and business continuity procedures, these firms ensure that backup data and systems can be restored in a timely manner with limited disruption of the business in case of a breach.

Increase Customer Experience with Cyber Resilience

Cyber resilience goes hand in hand with better customer experience. Cyber resilience measures give the end-user peace of mind. In turn, it increases the customer's trust in and satisfaction with a digital product, service or platform. We have noticed that

successful WM firms devise a customer-centric approach towards cyber security and their digital business model. They are able to reimagine the way both the client's relationship and cyber security are being optimized. This develops a connection with customers that feels safe. Examples of controls that add value to the customer experience and trust are:

- clear communication about the company's cyber resilience strategy;
- allowing users to choose between different levels of security (e.g. use of biometrics instead of passwords) while maintaining a secure company baseline;
- outstanding customer service for cyber security-related questions such as password resets.

Target Your Cyber Security Investments

Wealth managers must prioritize their cyber security spending when adapting a cyber resilience strategy. It is about building the right cyber security capabilities in line with the digitization strategy. This means that wealth managers should take a step back and look at their current state and future expectations. Next, they should target which areas to make their cyber security expenditures on. Many wealth managers will find that IT budgets are not only insufficient, but also being invested inefficiently.

A strong cyber resilience strategy includes both technology and business expertise. Change management is needed. The board and senior management must recognize that digitization and cyber security are top priorities. Risks should be mitigated from a business perspective by using preventive measures, and building holistic incident response capabilities. The focus is on investing in capabilities that can deal with risks from a people, processes and technology perspective.

Put the Customer at the Centre of Your Cyber Resilience Strategy

A customer-driven approach ensures a digitally and emotionally connected relationship. We observe that banks are moving away from one-size-fits-all approaches to protect their business. A discussion about customers' experience and security often leads to user access controls. User access controls are security techniques that regulate the authentication and authorization of resources in a digital environment. To match the specific needs of their clientele, banks are using customer segmentation methods in their security models. We believe that wealth managers should follow the same route. By using data intelligence, wealth managers will be able to analyse and understand how customers perceive the interaction of cyber security in their digital environment. The key is to take away cyber risks from the end-user, and to put the decision for a preferred level of security in that user's hands. This builds trust.

This brings us to a baseline security model. To implement a customer segmentation method, it is vital that a baseline is established. The baseline is the result of risk tolerance and a minimum level of security needed, and is predefined by senior management. We can imagine the baseline as a horizontal threshold line (e.g. "security level-1"). Under the baseline we will find investments in sophisticated security capabilities, such as behavioural analytics against insider threats,[2] cloud access security brokers[3] for user authentication of cloud solutions, and cyber intelligence to prevent ransomware and phishing attacks.[4] They allow for early prevention, detection and response against threats. Above the baseline, we can then enable the customer to choose their own security preferences in the digital environment (e.g. "security level-2", "security level-3", etc.).

The reason behind this is that customers are unable to distinguish good or bad security. And once customers are being segmented into groups, it is most likely that we will find end-users who either prefer convenience or security more, and a group of end-users that would not mind making trade-offs either way.[5] At face value, this process seems like a daunting task, but this is not the case. It does imply that it is critical that cyber security has been brought in early in the design of new products/solutions and customer journeys.

Wealth Managers Should Learn from the Technology Firms

In this chapter we discussed digitization with the emphasis on security, scalability and consumer experience. Cyber security is both a cost and an investment consideration. If only dealt with from an afterthought perspective, it can become a significant cost factor: a continuous stream of applying updates and patches is expensive, slows down operations and is ineffective against a determined malicious hacker. Wealth managers should take a cue from the playbooks of large banks and technology firms. Many firms that have implemented digital operations are considering themselves a technology company. For example, JPMorgan and Deutsche Bank consider themselves technology companies with a banking licence.[6,7]

---

[2] Algorithms and statistical analysis that detect anomalies from patterns of human behaviour and indicate potential threats.

[3] CASB are cyber security solutions that enforce company security policies on third-party cloud solutions.

[4] Cyber intelligence is used to blacklist internet domains that are used for ransomware and phishing attacks. Usually these domains are added to a spam filter to ensure that end-users do not receive emails from blacklisted domains.

[5] McKinsey & Co., "Is cybersecurity incompatible with digital convenience?" by Salim Hasham, Chris Rezek, Maxence Vancauwenberghe and Josh Weiner. www.mckinsey.com/business-functions/digital-mckinsey/our-insights/is-cybersecurity-incompatible-with-digital-convenience.

[6] Business Insider, "JPMorgan: 'We are a technology company'" by Portia Crowe and Matt Turner. www.businessinsider.com/marianne-lake-says-jpmorgan-is-a-tech-company-2016-2.

[7] CNBC, "Deutsche Bank's CEO says technology will be key to banking in the next five years" by Matt Clinch. www.cnbc.com/2017/01/17/deutsche-banks-ceo-says-technology-will-be-the-key-to-banking-in-the-next-five-years.html.

From a cyber risk perspective, all major banks and technology firms have a way to test their cyber resilience strategy. This is also a starting point for a wealth manager: test the firm's cyber security controls and proactively search for advanced threats in the company's IT network that can be exploited, so-called threat-hunting. Any cyber resilience strategy that does not test all layers of the organization is both inefficient and ineffective. The security of large banks and technology firms is tested structurally and periodically by technical penetration testers, social engineering experts and IT auditors. These experts evaluate people, processes and technologies against best practices. They leverage their experience and creativity from a hacker's point of view to reveal vulnerabilities.

Ultimately, we believe that the change digitization brings should be holistic instead of incremental. This means doing cyber security right from the start.

111

Digital Platforms, Products and Ecosystems

4

Wealth Management as a Platform

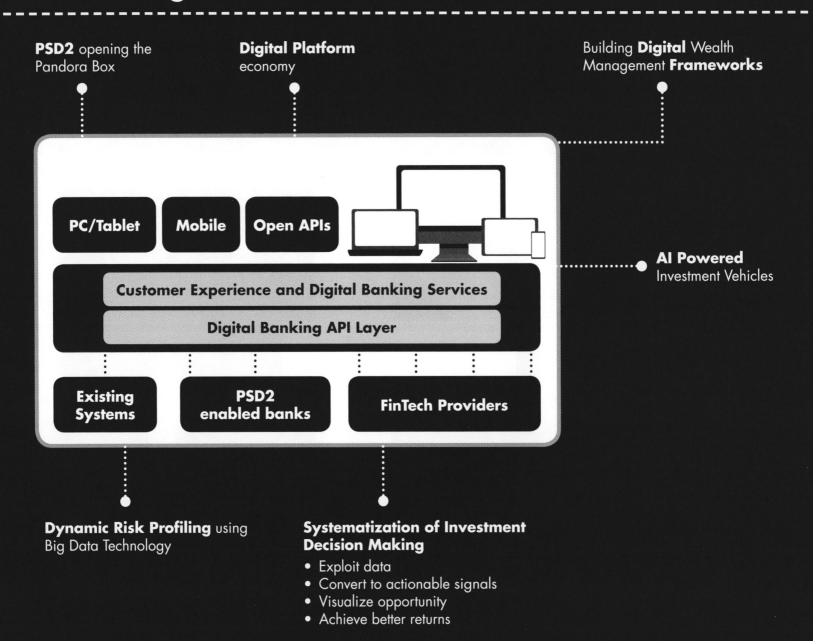

PSD2 opening the Pandora Box

Digital Platform economy

Building **Digital** Wealth Management **Frameworks**

PC/Tablet

Mobile

Open APIs

AI Powered Investment Vehicles

Customer Experience and Digital Banking Services

Digital Banking API Layer

Existing Systems

PSD2 enabled banks

FinTech Providers

Dynamic Risk Profiling using Big Data Technology

Systematization of Investment Decision Making

- Exploit data
- Convert to actionable signals
- Visualize opportunity
- Achieve better returns

Executive Summary

The wealth management industry is experiencing enormous pressure from increasing regulatory requirements, low portfolio returns and fierce industry competition. There is an increasing need to reduce costs and deliver industrial-scale wealth management propositions. To maintain and grow market share, wealth managers need to boost portfolio returns, adapt to regulatory requirements, and generate cost and scale efficiencies in their investment process. This part will look at some of the ongoing trends and changes in the financial services industry and how asset managers can (or should) be transforming themselves to stay relevant and "ahead of the curve". This will include an overview of different technologies, including the buzzwords "du jour" such as artificial intelligence (AI), machine learning and cloud computing.

PSD2 will fundamentally transform the banking landscape as we know today, and we see it as the first step towards openness in the financial industry. Platform strategy is a solution that has demonstrated its value by creating high-value marketplaces. That strategy can be different for each firm, but will require leadership and self-awareness from senior management to embrace the unknown. The wealth management sector has been one of the last bastions resisting innovation, and investment managers and private banks should consider PSD2 as their wake-up call. We will also discuss changing client behaviours and the demands these will have on traditional wealth management.

One chapter is dedicated to alternative lending. Many FinTech companies born in the last decade have new innovative solutions in alternative lending, with the aim of gaining market share by replacing bank lending. They have an attractive value proposition. However, scaling up the initial success remains a challenge and only a selected few managed to expand their businesses. This chapter explains how to gain market share in alternative lending and describes the most important factors for success.

AI is changing every aspect of human life – creating ways to develop precision solutions that were not possible before. The application to personal finance is one that is democratizing access to high-quality advice, and transforming how people save, invest and think about their financial future. The capital markets constitute a complex system with increasing amounts of data, that evolves beyond established theories and thus cannot be explained and predicted by traditional models. Adaptable, self-learning systems are needed to model and forecast the changing markets. AI and deep learning allow us to model the markets without human-derived assumptions and to identify patterns and relationships in stock market data to generate ranked forecasts. The forecasts provide investors with important insights when managing their wealth and are also utilized in the development of AI-driven trading and allocation strategies and structuring of corresponding investment vehicles.

Computers can be clever, but surely they lack any inherent sense of self, humanity or ability to act fiduciary? Hot on the heels of robo-advice, robo-selection – as it relates to the selection and research of mutual funds – is the next frontier for FinTech. As more assets move to index-based and systematic strategies, so the dynamics of fund research are changing. One chapter will focus on how robo-selectors can put the client above all others.

Finally, we will address the lack of diversity in finance. We see measurable action with the launch of Bloomberg's Gender Equality Index (GEI). The final chapter in this part will outline the development and creation of the GEI and insights derived from the data. It will also discuss how encouraging disclosure across industries, as the GEI has done in financial services, can get us closer to gender parity by catalysing a virtuous cycle – where disclosure and transparency can lead to changes in practice and behaviour; and when behaviour changes, culture follows; and when culture changes, it can change reality.

Wealth Management-as-a-Platform – The New Business Architecture with PSD2

By Pierre-Jean Hanard
Partner–Startup Advisor, The Startup Platform

Platforms are Taking Over the World

New "household" names such as Uber, Facebook, Amazon, eBay, YouTube, Wikipedia and Instagram all have a few things in common: they are recent, grew rapidly and took over long-standing players without the resources seen as critical to their success. The reason they took sectors and industries by storm is that they connect participants – people and organizations – with their respective resources and allow them to interact using technology. They are platforms, and value is extracted through all interactions and actions made on that platform (e.g. Facebook gathers data on its users whenever they are on the platform).

External Resource Management

What is truly unique to platforms is how they use external resources. Indeed, in a traditional business model, companies use their internal resources to produce goods and services with features based on market research. Platforms, on the other hand, do not own or control any resources. Instead, they are marketplaces allowing participants not only to offer their resources to other participants seeking them, but also to act as both "producer" and "consumer" of value at different points in time. For instance, on Airbnb, any apartment owner (producer) can offer their apartment (value) to an individual seeking to rent it

(consumer). And while on holiday abroad, the very same flat owner can now seek to rent an apartment. With frictionless access and supply/demand at play, consumers have access to more products and services. As the community of consumers on the platform grows, feedback mechanisms (e.g. ratings) act as a filter, ensuring that the best products and services remain.

Network Effects

One key feature to explain the success of platforms is the existence of network effects. Airbnb is a prime example of such effects. The more people join the platform as guests, the more apartment owners are incentivized to become hosts, therefore bringing more competition and pushing prices down. Lower prices, in turn, attract more guests until large-scale market adoption. This is a classic case of *positive* network effects, since both sides of the platform keep growing as they reinforce each other (positive feedback loops). A *negative* network effect is a negative feedback loop, whereby as more users leave a platform, more users follow through. For instance, at the height of the Blackberry's success, complacency combined with the emergence of the iPhone convinced some users to abandon Blackberry, triggering more users to do the same.

Why Banking as a Platform has Failed to Emerge

Bank and Platform: A Not-So-New Phenomenon at First

At its core, a bank is a platform, connecting providers of capital (lenders) with receivers (borrowers). However, instead of letting market forces drive the terms of engagement (rate), banks decided to set the terms themselves. As new products and services – as well as new lines of business – were added, banks grew with an inward focus on tightly knit processes, procedures and policies, ensuring not only the ownership of the value creation but also its full control. Over time, as technology became more sophisticated, banks started to outsource part of this value creation to third parties ("procurement"), with the aim of reducing and controlling costs. But, by and large, banks are about control.

The Absence of Network Effect

While ATMs are a prime example of how a large branch network can capture more deposits, they are also the only one. In the current organizational architecture, clients do not extract more value from their bank as the number of clients grows, as banks capture that increase.

Weak Competitive Environment

Incentives to innovate are often related to the intensity of the local market. In the UK, where a handful of banks control 80% of the market share, it is not surprising that innovation has a hard time taking off, despite banks' best efforts. Market shares are stable and there is no incentive to start a "war" with competitors. It is therefore also unsurprising that banks fail to truly revamp their client experience with the millennial generation in mind, now the largest segment in the western world.

This generation has grown up with Facebook, a social network with a user interface second to none. They never experienced computer freezing. Whatever they want, they do under their own terms. When banks refer to the digitization of their offering, they are in fact digitizing the client experience for the parents of the millennials.

Failure to Understand the Nature of Innovation

Innovation labs/centres have emerged, often as a me-too strategy, with inadequate senior management reporting lines, insufficient financial resources and unrealistic key performance indicators

(KPIs) (and their frequencies). Moreover, virtually no one in these labs has start-up experience, therefore failing to bring agility and in-depth cultural awareness when dealing with start-ups, leading to slow reaction, poor communication and tedious start-up onboarding processes with time-consuming operational and legal burdens.

PSD2: Opening Pandora's Box

The Second Payment Services Directive (PSD2), effective since January 2018, aims to harmonize the EU payment landscape with a common legal framework. With client consent, it enables third-party applications with a trusted licence to access bank account data and payment systems. PSD2 is quite revolutionary, because it forces banks to open up client data to third parties, therefore rebalancing client data in favour of the clients themselves, increasing competition by forcing incumbent banks to innovate faster and providing more choices and seamless experiences to clients.

Banks often see PSD2 as yet another compliance issue to solve. Without understanding the impact on its revenues, disintermediation is the likely outcome, as third-party solutions will take over the client relationship while traditional firms will provide infrastructure services (if they still exist – revenue will go down and fixed costs up). PSD2 also represents a unique opportunity to revamp the architecture, opening up access to new customers and to complementary services, therefore creating new revenue streams for the bank.

Seeing PSD2 as a retail banking problem would be short-sighted – after all, wealth management is a highly sophisticated and personalized retail banking proposition. Both business lines share common products and services, including payments. We believe that PSD2 is the first step of a series of forced openness in the financial industry. Wealth management firms should also take the view that their business model is at risk without proper review of their architecture.

Platform Roadmap

Building a successful platform requires strategic, cultural and security considerations. Being open without addressing them is the sure solution to disintermediation.

Strategic Considerations

At a high level, three discussions need to take place:

- **The vision and core focus of the firm.**

  - The vision of the firm is probably one of the most difficult conversations to have. Wealth management being an "old-fashioned" industry, it is tempting to continue defining the firm with an old mindset and customer profiles in mind, stressing company values, tailored wealth management solutions and specific market segments. The next generation of wealth are millennials, used to 24/7 availability, social networks, interconnectivity and interoperability, and with expectations of how, when and where products and services are consumed that are different from the previous generations of clients.

  - Defining the core focus is critical and requires a hard and honest look, as some wealth management firms are more likely to control the entire value chain. As we explained earlier, the value now resides within data, hence firms should look at each stage of the value chain and analyse whether it could build a sustainable and cumulative competitive advantage through data. Risk management is the most obvious function meeting the criteria for all firms, but other functions are firm-specific. Once the core asset is identified, it should then stand at the heart of the platform and new technologies and application programming interfaces (APIs) should be built on top of it, not integrated with it. Indeed, as consumer needs and technology evolve, the firm wants to maintain its agility by keeping the core asset(s) technology-neutral.

- **The degree of openness.**

  - Successful platforms are truly open, allowing any producer and consumer of services to join them. Three scenarios could be envisioned:

    - Little openness, where the firm is passive in its strategy and partners with any third parties qualifying for its APIs, with the risk of being disintermediated.

    - Firm-wide openness, where the firm actively seeks to create an ecosystem of APIs by actively opening up its (anonymized) data at all stages of the value chain, therefore creating its own app store with third-party apps complementing its existing service offerings and/or providing more efficient alternatives to existing internal processes (e.g. know your customer – KYC and artificial intelligence – AI). Apple's iPhone and its app store is a perfect example.

    - Industry-wide openness, where all wealth management firms cooperate on a common standard in APIs for their industry. Google's Android is a case in point – this operating system and apps are now used by numerous brands and phone devices.

- **The rules of engagement.**

  - For a platform to be successful, any participant should be able to join easily. As the number of third-party solutions increases, so do the interactions which generate data and therefore value on the platform. However, some third parties may be of poor quality and destroy value in the process. If not quickly identified, these solutions can harm the platform and proper curation and rules of engagement are therefore essential. As mainstream platforms, wealth management platforms should rely on their own community of users for review and ratings.

Cultural Considerations

As wealth management firms are about to enter a new era, self-awareness of senior management will be a decisive success factor. In the end, nobody knows what the right thing to do is, until it is tested and proven. Therefore, a culture of experimentation and tactical bets is necessary to discover what works specifically for a firm. Failing fast and often should be the mantra of each wealth management firm when embracing the unknown.

Security Considerations

Cyber security deserves a chapter on its own. Identity theft remains a risk whenever a client shares his or her bank account credentials with a third party. Strong customer authentication is therefore critical, as well as secured communication.

Conclusions

We believe that PSD2 will be a game changer in the financial sector. We expect some initial resistance by incumbent banks, raising cyber security risk and consumer protection as reasons to water down the current version of the Directive. But ultimately, PSD2 will fundamentally transform the banking landscape as we know it today, and we see it as the first step towards "forced openness" in the financial industry. In a world of openness, platform strategy is a solution that has demonstrated its value by creating a high-value marketplace with limited asset ownership. That strategy can be different for each firm, but will require leadership and self-awareness from senior management to embrace the unknown. The wealth management sector is one of the last bastions resisting innovation, and should consider PSD2 as its wake-up call.

Wealth Management – Preparing for a Digital Revolution

By Stephen Ong
Founding Partner, The Hub Exchange

Wealth management is the latest financial industry to face the opportunities and challenges of technological disruption. Dramatic headlines such as "Traditional wealth management is gone" point to the transformation of a historically opaque industry. The digital revolution is driving incumbents to decipher how the industry will be transformed and how traditional wealth management needs to adapt to be able to thrive in this rapidly evolving world.

The two most fundamental forces driving change are the shift in client behaviours and the evolution of technology. These forces complement each other in their pace of change and are often intertwined, having impacts on each other.

Changing Client Behaviours

The rising affluence of millennials is a key focus for the future success of the wealth management industry. These millennials have entered the work force and are now beginning to accrue wealth. It has been estimated that they will also inherit $30 trillion via generational transfer in the decades ahead.

For wealth management firms to remain relevant, incumbents face the challenge of continuing to service their existing clients, while having to adapt to new client behaviours and strategically positioning themselves to engage the next generation. There is a common misconception that millennials respond almost exclusively to social media and digital tools as methods of engagement. While they are mobile centric and tech savvy, it is key to understand that they demand the standard of service they are accustomed to receiving from leading social media technology.

A more nuanced view of their motivations is needed, which requires adapting the application of digital technologies to meet these needs. Often called "generation sceptic", millennials tend to have a mistrust of traditional financial services. Factors such as student debt and recent financial and banking-related scandals, since 2008, all contribute to general scepticism of the industry. Transparency is consequently a key quality that millennials are demanding from wealth management. There is a trend which no longer finds it acceptable for financial professionals to hold clients at arm's length and build trust solely on the notion that the wealth manager is the expert: they need to add real value.

Millennials have grown up in a relatively transparent world of information, where they can access it usually for free. Like many other industries, the finance and wealth management sector has grown rich by creating barriers to information, keeping the end customer in the dark and enabling wealth managers to add layers of fees, giving clients a perceived greater sense of value. Technology is enabling the new generation to break down these barriers by accessing new channels of information and providing them with the tools to engage more directly in the management of their own wealth. As incumbents seek to learn from the emerging new WealthTech competitors, they need to balance pivoting completely and shunning their existing client base.

Typical behavioural traits of the new generation include being fluid in their choices and wanting to have an impact through engagement. Wealth management has traditionally focused on long-term relationships, often with long-term investment strategies. With millennials happy to switch providers at a whim and wanting to be engaged directly in their investment choices, the role of wealth management is shifting to a more focused advisory role, providing the tools for end clients to execute. With investment products being increasingly commoditized and accessible, wealth managers are having to go the extra mile to find unique and interesting investments to show their value.

Furthermore, regulatory compliance is an increasing burden on wealth management firms, driving up their costs. Historically, the industry underinvested in operations, opting to invest in client-side relationship management. With increased regulation, a fickle client base – where relationships mean less than they used to – and the demand for services in real time, forward-looking wealth management firms are focusing on investing in their own operations, where technology makes the biggest impact.

Emergence of New Technology

The emergence of robo-advisory and alternative investment platforms is reducing inefficiencies and operational costs, while providing the next generation with digital and mobile channels to invest through. Technology, in particular robo-advisory, is broadening the addressable market for wealth managers by offering services to smaller investors. Where they were previously shunned due to low return on investment, technology allows wealth managers to offer their products to less wealthy individuals through more automated channels. Young tech companies such as Wealthfront, Betterment and WiseBanyan are now establishing themselves as a significant source of competition to the traditional wealth management firms who rely heavily on manual operations.

Many forward-looking wealth managers are finding that by combining robo-advisory with face-to-face client management, they can achieve the personal touch with lower operating costs. As robo-advisory becomes both more sophisticated and more accepted, an increasing number of high-net-worth individuals (HNWIs) are taking the automated investment route for part of their finances. With technology automating many processes, such as data crunching, wealth managers have more time to analyse investment opportunities and provide value to their clients.

Beyond the high-level forces described above, there are specific areas where technology is driving efficiencies within the wealth management industry.

1. Digital Client Onboarding Process

Customer onboarding is an important process and crucial in identifying and establishing the suitability of products for new customers. Historically, the onboarding process has been heavily manual and required extensive face time with advisors, which is costly. Furthermore, the increasing regulatory requirements – coupled with the advancement of automation technology, document management and analytics and emerging mobile capabilities – has resulted in a growing trend towards digital onboarding. Digital point solutions cover a whole range of processes, including fraud detection, identity verification, analytics, e-signatures and customer communication management. A digital automated onboarding process helps drive efficiencies, leading to increased revenue through a better allocation of resources.

2. Dynamic Risk Profiling Using Big Data Technology

Traditional risk profiling has been relatively basic and static, based on estimates extrapolated from past data and subjective human interaction. Big data advances have the ability to process huge amounts of data, leading to dynamic, near-real-time updates with more accurate profiling, while performing scenario and stress tests at portfolio level. Technology advances enable wealth managers to dynamically risk profile their clients by constantly reviewing their existing portfolio and adjust for clients' attitude to – and capacity for – risk, with real-time value at risk adjustments based on live market conditions.

3. Open API Approach

The rise of point solutions, such as know your customer/anti-money laundering (KYC/AML), has enabled the integration of financial data through application programming interfaces (APIs). Open APIs allow free linking of multiple apps, elimination of manual data entry and limited mistakes during data transfer and updates. Most platform providers and marketplaces now build their own infrastructure, so point solutions can be integrated through APIs. Open APIs have accelerated new app development and exposed new channels of engagement. In an increasingly integrated digital world, open APIs encourage innovation by enabling newer solutions to evolve and improve existing services in an integrated, seamless manner on top of the larger frameworks. It has been demonstrated that companies which build an ecosystem of solutions around them have provided a wider variety of solutions for the end user, providing services which prove more popular and, as such, are more aware of changing consumer trends. These third-party developments, which connect through an open API, also provide benefits by essentially outsourcing R&D while turning developers into brand advocates.

4. Increasing Demand for Post-Investment Tools

Client demand for transparency has led to the growth of new tools that cover three areas: market intelligence and reporting, investor relations, and communication. The number of new innovations is vast, ranging from tracking macro factors driving the industry, to identifying the metrics investors use to gauge value, analysing and evaluating the company and competitors, obtaining investor profiling solutions, and activity monitoring and performance benchmarking. The latest technology provides several post-investment tools, which have been traditionally served through manual paper-based processes. These tools can reduce timelines where companies need to make decisions (e.g. corporate actions), by allowing voting on company matters in an instant via mobile, as opposed to waiting weeks to receive a response by mail from shareholders.

Emergence of Digital Platform Economy

As the marketplace of point solutions continues to grow increasingly crowded, there is a rising need to organize it through frameworks, leading to the emergence of platforms with an open architecture. Companies such as Google and Facebook have created ecosystems of apps that grow and thrive from their communities. However, platforms designed with an open architecture and well-thought-out frameworks are not yet commonplace in the wealth management market, due to the complexities of regulation and the resistance to change within the industry. Platforms that are secure and provide efficiencies through standardization and automation of manual processes will transform the market as we know it today.

An example of such a platform is THE HUB, which provides private, invite-only, secure environments with all the tools to manage a whole investment community. The technology matches investor preferences to available opportunities ensuring relevance, saving investors' time and driving a higher likelihood of investment. Investors can express their interest in opportunities and even register their interest to sell their positions, providing the basis for a secondary market. Unlike most platforms, we do not market investments to the masses, but restrict the ability to promote an opportunity to the deal originator so they are always in control of who sees it.

How to Digitalize Wealth Management at Banks

By Sascha Freimueller
Managing Partner and Founder, Dufour Capital AG

Ryan Held, PhD
Managing Partner and Founder, Dufour Capital AG

and Dr Roman Timm
Partner, Dufour Capital AG

Digital Financial Battlefield

The digitization activities of established banks who dominate the market in wealth management are quite different from those of new entrants like robo-advisors. While robo-advisors go digital in the channel (web and mobile) and the content (origin of advice), the digitization efforts of banks are mostly focused on customer interfaces (channels) and cost-saving back-office automation. However, wealth management decisions – such as asset allocation, investment selection and portfolio/risk management – are done the traditional way, based on expert human judgement. The use of algorithms for running these core business processes is not something banks appear eager to do yet. However, by sticking to traditional wealth management methods, banks will lose ground vis-à-vis more data and innovation-driven new market entrants or early adapting trend-setting banks. Digitization of wealth management is in full swing now, and will change the landscape of the financial industry fundamentally.

Traditional Wealth Management Frameworks Under Attack

Forecasting market developments, as required by traditional wealth management concepts, turns out to be a challenging task and often has not met expectations. Human emotions – such as greed and fear, dynamic money flows, speed of information transmission and the complexity of financial markets often lead to misleading evaluations. The technology bubble of 2000, the financial crisis of 2008 and many other events have shown the limitation of financial professionals to foresee market responses. Because forecasting is so difficult, classical investment solutions from banks tend to be less active, which limits their ability to differentiate products. They usually stick closely to passive benchmarks to reduce the risk of "being wrong". Nevertheless, such offerings are promoted as active solutions and thus expensive for end clients, as banks need to cover their high fixed costs. Serious digital competition and investors' awareness of alternatives puts pressure on this product strategy now. Today, this model is attacked by disruptive players at the fund level (exchange traded funds (ETFs) and index funds) and at the asset allocation/portfolio construction services level (robo-advisors run by start-ups, but also by global giants such as Vanguard). They provide similar solutions at a fraction of the cost.

For this reason, it will not be enough to simply distribute traditional solutions over digital channels. In order to thrive in a digital world in terms of client satisfaction, profitability and competitiveness, banks will need new digital wealth management frameworks, integrating these into new business models and transforming their wealth management business.

Digital Wealth Management Frameworks: New Powerful Strategic Tools

Digital frameworks are based on algorithms and are fundamentally different from traditional concepts. As digital frameworks are free from emotions and do not rely on uncertain market forecasting, they are suitable for active investment solutions deviating from passive benchmarks. Such solutions protect, for example, capital in a crisis or profit from attractive conditions in bull market phases. To achieve this, digital wealth management frameworks must integrate strategic and tactical asset allocation, security selection, portfolio management and risk management. Portfolios can be created from simple building blocks such as ETF, single stocks or active funds where appropriate. This enables new applications and solutions well aligned with the needs of end-clients and banks. Such digital frameworks enable banks to provide clients with compelling solutions tailored to their needs. Production is highly scalable and costs can be kept low due to process automation and coverage of a broad investment universe within a single framework. Digital solutions can be offered for both self-directed and delegated client mandates. Therefore, they integrate well in today's landscape of banks' products and services. Digital frameworks are beginning to take roots and they will eventually move into the mainstream of wealth management.

Survival in Wealth Management: Hybrid Transformation Options for Banks

If banks want to secure their position in the landscape of future digital wealth management or even shape the industry, they need to transform their wealth management core business processes and implement new digital frameworks and business models. Transformation will need to integrate not only the way advice and products are transported to the client (from classical to hybrid to digital), but also the origin and frameworks of how advice and products are created (from classical to digital).

Solutions with a digital origination can be integrated in a straight and value-adding way into a comprehensive wealth management business model (see Figure 1). Digital solutions can be distributed across client segments via traditional client-facing channels, digital (non-client-facing) mobile and web channels or, in advanced hybrid forms, by combining personal advice, digital aids and digital wealth management solutions. This will allow banks to provide prospects and clients with both traditional and new digital products and services via their preferred channels. The authors are clearly of the opinion that industry-leading banks will opt for an advanced and highly interactive model, covering both classical and digital content. Advanced hybrid approaches will become

predominant, as machine-based advice will bring the client experience to new levels.

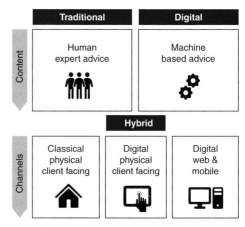

Figure 1: Emerging best practice business model for wealth management at banks

Source: Dufour Capital, Internal Research, Spring 2017

Algorithms or machines will therefore not replace finance experts and relationship managers in wealth management; however, their roles will have to adapt using their expertise for developing and governing processes and for explaining and communicating with clients and other stakeholders.

The "digital" element in the business model covers new client needs and thus offers growth opportunities. Due to the scalability effects from process automation, it also enhances the cost–income ratios of banks, which strengthens their profitability and competitiveness. Furthermore, this is well beyond what today's robo-advisors have to offer – focusing solely on low-cost passive digital solutions and distribution – and thus is clearly differentiated. Such a transformation also puts banks in a strong position to compete with innovative new market entrants.

Digital transformation of business models is always challenging. However, banks are in a very good starting position as they have essential ingredients such as a large client base, capital and established brand recognition already. All that fuels a powerful start to the required transformation, making their position sustainable.

Building Digital Wealth Management Frameworks: Dealing With the Complexity of Financial Markets

The sheer complexity and dynamic, ever-changing nature of the financial markets makes successful investing very challenging. For building digital frameworks, "rule-based" approaches are the option of choice. It is a rapidly growing investment category, where investment decisions are taken based on clear and evidence-based rules (i.e. what has proven to work). This approach fulfils three key requirements:

- **Automation.** Rules can be coded into algorithms.
- **Robustness.** Unlike complex quant models (where model parameters are continuously (re-)calibrated with historical data) or AI approaches (where investment decisions are determined by algorithms based on unknown criteria), rules are fixed, simple by nature and can be well understood. Thus, they are no "black boxes". Counter-intuitively, the simplicity of rules makes them also more robust to cope with the highly complex financial markets.
- **Cost efficiency, transparency and liquidity.** Portfolios can be composed from the huge universe of available ETFs, index funds or single stocks and bonds.

Three Steps to a Digital Wealth Management Framework

A suitable framework must be able to produce a wide range of active, value-adding and tailor-made investment solutions

(see Figure 2). Furthermore, suitable frameworks must be modular and scalable. A framework can be built in three steps:

- access to financial/news data
- extraction of valuable information out of data (noise filter)
- construction of portfolio solutions.

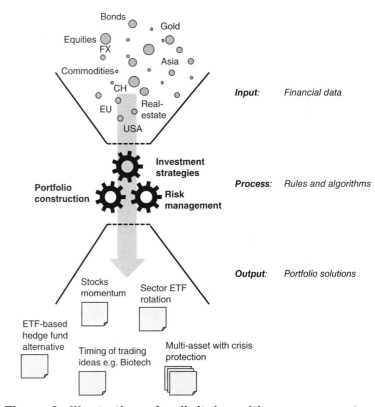

Figure 2: Illustration of a digital wealth management framework

Source: Dufour Capital, Internal Research, Spring 2017

The first step when building a framework is to source financial markets data. In the second step, data gets used as input for rule-based investment strategies. These strategies must cover all portfolio levels and collectively steer long-term strategic asset allocation, tactical asset allocation (under- and overweighting markets to manage risk and return) and, if desired, security selection (e.g. high dividend or momentum stocks). Strategies must be purely rule-based to take out emotions from the decision-making process. Testing and ensuring the validity of strategies over different market phases is critical during the development phase. At the third step, strategies are combined into portfolio solutions. The weight of the single strategies depends on and must be aligned with the investment objectives (strategies are used as portfolio "building blocks"). For example, if capital preservation is an important objective, then strategies which tactically reduce risk in phases of market stress should be given a high weight. The combination of different strategies means that the portfolio is managed according to different rules ("multi-strategy") and, thus, is diversified beyond asset classes, which enhances robustness. An integrated risk management process ensures that portfolios adhere to desired levels of risk (e.g. concentration limits or volatility). Lastly, ongoing management of portfolios covers regular adjustments from strategy outcomes and, at times, rebalancing.

Keeping the "Time-to-Market" Short is Important

The time to develop and build digital frameworks must be kept as short as possible to make progress quickly in executing the transformation strategy. According to the authors' experience, after having gained insight and collaborated with many financial institutions, two critical levers drive the "time-to-market". Initiatives must be driven from the top down. Bottom-up innovations do not work, due to the need to integrate such initiatives into a proper business-wide strategy. Furthermore, fear from competing approaches can cause political resistance in the organization. Secondly, it can take even well-resourced banks a few years to develop digital frameworks and the necessary IT systems. Specialized sourcing providers can help accelerate this process significantly.

Key Success Factors in Gaining Market Share and Scale in Alternative Lending

By Gabriella Kindert
Head of Alternative Credit, NN IP

Many FinTech companies born in the last decade have new products and innovative ideas in alternative lending with the aim of gaining market share and replacing banks. On paper and as a prototype, they seem better, faster, more efficient and with an attractive value proposition. However, scaling up the initial success remains a challenge. There are over 2000 FinTech start-ups globally, but only a selected few managed to expand their businesses. Several promising companies struggle to achieve the so-called tipping point.

So, *how does one gain market share in alternative lending? Is there a winning formula? What are the most important factors?*

This chapter builds on extensive research and insights obtained via over 20 direct interviews with various experts of tier-one alternative lending platforms and thought leaders in the industry. Their unique experiences and observations allowed me to identify several common themes, which I outline in Figure 1.

Key Ingredients to Achieving Scale: TVFO

Trust

Because financial products are intangible and often complex, trust remains the lifeblood of the industry. Still, nearly a decade after the financial crisis, confidence in the industry remains at painfully low levels. Although many marketplace lenders attempt to position themselves as different from old business models, the situation

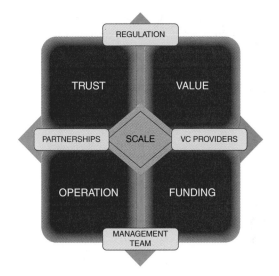

Figure 1: Gaining market share in alternative lending

Source: Gabriella Kindert, Spring 2017

is the same – and potentially more severe – for the newcomers. Many investors have concerns about the loan origination and due diligence processes employed by alternative lenders. Relevance of new sources of data is unproven, and so are the risk pricing models. Large-scale investors do not want even the lowest level of risk when dealing with unscrupulous business practices.

There are several ways in which marketplace lenders can build trust. For example, improved transparency and disclosure can facilitate risk assessment and cross-platform comparability. In principle, investing through marketplace lenders should require fewer resources to assess loans. For that to be feasible, platforms need to disclose comprehensive information about their credit assessment processes and loan portfolios. Industry-wide standardization can also boost trust. It is natural for people to approach novelty with suspicion. Indeed, many platforms report that fear remains a significant obstacle. They can combat these legacy hurdles by focusing on familiarity, which is anchored to existing trustworthiness. Small and medium enterprises are used to a particular way of approaching things, and it is often easier to deal with the current trusted ecosystem rather than promote change.

Approaching companies from the right angle should be a tactical decision. For example, accountants and other professionals familiar with processes involving sensitive data can be much more receptive to platform offerings. A retail client is likely to choose one of the biggest platforms, those that appear most familiar and long-standing, and are accepted by friends' networks. Potential fraud, cybercrime and privacy concerns exacerbate trust issues, particularly given the lack of proven track record among marketplace lenders. Therefore, security remains a crucial factor in building greater trust. To be scalable, marketplace lenders should have strong standards with regard to compliance protocols and risk management. They should strive for constant improvement of their security systems and protocols, and be able to tailor them towards specific threats relevant to the company profile.

Value

Platforms need to have disruptive and scalable offerings:

1. Offering a clear value-enhancing proposition (cheaper, faster, more convenient). The core product should have a sustainable competitive advantage (to be tested by consumers, investors). Value offering could also imply a niche strategy, a tailored proposition targeting specific groups that are most receptive to their offering. They can also benefit from focusing on what they do best – originating and underwriting loans – and outsourcing other operational processes to FinTechs that can do them more cost-effectively. For example, instead of spending money on building the reporting infrastructure themselves, platforms can outsource it to outside service providers like Orchard, which are capable of doing it more inexpensively because they perform the same service for a number of other lenders. Platforms can make their businesses significantly more profitable if they are willing to give up a certain portion of that value chain and outsource it.

2. Scalable: start on day one with a scalable proposition. Small regional markets do not attract the best capital providers, investors and suppliers.

3. Moving up: obtain first-mover advantage (involving funding, open architecture).

Marketplace lenders often focus on the technological aspect of their platforms. However, in-depth financial competence remains a critical factor (improved risk pricing models).

Funding

Entrepreneurs in FinTech spend substantial time on attracting capital. We know that from the thousands of companies, only some will survive. The lack of fully funded business plans might chase off large investors to give a proper consideration to the value proposition. The risk can be mitigated through early acceptance by top-tier capital providers. Obtaining funding from leading venture capital providers can create a snowball effect for scale. Due to internal resource constraints, many investors cannot allow themselves to look at investment opportunities below a certain size. For many, the size of the market in online lending is simply not deep enough to be considered at this stage.

My advice: Show the value, show the transparency, show the scalability and work with the best. We are increasingly living in a world where being second tier does not pay off. Capital providers know that. They do not have the time to try – they look for confirmation. Who do you work with, who are your suppliers, who is funding you – these all translate into: who trusts you already?

Operation

Plans without excellence in operational executions are meaningless. Agility is essential, not only in IT but also in marketing. Platforms often find themselves constrained by business models which lack operational flexibility – the ability to adjust to sudden spikes in demand and supply quickly. I observe many alternative lenders underestimating the importance of a borrower acquisition strategy.

They rely heavily on investors'/lenders' growth – how many investors they are able to attract to their platforms. This approach restricts their growth potential. Platforms should strive to achieve greater operational flexibility by developing the ability to "turn the tap on and off" on both the lending and investment sides, and ensuring that the two are always in balance. Only through that can they preserve the growth momentum without being held back by the lack of lending or investments.

Unlike the incumbent players, marketplace lenders also do not have an existing customer base, and need to build it from scratch. This highlights the importance of a cost-efficient customer acquisition strategy and finding scalable customer acquisition channels with a positive contribution on a unit-by-unit basis. Platforms need to be extremely smart about their marketing budgets and optimize their channel mix. This will require clever use of data, technical capabilities, corporate culture that encourages mistakes, a testing mindset and an ability to pivot. For example, by leveraging digital marketing capabilities, platforms can develop smart marketing models, allowing them to change their message on a short timeframe, thus creating a fine interplay between scale and price.

See Table 1 for an overview of the key ingredients to achieving scale.

Table 1: Key success factors in gaining market share

Element	What it implies	How to achieve it
TRUST	Transparency Security Familiarity	Consistent transparent setup (disclosure of returns) Audit by top-tier firms Involve accreditation from the existing ecosystem Leading financial industry players as business partners and vendors Uncompromising standards, risk management and compliance Facilitate processes that are easy to understand
VALUE	What is in it for the customers? (cheaper, more convenient) Is the advantage scalable?	Offer and protect sustainable competitive advantage Critical assessment of value proposition (is it truly better than the status quo?) Think big and protect the value via first-mover advantage Open architecture with ability to "plug in"
FUNDING	Funding to achieve scale Does the company have access to capital at appropriate cost level?	Fully outlined scalable business idea: the entire business is to be built on scalable business proposition Network impact: obtain funding from leading venture capital providers and respected names in the industry (Intel Ventures, Khosla Ventures, Index Ventures, KPCB, Sequoia, Accel Partners) Advisory board with people who have access to growth capital Obtain an appropriate balance between taking and controlling risks and refrain from aggressive milestones
OPERATION	Does the company have the capability to execute ideas into reality? Does marketing support the business plan with appropriate actions?	Agile, flexible management style, but disciplined Flexibility in marketing and strong focus on consumer acquisition Consumer acquisition price and execution Managing conflicts of interest

Source: Gabriella Kindert, Spring 2017

The Linking Pins and Enablers: PRVM

The points discussed above – trust, value, funding, operation – are not standalone factors. Platforms should approach them holistically. Based on research and interviews, I identified four key enablers that boost the ability to achieve scale.

Partnerships

Partnerships with established, reputable leaders can validate platforms, thus augmenting trust in the industry. There are several examples of this: British Business Bank–Rate Setter; Lending Club–Union Bank; Funding Circle–Santander; JP Morgan–OnDeck. These partnerships can be with vendors, IT system providers, back-office facilities and investors. They can also serve as a marketing channel or help attract capital, thus contributing to the creation of trust and subsequently promoting greater scale. Partnering with bigger, established players not only promotes better disclosure, but can also help to early identify potential breaches in security and operational processes of the platforms due to strong due diligence requirements conducted by these entities.

Regulations

Regulations facilitate trust in the sector and, at the same time, provide a fundamental framework for the creation of the robust ecosystem. At present, uncertainties regarding future regulatory developments are one of the key obstacles. It is often difficult to navigate regulatory complexities, especially when operating across several jurisdictions. In retail investing, regulation can act as a "stamp of approval" and safeguard the ecosystem, given the limited extent to which a crowd can assess credit risk. Some platforms (e.g. Zopa) have recently applied for a banking licence, which shows the importance of building trust and being a source of familiarity through the perceived safety of investment within a bank. Lack of any form of authorization can preclude certain types of investors from greater engagement.

Venture Capital Providers

Platforms require two forms of capital: lending and equity capital. When it comes to the latter, partnering with the right venture and private-equity sponsors is immensely important, as they bring not only the capital itself, but also recognition, validation, experience and skills. Entrepreneurs often tend to fall in love with their ideas and have several biases. An early-stage validation of a business idea via a reputable outside firm, which assesses thousands of business plans and selects only a few, can be a major achievement. Attracting names like KPCB, Sequoia, Andreessen Horowitz, Khosla Ventures, Spark Capital, etc. can offer critical support in marketing, operation and access to funding at a later stage. Similar to commercial firms, some business schools (INSEAD, IESE and Stanford) have venture capital funding arms that could help with content validation and recognition, given their unique insight and enormously valuable networks.

Management Team

Finally, a diverse management team makes the difference. The most capable entrepreneurs may see their limitations. Starting a business requires a very different skill set than scaling up a business. It might be an emotional decision and difficult for many founders to recognize. Involve professionals with outside views. This is often easier said than done, due to resource constraints and emotional attachments. Nonetheless, nobody can master all the skills required to run a successful alternative lending platform on his own. Those entrepreneurs who share their upside with a professional multidisciplinary team are most likely to succeed.

Interdependence Within the Ecosystem: Vulnerable to Contagion

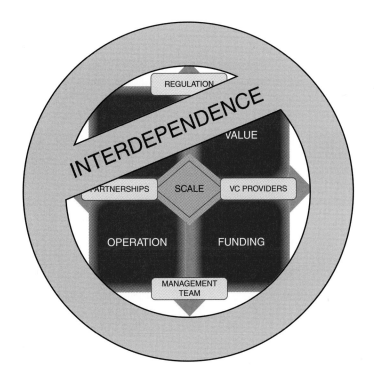

Figure 2: Interdependence in the ecosystem

Source: Gabriella Kindert, Spring 2017

Marketplace lending is a relatively new area, which has not yet been tested throughout the full economic cycle (see Figure 2). The platforms emerged in a period of favourable economic environment and many institutional investors voice concerns regarding their performance should the economic conditions worsen. This is heightened by the fact that some platforms have recently reported higher loan default rates and questions remain about the outcome when the interest rates begin to rise. Business models in alternative lending are still fragile, and because of the trust issues highlighted above, they remain highly vulnerable to contagion: a failure of one company can damage the entire ecosystem.

Platforms should commit to creating a robust ecosystem, resilient to adverse economic and reputational damage. At present, high reputational risks (e.g. money laundering) may deter investors from engaging with the platforms. For many, it just might not be worth it. Platforms should strive to develop deeper relationships with their stakeholders (above all, borrowers) and work towards greater, consistent disclosure, reduce information imbalances and ensure the provision of clear information about underlying risks. Maintaining discipline and high standards is critical and should come from all parties in the value chain. Understanding this new industry still remains in its infancy, with many areas requiring further research (the importance of first-mover advantage, measuring key success factors, understanding and measuring the role of partners).

Conclusion

Disruptive offerings may bring better value proposition to stakeholders than seen before. Their success often boils down to their ability to scale up to ensure the sustainability of their businesses. Achieving scale is an arduous challenge and many factors point to there being significant first-mover advantage present in this space. By fostering the right components outlined above, alternative lenders can significantly increase their chances of achieving this.

My advice: Ensure you have a product that offers clear value, team up with tier-one stakeholders, obtain funding from the best players and constantly challenge your beliefs. We are in a world where complacency and mediocracy offer no chance of winning.

Personal Financial Intelligence – AI and the Future of Money Management

By Catherine Flax
CEO, Pefin

With all the innovation that has occurred in the lives of consumers because of artificial intelligence (AI), very little has been done to meaningfully change how people manage their personal finances. As a society, we will benefit from approaching personal finance in a fundamentally different way to motivate good long-term habits. Fear of bankruptcy, hope of having enough money for retirement, inability to plan to put the kids through college, counting on the stock market rising is for many people the current – but wrong – way to address these important issues. Hope is not a strategy.

We can now impact the way we interact with money, rooted in a deep understanding of the complex equation that is an individual's financial situation, their goals, the economy, markets, tax rules and many other factors. A new model exists for how people can have an informed relationship with their finances, and take control of this important aspect of life. A new form of information and education can be economically adopted by the public at large, resulting in the acquisition of new habits. The challenge of economic illiteracy that plagues most of society – even our most educated citizens – can be addressed with AI. Today, only individuals with substantial net worth can access the services of professional financial advisors to approximate this level of service, but even those insights are not as comprehensive or tailored as what today's computational and machine learning power can create. A human financial advisor cannot process the hundreds of financial decisions that their clients make, let alone layer on top of that the changes occurring in state and federal tax codes, changes in inflation, the stock market and many other variables – as well as the interplay among those variables. Only advanced computational technology that can process millions of data points per client can adequately digest this web of interrelated information – and make sense of it. Because each person is unique financially, there is no "rule of thumb" or general guidelines that can give an individual the right advice for them. It must be highly tailored to have value.

Because of the transformational changes in technology (including computational power, cloud storage, smartphone and interactive browser technology), we are on the cusp of using well-known AI techniques to build remarkably low-cost, 24/7, fiduciary AI-powered financial advice for the public. Some of the important AI methodologies include:

- **Feedforward neural networks** – modelled on how the human brain works. These are able to process interrelated information and understand relationships between many different variables which have complex relationships. Humans are limited in how many of these relationships we can analyse; however, we make decisions that mimic a feedforward neural network all the time – we understand intuitively that if we want to send our children to an expensive college we may not be able to buy the house we want, and retirement may be delayed. What we are unable to do, given the limitations of the human brain, is to layer in other continuously changing factors, such as inflation rates, tax rates and other expense changes, to quickly determine the full range of choices at our disposal and the most optimal combination of these choices for us. These techniques are also able to consider things like short-term vs long-term trade-offs, which are of course inherent in financial decision-making. In short, the feedforward neural network is a highly sophisticated "brain", which can process and make optimal decisions across a nearly infinite number of variables and their relationships with one another.

- **Reinforcement learning** – the next layer that can be added in AI methods to truly provide individualistic and specific advice unique to each user. Reinforcement learning takes the details of one individual's behaviour and feeds that into machine learning algorithms – creating a growing insight into the objectives and behavioural patterns of that individual user. Rooted in behavioural psychology, this aspect of machine learning is very important in moving away from generic advice and into more complex problem solving with unique outcomes.

- **Collaborative filtering** – a term that may not be familiar, however, we are all quite accustomed to how it works in our lives, such as books being recommended on Amazon in the "if you liked this book, you may also like these" format. It is the ability to make predictions about the interests of a user by collecting the preferences of many users. This becomes relevant in many areas of life, including things like managing expenses, planning for family vacations or determining objectives for investing. While extrapolating preferences from a large sample of general information is a good start, it is not tailored enough for appropriate financial planning. The financial advice each person needs must be based on their own unique data and circumstances.

- **Proliferation of interface AI for speech and language** – simplistic interface AI is a familiar part of the user experience in many aspects of everyday life. Consider the verbal phone "bot" that allows you to speak your information as you navigate through an automated menu of options when you call your bank, or other large company. While most AI bots today seek to understand and communicate simple instructions like "What is my balance" or "What's my spending on coffee?", we can now answer more complex questions, like "Am I saving enough?", "Can I afford to send my child to an Ivy League University?", or "Can I retire at 60 instead of 65?" Linking interface AI with computational AI can both understand the question and provide complex answers with detailed reasoning, at your fingertips.

Combining these interfaces with an AI financial advisor is a ground-breaking and important advance, because ultimately people want to receive information in a way that is familiar – as if they were speaking with a human being. Leveraging tools like Amazon's Alexa or Siri adds a dimension of ease – and is also an important advancement for users who are visually impaired or have challenges with dexterity. Fundamentally, when people can no longer distinguish between speaking with a human or with a machine, it becomes easier for the machine to be leveraged

inexpensively and with scale – and across many languages. This also allows the machine to proactively reach out when there are issues, changing the dynamic from a person having to sift through their financial accounts to ascertain whether they need to worry about something, versus a new paradigm where your computer, phone or Alexa can tell you "hey, take a look at your bank account, it looks like you may have double paid a bill", or "those new tax laws that were just passed by Congress will have a negative impact on your retirement savings, unless you consider retiring in a more tax-friendly jurisdiction, you will run out of money sooner than anticipated". This is the sort of "nudging" that we really need from our automated AI-driven financial advisor, and we are on the verge of this being a reality.

Advances in computing power are one of the main drivers to leverage data and to change how we incorporate AI into our lives. The advent of the cloud has enabled inexpensive and large-volume computations. It has made enterprise-grade infrastructure security standards and military-grade encryption more easily accessible, enabling companies of all sizes to have substantially higher levels of security than most people experience with their financial institutions today. It is worth noting that many large corporations must redo decades of relatively open security, while newer companies can build from the start using sophisticated encryption techniques and other methods that greatly enhance security.

How does regulation keep up with these technological changes? What many regulators are beginning to understand is that advanced technologies are the best hope of delivering unbiased, appropriate and fiduciary advice – such as what is required by the US Department of Labour (DOL) fiduciary ruling, a rule which expands the "investment advice under the fiduciary" definition under the Employee Retirement Income Security Act. Unlike humans who – even with the best of intentions – come with biases, an AI financial advisor can be programmed to be a fiduciary and must only give unbiased advice by design. This is a huge protection for the consumers of financial services, and one of the most important dimensions of how technology will impact this sector. We are not far from the day when advice given by a human advisor will be compared with what an AI-based advisor provides, and it becomes increasingly complex to justify the cost of human advice. This is like investment management, where studies have shown that over the last 20 years up to 92% of actively managed mutual funds underperform an index to which they are benchmarked.

The future lies in intelligently harnessing the power of these tools to provide AI-based, user-friendly solutions, especially for complex and expensive problems like holistic financial advice. Given the acute need for reasonably priced approaches to solve the questions that people have about their finances, it is AI and only AI that can provide this. The future of financial advice is personalized AI, and it is the power of imagination that makes the impossible happen.

Financial Forecasting and Portfolio Optimization in the 21st Century

By Dr Jeremy Sosabowski
CEO, AlgoDynamix

"Diversification is the only free lunch in town", so the saying goes… but is this still really the case? And if not, how are newer technologies changing, or more likely transforming and disrupting, some of these traditional asset management industry assumptions?

This chapter will look at some of the ongoing trends and changes in the financial services industry and how asset managers can (or should) be transforming themselves to stay relevant and "ahead of the curve". This will include an overview of different technologies, including the buzzwords "du jour" such as machine learning and cloud computing. The predominant focus will be on asset managers active in the equity markets, as this asset class has over and over again demonstrated long-term capital growth potential; this is obviously subject to appropriate portfolio management, including de-risking and using the right technology choices at the right time.

A Very Brief History of Time and Technology

Advances in technology have been at the forefront of financial services, especially if these solutions can demonstrate a clear competitive and economic advantage. Already, back in the days of the Crimean War, competitive advantage was gained from improvements in communication speed by using carrier pigeons instead of horses. The modern-day equivalent has been to build direct microwave radio point-to-point links between stock exchanges to avoid the latency introduced by fibre-optic cables. The laws of physics suggest that this "arms race" is probably

over for now. The next new kid on the block could be quantum entanglement, although this zero-latency communication concept is currently still only part of academic and philosophical society debates.

Likewise, computational processing has always been an enabling tool in most parts of financial services, and even more so within the asset management industry. Research, portfolio construction, stochastic modelling, scenario testing, probabilistic (risk) calculations and many mathematical models – including option-related calculations – are very computationally intensive.

Once again, technology is coming to the rescue: cloud computing is streamlining existing infrastructure and at the same time enabling many new, previously unimaginable or unimplementable, applications. Many FinTech start-ups would simply not exist without this democratization of computing resources. In addition to the currently available near-unlimited, on-demand cloud computing, recent progress in quantum computers could soon provide the next disruptive chapter in humanity's unbounded appetite for computational processing.

"Quant Funds", Machine Learning and Other Trending Technologies

Like in many other areas, it is not clear if the dog is wagging its tail or vice versa: the answer might be a bit of both with regard to technology innovation, including machine learning enabling the more ubiquitous rollout of quant funds or vice versa. Nonetheless, the trends are clearly there, with even the larger household names such as Blackrock[1] and Morgan Stanley moving away from discretionary stock picking and equity analysis to more and more "software-driven" asset management decisions.

---

[1] https://www.nytimes.com/2017/03/28/business/dealbook/blackrock-actively-managed-funds-computer-models.html.

Regardless of methodologies and technologies, asset management investment objectives usually always include long-term outperformance and appropriate diversification to de-risk the portfolio and reduce shorter-term volatility. So, how can machine learning help with some of these overarching objectives?

Before delving into further asset management details, let us first explore in slightly more detail the different nuances of machine learning. Not only will this help demystify some of the concepts and terminologies, it will also help identify the key areas where more "value-add" automation can provide substantial benefits. Machine learning is sometimes more generically referred to as artificial intelligence (AI), a catch-all term that often elicits ideas of terminator-style machines going out of control. Out-of-control self-learning algorithms can certainly cause major havoc, though like everything else in life it is never black and white, however much the popular press likes to imply otherwise. Like any other new technology making its way into "everyday life", the adoption phase and transformative implications are not always clear and certainly not in everybody's best short-term interests. Unsurprisingly, there will be resistance from some quarters, much like the Luddites of old. Note that economic prosperity and productivity increases enabled by technology go hand in hand. This also means that companies which are slow to adopt such technologies may find themselves at a competitive, and therefore a financial, disadvantage.

Supervised and Unsupervised Machine Learning

Probably the more ubiquitous machine learning technology out there, and the one most associated with "self-learning" and "self-reinforcing", is known as supervised machine learning. These algorithms rely on some human element to label the input data (i.e. add some structure to the data) and the machine learning algorithms can then subsequently be trained, with ideally as much relevant input data as possible. Typically, the input data is segmented into learning data sets and validation data sets. Once

properly trained, the live out-of-sample performance of these trained algorithms will ideally provide some robust long-term predictive capabilities subject to some (ongoing) tweaks and retraining. Very good examples of supervised machine technology applied to real-world problems include "speech character and image recognition" and "search and recommendations", especially in e-commerce.

The predictive powers of these well-trained algorithms will depend on numerous factors, though generally speaking performance will improve with more quality input data, as long as there are no "regime switches". In the above examples, somebody starting to speak in a new language when the algorithms were only trained on the English language would be a "regime switch" most probably requiring new training data. Another limitation of supervised technology is the inherent assumption that future patterns are an amalgamation or a repetition of historic data.

Unsupervised Machine Learning

The unfortunate reality is that a lot of financial time series are very prone to regime switching and the past is not always a good (or indeed any) indication of future events. Examples of regime switches could include changes in interest rates (even negative interest rates these days!), never seen before quantitative easing programmes, new regulations and the introduction of new financial products (CDOs, etc.). Generally speaking, the more random and less repetitive the input data, the more difficult it is to learn anything from the past.

Thankfully, not all machine learning algorithms require historical data set training, human labelling and non-regime switching data universes. In addition to supervised machine learning technology, its younger, more recent unsupervised machine cousin is exceptionally good with the realities of financial markets. Working on the assumptions that Brownian ("random") motion models are applicable to describe some of the pricing behaviour of traded financial instruments, can we use unsupervised machine learning for forecasting capabilities? The short answer is a big "yes", although only under some circumstances, specifically when financial markets are experiencing "regime" switches and moving away from non-Brownian motion states. Using limit-order book information from global financial exchanges, complex clustering and characterization algorithms and distributed cloud computing, AlgoDynamix is providing forecasting solutions to asset managers and other global financial institutions all around the world.

Putting it All Together, Portfolio Sciences for the 21st Century

So, are Smith's invisible hand, the efficient market hypothesis[2] and portfolio diversification still applicable concepts moving forward? Probably yes, but like everything else, a lot of things work a lot of the time until they don't… Extreme events in financial markets, aka tail risk losses (or returns!), have historically been impossible to predict with any sense of consistency, and most of the money is either made or lost during these extreme events.[3] Moving forward, it is now possible (and even more important) to stop using predictive technologies based on existing models and past events. Newer technologies, including the AlgoDynamix directional market risk forecasting solutions, are already being used by asset managers and other financial institutions globally. Looking at the current FinTech revolution and the increasing rate of technology adoption in all areas of financial services, the future does look good for the right types of AI in the right places.

---

[2] https://www.winton.com/en/davids-views/february-2016/efficient-market-theory-when-will-it-die.

[3] http:// http://mebfaber.com/2011/08/12/where-the-black-swans-hide-and-the-ten-best-days-myth.

AI-Powered Wealth Management Products and Investment Vehicles

By Yaron Golgher
Co-Founder and CEO, I Know First

Dr Lipa Roitman
Founder and Partner, I Know First

and Dmitry Neginsky
Senior Research and Strategic Analyst, I Know First

Complexity of the Financial Markets and Big Data

Institutional and individual investors and financial advisers are looking for advanced technologies which not only help them in making investment decisions or recommendations with more confidence, but also offer a different perspective on the financial markets. The capital markets constitute a very complex system that continuously evolves beyond established theories and thus cannot be sufficiently explained and predicted by traditional models. Moreover, market participants are overwhelmed by the increasing amounts of (big) data that needs to be digested and understood to be able to navigate through all kinds of market environments successfully.

Even the supposedly best professionals in the industry seem to fail to adapt quickly enough to technological advancements, rising competition and the constant flow of new market moving information. This can be seen from the irregularity of hedge fund returns and their declining ability to generate alpha over the last 15 years. Therefore, more complex self-learning systems are needed in order to model the financial market and adapt to the changes it continuously goes through.

AI and Deep Learning: Adaptable and Self-Learning Capital Markets Modelling and Forecasting

I Know First's system incorporates multilayered neural networks, allowing it to model the markets without human-derived assumptions and maintain flexibility. It applies artificial intelligence and machine learning techniques to find patterns in large sets of historical stock market data and, based on these, can generate ranked forecasts. The algorithm learns from the most updated data and evolves with it. It adapts to new conditions and features and has enough learning experience and intelligence to be able to make predictions in circumstances not observed before.

This forecasting algorithm models the markets as non-stationary chaotic systems with fractal properties. It uses multi-representation, meaning multiple points of view and multiple data variants for each forecast, and data munging[1] to expose important features. Through explicit regularization processes – introducing additional information in order to solve an ill-posed problem or to prevent overfitting – and a fitness factor used to optimize the learning process, it is able to make predictions based on new data that the algorithm was not exposed to in the machine learning process. Moreover, principal component analysis is used to identify important (information-carrying) inputs and separate them from unimportant ones. It makes the data easy to explore, visualize and learn.

A genetic adaptable algorithm[2] is then constantly refining the predictor pool – an assembly of predictors used to create a

---

[1] Data munging is the process of transforming and mapping data from one "raw" data form into another format with the intent of making it more appropriate and valuable for a variety of downstream purposes such as analytics.

[2] In computer science and operations research, a genetic algorithm (GA) is a metaheuristic inspired by the process of natural selection that belongs to the larger class of evolutionary algorithms (EA). Genetic algorithms are commonly used to generate high-quality solutions to optimization and search problems by relying on bio-inspired operators such as mutation, crossover and selection.

forecast. The genetic algorithm repeatedly modifies a population of individual predictors, selects the best ones and rejects the worst ones. When the fitness criteria are changing, it adapts to new conditions. This method for solving optimization problems is based on natural selection, inspired by biological evolution.

Partially Versus Purely AI-Driven Investing

In the context of trading and investment management, one can differentiate between two main use cases of artificial intelligence. In the first one, the main goal when applying the techniques is to perform a certain analysis of capital markets data, for example price and trading volume pattern matching, detecting various market anomalies, interpreting sentiment via natural language processing (NLP) and finding relationships in order to come up with a set of outputs that are machine learned observations and conclusions on the current market environment. The big data is effectively condensed in that case into much smaller and more meaningful pieces of information. This first level of analysis can then be interpreted and eventually turned into action through a human filter (manager) or a strictly defined set of rules external to the AI module. Important to note is that the purpose of the outputs and their future application should be clearly defined in advance, when deciding on the setup of the AI module, in order to know how to make use of what the machine has learned.

From a business point of view, the machine processed and condensed information, along with corresponding descriptions and instructions, already provides additional insight into the markets and thus can be customized and sold as a product to the end-users, who are interested in integrating these insights into their investment decision-making processes.

In the case of I Know First, the condensed information pieces are the daily updated stock market forecasts. These are represented through positive or negative signals of different strengths to assess

the investment opportunity, and the predictability level for each asset and forecasting timeframe. The unique predictability indicator is a confidence/quality measure of the respective signal. It is used to identify and focus on the most predictable assets according to the algorithm, and thus achieve risk-adjusted outperformance.

The advanced algorithmic forecasting system helps to detect the best investment opportunities and monitor current portfolio holdings when integrated into clients' investment processes. Financial institutions, such as banks, wealth management companies and advisors, as well as brokers and online trading platforms, have the flexibility to customize the forecasting universe specifically to their needs and integrate the predictions into their research and advisory process or to offer it as a trading ideas generating tool to their clients. Through additional standardized subscription-based services, the AI-based forecasts further empower individual investors who usually do not possess the resources and expertise needed in order to develop, maintain and take advantage of AI technology when managing their wealth.

AI-Powered Investment Vehicles

The above-mentioned type of "intelligence" product can be extended to an investment vehicle. In this case, clients do not use the AI-based analytics by themselves but rely on their added value being optimally utilized in the implemented vehicle, which can easily be invested in. Here, AI prediction-based portfolio construction can be used. Algorithmic forecasting indicators are utilized in the development of systematic long-biased or long/short trading and allocation strategies. Depending on the chosen risk and trading activity profile, these strategies can be used to launch hedge funds, mutual funds or structure smart-beta or actively managed exchange traded funds (ETFs).

Opportunistic, more aggressive and frequently rebalanced strategies take the most recent changes in the daily updated forecasts into account and focus on the most predictable assets which offer a higher upside.

"AI-Smart"-Beta ETFs

In contrast, smart-beta products invest in a predefined set of companies, often constituents of a certain (sector) index or fundamentally sound "high-quality" companies, where, however, the default market cap allocation is adjusted according to the opportunities discovered by the predictive AI algorithm. The rebalancing happens either with a predefined frequency or in case a significant change in the forecast exceeds a threshold. Hence, the exposure is attained with the same assets as in a passive index-tracking (sector) ETF, with the weighting being adjusted to take advantage of the AI-driven predictive capabilities.

With these algorithmic forecasting and ranking systems, investment opportunities are assessed through predictability levels, signal directions and strengths, which are generated for various timeframes for each of the assets covered.

AI-Driven Sector (ETF) Rotation Strategies

A "bottom-up" built system allows us to separately follow the individual securities' forecasts as well as group these by sectors and industries in order to derive "macro" conclusions and trends. A higher level of allocation decisions can be made through such "aggregated" forecasts and finally implemented as a sector (ETF) rotation strategy. Here, an ETF portfolio is constructed by investing in more promising sectors – as suggested by the predictive AI system on the constituents' level.

Autonomous, Pure AI Hedge Funds and Reinforcement Learning

So far, we have covered the application of AI and machine learning technology on large and complex data sets in order to come up with outputs that give additional insights and are then used externally by managers in investment and by advisors in recommendation processes. A logical next step is the construction of a complete and closed AI-based "analysis-to-decision-to-execution" system, with minimal to no input from the fund manager. Reinforcement learning is used to transition to trading signals, and it can be seen as the integration of supervised learning and backtests.

Whereas, in supervised learning, a fitness function is optimized in the learning process from a training data set consisting of input–output examples, reinforcement learning is analogous to how a child learns from their mistakes. A machine explores the possible actions in a given environment and learns which ones give a desired result. A reward function is used to measure the success of learning. It can be singular (one step at a time), or cumulative. The best possible decision in any given state (current portfolio) is made and executed by the algorithm based on its learning experience up to this point. Such a system is not simply identifying, but predicting and adapting to the trends while making decisions in real time going forward, whereby the manager's discretionary control over the investment process is removed. Of course, this could lead to certain transparency and thus regulatory issues, making pure and complete AI trading less feasible for publicly traded funds.

Plurality of Uncorrelated AI and Alternative Data-Driven Strategies

A recent study conducted by Eurekahedge[3] on the performance of AI/machine learning hedge funds since 2011 indicates a low or even negative correlation to trend-following strategies and the average hedge fund returns, respectively. It is evidence of the

---

[3] Eurekahedge Pte Ltd, "Artificial Intelligence: The new frontier for hedge funds", January 2017, http://www.eurekahedge.com/NewsAndEvents/News/1614/Artificial-Intelligence-AI-Hedge-Fund-Index-Strategy-Profile.

ability of AI-based technology to find patterns and relationships in the data not identified by traditional models and not used in static rule-based strategies. By exploiting the rapidly growing computing power and the increasing amounts of new data sources, one can expect an even larger diversity of uncorrelated machine learned strategies and corresponding funds launched in the future.

Alternative data – such as, for example, high-quality satellite images revealing retailers' parking lot traffic, oil tanker and other cargo movements, number of vehicles in industrial areas and facilities, crop field colour, etc. – can have predictive value for the retail market, manufacturing sector, agriculture and more. Furthermore, advances in NLP now allow us to better understand, check for consistency and use valuable and predictive information from immense amounts of unstructured (not organized, text-heavy) data. Investor and consumer sentiment shifts can be cost-efficiently measured through machine analysis and interpretation of data extracted from different news sources, articles, reports and blogs, social networking and sharing applications. These so far insufficiently used or ignored data points, if correctly and comprehensively extracted, interpreted, analysed and traded on via AI in a timely manner, will give the advantage of being ahead of the crowd until this information is "priced into" the financial markets and generates additional alpha.

AI and the Future of Finance

Independently of applying AI to generate predictive information and trading ideas to help market participants with their active investment decisions and trading strategies, utilizing it in the construction of smarter AI and alternative data-driven allocation schemes within more passive investment vehicles, or going "all-in" by allowing the machine to also take over the decision part and learning from its experience, artificial intelligence's role in the investment management industry is on the rise and will become industry standard. Thus, it will be difficult to stay competitive without understanding and starting to incorporate this technology now, be it in the search for new alpha sources, the detection of risk events or in order to save costs and reduce fees.

Wealth Managers Can Deliver Effective Client Outcomes with a Data-Driven Investment Process

By Giles Adu
Co-Founder, ClearMacro

At the heart of the wealth management industry is the mission to deliver agreed investment outcomes subject to a client's attitude to risk. Wealth managers' investment processes and approaches to decision-making are a significant driver of the outcomes for millions of individual savers and retirement plans. While the wealth management industry continues to grow, it is experiencing enormous pressure from increasing regulatory requirements and a low environment for returns. While industry competition is fierce, there is also an increasing threat from low-cost robo-advice. To maintain and grow market share, wealth managers need to boost portfolio returns, adapt to regulatory requirements and generate cost and scale efficiencies in their investment processes. Recent innovation allows wealth managers to reduce costs, and become more efficient at generating portfolio returns with a disciplined, systematic process. Cutting-edge applications and tools enable wealth managers to capture a broader range of opportunities, more frequently to sustain long-term portfolio returns.

The industry needs to solve the problems of efficient data sourcing, processing and visualization to address portfolio opportunities and threats in real time to sustain portfolio performance. Best practice can now incorporate a data-driven investment approach with significant systematization of the analysis and decision-making process to drive portfolio returns, enhance communications and reduce business risk.

Systematization of Investment Decision-Making

Wealth managers need to systematize how their investment management teams exploit data, convert to actionable signals and visualize the global multi-asset opportunity set. The winners will be those investors who are able to effectively utilize multiple data sets to extract forward-looking information content that can be analysed within a robust, disciplined framework that generates frequent, high-quality portfolio ideas while taming risk.

Investment managers are currently drowning in ineffective data, leading to sub-optimal portfolio allocation. Decision-making is often predicated on "he-who-speaks-loudest" information from multiple data sources, formats, types and media processed inefficiently by multiple unconnected systems and human analysis. Sub-optimal data processing and evaluation of complex information mean that investment managers struggle to effectively convert noisy data into actionable signals and thus limit portfolio investment performance. Investment managers will need to actively consider data and processing as never before. They will have to address questions such as:

- What data sets are the most impactful for portfolio returns?
- Which data sets convey high-impact information content and which do not?
- How do they source effective data?
- Which data sets should be incorporated into their investment models?
- How do they process the data and convert it into reliable, effective signals?
- How to allocate their data and research budget?

Given these pressures, to be effective, wealth managers' investment decision-making processes need to be re-imagined and re-engineered.

Technology solutions are now available for bespoke portfolio solutions for wealth managers to utilize best-of-breed data to drive a complete framework for global, multi-asset strategic and tactical asset allocation decision-making. This can provide a framework for wealth managers to industrialize their investment process to deliver high-quality, scalable client portfolio solutions more cost effectively.

Investment managers can access systematic, transparent, back-tested, verifiable signals to provide reliable inputs to enhance portfolio return. Wealth managers can generate significant operational efficiencies and improve the quality of investment decision-making.

Research and Data

The European Markets in Financial Instruments Directive II (MiFID II), the European Union legislative framework for investment intermediaries, takes effect from January 2018. Wealth managers will be subject to new constraints and heavy burdens to unbundle research and execution services. Wealth managers can no longer use execution fees in return for fees. Research for the benefit of client portfolios will now have to be paid for explicitly by the wealth management firm, or a charge levied on client portfolios. Wealth managers will be required to quantify research and data costs, and the value that they provide to the portfolio for the first time.

Best-in-class wealth managers can seize opportunities to gain efficiencies, reducing research and data costs through utilizing smart technology to innovate. Winners will be those who address the questions of how to effectively combine the explosive growth of new "big data" insights from "traditional" sources. AI and machine learning-derived sets are already impacting forecasting techniques and being incorporated into analysis. Wealth managers need efficient, cost-effective analytics in order to continue to deliver acceptable client returns while reducing their own costs.

Skill sets and tools to utilize big data efficiently will become one of the most important skills for wealth and investment management teams in an industry driven by the relentless amount of data delivered at an increasingly rapid pace.

Imagine – wealth managers access the most insightful data providers through a single integrated application, where data is converted into fully transparent, back-tested, market predictive signals. These forward-looking signals drive performance and provide a source of competitive advantage (see Figures 1 and 2).

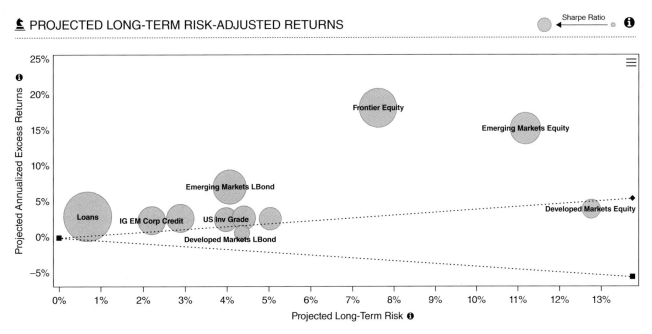

Figure 1: Projected long-term risk-adjusted returns

Figure 2: Emerging markets equity

Source: ClearMacro DashBoard for Investors, May 2017

The analytical platform incorporates curated, best-of-breed data content, including AI, machine learning and social media, across all information categories that wealth managers would consider when assessing tactical market opportunities, such as capital flows, liquidity flows, inflation and economic activity globally.

Investors are able to evaluate and rank data sets quickly and effectively with clear, high-impact visualization and analyse which data sets are most impactful on asset classes, markets and sectors (see Figure 3).

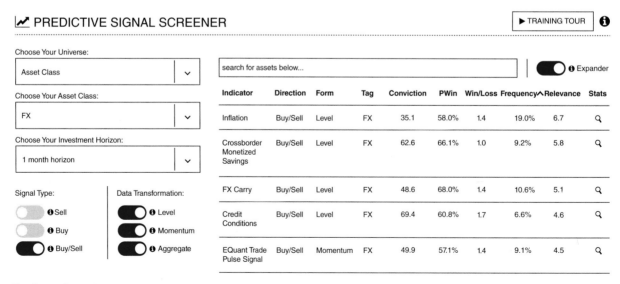

Figure 3: Predictive signal screener

Source: ClearMacro Predictive Signal Screener, May 2017

DIGITAL PLATFORMS, PRODUCTS AND ECOSYSTEMS

Imagine – wealth managers consume bespoke, tailored, impactful data curated to reflect their in-house investment approach, philosophy and requirements, to maximize the likelihood of meeting their customer portfolio objectives.

The result – a significant reduction in wealth managers' research and data subscription costs. Tools to evaluate with precision which data is adding to investment decision-making and contributing to portfolio returns. This functionality will enable wealth managers to discharge the upcoming MiFID research budget account requirement and demonstrate the value of the data providers in the research budget. They will have access to a rigorous and disciplined process while reducing human behavioural bias in the investment process.

Imagine – innovation delivered through a transparent, bespoke asset allocation framework across strategic and tactical asset allocation processes which enable investment managers to "connect the dots". Investment managers can capture and harvest regular, high-quality portfolio opportunities.

Investment Technology and Communications

Wealth management is inherently a people business. Internal teams and external advisors interact to form investment views and client advisors communicate with clients to develop and maintain relationships. Technology can enhance the quality and outcomes of these communication processes. Wealth managers typically make investment decisions slowly, while market opportunities occur rapidly. This can result in sub-optimal performance. If wealth managers can speed up investment decision-making, they can participate in more portfolio opportunities.

Imagine – investment decision makers at wealth management firms have access to curated, bespoke, high-quality data and analytics transformed into transparent, actionable, forward-looking signals. Decision makers being able to access the global opportunity set across asset classes, strategic and tactical frameworks in a single user interface driven by impactful data.

Investment decision makers and investment committees can build conviction for portfolio allocations armed with robust, complete analytics, with clear visualizations driven by data. The committee can spend more time discussing strategic and high-impact portfolio issues and implementation rather than collating projections and debating differing theoretical assumptions.

The impact – a huge saving in time and higher-quality communications, all leading to higher-quality, transparent and defensible decision-making.

Imagine – client advisors access real-time client portfolio content tailored to predetermined client suitability. Powerful visualization with scenario analysis and portfolio upgrade suggestions to address potential threats can be accessed from face-to-face meetings, tablet or mobile. The quality of client interactions can be significantly enhanced by real-time access to client portfolio information, house model portfolios and recommendations based on a forward-looking library of content and analytical tools driven by data.

Risk Reduction

Recent regulatory reprimands against wealth management firms for "unsuitable" advice by the UK regulator can be avoided by incorporating bespoke systematic "suitability" rules into the investment decision-making process.

Imagine – client advisors access data-driven, opinion-free, strategic and tactical investment recommendations that can only be allocated to clients if they are "suitable" for the particular account holder according to pre-assigned criteria. The client advisor can never inadvertently allocate a client portfolio to a transaction that is "unsuitable". The advisor can manage their book of clients more effectively, knowing that they can both meet suitability requirements and increase the number of clients covered and the quality of input.

Wealth managers substantially reduce their risk of censure and reputational damage with a solution that is highly scalable. Wealth managers can utilize technology to be able to demonstrate accountability ex-post for client recommendations through data-driven, verifiable investment decision-making. Decision-making will be demonstrably defensible and transparent.

In conclusion, in a world of increased regulation and competition, wealth managers can boost portfolio returns and business profitability with data-driven tools that systemize and industrialize their investment decision-making processes. Systematized data-driven processes enhance and streamline communication, while minimizing risks from inappropriate client advice.

The Business Case for Gender Equality

By Angela Sun
Global Head of Strategy and Corporate Development, Bloomberg

The Case for Gender Equality

The conversation around gender equality in the workplace reached a crescendo in early 2017, as millions marched for women's rights around the world. A few weeks later, an international strike urged women to forgo their paid and unpaid responsibilities and show the world the impact of a day without women. And, on the eve of International Women's Day, a bronze statue of a young girl appeared on Wall Street, defiantly facing the iconic charging bull. This "Fearless Girl" symbolized State Street's campaign to increase the number of female directors, calling on the thousands of public companies it invests in to take action.

Collectively, these protests and campaigns reflect a growing sense of frustration around the glacial pace of women's progress in the workplace and global economy. A 2015 McKinsey study showed that if women's participation in the labour markets matched that of men's, as much as US$28 trillion could be added to the global annual GDP by 2025.[1] Companies are beginning to recognize this untapped potential, and what's at risk if they fail to provide a more gender-equal and inclusive work environment: access to the widest pool of talent, more productive and innovative teams, and ultimately, stronger financial performance. Underlying this is the message that, increasingly, investor dollars are also at stake – and that gender equality can be a powerful financial incentive.

[1] http://www.mckinsey.com/global-themes/employment-and-growth/how-advancing-womens-equality-can-add-12-trillion-to-global-growth.

An Investment Imperative

What began as an ideology – equal rights for women – has become an undeniable economic and investment imperative. As investors seek alternative drivers of risk-aware alpha in a challenging market environment, and companies look for new ways to demonstrate sound governance and attract capital, the demand for transparent data regarding gender equality and diversity practices has never been greater. Bloomberg launched its Financial Services Gender-Equality Index in May 2016 to meet this growing demand, providing standardized, aggregate data to measure where companies stand on gender equality.

Demand for ESG and Gender-Based Data

Gender data is part of a broader set of information known as environmental, social and governance (ESG) data, traditionally used by investors focused on strategies variously labelled as sustainable, responsible or ethical investing. Over the past decade, demand for ESG data and socially responsible investment strategies has skyrocketed, driven by six key stakeholder groups:

- **Institutional investors** are relying on ESG data to assess firms' ability to mitigate operational risk and maintain corporate competitiveness.
- **Asset managers** are acknowledging the difficulty of capturing alpha from traditional, commoditized financial datasets, and looking to ESG factors to better understand a firm's or portfolio's outperformance potential.
- **Millennials, high-net-worth individuals and women** are more likely to use ESG data to align their investments with their values.
- **Companies** are using the data to inform policies and practices and attract talent.
- **Exchanges and governments** are demanding more robust data to encourage regional corporate competitiveness and attract more foreign and domestic capital.

- **Media and journalists** use ESG data to support their reporting on the business imperative behind diversity, inclusion and other topics.

In 2016, membership in the US Principles for Responsible Investment grew to over 1500 members, with US$60 trillion in assets. The Global Sustainable Investment Alliance reports that nearly US$23 trillion – 26% of assets under management globally – is currently invested in assets incorporating ESG investment strategies.[2] Rising interest in gender-lens investing specifically is also reshaping the ESG landscape. A 2016 study from the SIF Foundation tracked gender-lens investing for the first time, reporting that US$397 billion in investor assets "had an explicit focus on products or companies that actively support women's social and economic advancement".[3] In response, firms have developed products like State Street's SHE ETF, tracking companies with female leaders, and the Pax Ellevate Global Women's Index Fund, which invests in companies advancing women's leadership. Institutional managers are also seeking robust and widely available gender data to help inform these and other strategies.

Methodology: Measuring the Gender Ecosystem

The Bloomberg Financial Services Gender-Equality Index (BFGEI) expands the universe of available data, arming investors with information far beyond current disclosure requirements. Its unique, holistic datasets provide transparency across the entire ecosystem of gender data: (1) internal company statistics; (2) employee policies; (3) external community engagement;

and (4) gender-conscious product offerings. Each measures an element crucial to reaching gender parity. Internal company statistics, such as the percentage of women executives or the percentage of women in the top 10% of compensated employees, demonstrate a firm's commitment to promoting women into senior-most leadership positions. Employee policies, such as fully paid parental leave and equal pay for women, illustrate how firms are cultivating that advancement and encouraging a diverse working environment. A firm's sponsorship of financial education programmes, or support for public advocacy organizations and legislation, also offers a strong indication of its engagement with the community. Similarly, the availability of gender-conscious product offerings measures how firms are advancing gender equality within the larger economy, by providing financial resources and access for women clients and women-owned businesses.

Each company included in the BFGEI is required to submit an annual survey[4] and score at or above a global threshold established to reflect disclosure and the achievement or adoption of best-in-class statistics and policies across all four categories. Created in consultation with third-party experts such as Women's World Banking, Catalyst and the National Partnership for Women & Families, survey questions are updated annually to better reflect trends and demand from the investment community, as well as new developments in diversity and inclusion practices. And, as interest from both companies and investors continues to grow, future iterations may focus on additional industries and metrics (see Figure 1).

---

[2] https://www.bloomberg.com/professional/blog/sustainable-investing-grows-asset-owner-demand/.

[3] https://www.bloomberg.com/news/articles/2016-11-14/sustainable-investments-surged-by-third-to-8-7-trillion-in-2016.

[4] 2017 index eligibility required a firm to be classified as "Financials" under the Bloomberg Industry Classification System (BICS), a public company trading on a US exchange including ADR listings, with a firm market cap greater than or equal to US$1 billion. A complete list of eligibility criteria can be found within the 2017 BFGEI methodology documentation, https://data.bloomberglp.com/professional/sites/4/2017_BFGEI_Overview.pdf.

The 2017 Bloomberg Financial Services Gender-Equality Index is comprised of 52 firms headquartered in 17 countries

HOW BFGEI MEMBERS ADDRESS GENDER ISSUES AROUND THE GLOBE

84%
of Americas-based BFGEI member firms have a supplier diversity programme

80%
of Europe-based BFGEI member firms conduct compensation reviews to identify gender-based variations in pay

93%
of Asia-Pacific-based BFGEI member firms offer unconscious bias training

Figure 1: Insights – how BFGEI members address gender equality around the globe

Note: In less than a year, the BFGEI doubled in size to include 52 firms headquartered in 17 countries

This expansion is indicative of companies' growing desire to assure both investors and the public of their commitment to establishing gender equality and strong corporate governance. The index highlights a number of initiatives firms have engaged in to increase their pipeline of female leaders, and better recruit and retain women: 75% of index member firms provide return-to-work programmes for women; 73% require a gender-diverse slate of candidates for management roles; 83% offer or sponsor financial education programmes for women in their communities. The BFGEI 2017 member firms have an average of 26% female representation on boards, double the total financial services average of 13%.

The 2017 BFGEI's global footprint also provides insight into how different regions are addressing gender equality in the workplace. Among index member firms, 84% of Americas-based member firms implemented a supplier-diversity programme, 80% of Europe-based member firms incorporated gender-specific compensation

reviews and 93% of APAC-based member firms offered unconscious bias training. As global membership grows, the index will also capture how companies are meeting regional challenges, such as parental leave benefits in the USA, return-to-work programmes in Europe, elder care in Japan and childcare services in Australia. And, as exchanges and governments consider the merits of encouraging or requiring disclosures or the adoption of specific policies, the ability to standardize data across regions and multinational companies will be critical to that debate.

Setting New Standards for Gender Equality

In addition to measuring how well firms are progressing towards gender equality, the BFGEI can help identify potential factors contributing to an organization's success. Its holistic nature – offering insights into previously opaque areas like the prevalence of mandatory diverse candidate slates or the percentage of women among a firm's highest compensated group of employees – helps investors and the firms themselves measure progress, examine potential correlations between these unique sets of information and draw comparisons against peers.

By featuring firms with a demonstrated commitment to gender equality, the index is helping to set a new standard for the industry and beyond, encouraging companies to re-evaluate their own policies and practices. Over the course of a year, one firm included as a member of both the 2016 and 2017 BFGEI began requiring unconscious bias training for all managers, started covering fertility services and implemented a supplier-diversity programme including women-owned business. Another member firm increased its maternity leave by four weeks, extended paternity leave by seven weeks and started offering return-to-work programmes for new mothers. And in perhaps the most tangible sign of progress, Bloomberg's 2016 inaugural BFGEI member firms collectively increased the average number of women across all levels of leadership between FY 2014 and FY 2015.

Financial Performance and the Way Forward

The BFGEI catalyses a virtuous cycle, as index membership and investor demand continues to grow. More data allows investors to build stronger, more robust strategies targeting companies with diverse workforces and inclusive environments. It is also helping them achieve stronger returns. One strategy – investing in S&P 500 companies with the most women in board, management and workforce roles – has outperformed the benchmark by 141% over the past 10 years.[5] Similarly, the Pax Ellevate Global Women's Index Fund outperformed the MSCI World Index for a two-year period ending 30 June 2016.[6] In turn, companies are encouraged to implement and improve upon the practices and policies understood to drive gender equality, and disclose the data around those changes. As the BFGEI grows, it will reflect the leadership and progress of corporations, the investment community, media, exchanges and governments, working collectively towards gender parity. And, as one influences the other, we'll continue to build on transparent, actionable data to better measure – and drive – the financial and human impact of diversity and inclusion in the workplace.

[5] Vignesh, R. S. and Cosereanu, C., "A gender-focused strategy beat the S&P 500 by 141 percent", https://www.bloomberg.com/news/articles/2016-06-16/a-gender-focused-strategy-beat-the-s-p-500-by-141-percent (16 June 2016).

[6] http://www.paxellevate.com/resources/news/detail/86.

Fiduciary Robo-Selection is Possible in a New Fund Order

By J.B. Beckett
Author and Founder, New Fund Order

Computers can be clever, yes, but surely they lack any inherent sense of self, humanity or ability to act fiduciary, at creation? Could they? Hot on the heels of robo-advice, robo-selection, as it relates to the selection and research of mutual funds, is the next frontier for FinTech. As more assets move to index-based and systematic strategies, so the dynamics of fund research are changing. How then can robo-selectors put the client above all others? Friedrich Nietzsche wrote that *morality was the herding instinct of the individual*. If true, then that herding behaviour could be defined and mapped.

The concept of "fiduciary" certainly goes well beyond selecting the cheapest passive fund and leaving it there for 25 years. Fiduciary has also expanded into political, society and environmental levels through industry initiatives like the UN Principles for Responsible Investment (PRI) and Sustainable Development Goals. However, the very discharge of fiduciary itself could be more transparent, for example does an investor require a human to offer a fiduciary service or indeed to be a fiduciary fund selector? Could computers act in a fiduciary manner? First, consider that human decisions litter history with malfeasance: Madoff, Arch Cru, boiler rooms, LIBOR-rigging, flash boys and so on.

Computers are not predisposed to wrongdoing, only programmed to do so – a thought for the rapid proliferation of robo. With the rise of the robots, the battle for white-collar roles has begun. White-collar roles by and large have little physicality to overcome, lots of talking, thinking, writing reports and drinking coffee. Martin Ford's book[1] aptly summarizes the bleak outlook for white-collar

finance professionals; a second digital age if you will. The asset management industry ("the City") is actually one of the last bastions of human industrial intensity, be it actuaries, fund managers, brokers, consultants or professional fund investors, and the myriad of pseudo-executives and support staff in between.

What does being a fiduciary require? Empathy, diligence, determination, trustworthiness, expertise, judgement. Putting the investor before yourself. These may seem all too human and a realm beyond digitization yet, but when Google's DeepMind AlphaGo program beat South Korea's Lee Sedol 4–1 in the first of a series of games in Seoul in March 2016, the fiduciary opportunities from adaptive artificial intelligence (AI) took a huge step forward.

Over 2500 years old, in terms of rules, Go has considerably simpler rules than chess. Black and White sides each have access to black and white stones on a 19×19 grid. Once placed, stones don't move. The aim of the game is to completely surround and capture opposite stones, which are then removed from the board. Here the complexity and artistry arises – organic battles from the corners to the centre of the board. Given that a typical chess game has a branching factor of about 35 and lasts 80 moves, the number of possible moves is vast, about 35^{80} (35 to the power of 80) possible moves, aka the "Shannon number". Go is much much bigger. With its breadth of 250 possible moves each turn, and 150 likely moves, there are about 250^{150} (250 to the power of 150) possible moves.

In many ways the computations of a fund selector are far more complex than a Go stratagem, but the small judgemental biases are similar. Asset allocation, over- and underweighting assets against a "neutral", giving rise to tactical positions, has its very roots in war strategy and hence Go. Of course, fund selection is neither science nor art, it combines fuzzy logic with data inputs into a decision.

Imagine if fund selection can be derived from software: a neural network computing program that can screen thousands

---

[1] Ford, M. (2015). *Rise of the Robots*. New York: Basic Books.

of funds and make judgements, shortlist recommendations, assess suitability and compatibility against a mandate or investor needs and monitor the outcome of those decisions, all the while underwriting the capability of a fund manager based on a model, new information and past data, recommending changes while simultaneously weighing the impact on the portfolio and topical metrics like turnover, cost, etc. Performance analysis has already been digitized; other types of information can be stored and used for learning, algorithms can replicate judgemental nudges and biases based on common material changes like manager experience, tenure, benchmark, fund changes, moving firm, news flow and so on. In many ways software can far better interpret the signals, and its significance needs to lay a good starting baseline for self-learning. In many ways the components already exist as separate FinTechs, simply needing a complex adaptive algorithm to link it all together.

The other challenge is the retention of experience, digital wisdom if you will. Here AlphaGo solved through coupling self-learning with a *differentiable neural computer* (DNC). Memory requires memory, literally. The DNC architecture differs from others by selectively writing memory as well as reading, allowing iterative modification of memory, according to its developers. All mind-bending stuff for a mere fund analyst!

Firstly, robots follow three guiding laws: the three Laws of Robotics ("Asimov's Laws") devised by the science fiction author Isaac Asimov. These have come to be fundamental guiding principles for the robotics industry and so too should apply to the fiduciary robo-advisor and robo-selector:

- A robot may not injure a human being or, through inaction, allow a human being to come to harm.

- A robot must obey the orders given it by human beings, except where such orders would conflict with the first law.

- A robot must protect its own existence as long as such protection does not conflict with the first or second laws.

The fiduciary duty thus falls to the programmer of the algorithm, who instructs the programme to make decisions. Taking these laws, it is not unfathomable that computers can be programmed and learn to put the interests of the client first and foremost.

1. Uphold a fiduciary standard; all conflicts of interest must be disclosed. A computer has no conflicts unless they are first programmed. Like a driverless car, its function is to serve the purpose without question.

2. A fiduciary has a "duty to care" and must continually monitor not only a client's investments, but also their changing financial situation. A computer can monitor 24/7 continuously and is not restricted by fatigue or the adviser's/fund selector's diary. A sequence can be included if the client does not supply an update within x days or could be linked to the client's accounts, email, diary and so on.

3. Understand changes to a client's risk tolerance, perhaps after a painful bear market. Perhaps there was a family change. Under the suitability standard, the financial planning process could begin and end in a single meeting. For fiduciaries, that first client meeting marks only the beginning of the legal obligation. We have seen the term "orphan clients", and humans have a great track record of dropping less profitable clients (value pools).

4. Monitor, learn, adapt and assess fund changes. The reality is that many fund investors do not monitor their decisions often enough or with objectivity. They are susceptible to heuristic biases. Yet a computer can continuously monitor cost, turnover, risk, changes and performance. It can monitor RSS feeds, performance, fund manager commentary, portfolio positions, information supplied by the client, instructions, deal flow, thousands if not millions of data points analysed through neural networks.

From the above, the algorithm can include a core hierarchy of neural paths and decision trees: efficacy of active management versus benchmark/passive based on a learning empirical algorithm and relative valuation of index momentum, the carbon impact of a portfolio, the environmental, social and governance score of the fund and underlying stocks, Stewardship score, economic value comparison of available universes and fund structures, risks relating to the firm – like fines or corporate restructures, rating changes, flow data, people changes, process issues, significant portfolio turnover or positioning changes, risks, performance issues, ongoing costs. From these broad sections, the algorithm can create thousands of rules, rankings, logic maps and decision points driving further questions or a BUY, HOLD or SELL decision.

The move towards more fiduciary transparency is an important step towards digitizing robo-selection. The danger is that self-learning AI itself compromises the fiduciary obligation to the investor and it is here that Asimov's laws need to be hardwired, tested and continuously measured. Perhaps the answer is more symbiotic than we might be led to believe. A third way? If you feel the notion of digital fiduciary is still more science fiction than threat, then you may be right but we do well at becoming better "cyborgs"[2] – using technology, using the cloud, the crowd, to generate positive fiduciary evidence for the value added by human fund selection. Robo is Go, your move!

---

[2] Cyborg: in science fiction stories, this is defined as a creature that is part human and part machine.

Blockchain Applications in Asset and Wealth Management

Embedding distributed ledger technology

A distributed ledger is a distributed database that records ownership through a shared registry

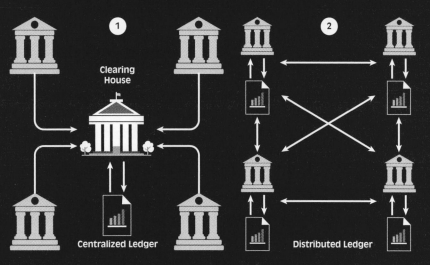

Clearing House

Centralized Ledger

Distributed Ledger

By enabling the digitization of assets, blockchain is driving a fundamental shift from the "Internet of Information" to the "Internet of Value", where we exchange assets.

Bitcoin currently is the best existing use case for Blockchain technology.

No single entity owns or controls these digital records. No customer service, no regulatory oversight exists!

Blockchain can provide new technical standards for transparency, openness and user content. Besides creating a global system of digital IDs, it could also provide users with self-sovereign identity and solutions in Asset Management.

1. Today we have central clearing houses and centralized ledgers.

2. Distributed ledgers (DLTs) do not need central authorities to certify ownership and clear transactions. DLT can be open and verify anonymous actors or closed (actors have to identify themselves before joining).

Ecosystem of Blockchains:

- Private
- Public
- Consortium blockchains
- Zero-knowledge proof chains
- Superfast blockchains i.e. for high-frequency trading

Blockchain Fund Subscription Model:

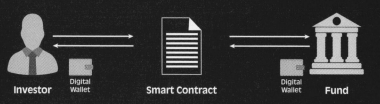

Investor — **Digital Wallet** — **Smart Contract** — **Digital Wallet** — **Fund**

Main opportunities to leverage DLT for Asset Management are Trust and Safety, i.e. digital identity, asset safe-keeping and fractionalization.

Executive Summary

Blockchain is driving innovation in asset management. The asset management industry is characterized by many intermediaries providing different kinds of service, like settlement of securities. Thus, wealth managers have historically exploited trust arbitrage, and the information asymmetry between them and their customers. Blockchain by definition aims to decentralize transactions and thus may revolutionize the industry. While the first application areas focus on digitizing traditional tangible assets like Royal Mint Gold, more disruptive ones focus on fund management – like for example Melonport. The first very promising proofs of concept are being tested, and there are many trail-blazing start-ups entering the field. This is exactly what the asset management industry needs now – fresh ideas and real use cases to swing over all the stakeholders, including the regulator.

The main opportunities to leverage distributed ledger technology for wealth management centre on trust and safety. Offerings in the realm of digital identity and asset safekeeping, also for traditionally non-bankable assets, appear to be the sweet spot for wealth management firms. In addition, wealth management firms might want to look into offering additional DLT-enabled services as they mature and gain wider-spread adoption. Irrespective of the opportunities these services present, challenges remain for blockchain solutions to scale and inter-operate in a partially heavily regulated environment. The last chapter in this part argues that blockchain innovations have the power to democratize the whole investment management industry, due to its decentralized characteristics. In summary, there is no doubt that blockchain will disrupt how the industry works, leading to lower costs, faster execution and better services to customers going forward.

Summarized, this part discusses the basics of blockchain and soon dives into the possible ramifications of blockchain across the investment management and wealth creation realm from a capital market perspective where maximum wealth is created or lost. It speaks about the possibilities of digitization and benefits from eliminating intermediaries and ends with an extrapolation on the blockchain market share.

Cryptocurrencies and Blockchain

By Steven Dryall
Principal, Incipient Industries

What is "Cryptocurrency"?

Cryptocurrency is tamperproof digital money that can be traded openly. Cryptocurrency technology enables the ability to reliably create and exchange value over the internet without an intermediary. Bitcoin was the first viable example of cryptocurrency. Bitcoin proved the capabilities of cryptocurrency technology and initiated the digital economy.

Many other cryptocurrency technologies have emerged following bitcoin and more will be created. Different cryptocurrency technologies possess different attributes, but they all share the same ability to reliably exchange value. A "general-purpose cryptocurrency", such as bitcoin, is meant for use in open markets with no designated trade purpose or associated value.

What is an "Asset-Based Cryptocurrency"?

An asset-based cryptocurrency (ABC) is a cryptocurrency that uses digital tokens to represent a tangible pool of assets. The value of the digital tokens is based on the assets. An ABC uses the same underlying technologies as general-purpose cryptocurrencies, but is different in how those technologies interact with systems and people.

How is an Asset-Based Cryptocurrency Created?

ABCs have characteristics and challenges that are unique when compared with general-purpose cryptocurrencies such as bitcoin. An ABC ecosystem has a distinct set of requirements that define the success or failure of that ecosystem.

To be viable, an ABC, like any cryptocurrency, must establish the "Three Pillars of Digital Money Viability", as shown in Figure 1. An ABC can more likely build the pillars, since the nature of an ABC is more focused and targeted.

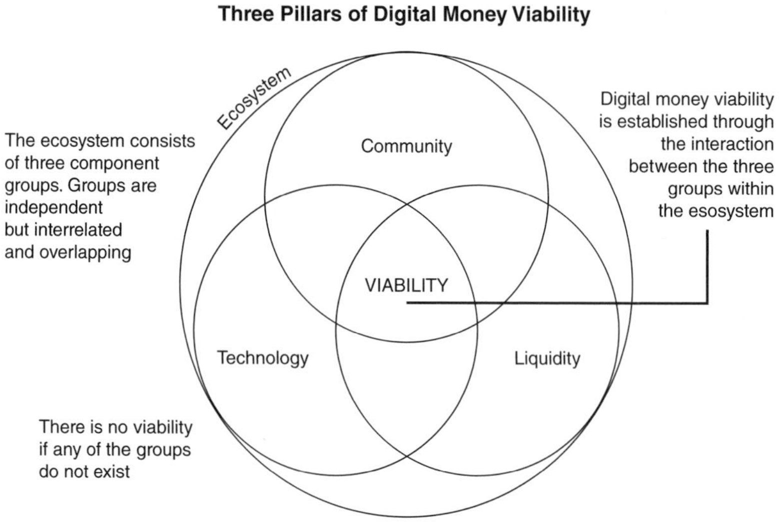

Three Pillars of Digital Money Viability

The ecosystem consists of three component groups. Groups are independent but interrelated and overlapping

Digital money viability is established through the interaction between the three groups within the esosystem

There is no viability if any of the groups do not exist

Ecosystem

Community

Technology

Liquidity

VIABILITY

Figure 1: Three pillars of digital money viability

The three pillars as applied to an ABC ecosystem are: network services, for the Technology Pillar; asset supporters for the Community Pillar; and token exchange for the Liquidity Pillar.

The differentiator for an ABC, compared with a general-purpose cryptocurrency, is the allocation of a pool of assets to be exchanged against the digital tokens. This distinction is significant and raises considerations that are unique to an ABC ecosystem.

Network Services

The ABC network services are the technology elements needed to support transactions with the digital tokens that represent the asset pool. Of critical importance to this functionality are the nodes in the network. Nodes are required for peer-to-peer network support, as well as being the foundation for related services. Services, such as exchange or redemption, require node communications for completing transactions.

The Network Platform

Cryptocurrency technology is based on open source software with different platform types available for ABC deployment. The benefits and drawbacks to each type are affected by the nature of the assets.

- **Dedicated platform.** A dedicated platform is purpose-built for the asset pool and surrounding applications. This type of platform has the benefits of being completely customizable and can be built according to the exact requirements of the assets represented. The main drawback is high development overheads.

- **Modified fork of existing technology.** Modifying existing technology provides the benefits of a proven history. Existing technologies have extensions allowing for more rapid deployment of services. This type of platform can have limitations or dependencies on previous development efforts that may not be aligned with the objectives of the assets being represented.

- **Sub-token on existing network.** Some existing cryptocurrency platforms allow the creation of separate digital tokens to exist on a network with other digital tokens. These tokens are independent in their represented value but are dependent on the existing network for functionality. There can be network effect benefits to using an established cryptocurrency network with a proven performance record. These dependencies can possess limitations, with customizations restricted to the specifications of the existing network technology.

The Wallet

Cryptocurrency tokens are accessed using software that is typically called a "wallet". The wallet provides an end-user interface for interaction with the cryptocurrency. Wallets use a semi-standard interface to enable consistent interaction and complete user control of their tokens. Wallet software is typically open source and can be a local client or online service. Wallet platform support is typically driven by the requirements of those interacting with the system. Support for wallets can include: desktop clients for Windows, MacOS and Linux; smartphone apps; web-based wallets; and physical wallets, such as paper or other printed versions.

The Block Explorer

Unique to cryptocurrency technology is the "block explorer". A block explorer is a service that allows users to view transactions in the network. This is done through an interface that allows easier access to the data within the network. The block explorer is not just used by people to view transactions, but is also the common application used for confirming transactions in commerce. Block explorers are typically web-accessed services.

Asset Supporters

The community supporting an ABC is vital to its viability, but may not be as robust as that of a general-purpose cryptocurrency. Those supporting an ABC will have more interest in the benefits of the underlying asset as opposed to the general benefits of cryptocurrency.

Market Opportunities

The benefits and opportunities created for asset managers when representing an asset pool with a digital token revolve around increasing markets through enhanced liquidity.

The deployment of an ABC creates new opportunities that are only possible through cryptocurrency. Using cryptocurrency, it is possible to exchange value that is represented digitally without an intermediary. This ability to reliably exchange digital value creates a new form of liquidity previously unattainable. More liquidity creates new market conditions that can facilitate previously unexplored forms of trade. Liquidity comes from the community and building liquidity also extends the community.

Community Building

The best efforts for building and maintaining a supportive community surrounding an ABC involve channelling participants. With an ABC the supporting community is likely already established, or is more easily rallied. The nature of the community will be directly affected by the nature of the asset pool associated with the ABC.

The community supporting an ABC will immediately consist of:

- asset managers
- token speculators
- liquidity providers
- aftermarket exchangers.

Existing interest should be leveraged by the ABC community building efforts. The supporting community affects the overall trust of the ecosystem. Having trustful entities responsible for important components in the ecosystem increases the overall trustfulness of the ecosystem.

Regulatory Concerns

The supporting community of an ABC is affected by regulation. Regulatory issues relating to cryptocurrency are regional, but cryptocurrency technology by nature is global. When dealing with an ABC, however, the regulatory issues can become more clearly defined. This can be affected by the nature of the assets represented by the tokens, in addition to the methods used for redemption.

Detailed aspects of regulatory issues surrounding ABCs are beyond the scope of this chapter. It is very important to take appropriate precautionary measures during the earliest stages of ABC development, to mitigate risk. Improper handling of assets can have severe regulatory repercussions, so be sure to seek legal counsel regarding any potential regulatory pitfalls that may exist.

Token Exchange

The value of an ABC comes from its association of value with the asset pool. The conversion of the digital token into the asset, or the reverse, is where implementation and logistics raise challenges. Liquidity and divisibility of the asset are the primary considerations for the deployment of an exchange system.

Security Mention

Cryptocurrency technology offers an inherent level of security regarding transactions and other aspects related to the supporting network activities. An ABC has dependencies on service components that have separate security concerns. The transactions stored within a cryptocurrency network are cryptographically secure, but the surrounding technologies are not secured by the same technology. A multidirectional approach to network security is critical to the establishment of trust and ultimately the success of an ABC.

Reconciliation of Value

Digital tokens used for exchange of value representing a specific pool of assets must have a consistent valuation for redemption. Although cryptocurrency technology does provide a very high level of security, the system is still vulnerable to human conditions. It is up to the asset pool manager to determine the value of associated digital tokens and how their redemption will impact the open-market value of digital tokens that have not been redeemed.

Redemption Logistics

Options for how to offer exchange of digital tokens for tangible assets – as represented by the cryptocurrency – are specific to the nature of the represented assets. The exchange of the digital tokens represents liquidity resulting from the assured value, but the practical liquidity of the underlying assets may not be as fluid. It is important for the asset manager to make allowances for (or restrictions on) the redemption of digital tokens as directly applied to the asset pool.

Conclusion

The development and deployment of an asset-based cryptocurrency offers challenges and benefits while creating new opportunities. ABCs can have economic effects that can only be realized as more become available. Viable ABCs can be used as part of digital economies that are built with cryptocurrencies and open markets. The ability to tokenize and exchange any value, reliably and without intermediaries, reshapes how assets function.

How Blockchain Drives Innovation in Asset Management

By Dean Demellweek
Senior Digital Transformation Manager, BNP Paribas

> The industries ready for transformation are all of those where the service is bad, the price is high, and the margins are high. So, that definitely will be finance, that's my own industry!

These are the words of Tim Draper, legendary Silicon Valley VC investor, who has invested US$10 billion in over 1000 companies so far. Another big name, Harvard Business School professor Clayton Christensen, when asked about disruption in financial services, replied:

> Banks will ultimately be the cause of their own demise if they limit investment in disruption innovations, and focus only on freeing up capital through tightening their belts and automating processes!

Neither of them mentioned asset management specifically, yet you would probably agree that both statements are equally applicable. There are reasons for optimism though! The first very promising proofs of concept (PoCs) are being tested (e.g. Fundchain Smart TA,[1] BNP Paribas Fund Link,[2] Funds DLT[3]) and there are many trail-blazing start-ups entering the field (e.g. Melonport,[4] Polychain Capital,[5] Blockchain Capital[6]). This is exactly what the asset

management industry needs now – fresh ideas and many more real use cases to swing over all stakeholders.

What's even more encouraging is the fact that in April 2017 the UK's financial services regulator, the FCA, launched a new phase of their Project Innovate with the aim of helping financial service firms tackle regulatory barriers to innovation, and develop new products and services. Furthermore, the FCA announced that it would work with other international regulators on approaches to innovation.

Challenges and Opportunities

The asset management challenges and opportunities are numerous:

- New technologies threatening to disrupt the existing business model – blockchain, big data and analytics, artificial intelligence (AI), cloud computing and mobile.

- FinTech start-ups leveraging these new technologies most effectively.

- Extremely complex structure of the asset management value chain with many intermediaries and operational processes resulting in high fees.

- Low beta returns due to sluggish economic growth in the developed world and slowing emerging-markets economies.

- Changing demographics across geographies and generations creating new classes of investors – millennials, women and the newly wealthy in emerging markets. Their behaviour, values and expectations are radically different. Millennials are, for instance, more risk-averse and socially conscious than previous generations. They expect to be served 24/7, on demand and via multiple channels and devices. Currently the largest segment of the labour force, they are also the largest investor group.

This chapter will concentrate on the impact of blockchain technology on innovation in asset management due to its potential

---

[1] http://fundchain.lu.

[2] http://securities.bnpparibas.com/about-us/news/development-of-a-next-generation.html.

[3] http://www.thefundschain.com.

[4] https://www.melonport.com.

[5] https://dailyfintech.com/2017/03/28/polychain-capital-a-hedge-fund-investing-at-the-protocol-layer-of-web-3-0/.

[6] http://blockchain.capital.

to completely transform business models in asset management and drastically improve the service the industry offers to clients, along with lower prices.

Blockchain can substantially reduce the costs and increase the speed of any digital transaction or interaction in the fund value chain by enabling investors and issuers to communicate and transact directly, without any intermediaries. Moreover, since all the blockchain transactions are time-stamped, immutable, transparent and auditable, even compliance processes will be greatly simplified.

Taking into consideration that smart contracts are executed as programmed, the data is secured by cryptography and there is no single point of failure, blockchain is also deemed reliable. Hence, the number of errors will also be dramatically reduced!

New Business Model

Figure 1 shows what the prospective business model of fund subscription could look like on blockchain.

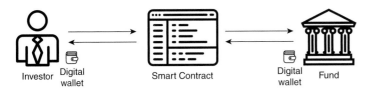

Investor Digital wallet   Smart Contract   Digital wallet Fund

Figure 1: Blockchain fund subscription model

Source: Dean Demellweek, Spring 2017

- The investor's fund subscription request sent via an application triggers the smart contract.

- In the first step, the smart contract performs all the required checks and verifications, such as client onboarding, AML/KYC, etc.

- Then, once the smart contract receives the computed net asset value from the fund, it verifies that all conditions are met.

- Subsequently, the smart contract executes the transaction – a newly created digital fund share is exchanged for a specified amount of digital currency, and both wallets are updated.

This is a pretty simplified version of the business model, but it is a very good illustration of how blockchain can streamline the complex operational processes performed on a daily basis by numerous intermediaries in the value chain.

Since everything is managed by smart contracts, all the costs associated with fund and cash processing, AML/KYC and due diligence, errors and reconciliations have been eliminated. Moreover, compliance is automated, since enforced by the blockchain. And the exchange of fund shares for payment is instantaneous.

It is worth mentioning that both the investor and the fund need digital wallets to store currencies and digital assets. Some physical assets, such as diamonds and gold, are already available as tokens on different blockchains (check for instance Everledger[7] and Digix Global[8]). No doubt many more real-world assets will, in the not so distant future, get tokenized. With that, their liquidity will also be greatly improved!

Other digital assets currently available are cryptocurrencies, digital coins and tokens granting holders access to a software or service. They are all becoming increasingly attractive to investors due to their remarkable growth over recent years. This year, investors will finally be able to gain exposure to an actively managed portfolio of blockchain-based assets – rather than just the major digital currencies – via Polychain Capital.[9]

---

[7] https://www.everledger.io.

[8] https://www.dgx.io.

[9] https://www.forbes.com/sites/laurashin/2016/12/09/andreessen-horowitz-and-union-square-ventures-invest-10-million-in-new-digital-assets-hedge-fund/ - 5e9712a75e97.

Ecosystem of Blockchains

Once assets are digitized and transferred onto different blockchains, we will be able to start trading across multiple asset classes in this new ecosystem of blockchains that will come in many different flavours: some private, some public, consortium blockchains, zero-knowledge proof chains, superfast blockchains and so on. They will match different requirements: for instance, a high-frequency fund will require a superfast blockchain. Besides, they will store different types of data such as identities, agreements, property rights, etc.

There will also be different blockchain platforms or marketplaces: for example, BNP Paribas is building Fund Link, dubbed "the next-generation fund distribution platform", with the aim of enhancing operational efficiency in the fund distribution by utilizing smart contracts and shared information. An excellent example is a speedy onboarding process for fund buyers – they will only have to upload their profile and investor onboarding documents once. This information will then be shared with the various management companies on the platform. BNP Paribas Fund Link will also help asset managers meet the demands of new regulations for higher levels of transparency, such as MiFID II. On top of that, the platform's analytics tools will enable investors to compare and select funds, and fund managers to fine-tune their distribution. In other words, BNP Paribas Fund Link will enable asset managers to sell funds directly to investors. (Funds DLT is another blockchain-based digital fund distribution platform for asset managers utilizing the powerful D2C business model.)

Adoption Stage

What the future business models of fund subscription and distribution on blockchain will really look like in 10 years is impossible to predict accurately. Not all intermediaries will disappear. Some of them will change their roles, since the new technologies and business models will create different requirements that will need to be met, whereby new roles will be

created – digital IDs will have to be created, stored and managed, as well as private keys; smart contracts will have to be built, issued and maintained; smart wallets will have to be managed and operated, etc.

We are still in the PoC stage of the development. The first results are pretty encouraging, although the transformation is going to last for years. Transitional models in this adoption stage will still need intermediaries, because many transactions will still be executed in FIAT currencies, digital wallets for currencies and assets are not yet prevalent, and the new blockchain processes will at first need solutions for integration with the existing infrastructure in asset management.

New Revenue Opportunities

So far we have discussed the huge cost savings and operational efficiencies blockchain will create. Let's now turn our attention to the new revenue opportunities it might generate. Lower trading costs, better liquidity, greater transparency and improved customer experience are all expected to considerably increase market participation. In addition, blockchain will certainly enable new product structures (e.g. digitized fund units). Analytics and real-time reporting will enhance value-added client services. And more complex instruments, such as syndicated loans for instance, are likely to become more economic.

Potential Disruptor

The picture of the current state of innovation in asset management would not be complete without mentioning at least one potential disruptor. Melonport's idea is to make it much cheaper and easier to manage assets, or set up a hedge fund or portfolio on blockchain. The start-up is building Melon[10] – open source

---

[10] Greenpaper: Melon Protocol.

software for asset management. Since the software is being built on Ethereum, accounting and security will automatically be taken care of, as well as any fund embezzlement or manipulation by fund managers.

Within a year, Melon will provide the first live release of a user-friendly interface and core tools. The first version will solely support crypto managers by enabling them to trade all ERC20[11] tokens, since Melonport firmly believe that crypto is the next asset class! Nonetheless, Melonport expect that within five years pretty much all assets will be collateralized. By then, the start-up will be capable and ready to help users build a well-diversified portfolio with a wider range of assets than in any bank portfolio today. And pretty much anyone will be able to manage their own portfolio on blockchain, invest in other portfolios or have others invest in theirs.

Exciting Times Ahead

Although a new operating and regulatory framework for the industry has not been defined yet, this is the right time for the players in the asset management industry to evaluate strategic investments in their own blockchain capabilities to ensure that they are able to compete and grow in the future.

165

---

[11] ERC20 tokens are created on the Ethereum network and conform to Ethereum's token standard. They are, therefore, easily exchangeable and able to immediately work with Dapps that use the ERC20 standard. To learn more, please check https://themerkle.com/what-is-the-erc20-ethereum-token-standard/.

Use Cases and Monetization Challenges of Blockchain Applications in Wealth Management

By Martin Hartenstein
Head WM OCM Strategy and Business Transformation, UBS

Dr Winifred Gutmannsbauer
COO Asia Pacific and Operating Head Wealth Management Asia Pacific and Head WM Omnichannel Management, UBS

Dr Dirk Klee
Chief Operating Officer, Wealth Management* and Joint Chief Operating Officer, UBS Switzerland AG and Member of the Executive Board, UBS Switzerland AG, UBS Business Solutions

Andreas Przewloka
Chief Operating Officer and Operating Head WM Europe, UBS Europe SE

Stefan Arn
Head of WM IT and UBS Switzerland IT, UBS Business Solutions AG

Andreas Kubli
Head Multichannel Management and Digitization, UBS Switzerland

Dr Veronica Lange
Head of Innovation Group Technology Office, UBS Business Solutions AG

and Peter Stephens
Head of Blockchain and UK Group Innovation, UBS Business Solutions AG UK

Digital Disruption in Finance via Blockchain Technology

Steve Wozniak stated, on the potential of blockchain technology: "It makes me think we're at one of those times

---

*Until 1 Feb 2018

in technological, economic and social history where the sky is the limit."[1] Additionally, a recent WEF report stated that blockchain will fundamentally alter the way financial institutions do business; with change coming from new processes and architecture, rather than Bitcoin or FinTech innovations.[2] Consequently, there have been numerous reports on finance use case proofs of concept progressing fast (e.g. in the area of smart contract-enabled trade finance or trading and fractionalization of digital assets, which also includes derivatives of non-bankable assets).[3] In addition, news is being shared on how consortiums are being set up to commercially leverage distributed ledger technology (DLT).

To assess the relevancy of use cases from a financial services perspective, the two questions "where to play?" and "how to win?" help focus on potential activity areas. Using these questions to analyse a portfolio of use cases enables identification of three innovation categories:

- **Evolutionary** – cases which address already served markets and audiences, optimizing existing offerings and operations.

- **Transformative** – cases which support new market entries and targeting new audiences, requiring the extension of the existing offering and infrastructure.

- **Disruptive** – cases which potentially lead to the creation of completely new markets and audiences through new business models.

For a universal bank, it makes sense to strive for a balance across all types of innovation to develop opportunities that enhance and extend existing products and services in core markets, but also build entirely new business areas. While the utilization

---

[1] Tapscott, A. and Tapscott, D. (2016). *Blockchain Revolution.* New York: Portfolio Books.

[2] McWaters, J. (2016). "A Blueprint for Digital Identity", https://www.weforum.org/reports/disruptive-innovation-in-financial-services-a-blueprint-for-digital.

[3] Lehman, A. (2016). "Building the trust engine", https://www.ubs.com/microsites/blockchain-report/en/home.html.

of smart contracts for payments, smart structured products, cryptocurrencies or trade finance might be of critical relevance to develop DLT applications in finance, such services are not necessarily key areas to "play" in from a wealth management (WM) perspective. They do, however, have relevance for wealth managers and their clients as users of such services.

Trust and Safety – A More Detailed Look at WM-Specific Use Cases

In an ever more digital world, WM clients have increasing expectations on convenience of service, provision of succinct digital information and insight, while at the same time also expecting improved speed and reduced costs for traditional banking and investment advice services. The results are eroding margins for WM firms, with revenue potential being forced ever lower in a race to the bottom. In order to compete, WM firms need to focus on providing differentiating, individualized advice and services for clients across complex digital investment portfolios, potentially also including advice on any form of digital asset, including but not limited to non-bankable assets. Advice in this scenario is provided in a convenient client-centric digital way, supported by first-rate human relationship management and advice if in line with clients' wishes. This leaves significant growth opportunities in traditional WM service fields, while also catering to new markets and audiences. Emerging technologies – like DLT, cloud computing, Internet of Things applications or machine learning and artificial intelligence progresses – are key enablers of digitization across a broad spectrum of assets and related services of interest to high-net-worth individuals. There are already numerous examples of DLT projects with relevance to WM:

- traditional tangible assets, e.g. Royal Mint Gold;[4]
- fund management, e.g. Melonport;[5]

- private equity funds, e.g. Northern Trust;[6]
- ownership and provenance of collectables, e.g. Everledger,[7] Verisart;[8]
- ownership and corporate governance of limited companies, e.g. Otonomos;[9]
- land registry and trading of real-estate derivatives and fractionalization, e.g. ChromaWay[10] cryptocurrencies – Bitcoin or Ether realized by various firms.

Trust, safety and interoperability are key aspects that will influence the adoption of such DLT-enabled services, from the perspective of a WM client as well as that of a holistic WM provider. Specifically, trust in asset registries and the safety of related services are core requirements, on top of which the question of how to best use and connect all of those services in a seamless manner, as required by a high-net-worth client's portfolio, arises. One way to look at opportunities to address each of these aspects might be found in the value proposition of WM firms: protecting and growing the wealth of individuals or families over generations. In addition, providing holistic advice beyond investments has become more important when serving wealthy individuals today. To gain and uphold a client's trust in this regard, the excellence of advice, physical and digital safety of their assets and personal information stored from a know-your-client (KYC) perspective and beyond are all equally important. As such, WM firms seem well positioned to be a key partner of choice for digital asset safekeeping, but also for being a trusted provider of identity and related data and documentation offerings in a DLT-enabled world.

In order to get there, the development of platforms for the management of identity and digital assets, potentially using the

---

[4] https://www.royalmint.com.

[5] https://melonport.com.

[6] https://www.northerntrust.com.

[7] https://www.everledger.io.

[8] https://www.verisart.com.

[9] https://www.otonomos.com.

[10] https://chromaway.com.

strengths of DLT but ultimately operating in a technology-agnostic ecosystem, appears to be a logical conclusion. Offering digital identity-related services to clients is a natural meeting point of core capabilities of WM firms with their clients' desire to rely on their trusted partner that already captures regulatory required data and invests heavily in security and safekeeping of assets and data. Offering digital identities and related services to clients is also an enabler to connect digital asset registries. Consequently, additional DLT services can also be enabled based on identity and KYC information provided (e.g. smart contracts for various financial but also other use cases).

In summary, the digitization of assets using DLT is an observable trend, however from a WM perspective it is not necessary to be at the forefront of actively driving the digitization in all cases. What is of key importance is being active in platform building and standard setting, with digital identity as the core that enables DLT and other digital offerings in a convenient and user-centric manner, helping clients to safely embrace the digital world.

This trajectory might also, either driven by client demand or regulation such as the European Union's General Data Protection Regulation (GDPR), increasingly enable clients to access and manage digital assets outside of traditional accounts at financial institutions. In this scenario, WM firm-enabled digital identity concepts, standards and platforms are key to infuse additional trust and allow interoperability between services and platforms. This would ultimately enable holistic advice across a broad range of definitions of digital wealth portfolios.

Challenges for Implementation and Monetization

To ultimately arrive at such a DLT-enabled digital world, WM firms can build on their existing clients' trust and address challenges of managing privacy, transparency and security requirements through smart combinations of hash codes, encryption keys, wallet usage and related cold-storage options.

For digital identity, asset safekeeping offerings for more traditional and non-bankable assets and integration into client ecosystems to become established, an additional implementation challenge must be solved: how should the various existing digital identity and asset registries or wallets be connected in a (for all parties involved) meaningful, efficient yet regulatory compliant way? Developing an identity management strategy within firms is essential to provide clients with transparency on what data is captured and handled on their behalf. Taken one step further, supporting clients in managing their data privacy beyond banking, with information about them being tied to their digital identity, provides additional business opportunities, but also significant additional challenges.

Resolving such challenges should lead to scenarios where various monetization opportunities emerge (e.g. via authentication services, shareable badges or attestations for certain data points, and protecting clients with regard to the use and re-use of their data across and beyond the finance industry).[11] In this regard, SecureKey's blockchain-based services are one example of giving customers the ability to control what classifying information they share with corporations.[12] However, the business model for providing such services is still unclear.

In a world where digital identities can be connected and digital assets in a wider sense are transparent to a client's partner of choice, revenue mechanisms for advice on those assets create opportunities for firms that are able to provide insights in a holistic and convenient manner. A non-traditional example, potentially relevant for younger WM clients, might

[11] Clark-Jones, A. and Yardley, P. (2016). "Digital identity", https://www.ubs.com/magazines/innovation/en/into-the-future/2016/who-will-we-be-in-a-digital-world.html.

[12] Lyons, C. (2017). "Blockchain-based identity service backed by Big 5 Canadian banks", https://www.crowdfundinsider.com/2017/03/97722-blockchain-based-identity-service-backed-big-5-canadian-banks/.

be online gaming. In this regard, digital asset safekeeping for online games has become a market with a value of more than US$46bn based on traded in-game items last year alone.[13] Individual collector depots of such items – including in-game digital gems, spells, weapons or additional health – are supposedly reaching valuations of US$100,000 and more. Connecting such assets to a client's portfolio and keeping all assets secure in a digital safe that could also include cold, offline storage options suddenly doesn't appear to be a far-fetched offering for a WM firm.

In summary, there are at least two key monetization challenges imminent: the first is the observation from the evolution of other digital technology offerings where value capture is usually not distributed equally among actors establishing the ecosystem. The second challenge relates to the network effect required to make DLT a success for all parties involved.

Conclusion and Way Forward

The main opportunities to leverage DLT for WM centre on trust and safety. In this regard, offerings in the realm of digital identity, asset safekeeping and fractionalization, also for traditionally non-bankable assets, appear to be the sweet spot for WM firms. In addition, WM firms might want to look into offering additional smart contract-enabled services as they mature and gain wider-spread adoption (e.g. smart product trading, trade finance, notarization, etc.), where agreements are described with pre-programmed rules and self-executing operations without the need for a person, clearinghouse or middleman to facilitate.

Irrespective of the opportunities these services present, challenges remain for them to scale and interoperate in a partially heavily regulated environment.

How value creation and capture is realized in a DLT-enabled world is still unproven. When trying to estimate when WM firms should start taking a reflected and proactive position on where to play and how to win, a classic Silicon Valley mantra might be of inspiration: "If you think it's too early, it's probably too late already."[14] For those of you alarmed by such thoughts, Bill Gates reiterates the importance of action, but also offers some consolation with regard to timelines: "We always overestimate the change that will occur in the next two years and underestimate the change that will occur in the next ten. Don't let yourself be lulled into inaction."

---

[13] Rohwetter, M. (2017). "Cash, Boom, peng! Virtuelle Waffen sind ein Milliardengeschäft – aber wer mitverdienen will, sollte sehr vorsichtig sein", *Die Zeit*, 3 April 2017, p. 12.

---

[14] Von Kittlitz, A. (2017). "Fuck you, Silicon Valley!", *Die Zeit*, 26 January 2017, p. 52.

Blockchain as a Backbone to Asset and Wealth Creation

by Denis Thomas
Associate Director, KPMG

Demonetization has been the most tweeted topic for India in 2017. It has been touted by many as a classic case of execution failure, failed governance and lack of overall strategy execution. True. Mostly. However, the push for demonetization has nudged the creation of modernized infrastructures that could support digital transactions, buy-in from senior management and better governance, which eventually shall propel the country towards an eon of cashless transactions. As the amount of wealth increases in the system, newer forms of investment instruments and even newer forms of investment patterns emerge. This in turn gives rise to an era of WealthTech that in turn exponentially inflates the amount of data across computing platforms. This proliferation of data is what emanates the need for faster transaction processing and faster authentication mechanisms. Voila! A technology that resides on the cusp of this is blockchain. Let's try and decode it before diving deeper.

Blockchain

If you ask me, I'm biased towards blockchain and I'd say blockchain was the star child hidden behind bitcoin. But is that also an unbiased opinion? How many people understand blockchain? Many people confuse it with bitcoin, but it is far from that. Bitcoin is an encrypted digital currency, while blockchain is the base technology required for bitcoins to function. Currently, most people use a bank as a middleman to make money transactions – either via digital wallets, credit/debit cards or cheques. Blockchains allow consumers and suppliers to connect directly, as they completely eliminate the need for a third party (significantly driving down costs and dramatically improving turnaround times through the reduction in steps involved). Let's explain blockchain in simple words for the benefit of everyone.

Blockchain is primarily a ledger of all transactions that have been executed, which are stored cryptographically on a distributed database. A block can be single or multiple transaction/s. Each time a transaction is completed, it is linked to a chain, with every block containing a hash of the previous block in a chronological sequence. The fact that it is distributed and secure makes it impossible for any hacker to hack into it, as hacking or manipulating it would require updates to all the blocks within the blockchain at the same time in real time, making an attack almost impossible with the available sets of technologies currently available.

Some of the benefits to using blockchain technology include, but are not limited to:

- blockchain records are secure and reliable;

- blocks are immutable and this prevents hacking;

- it discards the need for a third party or central party to validate transactions.

Some of the banks/financial entities involved in investing, "proofs of concept" in the blockchain space, include players like Nasdaq, Visa, Standard Chartered Bank, Citibank, DBS, BNY Mellon, UBS, Santander, Barclays, Deutsche, BNP Paribas, Euro Banking Association, Fidor Bank, LHV Bank, Goldman Sachs, and many more.

Applications in Asset and Wealth Management

In order to dive into the applications for blockchain within asset and wealth management, let's look at typical asset and wealth management functions and shortcomings. Insights into the current problems will provide clarifications on solutions that can be addressed by blockchain.

Let's look at the current processes within a capital market, apart from the typical usage of bitcoin for bad versus good. Figure 1 explains the typical processes involved.

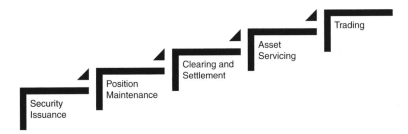

Figure 1: Capital market and processes
Source: Denis Thomas, Spring 2017

The issuance of securities is a critical path within capital markets and securities could be issued as debt (bonds) or equity (stocks) based on the company's need for capital alongside other financial considerations. This issuance in turn requires the creation, management and distribution of physical documents like stock certificates and bond notes. Post-issuance, these are traded over securities exchanges. Some of the key players involved in the securities issuance process include investment bankers, asset managers, lead managers, regulators, syndicate members and issuers.

The involvement of multiple entities and intricate processes leads to multiple versions of the truth, longer settlement times and many other problems, as depicted in Figure 2.

Blockchain as a Backbone

Public and private security issuance can be managed via blockchain technology and physical documents can be fully

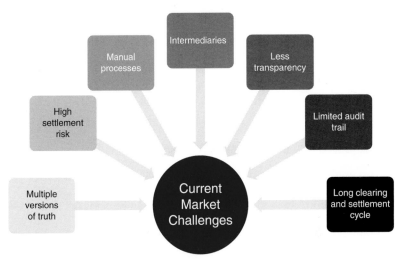

Figure 2: Market challenges
Source: Denis Thomas, Spring 2017

digitized via smart securities. Smart contracts can be put in place that reduce the number of intermediaries involved between customers and producers, and dramatically improve efficiency. The smart contracts are an integral part of maintaining and establishing smoother supply chain cycles without the need for human intervention.

For example, a tulip flower buyer can utilize a smart contract in conjunction with a thermosensor that is directly linked to the smart contract. The moment the temperature increases to a non-acceptable level in the shipping container, the contract is cancelled and the shipment will be routed back without the need for checking, validating or negotiating return/payment terms. This ensures the consumer gets what he pays for and the producer in turn ensures safer transportation with better packaging mechanisms to guarantee reliable delivery.

Drawing a parallel with the stock market, blockchains would help with the transfer of securities from one party to another via a distributed ledger through secure transactions, allowing direct dealings between issuers, syndicate members and investment banks while providing tracking of real-time ownership of underlying securities. This would also drive down costs, as the need for multiple intermediaries is eliminated. A blockchain would thus help resolve all the current market challenges via the following routes:

- All the parties involved view a single version of the truth via the distributed ledger and common blockchain platform.

- The settlement risk is reduced as clear visibility on ownership is provided and time to execute transactions is significantly reduced.

- Manual processes for issuance, settlement, validation and clearing are automated via the use of smart contracts.

- The clearing and settlement time is currently three days in America and two days in Europe, which can be reduced to less than 10 minutes using blockchain.

- The entire process is online, immutable and available via the distributed ledger of transactions, which makes auditing mechanisms and tracking extremely simple and transparent.

Blockchain Market Opportunities

In order to make this chapter more exciting, I dive into the possible ramifications of blockchain (positive or negative), examples of its use across the domestic and international markets, and a glimpse into the possible market size for blockchain, which is extremely relevant and exciting for bankers, insurers and venture capitalists, to name but a few.

The other potential area for blockchain disruption is trade finance, as this space includes multiple entities – importers, exporters, government agencies, logistics operators, shipping companies

and related insuring companies. Blockchain can be used in the above example to create legal smart contracts, digital sales processes, facilitate monitoring of goods via ubiquitous computing sensors and payment processing/clearing in real time. For example, R3 CEV (consortium of 50 + global banks) investigating blockchain applications in the financial services space has up-voted the trade finance use case as the most promising and core area of focus.

Some other areas in the non-financial realm that are witnessing a disruptive blockchain presence include ownership proofs for application development, origin sourcing for diamonds to tell apart blood diamonds, digital identities that could flow across applications in the digital and physical world, end-to-end verifiable blockchain voting software that ensures power resides with the voter and not the vote counter, a global healthcare identity that maintains your identity across providers and geographies using "elliptic curve cryptography" (an encryption feature used with bitcoin ownership), and a distributed cloud storage system that encrypts all data stored on the cloud and only allows the owner to view his/her data at a per TB price for storage and bandwidth consumption that's cheaper than Amazon Web Services S3 and Microsoft Azure.

Blockchain savings in the security issuance and regulatory aspects easily add up to US$10–12 billion, merely by applying it to the settlement use case. It would also help free up capital for banks and other entities that currently need to store several billions for trades that are currently being settled due to clearing, settlement and possible counterparty risks. Extrapolating this example by including all banks, financial entities, related players and extending the applications of blockchain across applicable supply chains in financial and non-financial realms, we are on schedule to behold a major disruption.

Let's hop on to witness a trillion-dollar industrial revolution together.

Dreaming of a Ledger-Free, Globally Connected Wealth Management Industry

By Anni Kristiina Salo
Marketing Communications Manager, FA Solutions

The last 20 years have shown us technology-driven disruption across a variety of industries: Amazon making online shopping mainstream; Netflix superseding traditional TV broadcasts; Airbnb enabling anyone to turn their flat into a tourist guesthouse; Uber redefining transportation… Meanwhile, the foundations of the wealth management industry have remained nearly the same since Harry Markowitz published his modern portfolio theory paper in 1952.

Disruptive businesses typically have the characteristic of simplifying previously highly complicated and costly operations. And this, as I see it, is the problem in the current wealth management scene. Operations are highly manual with heavy, complicated processes, resulting in high costs and inefficiencies, which in turn whittle away the investment returns. What is also a concern is that as long as there are institutions too big to fail, they do not have to develop truly customer-centric services. The industry will need to change – and will change – a lot during the next few years.

I would like to see the financial industry as a network of services, where each of the services are designed to work and integrate with other services, forming value networks. There can be bigger "umbrella networks" around a certain geographical location or industry, or bringing together multiple locations or industries, maintained by regulators and institutions, for example. But what is more interesting are the smaller value networks between agile service providers, creating customer-driven service entities. Within these networks, each of the service providers concentrates on their own core business, taking care of different tasks required to deliver certain services within the network, while information between these service providers is transferred automatically, safely and in real time through open application programming interfaces (APIs). Technology for creating these networks already exists, which we call "roboblock". As the name suggests, "robo" refers to automation and "block" to the technology used, similar to blockchain technology.

What is Roboblock?

A roboblock network can be established by any player in the industry. It is a closed network, where only those invited by the founder are able to join. Using roboblock removes the need for extra middlemen and therefore enables significant cost savings for network participants. While each of the network participants can concentrate on their own core business, data is transferred automatically and efficiently between interfaces. Roboblock offers all participants in your network up to date information on customers, holdings, transactions, model strategies and so forth, with the possibility to define and restrict what kind of data is shared. For example, if you wish not to hand over customer identification data, then portfolios can be tagged with identification numbers instead of a customer's personal information. And of course, all the actions carried out within the roboblock network are recorded as required by the regulator.

Furthermore, interactions with third parties in the wealth management business are getting increasingly digital – as it should be to eliminate unnecessary manual processes and inefficiencies. Consequently, in addition to connecting with business partners, you should also integrate with the relevant third parties, such as market data providers, trading platforms, authorities and so forth. This is also easily done by utilizing APIs for automatic information sending and receiving.

Differentiating Roboblock From Other Distribution Models

Currently, the system of distribution is based on central electronic ledgers where banks act as general ledgers. Furthermore, probably everyone working with technology or finance has heard about the distributed ledger model, blockchain. A public blockchain is an open network that anybody can access, and where the digital ledger of transactions is shared, transparent and run by all parties. However, public is fully public, and in that sense also uncontrollable, so today the most preferred type of blockchain for tier-one investment and retail banks is a private blockchain, only accessible by invitation. However, this is fairly close to the current system of central electronic ledgers, only adding some cryptographic auditability.

Roboblock, in turn, utilizes private blockchain technology to enable a value network for independent players to share information and distribute advice globally among each other and with the other parties invited (see Table 1). It enables companies to outsource asset management operations partly or fully while retaining a transparent control and audit trail of everything. Asset managers gain an opportunity for setting up additional distribution channels for their services, while they can focus on their core profession, asset management, instead of distribution. Furthermore, all parties can benefit from a full-scale know-your-customer (KYC) process, automatic data transfers and digital compliance.

The current system of distribution is seriously outdated, both process-wise and cost-wise, for serving the novel and agile network-based financial industry. And when it comes to blockchain, there is a lot of buzz around it, but having real, functional solutions is still somewhat distant. The concept of roboblock, first of all, was born from real customer need; second, it is already used by asset management and advisory companies. So, it is not something that would be nice to have *some* day, but something that is already possible and in use.

Table 1: Difference of roboblock from other distribution models

	Manual processes	Current technology solutions (e.g. SWIFT)	Roboblock
Distribution benefits	—	Current standard model of distribution	Qualified products and services available for public more efficiently
Coverage of data	Too laborious and risky	Transactions	Transactions, securities, KYC data, portfolios, model portfolios, analyses, reports
Speed	Slow, depends on workforce	+2 days	Real time
Costs	High	High	Low
Audit trail	Lacking	Yes	Yes
Openness	Theoretically open but highly laborious	Theoretically open but highly expensive for non-members of the network	Open for everyone with APIs (invitation holders)

The roboblock technology already exists, and we at FA Solutions are currently working with it on real-life customer cases. In our model, the roboblock network (see Figure 1) is run in our portfolio management system (PMS) by our customer, who is using the system for their daily portfolio management purposes. The PMS is then connected to their partners' systems with APIs, regardless of whether it's ours or someone else's PMS. But I want to highlight that the model – how we are doing it – is just one way to do it. Roboblock itself is a universal concept that can be implemented in different ways.

Figure 1: API data transfers in roboblock network

Setting Up a Roboblock Network

The key for implementing roboblock is to have an open technical architecture. This enables us to integrate all systems, and is the basis for a fluent information exchange. The lightest setup of a roboblock would be an open network for advice exchange (see Figure 2), where Company A would take care of their customers and manage their portfolios, but with model portfolios provided by Company B. In this model, information flows one way from Company B to Company A, and Company B does not have any information about the end customers. Company B is only responsible for managing different model portfolios and making investment decisions related to these. Company A then has wider responsibilities, such as taking care of customer relationships, customer portfolios, trading and reporting.

Figure 2: A roboblock setup sample 1

The next possibility is a closed peer-to-peer model, where (see Figure 3) Company A can take care of customer onboarding, giving investment advice and managing customer relationships, but where portfolio management itself is handled by Company B. When a new customer is acquired and advised by Company A, information flows automatically further to Company B for portfolio management purposes. Company B will then use its own facilities and expertise to manage the client portfolios, and all the relevant information, such as portfolios, transactions and securities, are continuously updated in Company A's portfolio management system. Company A has all the information available in their own system in real time for internal monitoring and external reporting purposes.

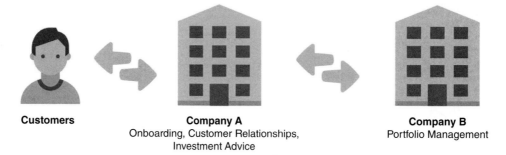

Customers

Company A
Onboarding, Customer Relationships,
Investment Advice

Company B
Portfolio Management

Figure 3: A roboblock setup sample 2

The most exciting model, as shown in Figure 4, is extending the peer-to-peer model into a multi-manager model. Here, referring to the previous example, Company A (advisor) has connected with multiple asset managers and fund managers similar to Company B. Also, Company B as an asset manager might have other advice and sales channels in addition to Company A. This results in a many-to-many model, even though information exchange may still be peer-to peer. This model enables companies to effortlessly and efficiently offer a wider range of services to their customers in multiple locations or different segments.

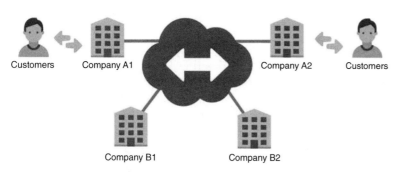

Customers   Company A1   Company A2   Customers

Company B1   Company B2

Figure 4: A roboblock setup sample 3

Conclusion

New emerging technologies enable a situation where your imagination is the only limitation. Who will be the first to create "the Amazon of financial services"? Why can the financial industry not work with the same principles – transparency, trust and peer reviews – as Airbnb, Uber and Amazon?

We are working for a more agile, open and transparent finance industry. We believe that the future of wealth management lies in agile value networks that bring together experts from various fields. We believe in a globally connected wealth management industry, and want to challenge you to join in!

As final words, I want to say thank you to my colleagues at FA Solutions, Hannes Helenius for being the father of the concept and Juha Lehtonen for providing unfailing technical know-how.

Trust Arbitrage and the Future of the Wealth Manager – How Blockchain Innovations Can Crack the Code

By Partha Chakraborty, PhD, CFA
CEO, Switchboard Systems, Inc

The firm has historically exploited trust arbitrage, especially true for wealth managers. Autocracies, a beneficiary of trust arbitrage, lost ground to democracy when the "founding fathers" endowed certain rights to the individual. We argue that blockchain innovations potentially bestow the same attributes to economic agents at an atomic level, thus reducing the impact of trust arbitrage. If and when that happens, performance and client service remain the two levers a wealth manager can work with. Will it be back to the basics or the doomsday ahead for today's wealth managers?

The concept of the company, "the firm", persists and prospers even when other authoritarian experiments have failed in history. Utopian visions of "productive agents" coming together to perform one economic task only to regroup thereafter has not happened, even in a "networked/connected economy". It has been a secular trend that authoritarian constructs have given way to political constructs that explicitly allow for reasonably free association and commerce. Public space is by and for the people.

It can be argued that many public goods could, individually, be produced by profit-seeking private entities more efficiently. That said, nobody wants a return to authoritarian disbursal of essential public goods – no privatized police or judiciary is contemplated.

The firm as an autocratic construct prospers in the economic domain. This is because the founding fathers caused a rupture by granting a few rights that we hold so dear. We will argue further that the latest technological advancements, especially in the blockchain space, will make a similar disruption possible in the commercial sector.

Founding Fathers Ring the Death Knell for Autocracy with a Pen

The founding fathers gave individuals the right to determine their own destiny. The fathers bestowed on us an identity, a right to organize as we please, (in effect) an institutional memory to look back and take away lessons. Combined, we create reputation for and by ourselves, which in turn empowers us to choose our representatives.

- **Right to freely assemble and organize.** Existence of the manager precludes free organization, in turn the absence of free organizations necessitates supervision by managers.

- **Self-sovereign identity.** The individual is considered sacrosanct in a democracy – you do not have to depend on recognition by a ruling person/body.

- **Institutional memory.** The implicit or explicit authority to act on decisions essentially resides in the manager, the same as in feudal societies.

A self-sovereign identity is at the core of what the founding fathers did; they took the privilege away from the lordship. Complemented by institutional memory, hence the capacity to recognize what's good for them, and the right to freely organize, people were truly empowered to be masters of their collective public domain. In our view, the same three self-enforcing themes, or specifically the lack thereof, bestowed the firm with the power to prosper against reasonable odds.

The Story of the Firm, as Told by Economists

The firm is notorious for the inefficiencies it represents. Economists have tried to explain why.

Ronald Coase[1] (and subsequently others) attributed the success to a cost–benefit analysis. Costs were classified as

- information/search cost
- contracting cost
- cost of administration/allocation of resources.

Technology has already reduced the comparative advantage the firm enjoyed on two of these. Information/search cost has been minimized with Google (for example) – equally available to a firm and outside. Contracting cost – the cost to enforce and supervise execution per terms agreed – is arguably lower outside a firm for most plain vanilla economic transactions. The firm fosters inefficiencies, not the opposite.

Allocation of resources is the single biggest argument for the firm to exist, thereby raising questions of agency costs (e.g. Holmstrom,[2] Jensen and Meckling[3]). The market allocates resources most efficiently wherever there is a price. Arguably, within the firm there is no clear quantifiable metric for most purposes. The "manager" is tasked to allocate resources (tasks) because the effect of individual decisions towards the objective of the firm (profit maximization) may not be immediately evident.

[1] Coase, R. H. (1937). The nature of the firm. *Economica*, 4(16), 386–405.

[2] Holmstrom, B. (1999). Managerial incentive problems: A dynamic perspective. *Review of Economic Studies,* 66(1), 169–182.

[3] Jensen, M. and Meckling, W. (1976). Theory of the firm: Managerial behavior, agency costs and ownership structure. *Journal of Financial Economics*, 3(4), 305–360.

In our view, the "manager" represents the "lord" in an autocratic political system. The manager holds the same power of resource allocation, including preservation of memories, recognition of identities and intermediation of most commercial activities within the borders. These powers are mutually self-enforcing, and the efficiency of management is often hard to judge.

Blockchain Innovations Can Make the Firm Feel the Pain

Blockchain innovations replicate in the digital world the rights that the founding fathers bestowed on us.

- **Capacity to freely assemble and organize.** Exciting new work is being done in the blockchain space in this area. Protocols developed at the MIT Media Lab and elsewhere make it technologically possible for a decentralized autonomous organization (DAO) to form teams, who will themselves have the power to associate and organize. In addition, these teams have the power to execute smart contracts that can be written as an overlay, just as in the "real" world.

- **Self-sovereign identity.** Identity is derived from our past and memory of the same. Every agent in a digital ecosystem has the power to be whatever they want to be, so long as their subsequent actions validate their identity.

- **Indelible memory.** Blockchain, by design, endows systems with the power to remember. It is the invisible secret sauce that binds everything – providing recognition to enable a self-sovereign identity.

A parallel can be drawn between the rights the founding fathers gave us and the attributes blockchain promises for an economic agent in the digital world. Autocratic regimes crumbled in front of these three rights, while the absence of the same allowed companies to exploit a trust arbitrage. It is highly likely that traditional company structures and management layers will become obsolete.

Wealth Managers are Especially Vulnerable to – and Benefit from – Trust Arbitrage

For wealth managers, trust arbitrage has been absolutely essential for their business. As a result, this makes them particularly more vulnerable.

- **Sine qua non.** Hand me your money smilingly, said no (wo)man ever – except your wealth manager.

- **Perception.** Wealth managers are good at creating an aura of aspirational quality. Not that there's anything wrong with that, but the reality does not always match the customer's expectations.

- **The good steward.** All things considered, the main value proposition of wealth managers still remains a claim to be "the good steward" of client capital, as evidenced by safety and reasonable growth.

Metrics of reasonable growth abound; academia and practitioner associations proffer many that are suitable for various client profiles. However, business realities creep in, and delivering consistently on the metrics of being "a good steward" is nearly impossible. Which leads us back to the trust arbitrage question – if true alignment of interests is hard to find, how do we cultivate trust by our clients?

Smaller Wealth Managers are Getting a Raw Deal

When trust is difficult to attain – and harder to communicate coherently – selecting large, established brand names becomes the default option.

- **History is hard.** One day at a time takes many days for history to be built – especially when you are young.

- **Façade is easier.** A good fall-back option is to create a façade giving clients a misleading or not completely accurate impression of one's true capabilities.

- **Performance is the hardest.** The good steward high-water is the hardest to maintain.

Even if a wealth manager is a good steward, the manager has to compete with the asset management leaders in the industry. It takes years for small investment managers to truly achieve scale and run a profitable business – thereby preventing entrepreneurial ventures.

The creative juices of American capitalism are being squeezed out, especially for new traditional and alternative wealth managers.

What If…

What if blockchain were to unravel trust arbitrage? Smaller investment managers could grow faster and customers could be in a better position overall.

- **The brash and the beautiful.** Self-sovereign identity will help the newcomer, the brash and the beautiful power to compete with the incumbent on the basis of performance metrics mostly.

- **The cream shall rise to the top.** Even in established firms, the performing few will have no reason to be in the company of a crowd that makes the herd. Firms as an association of many diverse people may exist only as an insurance mechanism, protecting all members against turns of the tide they have no control over.

- **Abundance to choose from.** For consumers, it shall be an abundant offering. Some operators may not survive the test of time. Notwithstanding, whoever survives will be there because they offered tangible value to the client.

In other words, blockchain innovations will disrupt the market as we know it. We will move to granular levels of tangible value added for customers. Creative destruction had no better example than this.

Predictions are Difficult, Especially About the Future

We predict that firms as a powerhouse of economic systems will be disrupted as blockchain takes away their raison d'être and capacity to exploit trust arbitrage. Further, wealth managers will be impacted because they have nowhere to hide but behind their performance, which has often not outperformed their peers or the index. In a world where digital and real existences merge, who says your next wealth manager will not be a machine?

Investment and Issuance Distributed in Blockchain

By Zeng Ziling
VP, ZONFIN China

Current State of Securities Practice with Pain Points

In the financial instruments issuing procedure lies an old problem. All institutions use their own heterogeneous information technology (IT) systems, which are incompatible with each other. If the bond and share securities are not traded in exchanges, which we call over-the-counter (OTC) trading, there is no dominant system to link the trading parties together. The participants of this procedure include the securities issuer, the subscriber, the funds, fund of funds (FOF), or other types of financial intermediary and the final investor. Some say that the most used "tech" here is Microsoft Excel. In most countries, we have exchanges or other types of information centres performing the task of bookkeeping and clearance. In practice, those central servers do not cover all securities businesses. Only part of standard commodities are allowed to trade.

Stock exchanges do not cover: some non-standardized securities or other types of financial instruments or fundraising activities (e.g. trust, unlisted bonds). The initial fundraising takes part in the primary issuing, but there can even be a multilayer structure of investment participants. We have multiple exchanges or other trading centres even within one country, which is a fractioned marketplace. Before blockchain technology, there was no good way to synchronize trading information among multiple nodes or centres.

Present efforts turn out to be just another system for a limited group of players. Time and money are wasted due to these barriers. We have witnessed some banks developing innovative services to bring the different stakeholders together to solve the problems above. What is unsolved: the participants need no bank regulation, they want to keep private.

Without a universal bookkeeping and clearance centre that is universally accepted, security participants are fragmented and human accountants need to do the bookkeeping, reconciliation and payment. Even if some incumbents claim they are fully connected with automation, it is only in their field and unrepresentative. The consequences are: in the closing period of fundraising, the issuer or secondary funds could wait for days because the trade is not confirmed in real time. The fundraising information is not automatically passed through the vertical structure of incompatible participant systems.

In the conventional issuing procedure (see Figure 1), the issuer passes on all debt, for example to the subscriber or an investment bank. The subscriber then sells the debt to several buyers. The buyers can be funds, trusts or other types of financial intermediaries. The buyer here may buy and pay for it or just promise to buy. The buyer may need to find a secondary buyer to buy. The secondary buyer may repeat this process until it reaches the final buyer. There is always the risk that the secondary buyer cannot fulfil their purchase promise. Therefore a confirmation period is needed, and marketing for a little surplus so that the full amount of fundraising at its required level can be met. The purchase and subscribing or payment information cannot pass through the nodes of financial intermediaries. The information between the nodes is heterogeneous data. This is the fundamental reason for the need for a long fundraising period, confirmation period and redundant accountancy.

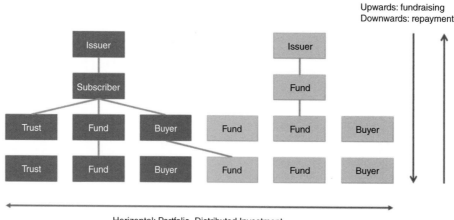

Vertical:
Upwards: fundraising
Downwards: repayment

Horizontal: Portfolio, Distributed Investment

Figure 1: The conventional issuing procedure

Future State of Securities Practice with Blockchain

The aim of this chapter is not to explain how blockchains or smart contracts work, but how they can be applied. With blockchain technology, no central instance for information consistency is required. Instead, the primary subscription and secondary transactions can be largely optimized. It is a universal and democratic way to synchronize all parties. To include all participants, the blockchain platform should not include a subjective rating. It only performs as a public technical solution. On a blockchain-based platform, the issuer, subscriber and all other types of financial intermediaries are connected.

In the fundraising/issuing process shown above, any participant in the vertical structure can be called a seller if they are above another actor and can be called a buyer if they are below another actor. Every seller creates a security entry in the blockchain, specifying the amount to be raised. The information of a subscription promise or purchase order of any buyer and

secondary buyer is immediately published and synchronized with the whole network. As a result, the issuer and subscriber know the status of the fundraising process throughout the participant network. Therefore, the time span of the fundraising and confirmation period can be reduced significantly.

In the repayment process, the work of a fund accountant causes the settlement time to be $T+n$. It must wait for repayment from the chain of subsequent sellers. The cash flow must go from the issuer through multiple financial intermediaries. In both the fundraising/issuing and repayment process of a blockchain structure, information can flow in real time.

In portfolio/distributed investments, especially with some non-standard or unlisted financial assets, the investment/fundraising and repayment process becomes so sophisticated that the bookkeeping and accounting becomes very complex. For example (see Figure 2), an unlisted fund invests in hundreds of unlisted non-standard financial assets. A compliance issue could result in certain jurisdictions. In the case of a fund or

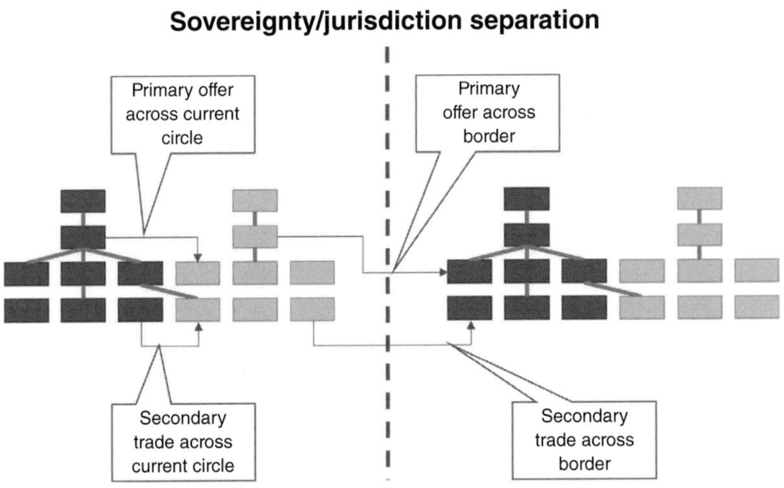

Sovereignty/jurisdiction separation

Figure 2: Sovereignty/jurisdiction separation

trust, the investor's money is pooled into the fund's account, the fund then invests the money into the portfolio or distributed assets. If all participants are equipped with blockchain and smart contracts, under the direction of terms defined in the smart contract, then the money can flow directly from the investor to the asset, bypassing the intermediate fund, and the money is not pooled in the fund's account. With this feature, further innovation is possible. [What do we mean by this? For example, a personal portfolio with no security from authority's regulation. A fund is regulated in any country to various degrees, which should acquire legal-body status at least. Now it may be totally free.] The benefits are:

- **Wider diversification.** We were discussing the convenience of a portfolio with blockchain above. Blockchain also enables participants to get connected to a wider range of counterparties if everyone is in the same chain. Investment diversified by geography is more convenient.

- **Asset seeking and sales.** An investment intermediary is always seeking financial assets. Due to information silos, a financial institute reaches a limited group of clients around it, so it knows

only a small fraction of the whole market, especially in unlisted non-standard assets. In the blockchain platform, all assets are listed under the permission of the issuer and broadcasted to the network. A search engine filters and thus helps investors to find any asset in every corner of the world. And vice versa, a fund to promote its products will easily broadcast the asset to the whole network. The agent intermediaries for promotion may no longer be needed.

- **Some financial instruments are issued worldwide.** Even if it was not issued globally, foreign investors can invest directly from abroad or through a financial intermediary arrangement. In this case, participants are from different sovereign countries, so stock exchanges or centralized marketplaces are beyond their reach. A blockchain platform overcomes these barriers. The trading information is not restricted by any country or bound by centralized marketplaces. In a minimal case, the blockchain record is just bookkeeping that encounters no regulatory restriction.

In the real world, all marketplaces – including stock exchanges – keep their ratings on trading participants. One reason is regulation. Another reason is that these marketplaces make the rating due to risk control and their own reputation. Value is added to a listed financial asset after the scrutiny of these marketplaces, but it also rejects some assets and therefore some participants choose the OTC route. Blockchain financial trading platforms offer the participants simplicity, privacy under their control and provide the convenience of listing. If a blockchain platform includes a rating, it will reject clients having any conflict with its standard. This creates a fraction with different value groups and is against the initial intention of blockchain or a decentralized autonomous organization. Therefore, the blockchain should not contain any rating. It should only perform as a neutral financial infrastructure, like the internet stands for neutrality and is built on protocols which do not care if you are transmitting text or video steaming. Since ratings create market fragments, trading participants will take jurisdiction shopping to seek for the most convenient marketplaces.

Conclusion

Blockchain technology provides a wealth of opportunities for the investment and asset offering sector: all types of participants are connected globally in a democratic way without a rating. OTC trading will be optimized, where the assets listed are broadcast to the whole network, so that asset seeking and sales promotion become global rather than local. Purchase and payment information can penetrate layers of institutions and all participating stakeholders within minutes rather than days of human operation. The fundraising, confirmation and settlement periods can largely be optimized based on real-time information.

Founders' Success Stories

6

Robo-advisors

- Automated investment platforms that leverage technology to reduce fees
- *B2C:* WealthFront, Nutmeg, **VestPod** (Improve women's financial literacy by addressing women-specific needs like specific lifestyle goals and lower risk)
- *B2B:* AdvisorEmpire
- *Both:* **ScalableCapital:** Offering a transparent solution to clients by taking both the "Fin" and "Tech" very seriously

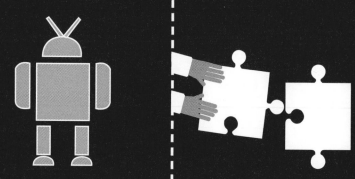

Digital Brokerage

- Include equity, bond funds and sometimes insurance i.e. MeDirect Bank, MoneyMeets.com, eToro
- **MeDirectBank:** a good product and service at a competitive price based on client centricity and partial rebundling
- **Moneymeets.com:** complete, customized and cross-vendor overview of customers' finances, bank accounts, investments in funds and insurance products

Founders Success Stories

Micro Investing

- More frequent, smaller amounts such as Stash, Acorn or Moneybox
- Chinese players include Jimubox, Tiger Brokers and Niu Jiao Sui

Investing Tools/Financial Services SW

- Kensho Technologies
- Wikifolio Financial Tech
- ClearMacro
- AlgoDynamix
- **SharingAlpha:** a rating platform to gather the views of a large group of advisors and to measure their success rate by moving from the current rating model where advisors work in silos to a more centralized approach in which their views are shared on a dedicated platform

Founders of the companies highlighted in **bold** above have shared their entrepreneurial journeys in this Part.

Executive Summary

WealthTech innovation is fuelled by entrepreneurship. One of the measures that demonstrate the importance of this is the increasing investment in start-ups in this field. This part shares the personal insights and stories of five entrepreneurs who set up their own successful WealthTech companies. Many of them left the world of financial services behind to found their own business – this part might guide and motivate you too to either join one of the many innovative FinTech companies around the world or launch one yourself.

Most often these entrepreneurs experienced challenges in the investment management industry, which were ignored and not addressed. These personal experiences inspired them to set up their own WealthTech businesses. In this part you will meet the following entrepreneurs and learn from their insights:

- CEO of **MeDirectBank** on how they built a challenger bank and became the pioneer in online wealth management in Belgium. Because trust is a major challenge for WealthTech start-ups, MeDirectBank followed a dedicated path around customer centricity and partnerships.

- CEO of **VestPod** on financial services for women who control more than $20 trillion in annual consumer spending and are predicted to be responsible for 75% of spending by 2028. The lack of diversity is a key challenge across financial services, including FinTech and the global investor community. VestPod's founder will provide more details on how to better serve 50% of the population.

- CEO of **Scalable Capital,** a European digital wealth manager with assets under management of more than £200 million. This start-up sees the critical success factor focusing on both "Fin", with a strong team who understand the financial landscape (both commercially and regulatory) and "Tech", with a core emphasis on building proprietary technology.

- CEO of **moneymeets,** the leading independent online platform for personal finance management in Germany. In order to win trust from its clients, the company consistently relies on user-centred processes and absolute cost transparency.

- CEO of **SharingAlpha,** a FinTech start-up focused on helping financial advisors build up their performance track records. For this, the SharingAlpha platform aims to gather the views of a large group of advisors and to measure their success rate.

So, get ready to be inspired and to learn how to set and scale up FinTech and WealthTech companies.

Launching MeDirect Bank as a Challenger Bank

By Xavier De Pauw
CEO, MeDirect Bank

After 10 years in the fixed income markets with Merrill Lynch in London, I joined three experienced fellow London-based bankers to start a new banking group in 2009. The aftermath of the banking crisis seemed to us the ideal time to launch a new bank with a focus on simplicity and transparency.

In contrast to a traditional (FinTech) start-up, a new bank requires substantial capital before it can be launched and thus we sought backing from a specialized private equity house, AnaCap Financial Partners, who provided the capital to start the venture.

Our initial focus was on simple balance sheet strategies to get the bank into profitability within months from start. As the bank grew, we shifted from wholesale funding to retail deposit funding and realized that our deposit clients were also interested in solutions to earn higher returns on their savings. We set out to build an online investment and wealth management platform within our challenger bank. The investments to build this platform came – and still come – from retained earnings.

Our strategy is based on partial rebundling. We built a WealthTech within a bank to offer a one-stop shop for savers and investors. From the WealthTech point of view, the rationale of this model is twofold: we achieve lower client acquisition cost and we self-fund the build-up of the business from retained earnings of the bank. In addition, from the savings and lending business point of view, offering investment products increases client loyalty and retention.

Over the past eight years, our approach to building the group has been quite atypical, yet many of the lessons we have learnt along the way are relevant to other WealthTechs. Especially over the past three years, we have established MeDirect Bank in Belgium as:

- the pioneer in online wealth management;
- the first open architecture platform for model portfolios and online wealth management;
- the most transparent platform for investing in mutual funds;
- the first platform to obtain a full banking licence since the 2008 crisis.

A Good Product and Service at a Competitive Price

Compared with most other B2C FinTechs, WealthTechs have an additional challenge to overcome when building a business: success requires convincing people to entrust their hard-earned life savings to a website or an app. This requires a lot more trust from a consumer than for them to, say, pay a restaurant bill with a payment app.

What do we mean by "a good product"? WealthTechs compete among each other but also with the incumbents. So it is interesting to look at why clients leave their wealth manager. According to a JP Morgan and Oliver Wyman survey, the top three reasons are dissatisfaction with service, poor investment advice and poor investment performance. Simplified, the three main reasons boil down to the client losing money or earning lower relative returns in comparison with their peers.

A good product for a WealthTech is one that generates good (relative) returns over the long term. Building trust and a solid reputation takes a long time, especially for unknown start-ups. At MeDirect Bank, our growth hack consisted of teaming up with Morningstar, one of the world's largest and most reputable independent investment analysis and advice companies. While such a partnership comes at a cost, it gave us instant credibility in terms of quality of product and independence of advice and product selection. Morningstar allowed us to offer a trusted high-quality product to attract clients and be confident that clients would stay for the long run. That is essential for enterprise value creation and to recoup your client acquisition cost over time.

We applied the same philosophy to many parts of the business. For example, for our equity trading platform we teamed up with Instinet to reliably offer best execution to our clients. When we found solid partners, we chose to integrate with their systems and infrastructure rather than build our own. In addition to building trust, it got us to market faster. Thanks to our digital distribution model, we are able to offer these quality products and services at a lower cost than incumbents, which plays a role in attracting potential clients.

The user experience (UX) and user interface (UI) of the platform are also important, and we strive to improve both to get and maintain an edge over our competitors. But they come third for a WealthTech in our opinion. Offering a good-quality and trustworthy product at a competitive price is essential to offering a great customer experience. I have seen many greatly designed WealthTech platforms, but usually wondered whether I could be an early adopter and trust my life savings to them. Good UX/UI is not enough.

Partial (Re-)Bundling

When we launched MeDirect Bank in September 2013, the idea of combining online savings and online wealth management was at odds with the FinTech trend of extreme unbundling: the tendency of FinTechs to focus on just one narrowly defined product or service.

Most B2C FinTech success stories to date are indeed mono-product businesses. Their narrow focus on a simple product is a key ingredient for exponential growth. They are low cost and have great UX/UI to onboard clients easily. They typically operate in less

strictly regulated environments and trust is less relevant, given the small transaction amounts involved. Wealthfront and Betterment have achieved fast growth, but they remain exceptions and account for only a fraction of their wealth management market.

Today, the concept of "partial rebundling" for WealthTechs is widely accepted and adopted. We have seen many WealthTechs team up with established partners, which can offer instant access to a sizeable client base and/or can add the element of trust to an unknown start-up. Such partners for WealthTechs can be established banks and fund managers, and even fast-growing and well-known mono-product FinTechs.

Such alliances are not revolutionary. It makes good business sense for both parties when a WealthTech with a high client acquisition cost plugs into an established client base.

For MeDirect, our attractive savings products allow us to grow a client base of potential clients for the WealthTech part of the business. Growing a deposit client base can be done at a lower cost of acquisition and at greater velocity than attracting online wealth management clients. Selling wealth management products to a client who already trusts us with their savings represents a materially lower barrier. The bank licence of MeDirect and implicit stringent regulation and oversight also helps create trust with potential clients.

At MeDirect, we took the (re-)bundling one step further. With our client-centric focused online wealth management, an e-brokerage platform, online savings, etc. essentially all answer the same client need for a return on their savings. We decided to offer a one-stop shop that encompasses these various interpretations clients may have of "wealth management and investments".

Testing and Pivoting

The co-founder of LinkedIn famously said, "if you are not embarrassed by the first version of your product, you've launched too late". The first version of the MeDirect online platform, launched in September 2013, offered good-quality products, but too many of them and with basic UX and UI. Importantly, the launch enabled us to get the first clients through the door, measure their behaviour on the platform, and start improving the site based on real client feedback.

We launched the online platform to the public with a broad spectrum of products and services that had not been offered online in Belgium (and Europe to our knowledge) before: innovative savings products; online wealth management in three options – a managed pension plan, a "monitor and advice" service and a full discretionary management service; an execution-only platform for funds, ETFs, stocks and bonds; and execution-only thematic model portfolios of funds.

We monitored and measured client activity and evolved the platform accordingly. The online "investment advice" service profiled a client, recommended a portfolio of funds and could make alterations to that portfolio, including changing the weights of individual funds and switching individual funds. The client could even replace an equity fund with the individual underlying equities and then change these equities. The platform would monitor such portfolios and regularly make recommendations to the client based on their profile, and show a gap analysis between the recommended portfolio composition and the one chosen by the client. Technically very advanced, and offering great flexibility to clients. But such flexibility created several UI and regulatory challenges. Too many options created "choice-stress" for clients, with negative consequences for conversion rates. Client appetite remained very low, despite several iterations, and we decided to remove the product to simplify the platform and focus our scarce resources elsewhere. The MeDirect "pension planner" followed a similar faith.

In contrast, we observed a fair and growing level of activity from our clients on our execution-only open architecture fund platform. The MeDirect "fund supermarket" clearly appealed to the retail and mass affluent audience we were targeting. The breadth of our offering, together with the low and transparent costs, earned

us accolades in the press as best and most transparent platform for mutual funds. Client centricity was a key factor in this. For example, we started offering 250 mutual funds on the platform. Within a few months we were distributing three times as many, mainly as a result of client requests to add new funds and fund managers. Requests which we were able to meet within a few days thanks to our efficient operational setup. We clearly had identified a need in the market and had a platform that met that demand better than most (the observant reader will have noticed that adding and settling funds in a few days gave us an edge over competitors; clearly there is much more innovation possible in this space, but that is beyond the scope of this topic…).

In parallel with our growing fund supermarket, we also saw encouraging interest by clients in our execution-only model portfolios and discretionary wealth management service, both of which built on the basis of our open architecture mutual fund supermarket.

Clients like the execution-only model portfolios for their convenience, combining a number of funds in a handy shopping basket according to an investment theme. The ability to contribute monthly amounts to that basket of funds, and the fact that we do not charge any transaction costs, make this a popular product. The partnerships with several recognized and trusted partners, such as Morningstar, to construct these thematic baskets effectively created the first open architecture platform for model portfolios of funds.

The straightforward discretionary management service also appealed to clients because of its simplicity, transparency and convenience – in addition to its strong performance. The online profiling questionnaire, including MiFID questions, makes for a longer conversion funnel than the execution-only model portfolios. But clients understand that this additional step provides them with a personalized portfolio which is managed for them. They are willing to pay the additional management cost for this service (0.3–0.6% depending on the amount invested). We charge no other fees (no entry fees, no exit fees, no transaction costs, etc.), and thus the cost of our discretionary wealth management is well below that of traditional wealth managers (and online players). The entry threshold of minimum €5000 also makes this service available to a population that cannot or will not invest the minimum €300,000–500,000 that incumbents require to open an account. So in the months following our first launch, we took a number of decisions that shaped the platform as it stands today, following the adage that "less is more":

- We drastically simplified the wealth management offering from three products to just one.
- We followed our clients and allocated most of our resources to further improving the products, services, UX/UI and operations associated with our open architecture fund platform.
- We set out to redesign the platform to drastically improve UX/UI and reflect the evolved product and service offering.

Growth!

During our first year of activity in 2014, we spent half of our time learning from client feedback and A/B testing. We tested many product, design and UX/UI features with an eye on client engagement and conversion rates. This provided valuable inputs in the parallel work that was ongoing to launch a completely revamped online platform in the last quarter of 2014.

The following year (2015) was one large test. We had just launched the new version of the platform with a refocused business strategy. Client activity grew noticeably and trends in that activity became clearer with increasing assets under custody/assets under management. Our decisions from 2014 were confirmed and we persevered in establishing MeDirect as the main platform for investments in mutual funds in Belgium with a fund supermarket, execution-only model portfolios and online discretionary wealth management.

During 2015 we launched several marketing campaigns. We realized that the energy, time, creativity and money invested in product and service innovation had to be met with equal investments in clever marketing. We tested various messages,

channels and incentives to attract investment clients directly and to convert depositors to investing part of their savings.

Here we also tried growth hacks to stretch our budget. For example, we rented a tram plus conductor in one of the major cities and made it free for everyone to use during the Christmas shopping month. We wrapped it in our logo with the slogan "On this tram you don't pay entry or exit costs, just like in the MeDirect fund supermarket". The originality meant that everyone was interested and had an opinion about it. Five national newspapers covered the story and we shot a TV commercial on the tram to reinforce the message.

Client Centricity

We pride ourselves on being extremely client centric in terms of transparency and service. For us this means doing a few things well. Not doing everything for everyone.

Client centricity is an important differentiator. For example, even though we distribute our products and services digitally for scalability, we also make a contact centre available for our clients. They take phone calls and email messages. For some of our clients, having the option to speak to a person is important. Our contact centre staff fully subscribe to client centricity and we are convinced that they contribute significantly to the 96% client satisfaction rate at MeDirect.

We are about to launch the next version of the platform. Again, this will incorporate new functionalities based on client feedback. They really appreciate it when they talk to us or meet us at a seminar and see that their feedback makes it onto the platform. We are also having more conversations with potential new partners to continue to improve our client offering with new products and functionalities. Very much like a post-Payment Services Directive 2 (PSD2) platform that will distribute many banking services, we have built an open architecture platform to distribute a variety of savings, investment products and services.

Empowering Women Financially – The Why and the How

By Emilie Bellet
Founder and CEO, Vestpod

Why is it Important to Empower Women Financially?

Women are the future of the economy – controlling about $20 trillion in annual consumer spending (in 2009), and that figure is expected to rise to $28 trillion by 2018.[1] By 2028, women will control 75% of discretionary spending worldwide.

Moreover, the proportion of working women carrying the primary financial responsibility in their families has risen from 23% in 1996 to 33% in 2013.[2] Yet, there are plenty of reasons to be concerned: according to the Institute of Fiscal Studies,[3] women, on average, earn 18% less than men – with the gender pay gap being particularly hard on mothers. Such a wage disparity has a direct impact on the way women save for retirement: the median level of wealth held by men in pensions is more than twice that of women.[4] The statistics on savings, investing and levels of debt show a similarly bleak gender divide.

Consequently, there has never been a more important time for women to get serious about understanding their finances and for the industry to start serving them better. If we give women the tools to rise above their challenges, we can help them earn more and save more, giving them the freedom to live their lives on their own terms. Financially empowered women also have a positive impact on the economy, helping improve living standards, bettering education and boosting jobs.

However, impediments stand in the way: professional financial advice is expensive, intimidating and not well adjusted to the challenges that women face in the contemporary world. This gap in financial advising has been clearly identified in the UK – both by the Treasury and the Financial Conduct Authority[5] – and it only keeps growing. Second, financial products are becoming more complex and difficult to understand, resulting in a sense of overwhelmedness.

It sounds dismal, but it doesn't have to be. So, how best can we empower women financially?

Empowering Women Financially: How?

Improve Women's Financial Literacy

A recent survey by the OECD[6] showed that most countries score abysmally low when it comes to financial literacy. As defined in this report, "*financial literacy is a combination of awareness, knowledge, skill, attitude and behaviour necessary to make sound*

[1] Silverstein, M. J. and Sayre, K. (2009). "The female economy", *Harvard Business Review*, Sept. https://hbr.org/2009/09/the-female-economy.

[2] Cory, G. and Stirling, A. (2015). "Who's breadwinning in Europe", IPPR thinktank. http://www.ippr.org/files/publications/pdf/whos-breadwinning-in-europe-oct2015.pdf?noredirect=1.

[3] Institute of Fiscal Studies (2016). "The Gender Wage Gap", https://www.ifs.org.uk/uploads/publications/bns/bn186.pdf.

[4] ONS (2014). "Private Pension Wealth, Wealth in Great Britain 2010–12", http://www.ons.gov.uk/ons/dcp171776_362820.pdf.

[5] FCA (2016). "Financial Advice Market Review", https://www.fca.org.uk/publication/corporate/famr-final-report.pdf.

[6] Atkinson, A. and Messy, F. (2012). "Measuring financial literacy: Results of the OECD/International Network on Financial Education (INFE) pilot study", OECD Working Papers on Finance, Insurance and Private Pensions, No. 15.

financial decisions and ultimately achieve individual financial well-being". Women scored lower than men in almost every country studied (in the UK, 67% of men gained a high score (6 or more on the knowledge measure), and just 40% of women achieved the same). As financial markets become increasingly more sophisticated and households assume bigger risks and responsibilities, financial literacy becomes even more pertinent.

An individual's financial literacy plays a crucial role in shaping wealth equalities. Having sound financial knowledge helps us make well-educated decisions, save more for retirement, carefully manage investments and better manage household finances. On the other hand, the financially ill-informed rarely make efficient choices and are more likely to incur more debt, save less and be more prone to fraud.

Evidently, the focus needs to be on providing better and greater access to financial education, which should trickle down to schools and universities. Financial literacy training should also be provided in the workplace, but it is important to note that this alone is not enough – the majority of new freelancers (55%) today are women,[7] and they too need financial support outside the workforce.

Vestpod's mission is to empower women financially by making it easier to be smarter about money and take action to better manage it. We are continuously exploring ways to communicate with women in an engaging and relevant manner. Our weekly newsletters see high engagement rates and the feedback we get is extremely encouraging.

Engage Effectively: Address Women-Specific Needs

Women have a different approach to wealth building. For example, women save and invest with specific lifestyle goals in mind, while men are more inclined to focus on the products and investment outcome. Due to this variance, women benefit from a more holistic and personalized financial strategy: understanding their values and beliefs is key, as is delivering advice in an accessible, clear, concise and friendly manner.

Women are also less likely to engage in perceived risky trading, are more diligent in their research, make more diversified investments and are humble when it comes to admitting mistakes. Indeed, women make good investors, but their financial drive is yet to be fully understood and effectively addressed by traditional financial institutions.

Finally, women are in need of a good confidence boost. A study by Annamaria Lusardi and Olivia S. Mitchell[8] revealed that while women scored lower than men on financial literacy tests, when the option of answering "I don't know" was removed, they scored just as high as men. Thus, understanding and addressing women's values and beliefs, while helping them build their confidence, is vital to engaging women with finance.

Help Women Take Action Through Innovation

While financial literacy is important, it is only part of a much larger picture. Effectively empowering women and helping them take action will have a direct impact on their financial independence and a positive outcome on their lives. In order to achieve this, we need to consider the gap in financial advice.

At present, professional financial advice is unaffordable for most segments of the women gender group. In addition, financial products are complex and their jargon is often intimidating. The industry is also historically heavily targeted at professional males: finding an understanding advisor able to genuinely connect with women's needs and concerns is not easy.

[7] Kitching, J. (2016). "Exploring the UK Freelance Workforce in 2015", IPSE report, https://www.ipse.co.uk/sites/default/files/documents/research/Exploring-uk-freelance-workforce-2015-report-v1.pdf.

[8] Lusardi, A. and Mitchell, O. S. (2011). "Financial Literacy Around the World: An Overview", NBER, http://www.nber.org/papers/w17107.

To further complicate things, a lack of trust plagues the financial industry, with the millennial generation being particularly sceptical of traditional institutions (only 8% trust financial institutions according to a Facebook survey of millennials aged 21–34 in the USA).[9] The FinTech scene has been swift to address this opportunity: internet banks are growing in popularity, while robo-advisors and investment managing apps continue to gain traction among them.

At Vestpod we offer a unique, user-friendly platform tailored specifically to women's needs, helping towards taking steps to save and invest. We believe in helping women break the taboo associated with "money talk" by communicating digitally and leveraging online communities.

With start-ups geared to disrupt the financial space, it is vital for banks and traditional institutions to respond and step up their game, which in turn will benefit women. Financial institutions can start by improving how they communicate with customers and focus on personalization. With a more targeted approach, banks will be better placed to understand and address women's needs. It is important that they particularly take into account the wide-ranging segments and financial backgrounds to which women belong.

As such, innovation is imperative when it comes to bridging the gap in financial advice, regaining consumer trust and targeting the mass market. Financial institutions need to adjust to the demands of consumers, particularly those of women and millennials, and solutions need to be cheaper, more relevant and accessible.

It matters. Why?

Empowering women financially is a win–win for all. Financial independence gives women the freedom to live their lives on their own terms and boosts their confidence, which in turn helps their families and future generations. It also helps close the gender-based disparities in retirement savings and pay. But empowering women is also smart economics – closing the gender pay gap is important both for policymaking and development. Research has shown that greater gender equality enhances economic productivity and helps make institutions more representative, while greater spending power helps shape consumer markets. What is more, charities and philanthropic causes are also likely to benefit from female empowerment – studies show that women are more generous than men when it comes to charitable giving.

Finally, greater female empowerment means added financial security for families. In the past 20 years, the number of women who carry the primary financial responsibility for their family has increased dramatically – something that was unthinkable in previous generations. So, while much remains to be done, the world is slowly adjusting, adapting and embracing the idea of empowering women financially. It is our collective responsibility and benefit to ensure we continue the positive trend, and fill in the gaps sooner rather than later.

---

[9] Facebook (2016). "Millennials + money: The unfiltered journey", https://fbinsights.files.wordpress.com/2016/01/facebookiq_millennials_money_january2016.pdf.

Why I Left Goldman Sachs for FinTech

By Adam French
Founder, Scalable Capital

I spent a lot of time thinking about the best title for this chapter, and I wasn't sure if it should be "Why I Left Goldman Sachs for FinTech" or "Why I Left Goldman Sachs to Join the Robots". Although many are fearful of our robot overlords, I was a child of the Johnny 5 and R2-D2 era and thus grew up with a love of technology. I ultimately decided that FinTech is probably the more popular option – a sign of the times. I hope my story proves useful as a source of insight for someone looking to leave the world of financial services and join one of the many innovative FinTech companies around the world. To give you some context, I studied at the London School of Economics and read Business Mathematics and Statistics from 2004–2007. Over the summer of 2006, I applied for a number of internships within the world of finance, and I was fortunate enough to spend 10 weeks of that summer working at Goldman Sachs. This is where the story begins.

By the time I started the internship in July of that year, the S&P 500 had rallied up to 1250 from the lows in 2003. I found the internship exhilarating and was excited to go back to university for the last year of my studies with a job offer under my belt. It so happened that when I joined the firm again for full-time employment in September 2006, equity markets were still firing on all cylinders; the S&P 500 was now around 1500. A personal bull-market highlight at the time was going to New York for 10 weeks of training while sterling was trading above two US dollars. At this point of the story, things took a different turn. Eighteen months later and the S&P was down over 50% and the future looked very different to the rosy past we had left behind.

At Goldman Sachs, I worked as part of a derivatives trading team that provided solutions to retail banks across all asset classes.

The team was very much at the forefront of automation within the trading division, as we used technology to scale the business up from doing a few thousand trades a day to tens of thousands of trades a day. All while reducing the trading team from twelve people to just four. It was this type of technological disruption within institutional financial services that left me wondering why retail financial services seemed to be operating in the Stone Age. There was no Eureka moment but, in 2014, I quit my job to enter the world of FinTech. I finished my Goldman career on a "high"; a full market cycle complete, the S&P was now above 2000, 100% above the lows in the depths of the market cycle – and I had a few grey hairs as proof.

A quick Google search on their trends tool shows that FinTech was barely a thing going back as recently as 2013. A quick look at the data from KPMG and CB Insights confirms that the venture capitalists (VCs) had yet to pick up on the trend at this stage as well; in 2013, only $2.8bn was invested in VC-backed FinTech companies. In just two years, this had exploded. Not only did the media pick up on the topic, but the VCs started to invest heavily in the sector. 2015 saw an almost fivefold rise in VC investment in this space, reaching $13.8bn. Fast forward to 2017 and the word FinTech is on everybody's lips. A day barely passes without a major publication covering the sector in one way or another.

So what does FinTech mean to me? Broadly speaking, consumer FinTech is about focusing on a particular financial service or product, putting the customer at the centre of the proposition and creating a solution that is ten times better than the traditional offering. By specializing in one thing, solving a niche client need and doing it very well, consumer FinTechs are building services that clients love. This means that traditional banks, which offer every product and service to their clients, are being disintermediated. We saw this with firms such as Transferwise (offering a great currency exchange service) and Funding Circle (offering a great way for people to lend directly to businesses they know and love). It is here that Scalable Capital, the company I co-founded, enters the picture.

Scalable Capital is a European digital wealth manager. We help our clients grow their wealth to reach their long-term investment goals. Not only does our use of technology allow us to make investing more accessible, more convenient and more competitively priced than many alternatives, but it also allows us to make investing better. We focus on risk management so that our clients can remain invested for the long term without having to put in hours of research themselves. By offering a transparent solution to clients who otherwise would have invested by themselves, we are giving them access to a service which was previously reserved for the top 1%. The idea behind Scalable Capital came about due to the sheer number of friends and family who used my financial expertise to ask "What should I do with my money?" The problem I faced was not having anywhere to send them. It was a challenge faced by my Scalable co-founders too, and as such we thought we should create the service that we knew people deserved, a service I would be happy to recommend to my mother. The founding team of four has rapidly expanded to what is now around 50 people. A little over two years since we left our old jobs, we now have over 5000 clients and manage more than £200 million. We are well on our way to fulfilling the dream of providing a superior investment service to many thousands of people.

Looking back on our experience so far, what do I think is important when looking to build a FinTech company? I think you have to take both the "Fin" and the "Tech" very seriously. The "Fin" comes from building a strong team who understand the financial landscape (both commercially and regulatory). The "Tech" comes from a core emphasis on building proprietary technology. At Scalable Capital, we have focused on both. The founding team spent almost their whole professional lives in finance and financial concepts (like portfolio construction). We need that technical expertise when looking into concepts such as the correlation of risk (there are periods where high risk follows high risk and low risk follows low risk), risk not always being rewarded in the short term and the observation that when markets get riskier, it is generally better to de-risk and not get punished for holding riskier assets. These are all observations which are well researched and understood if you have spent time working in the capital markets.

Then there is the "Tech"; we use technology to run millions of simulations so that we can optimize our client portfolios in all market conditions and in line with their risk tolerance. Our aim is to provide the best opportunity for long-term investment gains. Two years in and only 1% done. We cannot rest on our laurels. We have so much to do, so many innovations to bring to market and so many people to help. I am very excited to be a cog in the wider FinTech machine. There are so many other fantastic businesses who are building great services and helping people in ways which were previously impossible. I often get asked if I would rather have gone straight into FinTech or followed the traditional route of working for an investment bank. The new tough question for top students is "investment banking or FinTech?" For me, I look back on my time at Goldman Sachs with complete fondness. It was a great place and I worked with smart, driven people who ultimately had clients' best interests at heart and practised a philosophy of "long-term greedy". I do not regret working there for a minute and have many friends who still work there. I also do not think that Scalable Capital would be here today were it not for the groundwork laid at Goldman Sachs. It was there where we found the people able to build Scalable to what it is today; it was there where we found out about the investment problem that people had; it was there that we were able to think about the solution with the knowledge we had gained while working in the market.

Whatever you decide is the best place for you, I do not think you can go very wrong. Everything in life is a learning experience and as long as you are willing to work hard and solve problems, you will enjoy the challenge. If you are no longer learning and are thinking of doing something new, just remember this closing quote from Mark Twain. It certainly helped me to sail away.

Twenty years from now you will be more disappointed by the things you didn't do than by the ones you did do. So throw off the bowlines. Sail away from the safe harbor. Catch the trade winds in your sails. Explore. Dream. Discover.

Moneymeets.com – Germany's Leading Personal Finance Management Portal

By Dieter Fromm
Founder and CEO, moneymeets.com GmbH

Digitization Redefines the Rules of the Game

In the digitization of financial services, the German financial and insurance sectors are still at the beginning of these revolutionary changes. The current trend is not just mere innovation, but a real cultural change. The task of the day for the technical departments is not only to reorganize proven processes to make them quicker and to use paperless methods, but to completely rethink them. And of course, the new and the old world of finance are communicating in Germany as well: at least 87% of the banks surveyed by the Federal Ministry of Finance stated at the end of 2016 that they had cooperated with at least one finance start-up and that they were planning on continued cooperation or participation in the future. Banks, and of course insurance companies as well, benefit from the customer orientation, innovation and flexibility of the new digital players. FinTechs can, in turn, use the reputation of a bank or insurance company to their benefit. In the end, these synergies will remove any opposition and the result will be that it really does not matter where the customer gets his advice from.

How Two Bankers Became the Founders of a WealthTech

Everyone knows that challenging the status quo can sometimes have far-reaching effects down the line. In the moneymeets founding story, the crucial question was asked in 2010 by Johannes Cremer and it was: "Will client advisory meetings (client consultations) with our bank customers remain effective?" At that time I had more than 25 years of experience in customer services and before I resigned, I was responsible for the entire retail business of the Kreissparkasse Köln, Germany's third largest savings bank at the time, with total assets of approximately €25 billion. Johannes Cremer, my co-founder, had also gained more than 20 years of banking experience. Customer confidence in banks was low due to the financial crisis and the regulatory requirements had already been tightened. Banks and insurance companies were still largely untouched by innovations. We were soon in agreement that the trend towards digitization which had spread through other industries like trade and tourism a long time ago would not stop at the banking industry either. Why should it? We concluded that banking activities lent themselves well to digitization, and that an online marketplace for financial products could be promising.

Using our own funds, we commissioned an IT company with programming the portal and decided to leave the safety of our workplaces and the colleagues we had grown so fond of, to start moneymeets together. That same year we were able to win the support of two Cologne family offices, with their investment of a seven-digit euro amount in our business idea. At the end of 2012, the first version of the moneymeets marketplace went live – the first financial portal that offered a marketplace with real financial strategies for private investors, a community for exchanging financial strategy ideas, complete cost transparency, as well as the option to purchase more than 20,000 investment funds without an initial fee.

In 2014, the Handelsblatt publishing group invested via the Dieter von Holzbrinck Ventures in our business and moneymeets expanded their marketplace to insurance products. To this day, moneymeets is the only portal where customers can check more than 140 different insurance companies for statistics on annual sales commissions paid for their existing insurance contracts, and where they are able to receive a 50% refund automatically when integrating their current insurance policies with moneymeets or when signing up for new contracts. This offer is unique in the German market. In 2015, moneymeets expanded with a complete financial aggregation service and by offering asset statements for all their accounts, deposits, insurance instruments and other financial products. Irrespective of the bank or insurance company that the customers are maintaining their products in, they can be compiled and evaluated in the moneymeets financial overview. That same year the Swiss Woodman Asset Management Group participated in moneymeets and a new collaboration with Fidor Bank followed. They began to refer any customers expressing an interest in securities and insurance products. In 2016, investor integration from the largest Swiss retail bank (PostFinance AG) followed.

Wealth Management with Moneymeets

Today, moneymeets is the leading independent internet platform for personal finance management (PFM) in Germany. The platform makes it possible for anyone to set up their digital financial home easily and free of charge. Our platform has thereby become the digital alternative to the personal banking and insurance services consultations that are still so common in Germany. The customer's personal profile allows them to manage all their financial products from just one site. This makes it possible to establish a complete, customized and cross-vendor overview of their finances, their bank account, and even their investments in funds and insurance products. We offer great advantages not only in clarity, but the cost of doing business in investments and insurance products is also significantly lower than in the traditional commission-driven German financial market. Any efficiency gains thanks to our cost-effective digital processes are passed on to customers as a price advantage. In addition, service challenges such as opening hours or lengthy consultations are no longer an issue, as the services are available at any time. This makes our offering a much better fit

for the life reality of many customers, plus it provides banks and insurers with the added opportunity of targeting new client groups, or following up and reactivating customers from their existing customer base.

Of course, customer inertia and possible fears are just as great a challenge for the WealthTechs team to overcome. Great trust is required to share one's own financial information with a start-up business. And we also know that German customers may demand greater trustworthiness than users in other countries. To win this trust, moneymeets consistently relies on user-centred processes and absolute cost transparency. It is normal in the German financial sector to include commissions in the cost of the product without transparent disclosure to the customer. On moneymeets.com, however, all commissions, surcharges and fees for financial products can be compared with complete transparency – which is a novelty for the German financial market. moneymeets uses this to counteract the information asymmetries which exist between consumers and the financial sales sector in Germany. We voluntarily established true consumer protection. This was recognized by the prestigious German consumer protection organization Stiftung Warentest, which recommends moneymeets.

In addition, all commissions that we receive as product distributor are split with the clients. When buying new products, moneymeets forfeits up to 100% of the commission paid by the financial institutions; for existing products, which the user integrates into his moneymeets account, we pass on up to 66% of any regularly received annual portfolio commissions to our customers. This makes moneymeets the price leader for funds, deposits and insurance products in Germany.

Working with Regulators

Regulatory conditions do play a significant role in the growth and innovative power of the industry. In the UK, the Bank of England and the FCA are considered true pioneers. Since 2016, FinTechs in the

UK can apply to the so-called regulatory sandbox. As participants of this project they are allowed to test their business model for three to six months in the market and benefit from much looser regulatory provisions. A similar regulatory scheme is currently being tested in Switzerland. Do we need a "sandbox" in Germany as well to provide young entrepreneurs with an experimentation field? There is no doubt that some regulation in Germany does create difficulties for the young industry. And the German insurance and finance industry has a very hard time implementing European guidelines and opening themselves up to the market. In principle, we hold the opinion that regulation can be a real advantage as well. It forces all companies to play on an equal playing field and create insights through standardization of processes and product requirements, especially for innovative digital approaches. Last but not least, regulation does build trust and confidence, which can be a true benefit especially for start-ups.

Following initial reluctance, both the German regulator BaFin and the German Ministry of Finance are now striving for a constructive dialogue and the promotion of the German FinTech scene. In December 2016, BaFin successfully completed its project "FinTech". One of the project's aims was to ensure that FinTech start-ups gain assistance, in order to better understand the prudential perspective of BaFin. Depending on the business model, FinTechs also need permission from BaFin and have to meet the corresponding supervisory requirements. A newly founded unit in the BaFin presidential area will focus on new financial technologies and institutionalize contact with the FinTech industry. At the same time, the Ministry of Finance established the FinTechRat in March 2017, which is intended to advise the Ministry on issues relating to digital finance technology. The FinTechRat is so far comprised of 20 members. These are representatives of FinTechs, banks and insurance companies, as well as academics researching the digitization of the financial sector. The FinTechRat is supplemented by supervision and ministries.

I can only recommend that any FinTech founder engages actively with their local regulator as soon as possible, and supports the growth of their local FinTech ecosystem to counterbalance the influence of the traditional financial services sector.

How to Scale a Successful Team

After we began with two permanent members of staff in 2012, our team grew to 40 colleagues by 2017. Long-term personnel planning, an effective and efficient recruitment process, and the founders' decades of managerial experience were crucial prerequisites for our successful staffing. Attractive employer branding to target top talent and achieve long-term employer attractiveness have been part of our toolkit. We have an ideal network in the media and insurance capital of Cologne, and sought proximity to universities. For instance, we have been cooperating very closely with WHU – Otto Beisheim School of Management since 2015. As part of the joint research project VikoDIA, we conduct research into the investment consulting of the future. The project is funded by the European Regional Development Fund (ERDF). The aim of the project is to develop an innovative visualization concept for comprehensive digital financial advice. To plan and handle the workflow, we rely on agile scrum methodology not only for software development but also for product management and marketing.

Finding "Good" Investors

When we founded moneymeets in 2011, Johannes and I already had extensive experience in the banking world. This is certainly the biggest difference compared with other founders, who are often at the start of their professional careers or are attempting to position their business model in an industry environment that is new to them. As former executives, we were able to draw on a wide network when looking for investors. Our first two investors come directly from our network.

The further search for investors was surprisingly simple. We were one of the first German FinTechs, knew the industry and the investors involved there, and were able to offer a brand new concept. For young founders and start-ups who are starting out as newcomers in an already established industry, this means that they should invest a great deal of time in networking. Those who are recommended by the right people appear trustworthy. This makes a huge difference and significantly increases the likelihood that you will find an investor. Above all, business networks and start-up conferences are suitable platforms for entering into conversation with relevant decision-makers. However, pure industry events without a direct FinTech focus are also an excellent opportunity to become known and make contacts.

But what is a suitable investor? Someone who provides "smart capital". At a management level, a "smart" investor knows the many pitfalls that threaten a young company. He can use his experience as a kind of mentor and help to prevent founders from making many classic start-up mistakes. At the same time, he understands the business model and uses his expertise to help position the company correctly on the market and make the most of its opportunities. What's more, he is an important partner when it comes to further expanding his own network – for instance, finding additional investors. It is also extraordinarily helpful to put yourself in the investor's shoes and really understand his or her motivation for the investment before you sign the contract.

WealthTech Market Germany – A Small Excursion

According to McKinsey, 20% of all savings and investment products in Germany are purchased online. We expect this number to rise to 35% by 2020. According to the current

"FinTech-Markt in Germany" study, commissioned by the German Ministry of Finance and published in October 2016, about 1.2 million Germans currently use independent PFM systems to get a better overview of their finances and to manage their assets. The German WealthTech and FinTech industry functions in a very fast-paced and dynamic environment, with a variety of different business models. Since many companies, just like moneymeets, are active in a number of segments (PFM, insurance), their precise categorization is often not easy. Start-ups in the financial sector are developing rapidly, and they continue to boom. The total previous yearly market volume of the financial technology companies currently active in Germany was €2.2 billion; this figure was for their financing and asset management sectors alone. The market value of the German industry as a whole could possibly grow to €148 billion within the next 20 years. This is the forecast of Professor Dr Gregor Dorfleitner from the University of Regensburg and Junior Professor Dr Lars Hornuf from the University of Trier, based on their study on behalf of the Federal Ministry of Finance we mentioned previously. They are not quite a danger to the status of the established financial system yet, as their share is still too low in comparison with conventional finance in Germany. The researchers infer from their study and forecast as follows: "If the dynamic growth of the FinTech sector should continue to grow and their vast growth potential should eventually become exhausted, systemic risks could possibly develop." Their assumption is an enormous market potential for finance start-ups, currently estimated at €1.7 trillion for the financing and asset management sectors. According to the Federal Ministry of Finance, 346 active start-up companies makes the German market the second largest in a comparison of European countries, right after the UK. They also report growth of approximately 150% annually.

The 100 Trillion Dollar Market Failure

By Oren Kaplan
Co-Founder and CEO, SharingAlpha

The idea behind SharingAlpha had been boiling in my head for years. Once I decided it was time to execute, I called up my brother who is an extremely talented and experienced programmer and asked him whether he would like to join me on this journey. I have over 20 years of experience in the financial industry and I cover the "Fin" part. My brother, now aged 46, has been writing code since the age of 13 and comprises the "Tech" part.

Over US$100 trillion are managed globally by active managers. Most of the assets flow to managers who have performed well in the past and outflow from those that have underperformed, although research has proven time and time again that past performance is not an indicator for future results. It is not just a disclaimer at the bottom of every fact sheet, but actually a reality.

One might compare this with lottery players who decide to select last week's winning numbers, while most of us are aware of the fact that doing so does not improve their chances. In the asset management world, crowding behaviour might actually be harmful since every strategy has its capacity limitations and therefore, buying into what is known as "mega funds" that have performed well in the past actually decreases their chances of achieving outperformance in the future.

The natural question to ask is: "Why do investors behave this way, or in other words, what is the current market structure that leads to this market failure?"

Most investors do not manage their own savings, but rely on financial advisors. Naturally, those advisors need to have solid reasons for the selection they make on behalf of their clients.

Investing other people's money into a fund that has performed terribly, or has yet to gain a significant track record, would leave the advisor exposed in case post-investment performance remained poor. In order to avoid such a situation, most advisors prefer to play it safe and rely on some kind of past performance analysis, although, once again, the proof suggests that this strategy will not add value to the end investors.

Therefore, it is difficult for investors to select an advisor who has a proven track record of adding value to his or her clients in the past. An objective measurement is unavailable and as a result, advisor selection is dependent solely on factors such as service and presentation capabilities rather than hard and indisputable numbers.

Since historically, advisors were allowed to receive kickbacks from fund managers, clients were happy to receive "free" advice and this serious conflict of interest definitely did not work in the best interest of investors.

Prior to the 2008 financial crisis, regulators took a passive approach and did not interfere in the way this market was structured. In recent years, things have started to change and currently we see more and more countries in which retrocessions are a thing of the past. This dramatic change is placing plenty of pressure on advisors, who now need to ask their clients to pay them for the advice they can offer.

This regulatory change has led many advisors to move away from active funds – which could no longer pay them – to passive alternatives that require less research and more importantly are a safer bet, rather than having to explain later why they chose a manager that underperformed its benchmark when they could simply, and cheaply, buy the benchmark itself.

On the back of the above changes, we are currently witnessing one of the greatest movements of assets ever seen in the asset management industry towards cheaper solutions like exchange-traded funds (ETFs) and robo-advisors. Is this the beginning of the end for active managers and human advisors, or can this market still survive?

In my opinion, the only way forward is further transparency and the use of a platform that will enable advisors to select winning managers in advance and offer investors simple and objective tools to select the advisor that has a proven track record of adding true value to investors.

Since I couldn't find such a platform, I decided to take the initiative and create one. With the support of my brother, who has been writing code for over 30 years, we turned this idea into a reality. We called it SharingAlpha and that's exactly what it aims to achieve.

It's Time for a Rating Platform

The SharingAlpha platform aims to gather the views of a large group of advisors and to measure their success rate.

The greatest advantage that a platform of professionals using a user-generated fund rating platform brings to the market is the possibility to grow to scale more rapidly and effectively. This is done by moving from the current rating model, where advisors work in silos, to a more centralized approach in which their views are shared on a dedicated platform.

This change can be compared with the traditional encyclopaedias that were created through costly, complex and difficult-to-manage supply chains of academic experts, writers and editors. Using a platform model, Wikipedia has built an information source comparable to Britannica in quality and scope by leveraging a community of external contributors to grow and police the content.

The successful introduction of the platform model to the asset management industry creates plenty of opportunities for those members of this community that do adapt to the change. On the

other hand, investment advisors that fail to adapt will be taking on a serious risk of being left out. The sharp decline in valuation of the NYC taxi medallion (from over US$1.2 million in 2013 to less than US$300,000 today, due to Uber) should serve as a warning sign to firms and individuals that make their living from selecting funds. Unless they are able to hold proof of their actual added value, then their chances of keeping their current "valuations" is rather questionable.

This Leads Us to the Question: What Do Investment Advisors and Fund Selectors Have in Common?

Both have no independently proven track record to present to prospective and existing clients. This lack of track record has led many clients to choose cheaper solutions, known as robo-advisors. A user-generated fund rating platform offers to combat the robo alternative by offering investors a way to select investment advisers or fund selectors that have been proven to add real value. The platform ranks the individual raters in terms of their talent in selecting funds.

An additional feature enables investment advisors to build virtual funds of funds and in turn SharingAlpha ranks them based on their performance, not only as fund selectors but also as asset allocators. Their fund selection and asset allocation track record enables them to test their analysis, and if they choose, they are able to present their proven track record to existing and potential clients or receive better pay as an employed fund selector or asset allocator.

We have taken into account that putting people's professional ability online for everyone to see can be risky. For that reason we have put in place a policy that enables our users to remain anonymous. However, the assumption is that once advisors build a successful track record, they will probably be interested in showing their performance and at that stage they will decide that sharing their identity publicly is beneficial.

We launched the platform as quickly as possible, after less than six months of development. We later added further functionalities based on the feedback that we received from our initial users. Many platforms grow on top of other networks. Instagram and Zynga have achieved their growth by leveraging on Facebook as the underlying network. SharingAlpha has so far leveraged on my large network of connections on LinkedIn (currently reaching more than 20,000 people, mainly from the asset management industry). Like the rest of the successful platforms, we had to be open to suggestions from users. For example, eBay has moved from auction pricing to mainly regular pricing as a result of demand from their user base. Similarly, we have allowed users to keep their identity private while building their track record, hence providing our advisors with a free option where they have nothing to lose by starting out and building their proven track record in terms of fund selection and asset allocation.

Instead of seeking external funding, both my brother and I agreed that it would be quicker to simply withhold salary payments. The other costs have so far been covered by us; however, we are fully aware that not all founders can afford such a setup and are forced to seek external funding at a very early stage.

In summary, on SharingAlpha investment advisers or fund selectors can either:

- start building a track record, be successful and have a competitive advantage;
- start building a track record and constantly improve until they are successful; or
- do nothing.

Obviously doing nothing is very risky. Imagine – two years down the line and many of your co-workers or competitors have created a proven track record. They can be compared while you cannot even enter the playing field!

Enterprise Innovation

Types of Innovation

1. **Efficiency** – reduce the cost of making and distributing products and services

2. **Sustaining** – replace old products with new ones

3. **Disruptive** – transform organization and/or products and services

Asset Management

3rd most likely industry to experience disruptive impact of startups!

Source: PWC Global FinTech Survey

Partnerships Strategies

1. Labs / Academia

2. FinTech / WealthTech Startups

3. Tech Companies

4. Corporate Innovation Accelerator as an instrument to enrich bank's innovation potential

Startup Collaboration Models

1. **Detached** – sponsor start up events, offer mentorship programs, access to office space, etc

2. **Overlapping** – co-development with startups, conduct in-house innovation programs with startups

3. **Embedded** – setting up in-house digital innovation unit to explore, test and develop new offerings with external partners & intrapreneurs. Can also mean investment or acquisition of startups

Innovation Tips

1. Just Do It

2. Execution is the real game

3. Define goals / vision for collaboration

4. Foster entrepreneurial culture

5. Establish KPIs to track progress

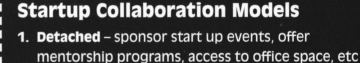

Executive Summary

Innovation has become a key priority for most banks and asset managers, however really transforming an organization and changing its culture into a more agile, entrepreneurial structure is easier said than done. Today's digitization efforts of banks mostly focus on client channels and back-office automation, thereby neglecting the creation of new business and revenue models, new innovative products and solutions, and digital content. Wealth management decisions are still predominantly based on expert human judgement. However, by sticking to traditional investment concepts, banks risk losing ground to more innovative new market entrants in the FinTech and WealthTech space and challenger banks. Banks who digitize their wealth management and offer digital solutions in coexistence with traditional ones will capitalize on growth opportunities and strengthen their profitability. In general, innovation has four core characteristics. First, innovations relate to an object like a product, a process or a business model. Second, innovations can either be incremental or radical/disruptive, depending on their potential to change existing products and/or industry structures. Third, innovations require a structured approach to a company's innovation management capabilities – like incubators, open application programming interfaces (APIs), etc. Fourth, innovations are relevant for companies if they can be transferred to the (mass) market. This part will provide an overview on enterprise innovation models and case studies from leading industry players, taking into account all four innovation areas.

The first chapter in this part ties up with the fourth characteristic and describes how companies need to implement a rigid corporate culture to execute innovative ideas. It argues that innovation is 1% inspiration and 99% perspiration. Thus, it involves different critical success factors like a do-it-yourself approach, involving the value chain and allowing failure.

The second chapter relates to the third core characteristic of innovation and provides an exclusive insight into how a leading European direct bank and a global investment manager face the aforementioned challenges and constantly work on innovating and further developing their service portfolio. It shows how companies can combine incubators, open API infrastructures and intrapreneurship to foster innovation. It also includes invaluable tips on how to empower internal entrepreneurs and visionaries (referred to as "intrapreneurs"), which every organization has.

The third chapter focuses on the first and second innovation characteristics, introducing three general models of innovation: detached, overlapping and embedded. As digital technologies increasingly disrupt the wealth management industry, collaborating with WealthTech start-ups has become a viable approach to identify, validate and scale solutions as a means to stay relevant and compete in the digital age. However, start-up collaborations bring a new level of complexity for incumbents. By following a blueprint of successful corporate–start-up collaborations from other industries, wealth management firms can avoid the pitfalls and focus on achieving the desired outcomes. The last chapter will provide a guide to collaboration and also show the necessity of assessing a firm's digital maturity.

We hope this part inspires all established players to see how innovation can be fostered in financial institutions globally.

Just Do It! Using the Buzz Around Innovation to Empower Banks and Asset Managers

By Konstantin Speidel

Program Manager Digital Transformation – Vice President, Allianz Global Investors

There does not seem to be a conference, town hall or announcement these days without executives speaking about the importance of innovation. Companies like Uber or Spotify have shown that digitization and technology can bring disruption into established industries. This, and the growing FinTech scene, are alerting executives in banks and asset managers. They are setting up different initiatives to understand how technology will impact existing business models. Hackathons, labs, think tanks, accelerators, incubators, outposts, dedicated functions and teams are all frequently seen examples of attempts to support innovation in the financial world.

Big banks and asset managers nevertheless often fail to create an environment which fosters innovation, even though they have talented staff and good ideas. I have seen a few successful projects and many failures, and detected something which Edison apparently already saw more than a hundred years ago: "Innovation is 1% inspiration and 99% perspiration."

I am convinced that the institutions are not missing the creativity, but the execution power to develop new things. The good news is that, from my experience, the failure of execution power is not about missing opportunities, or the funding, but boils down to a rigid corporate culture lacking the pragmatism to execute ideas.

The purpose of this chapter, therefore, is to provide readers, particularly bankers and asset managers, with some pointers to help them test and try newer models and concepts in the workplace, in the hope that many more ideas will be successfully executed, and to empower the internal entrepreneurs and visionaries – called "intrapreneurs" – in these organizations.

Always Strive to Generate Buzz When Promoting Your Idea Internally

Some of the advantages that bank staff and asset managers have over newcomers are distribution, funding, knowledge and regulations. As banks consist of educated and competent personnel who can generate equally good ideas as their competing newcomers, what bank staff need to bring these ideas to life is, well, buzz.

How do you generate buzz around your idea? Begin by researching what is trending in the finance and banking industry. Big data, robo-advisory, bots, artificial intelligence (AI) or blockchain are examples of currently often quoted innovations, which are, however, seldom completely understood by banks and asset managers. The end justifies the means, so use these trends to create attention and visibility. By augmenting your idea with these trends, you will most likely find more support to develop your idea. AI or big data are some good examples of trends which can easily be built into many ideas due to their broad definition. Almost any database can be big data, and I have seen a decision tree being sold as AI supporting a project. Important here is not to overdo it; focus on one trend, and be clear about how you will implement and leverage that trend. Take your idea, augment it with one of these trends and bring it to the newly created innovation functions within your bank or asset manager. They are waiting for ideas and people like you, and you have a fair chance of getting support.

The point here is to use these current trends to push and develop your idea, ultimately garnering the internal support you need. But securing the idea is just the start, as the most challenging part for financial institutions is successfully producing innovative products. Let us focus on patterns of successful innovation projects at big financial institutions first.

Execution is the Real Game

Many people might think that once you have secured support for the project the big work is done, but in fact it has not even really started. The support to execute is often the start of the struggle for banks or asset managers. In fact, hierarchies, legacy, regulation, guidelines, delegation, incentives or culture are all examples of disadvantages of established players versus new entrants when it comes to execution.

Here are some observations I have made after dealing with different innovative projects in wealth and asset management. These insights are presented to overcome the mentioned burdens and to help you successfully implement your idea:

- **MVP + (minimal viable product plus) approach.** The focus of all doing needs to be on building a real product, and leveraging part of the existing infrastructure. The faster something real can be shown, the higher the success probability. Important here is to apply Eric Ries' lean start-up methodology to the established corporate world. Avoid trying to build a perfect product from scratch; you will most likely fail. Innovation always involves uncertainty, so focus on getting something out and testing it. It may not be perfect, but unlike start-ups, you have existing products, know-how or infrastructure at your disposal. Get your idea up and running fast.

- **Less is more communication.** Visibility will lead to alignments, doubts and coordination efforts. Stay in stealth mode as long as you can. I have seen many innovation projects lose their lustre and ultimately fail because the project managers spent half of their time with internal bureaucracy, having no time to deliver. You can be sure that you will find many colleagues who want to contribute for different reasons, but remember that it is not

about talking, it is about execution. I sometimes avoid telling colleagues too much in the beginning, and if people approach me, I try to decrease their interest by making the project sound irrelevant.

- **Apply a do-it-yourself approach to tech.** Hiring an agency to support you can be useful, but hiring an agency to lead the development will be deadly. Technology is the core of any digital project, and outsourcing IT will ultimately not be successful. The most successful projects I have seen were those where at least part of the project management team was actually building the product. I am not saying that everything has to be done in-house, but what I have learned is that you need to be on top of technology for it to really work in the end.

- **Be bold.** Executives have already built labs, created teams and promised a lot. The likelihood that you will be their only justification for all this time and effort is quite high. Approach them directly, avoid the middle management (which is rarely supportive) and make them feel like they are part of the idea. Executives in banking or asset management spend most of their time building a legacy; they will surely support any exciting innovation.

- **Tackle, do not question.** Innovation is about improvement not perfection. Be disciplined but take failure as part of the process. Keep iterating, and the faster you do this, the quicker you will improve and, hopefully, be successful.

- **Do not forget your value chain.** There is a big difference in using technology to improve existing services, and in developing new technology. Banks are not basic research centres, and academia and entrepreneurship will most likely beat any corporate efforts in this field. Giving use cases to these fundamental researchers, on the other hand, can be highly productive. Just look at what is already in the market and think of new ways to use it in your industry or office.

- **Consider failure.** Nobody wants failure, but the success probability of innovation projects is significantly lower than the usual corporate projects. You are doing something which involves a lot of uncertainty and your stakeholders are aware of this. Do not get scared but try it – the attempt will always be a great experience and an enrichment for you. You might come to a point where you realize that your idea does not work as planned. Accept this quickly, pivot and go try the next idea you most certainly got while working on the initial project.

Summary

We only need to look to Kodak or Nokia, once major players in their industry, for lessons in failing to innovate. Banks and traditional financial institutions are not exempt from this and the signs are everywhere. New entrants from the FinTech world, changing regulations like the Payment Services Directive 2 (PSD2) and technological progress have all increased management's attention on changing business models, and intrapreneurs can use this momentum to drive change. Just remember, you first need to augment your idea with some of the trending disruptive movements in the market. Once you have successfully received the mandate, iterate as quickly as possible, test and prove your product. Failure is expected, but that should only spur you to refine the idea. After all, failure is better than not trying at all – so Just Do It!

Leveraging Corporate Innovation by Opening Banks to External Ecosystems

By Mariusz C. Bodek
Digital Transformation Executive, KPMG

and Jan Enno Einfeld
Head of Investing, Comdirect bank AG

Banks and other established wealth management players are facing an upcoming and more competitive market environment. With new players entering the market as well as increasing regulatory requirements and costs, the pressure to reinvent and further develop existing services is rising constantly. New technological solutions provide a unique opportunity to win new customer groups, like self-directed retail clients with digital and cost-efficient services (i.e. robo-advisors). In the last couple of years there have been few market "intruders" under the label of FinTech. Companies that are focusing on changing the market structure within wealth management are now becoming numerous and the market segment has received its own terminology: WealthTech.

In this chapter, we would like to offer a definition of the "label" WealthTech. Furthermore, an exclusive insight will be provided on how a leading European direct bank has faced the aforementioned challenges and constantly works on innovating and further developing its service portfolio. The first corporate innovation accelerator by a bank was founded in Germany, enabling cooperation between the bank and WealthTechs by opening the bank to external ecosystems and adding value to corporate innovation activities.

Definition of the Term WealthTech

The term WealthTech is a relatively new expression and is a derivative of FinTech activities in the field of wealth management. The authors provide the following definition of the term WealthTech to offer a basis for discussion regarding which contents and characteristics should be affiliated to the label:

> WealthTech consists of technological developments and services that are created to transform existing investing solutions, including subcategories like wealth and asset management or trading, and across all asset classes. It comprises solutions for the so-called advisory-seeking customer up to family offices, addressing its users' needs through digital interfaces and business processes.

As we present an insight into our current activities at a leading European direct bank, which offers a completely digitized banking experience, the focus in this chapter is on identifying and creating new innovative solutions for advisory-seeking customers as well as so-called self-directed customers.

Insight: The First Robo-Advisor by a Major German Bank

As a pioneering service within the German market, a robo-advisor was introduced as the first digital wealth management offering by a market-leading bank in Germany in 2014. It currently has the largest customer base among German robo-advisors and maintains the largest amount of assets under management. Thus, the bank is able to gain deep-learning insights regarding the adoption by customers and the marketability of such digital wealth management offerings based on reliable amounts of data.

As a digital bank, the vision in generating a transparent and comprehensible digital asset management service has been to enable customers with higher support requirements than the traditionally served execution-only customers to handle their investments online. The robo-advisor systematically allocates customer portfolios based on predefined rules and models, which monitor market developments and automatically adjust and optimize the portfolio structure.

As the solutions within the FinTech and WealthTech environment become numerous, the need to find a way to stay ahead of upcoming trends and market developments becomes eminent. Therefore, the bank founded a corporate innovation accelerator. Among other departments, the accelerator works closely with the bank's corporate venturing arm. The aspiration is to identify internal and external innovation impulses within wealth management and WealthTech that can be utilized to bolster the bank's strategic roadmap and fill the wealth management product development pipeline.

Corporate Innovation Accelerator as an Instrument to Enrich the Bank's Innovation Potential

To support the various internal innovation management activities and make use of the upcoming new business models and the entrepreneurial potential of start-ups, the bank founded a corporate innovation accelerator, named Start-up Garage, in 2015. The fundamental concept of this initiative was to provide an interface to the external ecosystem. Especially the corporate venturing department is a strong supporter of the initiative and uses the accelerator to gain access to WealthTech and to establish cooperation with new market players. Within Start-up Garage the bank cooperates for a predefined period of time with selected early-stage start-ups, which are actively developing innovative solutions in the market environment of the bank. The ambition is to provide a win–win opportunity for both cooperating partners:

• *The bank* gains added value by accessing new ideas and solutions by the start-ups and is able to enrich their own

innovation activities by using the pool of innovative start-ups as a cost-efficient addition to their research and development activities.

• *The start-ups* gain access to established banking infrastructure and are able to challenge their solutions with certified banking experts. This exchange with experts is especially valuable in the fields of special expertise like regulation, business modelling or IT.

Paradigms for a Beneficial Cooperation within a Corporate Innovation Accelerator

To ensure that both parties benefit from the cooperation, several paradigms have to be considered for the accelerator. The following criteria can be seen as universally applicable not only for the banking industry, but for all companies that plan to use a corporate innovation accelerator in order to complement their innovation activities:

Company perspective

The start-up:

• should be in close proximity to the company's own business model and/or be an economically reasonable addition by closing a capability gap;

• should be compatible with the company's ecosystem, infrastructure and customer base;

• should provide clear added value for the existing customer base and/or enable broadening it.

Start-up perspective

The company:

• should be able to provide the specific support needed to transfer the benefits of the start-up solution to the bank's ecosystem and vice versa;

- should provide an open infrastructure allowing interconnection with the bank's ecosystem with minimal frictional losses;
- should provide further support (e.g. by offering at least basic financial support to an investment).

The Need for Technical Interoperability within the Digital Banking Environment

The most time-consuming and critical factor for a successful cooperation between banks and external partners is the ability to connect both IT platforms. In order to be able to interconnect with numerous external services without developing a single interface for each partner, the bank has to develop a universal gateway that enables partners to gain simplified access to core banking processes. Thus, developing and operating an application programming interface (API) appears mandatory. In order to make use of the advantages of an API, banks have basically two options:

- The bank develops its own API(s).
- To minimize internal development efforts, the services of independent API providers can be used, providing universal APIs that enable interconnection of the bank not just with a specific start-up, but with a significant part of the FinTech ecosystem.

In addition, it is recommended to provide a test environment for the start-up in which the services can be tested regarding their usability and technical feasibility. In this environment, tests can be performed virtually or based on sample data, before final product rollout.

Intrapreneurship as an Option for Accelerating Corporate Innovation Potential from Within

While the cooperation with innovative start-ups within the accelerator focuses especially on making use of the external entrepreneurial potential of new market players, the introduction of an intrapreneurship initiative can also foster innovation potential.

Therefore, the bank introduced an intrapreneurship programme that makes use of the well-established recruiting concept "entrepreneur-in-residence (EIR)". Based on the concept of venture capital (VC) companies, EIRs develop their own business models – financially backed by VC – or support funded companies within the VC portfolio.

The bank enables the EIR to develop and/or launch business models within the bank's service portfolio. The EIR basically has two options:

- The EIR can develop his/her own idea and implement it with the infrastructural support of the bank.
- The EIR can further develop an idea that has been provided by the bank. Thus, the EIR is used as an additional resource to realize products from the bank's innovation pipeline.

In order to efficiently manage both initiatives, cooperation with external start-ups and intrapreneurship activities are combined as two complementary initiatives of the corporate innovation accelerator. Thereby, both initiatives can be monitored, mutual benefits can be explored and synergies can be utilized.

Conclusion

As the market environment within wealth management changes dramatically, banks have to adapt to new market dynamics and find ways to stay ahead of the shift of the market. By opening the bank to external ecosystems, several benefits can add value to the corporate innovation activities.

A corporate innovation accelerator is a successful method to leverage the external innovation potential provided by new market players, as well as fostering the internal innovation potential by enabling intrapreneur activities.

Wealth Management is Dead, Long Live Wealth Management

By Kamales Lardi
Founder and Managing Partner, Lardi & Partner Consulting GmbH

Wealth management is facing an unparalleled transformation as a wave of disruption sweeps across the industry. Although rapid technology developments are a significant driver, disruption has also been prompted by evolving consumer behaviour, emerging agile competitors, new business models, shifting regulatory landscape and democratization of knowledge. Additionally, client expectations have been transformed by superior interfaces and hyper-personalization offered by digital businesses across various industries such as Amazon, Netflix and Uber. Wealth management clients now seek immediate responsiveness, 24/7 information access, visualization of content, flexibility and control over data and decision-making. As wealth management firms grow to realize the true impact of disruption, many scramble to compete with young, innovative start-ups by adopting new technology solutions.

Although still a developing sub-industry within the overall FinTech ecosystem, the number of WealthTech start-ups has been growing steadily since 2012.[1] Asset and wealth management firms are struggling to achieve excellence in creating superior client experiences. As a result, WealthTech start-ups are utilizing emerging technologies to capitalize on the growing gap between consumer expectations and traditional players. Start-ups such as Wise Banyan, True Link and Personal Capital are demonstrating that consumers now have an alternative to traditional, outdated financial technology offerings.

WealthTech Start-Up Collaboration Models

In a recent global FinTech survey by PwC, the asset and wealth management industry was ranked as the third most likely to experience the disruptive impact of start-ups.[2] Furthermore, over half (60%) of asset and wealth managers surveyed believed that at least part of their business is at risk to WealthTech start-ups. It is becoming increasingly clear that traditional industry players need to explore start-up collaboration as a way to stay relevant, transform offerings and continuously connect with clients. Several overarching collaboration models exist in the market today, described as follows.

- **Detached**

  This model probably offers the easiest way for wealth management firms to get involved in the start-up scene. For example, organizing or sponsoring start-up pitch events offers a good way to build a presence in the start-up community and benefit from engagement with innovative teams. Additionally, wealth management firms could ease into start-up collaboration by offering mentorship programmes or free access to resources such as corporate office space, collaboration tools/platforms or key personnel.

  Organizations such as Startupbootcamp.org actively work to match start-ups with mentors from banks and wealth management firms who offer advice and feedback on their pitch, products and overall market. Specifically, financial institutions such as Santander, Rabobank and Deutsche Bank use mentorship to participate in the start-up ecosystem and draw open innovation to their organizations.

  This model allows firms to maintain control and independence, particularly if they are not ready for digital transformation or full start-up partnerships yet. However, it is challenging to stand

[1] CBInsights, "Spreading the wealth: Investment & wealth management startups see record deals". https://www.cbinsights.com/blog/fintech-wealth-tech-startup-funding/.

[2] PWC, "Blurred lines: How FinTech is shaping financial services". http://www.pwc.com/gx/en/advisory-services/FinTech/pwc-fintech-global-report.pdf.

out against numerous other firms also competing to make an impression in the start-up ecosystem.

- **Overlapping**

This model is suitable for wealth management firms looking to accelerate innovation and explore offerings through co-development or co-invention with WealthTech start-ups. Common approaches such as hackathons, start-up accelerators, incubators or innovation hubs offer great ways for traditional firms to participate in innovation initiatives outside of the existing organizational structures.

By sponsoring, participating in and/or conducting innovation programmes, traditional firms are able to rapidly and actively explore emerging technologies, new offerings, and collaboration partners, as well as potential acquisition targets. Additionally, these initiatives create an opportunity for asset and wealth managers to flex their creative muscles and explore entrepreneurial thinking in a fail-safe environment.

The overlapping model allows innovation initiatives to grow independently towards more aggressive goals, undisturbed by existing business constraints and boundaries. However, organizers may require specific experience in innovation models, such as Sprint or Design Thinking to ensure value-added outcomes are achieved.

- **Embedded**

This model is commonly applied by larger wealth management firms and involves two distinct approaches to accelerate innovation and explore emerging technologies or offerings. The first approach involves setting up an in-house digital innovation unit to explore, test and develop new offerings based on evolving market trends. For example, wealth management divisions of international banks such as UBS are actively setting up "intrapreneur" environments to generate innovative ideas and challenge existing internal processes. The second approach involves investment or acquisition of promising WealthTech start-ups to diversify or expand their firm's offerings. Acquisitions offer a quick way to get direct access to entrepreneurial teams/skill sets, new technologies and an evolving customer base.

This model offers the advantage of embedding innovation culture and entrepreneurial thinking in the organization, as well as owning new technology solutions, capabilities and digital skill sets. However, it is also the most complex approach, as it involves merging distinct organizations, teams and cultures.

Key WealthTech collaboration success lies in selecting a model that fits the strategic vision and business goals of the wealth management firm, as well as taking into account the critical cultural and team sensitivities.

Blueprint for WealthTech Start-Up Collaboration

Collaboration of any kind carries certain risks. However, collaborating with WealthTech start-ups has the potential to breathe new life into traditional wealth management firms, which is critical in these disruptive times. By following some critical steps, wealth managers will be able to create a win–win situation for the company and the WealthTech start-up.

Assess Digital Maturity of Company

Aspiring to collaborate with start-ups requires digital maturity on the part of the wealth management firm. Here, digital maturity refers to the willingness to explore possibilities created by new technologies, as well as the potential to adopt new ways of doing things. Incumbent firms need to be honest about their existing digital capabilities and readiness to collaborate with start-ups.

This may mean conducting an internal audit to develop a realistic assessment of the firm's own pain points and ability to survive in the digital age. The audit should aim to understand current capabilities and the technology landscape in the firm, as well as challenges or barriers relating to existing business operations. Additionally, an external audit of the digital maturity of peers and emerging client needs or expectations will act as a benchmark and provide best practices that could be applied.

Define Vision for Collaboration

An internal digital maturity audit will also provide incumbent firms with direction on where and how WealthTech can contribute to enhance offerings and client interactions. By identifying start-ups that align with the strategic direction and business goals, wealth management firms accelerate potential outcomes.

For example, in 2015 BlackRock acquired FutureAdvisor, a robo-advisor platform with US$600 million of assets under management at the time of acquisition. Although significantly smaller than other competitors such as Betterment and Wealthfront, BlackRock's decision to acquire the company was in alignment with its strategic direction to offer it as part of the BlackRock solutions technology platform to other financial institutions.[3]

Foster Entrepreneurial Culture

By design, WealthTech start-up teams tend to be nimble, bold and explorative. In order to thrive in the digital age, investment advisors, wealth managers and private bankers must develop the ability to constantly adapt, acquire new knowledge and skills, as well as embrace the potential of new technologies. By encouraging exploration and corporate innovation techniques, wealth managers will be better prepared to collaborate with start-up teams.

For example, the UBS Wealth Management Innovation Lab was set up to help teams focus on transformational trends.[4] The innovation function is deeply integrated within the organizational structure and collaborates with several divisions of the bank to promote a "permission-to-fail culture" that encourages exploration without pressures of failure or return on investment.

Establish KPIs to Track Progress

Irrespective of which collaboration model is used, it is critical to predefine key performance indicators (KPIs) to measure and track the progress of the collaboration effort. However, unlike traditional corporate success measures, the KPIs for start-up collaboration should focus on flexible outcomes, rather than quantitative investment/revenue returns.

For example, corporate members of the SIX Fintech Incubator F10 measure long-term success by the number of open innovation ideas entering their pipeline. Wealth management firms could also measure the number of new ideas generated by internal employees (indication of innovation mindset), efficiency in the WealthTech selection process, or even number of co-invention or co-development initiatives.

Future of Wealth Management in the Digital Age

As digital disruption sweeps over the wealth management industry, traditional firms need to explore opportunities for a sustainable future in the digital age by simulating, learning from and collaborating with innovative WealthTech start-ups. Some of the biggest barriers for effective corporate–start-up collaboration relates to lack of clear vision, organizational culture clashes and low digital maturity. By following a blueprint of successful corporate–start-up collaboration models from other industries, wealth management firms could avoid the pitfalls and focus on achieving the desired outcomes.

[3] Kitces, M. (2015). "Blackrock acquires FutureAdvisor for $150M as yet another robo-advisor pivots to become an advisor #FinTech solution". https://www.kitces.com/blog/blackrock-acquires-futureadvisor-for-150m-as-yet-another-robo-advisor-pivots-to-become-an-advisor-fintech-solution.

[4] UBS, "Innovation at UBS". https://www.ubs.com/magazines/innovation/en/about-us.html.

Global Overview of WealthTech

Global WealthTech Markets

Investment Management is a **massive global industry** which is expected to grow by 6% annually to $102 trillion in 2020

Source: PWC 2016

WealthTech in LATAM – grow wealth by increasing financial literacy among 65% unbanked population

Answers to Japan's demographic development and savings challenge: an online P2P direct financing real estate platform

Unlock WealthTech in Turkey by simple products and user interfaces to have better visibility over client's portfolios

Passive investing across both mutual funds and ETFs grows at the expense of higher cost, active funds

China: Ant Financial operates a money-market fund which has become the largest MM Fund in the world with $165B AUM

48% North America

52% Rest of the world

Global Asset Mix in 2020 by Geography

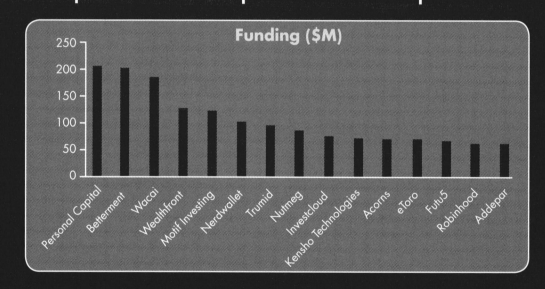

Funding ($M)

World's 15 Biggest Asset Managers

1. **BlackRock,** US: $4.6 trillion
2. **Vanguard Group,** US: $3.4 trillion
3. **State Street Global,** US: $2.2 trillion
4. **Fidelity Investments,** US: $2 trillion
5. **Allianz Group,** Germany, $1.9 trillion
6. **JPMorgan Chase,** US: $1.7 trillion
7. **Bank of New York Mellon,** US: $1.6 trillion
8. **AXA Group,** France: $1.5 trillion
9. **Capital Group,** US: $1.4 billion
10. **Goldman Sachs Group,** US: $1.3 trillion
11. **Deutsche Bank,** Germany: $1.2 trillion
12. **BNP Paribas,** France: $1.2 trillion
13. **Prudential Financial,** US: $1.2 trillion
14. **UBS,** Switzerland: $1.1 trillion
15. **Legal & General Group,** UK: $1.1 trillion

Source: Report by Willis Tower Watson in conjunction with Pensions & Investment

Executive Summary

This part is dedicated to giving you a global perspective on WealthTech innovation happening across China, Japan and Latin America and future trends in those regions.

While digital payments are dominated by debit or credit cards in many Western countries, China's consumers have jumped directly from cash to mobile. More than 70% of Chinese internet users say carrying cash is no longer necessary – payments are made with Alipay and WeChat. Few foreigners realize how fast and advanced the development actually is in new payment features and mobile financial services in China.

One chapter focuses on the development of WealthTech in emerging markets and especially in Latam, where activity has started and the potential for further WealthTech growth is huge. It may take some time before Latam embraces completely the benefits of digital wealth management platforms as we know them in the USA, but it is coming sooner rather than later.

One chapter focuses on Japan, which has (as in many other countries) a serious savings problem caused by the low financial literacy, and exacerbated by an unfavourable population demographics. In order to achieve societal break-even levels of savings, individuals will need to invest in potentially higher yielding, unsecured assets outside of bank savings deposits. The authors propose a WealthTech solution for this in the form of a peer-to-peer real-estate equity crowdfunding marketplace.

Another chapter describes strategies to unlock WealthTech in Turkey. Although the country is the 18th largest economy in the world, only a few WealthTech firms can be found so far.

Is the Future of WealthTech Already in China?

By Yvon Moysan
Master in Digital Marketing and Innovation Academic Director,
IESEG School of Management

China, the Largest FinTech Market in the World

According to the Pulse of Fintech Q3 2016 report by global audit and advisory firm KPMG,[1] venture capital (VC) funding in Asian financial technology companies increased, reaching US$1.2 billion – outpacing even the USA, where VC investment totalled US$0.9 billion. There are several factors driving this rapid growth. First, population: China has a population that is upwards of 1.3 billion. As a consequence, when addressing the Chinese market, one advantage online companies have is access to voluminous client and prospect data, which traditional financial service companies lack. Alibaba, for example, has more than 420 million customers,[2] who have provided the company with behavioural data for years. Second, economic advancement: China is first in terms of GDP (purchasing power parity) at over US$20 trillion. Third, the massive adoption of mobile technology: China has almost 1.3 billion[3] mobile phone users, many on 3G or 4G networks. In addition, and by 2020, the government plans to invest more than US$320 billion in broadband internet infrastructure, benefiting rural areas that lack established banking networks. Fourth, financial industry liberalization and regulatory acquiescence. Appropriately regulating financial services is challenging. If policies are too lax, investor risk increases. Too stringent, and innovation is stifled.

In China, regulations are supporting the FinTech industry. Unlike developed markets where regulations were instituted prior to technologies being invented, Chinese regulators are relatively young and are evolving with FinTech. In an Ernst & Young (EY) report, Douglas Arner and Jànos Barberis wrote: "China is formalizing this harmonious relationship between banks and Fintech players by creating a tiered regulatory regime (…). China is increasingly at the forefront of regulatory developments within Fintech, signaling a dramatic change in the origin of where regulatory standards may emerge from."[4]

Although regulatory scrutiny is increasing, Chinese officials have thus far been more liberal than in other markets. Although more stringent regulations could temper growth, the trend is towards greater FinTech adoption in China, driven by technology companies. As an example, Yú'é Bǎo was demand-driven, with Alipay addressing a market need and subsequently managing regulatory concerns. Porter Erisman, former Alibaba Vice President, said: "Our view was always, run ahead, do it, prove to the government that it will in the long run benefit the Chinese economy, and then ask for forgiveness later." The combination of all these factors created a real catalyst for FinTech adoption and numerous players from various industries have rushed to stake a claim on China's internet finance sector, with distinctive value propositions: the BAT giants, tech companies and traditional banks.

BAT Giant Tech Players Continue Growth by Moving to Other Markets Such as Banking

China has a uniquely competitive digital landscape dominated by a few digital companies that have established comprehensive multi-licensed financial ecosystems: the BAT (Baidu, Alibaba and Tencent).

---

[1] https://home.kpmg.com/xx/en/home/insights/2016/03/the-pulse-of-fintech-q1-2016.html.

[2] http://www.alibabagroup.com/en/ir/financial.

[3] https://www.statista.com/statistics/278204/china-mobile-users-by-month/.

[4] http://www.ey.com/Publication/vwLUAssets/ey-the-rise-of-fintech-in-china/$FILE/ey-the-rise-of-fintech-in-china.pdf.

In China, mobile wallets such as WeChat – provided by Tencent – have seamlessly integrated into people's everyday lives. Banks often look at disruption in terms of product impact; in other words, how general FinTech (including distributed ledger technology, P2P lending, third-party payments, etc.) will disrupt. In reality, the biggest threats lie in the changing structure of global markets. Currently, most FinTech start-ups pick existing financial verticals – such as lending, investments, payments or currency transfer – and then play within their four walls. Yet, ironically, what consumers and businesses are looking for is less fragmentation of their financial services, not more. When you start looking at the emerging tech players in China and their foray into financial services – Alibaba Group with Alipay and Tencent with WeChat – what's interesting is that neither company started out as a pure FinTech player or as a bank disrupter. Instead, after mobilizing millions of users through their respective platforms, they realized continued growth could be found by moving laterally into other markets, such as banking (like ApplePay and Facebook Payments in Western countries).

What's especially interesting about WeChat is that it delivers a nearly full and frictionless financial integration experience into a user's life, allowing for peer-to-peer (P2P) payments, bank transfers and wealth management alongside food delivery orders, taxi bookings and mobile phone top-ups. All from the palm of your hand. This is the WeChat experience; the ability to connect strangers, split bills, pay rent to a landlord, and all with the virtual human smile of an emoji or avatar at the other end of the transaction. What WeChat and Alipay have achieved through their mobile wallets is what PayPal has been struggling to do for years: seamlessly integrate their offerings into their users' everyday lives. For some reason, mobile wallets are still clunky and awkward in the West, hampered by a chicken-and-egg problem of usage and acceptance. In developed economies, there's also the dual problem of widespread card usage, which is still very efficient, especially since the introduction of near-field communication (NFC). In China, card usage lags. It would appear that Chinese consumers find it far more palatable to leapfrog plastic altogether, going from cash to mobile wallet in one fell swoop.

Tech Companies Also Emerge with Specific Value Propositions

Alongside these giants, smaller players have emerged in very different areas. The P2P lending platform Dianrong, the credit decisioning engine Dumiao, the intelligent financial services technology platform Pintec or the online mutual fund distribution business Hongdian Fund are some of the most successful FinTechs in China.

Dianrong is China's answer to US-based Lending Club – a P2P lending platform providing market-oriented borrowing and lending solutions for domestic and overseas financial services institutions, including banks. Dianrong utilizes information provided by third-party data and credit consulting companies to select assets based on a risk-weighting system. The company has also developed several other products including its e-wallet and its transaction processing system, as well as clearing and settlement services.

Dumiao is a digital consumer lending business that leverages technology and big data to make automated credit decisions. Dumiao's core product is a credit decision engine that enables high-speed lending decisions without the need for traditional offline human underwriting examination. By leveraging big data to increase the speed and accuracy of credit decisions, Dumiao enables the consumer loan decision to be made in real time at the point of sale, opening up a multitude of new product opportunities that were previously unavailable in the market.

Pintec is an intelligent financial services technology platform that uses big data and digital technologies to provide financial solutions for consumers and small businesses. It provides more advanced investment management services, robo-advisory, digital wealth or digital advisory services, blending investment recommendations from the robo-advisor with some client decision-making, which is especially well suited for Chinese investors who value lower fees and being involved in the process.

Hongdian Fund is an online mutual fund distribution business providing market access for retail investors and B2B partners through API connectivity. The company holds a licence issued by the China Securities Regulatory Commission for the online sale of mutual fund products. As of May 2016, the company has reached agreements with 53 different Chinese fund management companies to market 1645 different mutual fund products on the Hongdian Fund platform.

Traditional Banks are Developing FinTech Solutions In-House or are Acquiring Them

Although the BAT giants and tech companies are leading the initiative, traditional Chinese financial companies are developing FinTech solutions in-house or are acquiring them, enabling them to reach new clients, improve services and increase internal efficiency. Yet, strict regulations and relatively conservative mindsets mean that they are typically followers rather than leaders, at least compared with the BAT giants. That said, institutions such as Ping – an insurance group – are strategically entering the sector through subsidiaries, including Pinganfang, Ping An Puhui and Lufax, an internet-based wealth management platform. Lu.com aims to provide one of the most comprehensive wealth management platforms globally. Its services include providing risk management expertise, financial assets trading information

and related consulting services for enterprises, financial services institutions and other qualified investors.

In addition, large commercial banks are acting: for example, China Construction Bank and Industrial and Commercial Bank of China are now building their own e-commerce platforms. Others will inevitably follow. Traditional players also have several strengths that should not be underestimated: a legacy of strategic partnerships, comprehensive product offerings, professional risk-management expertise and physical branches.

The Future of Chinese FinTech

In the coming years, China looks set to continue to dominate the global FinTech industry with a very strong domestic market. Internally, the push and pull factors are clearly in place to catalyse the establishment of a leading digital finance sector. On the push side, capital investment is pouring in and the market is being bolstered by substantial government support for innovation. On the pull side, demand is being driven by underserved SMEs and tech-savvy, often unbanked, consumers keen to access financial services via their mobile phones. Overseas, Chinese FinTech firms will also play an increasingly important role in the global collaborations driving technological innovation. What these companies learn abroad, they will bring back to the domestic market, further fuelling the sector to stay ahead of the rest of the world.

WealthTech in Latin America

By Juan Manuel Vega Bellés
Chief Digital Officer, Principal Chile MANAGEMENT

As a member of Principal's international team, I have had an amazing and unique opportunity to follow the FinTech phenomenon very closely in various countries around the world. Working at head office in the USA, where FinTech has exploded, and visiting and researching countries like India, Brazil, Chile, Mexico, Malaysia, Hong Kong and China, has given me a unique first-hand view of the state of evolution on financial technology. For the purposes of this chapter, I will concentrate my comments on Latin America (Latam), and more specifically on Brazil, Mexico and Chile, which are the countries where we have operations.

What We Expect for the Evolution of FinTech and WealthTech in Latam

The big banks have fallen asleep. In Latam, the banks own most of the distribution of financial products, especially investment. Accounting for an average of 70% of mutual fund sales, they offer "closed architecture" (they sell only their proprietary funds, normally managed by their own asset management company). They offer poor customer experience and proprietary-only funds often not in the customer's best interest. When you look to the way

FinTech has evolved around the world, especially in the USA and Europe, you see big banks and incumbents applying an approach like that described in Figure 1, clearly trying to maximize their profit-creation products.

It is very easy to understand why incumbents are taking this approach, especially in Latam, where the biggest problem is a debt and overspending culture, where most people don't have any money to invest and big retail chains have flooded the unbanked customers with credit cards. And please, don't get me wrong. Banks and retail chains are not evil for doing this; in fact, they have given access to credit to people who never before had the opportunity to afford big purchases, and today those customers are enjoying bigger than they probably need flat-screen HD TVs, enormous refrigerators with ice makers and even cars. The problem is that with great benefits and credit access come great responsibilities too, and here is where the incumbents, big companies and especially customers have not done a good job.

Because of the speed of change, how fast we are learning from international experiences and local adaptation to market products and needs, in Latam we have seen an interesting acceleration of some of these categories in FinTech that don't necessarily match the US and European evolution. Based on our own exploration and scouting of the markets, we see a slightly different evolution in terms of start-up activity, as illustrated in Figure 2.

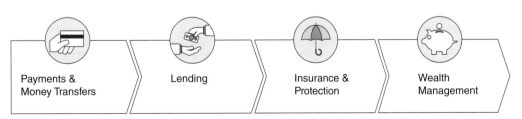

Figure 1: Evolution of FinTech solutions in incumbents in the USA and Europe

Payments & Money Transfers — Lending — Insurance & Protection — Wealth Management

Country	Payments	Lending	Insurance	Wealth Management
Mexico	1	2	3	4
Brazil	1	4	3	2
Chile	1	4	2	3
Latam	1	2	3	4

Figure 2: Evolution of FinTech solutions in Mexico, Brazil, Chile and Latam

Why We Believe There is a Different Evolution of FinTech Activity in the Region

There are a couple of reasons:

- **Unbanked population.** It is estimated that around 65% of the Latam population is unbanked, making it easier for start-ups to target a segment of the market that is underserved.

- **Overspending/debt culture.** Banks and retail chains have open lending opportunities to more and more customers, which is a great thing. The bad part is that these opportunities come to a population without the right knowledge, the proper understanding of interest rates and that is extremely financially illiterate.

- **Trust.** People realize that financial institutions for a long time have offered products and services in their own best interests, ignoring what is best for their customers. FinTech has started to change this, putting the customer at the centre of everything they do. But there is also a trust issue with start-ups, especially

critical in wealth management, where a customer may not feel comfortable saving or investing their money with a company that has 10 people and is funded by venture capitalists.

- **Privatized pension systems:**

  - In Mexico and Chile, with a highly regulated and privatized mandatory pension system, wealth is increasing every month. In these markets, since saving is mandatory, the employer deducts that saving every month out of the employee's payroll, so people view this more like a tax than their own saving effort. This is a big problem, because people don't feel this is their money, so they don't track it or worry too much about it. On top of this, the mandatory contribution rates are not sufficient to generate proper amounts of income in retirement, so people need to make voluntary contributions to their retirement accounts in order to have a 70–80% replacement ratio of their working day's salary in retirement, but less than 20% of active workers make such voluntary contributions.

  - Brazil is going through a difficult process, where the government is realizing that they cannot afford to pay pensions to all the citizens demanding one as their population ages (traditional social security pension schemes are bankrupt everywhere in the world). Discussions are going on right now to solve this pension crisis. International experience shows that from design, adequacy, integrity and sustainability perspectives, privatized pension systems like the ones used in Chile and Mexico are a better long-term solution. Banks are the go-to place for financial needs.

- **Extremely low financial literacy.** Money conversations are hard, and most people don't want to deal with the "hard" part of money, they just like to spend (who doesn't?). In Latam, too many people don't want to listen and understand that all the financial decisions we make (or don't make) today will have an impact on our future, and without the proper education and understanding of how the financial world works, it is very hard to make the right financial choices.

The Opportunity: To Grow Wealth We Need to Grow Financial Literacy First

The biggest challenge that we face in Latam, and probably around the world, is financial literacy. Everybody talks about money, everybody likes money but very few people understand how money works, especially in the long term. I am not even talking about investments, I am talking about basic understanding of personal finance, budgeting and expense tracking, debt management and credit cards, interest and long-term investing. No doubt the world is changing and we are changing as users and consumers too. As an example:

- My 9-year-old daughter does not remember a time when she was not able to talk to her family back in Chile using FaceTime. For her, phone communication is not only about listening to someone but also looking at the faces of her relatives and their non-verbal expressions. In her mind, there is no reason to go somewhere and meet face-to-face, unless it is a play date with one of her friends, but financial education and even financial advisors – when she grows up – are not in the "friend" category.

- My 12-year-old daughter rarely uses pen and paper in her school assignments. Her school (a US public school) uses Google Classroom technology, which allows the teacher to post all the assignments, homework and materials in the cloud, so she can access everything from her phone, tablet or computer, anywhere! The teacher also uploads videos of classes and exercises, so if she is in doubt on any topic, my daughter can always go and review the class. Why would she go anywhere else to get the content and information she is looking for? Financial education should be delivered in the same way, with fun and relevant content, on the platforms we are using today and in a cool way.

- My 15-year-old daughter received her first allowance a year ago. Like my dad did with me, I got her a piggy bank and gave her a bunch of bills and coins. I told her that from now on, she was going to start needing and using money, and I wanted her to start saving a little every time she received some money by putting some bills in the piggy bank. She was surprised, and I thought great, she likes this idea! The surprise was mine when she told me that she needed "digital" money instead, because most of her purchases were made on her phone (apps, music, Amazon, Starbucks… and she was using MY credit card for that!). It seems pretty obvious, but I must be honest, I didn't see that coming, even with all my research on digital behaviour. So, how do you teach a teenager to save and manage money in a world where she doesn't see money, where the touch ID button on a phone is used exactly the same way for a US$3 purchase as a US$100 purchase? How do you make them keep track of their expenses and account balance on their cards and accounts if they just erase the bank app every time they need extra space for more photos, videos, music or apps? As you can imagine, I have not solved the problem yet!

So, in order to grow wealth, we need to grow financial literacy. And in order to grow financial literacy, we need to find a way to make it cool, fun, simple, direct and relevant, and as early as possible in life. I am optimistic that technology will help us get there faster, with solutions that are generating some traction in the USA. (For full disclosure, I am not trying to promote any company or receiving anything from the companies mentioned. The examples are just for illustration purposes and to help the reader understand the point I am trying to make):

- **Expense management or personal finance management (PFM) apps.** A key part of financial education is understanding where your money goes. With people too busy to organize and follow their expenses, this type of app follows your expenses through your current account and credit cards, in one or many accounts, and keeps track of your expenses and budgets in real time with cool graphics and UX, phone and watch apps. Some of them will even send you information comparing your peer group, people on your income level, living in your area and even in your age group (e.g. www.mint.com).

- **Robo-savers.** There are some start-ups that use artificial intelligence (AI) to keep track of your expenses and money movements in your current accounts. The app will pull money from your current account into a savings account without you noticing the saving effort. In other words, it automates the act of saving, especially for people who say "I don't have any money to save". These apps help you find small amounts that add up in the long run. The one I use in the USA has already saved more than USD$500 billion in 4 years for their users (e.g. www.digit.com).

- **Micro investing.** This type of app is more spread around the world, and they work by basically linking your current accounts and allowing them to round up every purchase you make. You can also add other rules to increase your savings, for example shopping in certain stores, making big purchases or just getting your payroll. Again, the idea here is start small (average weekly savings of USD$5) and show people that progress can be made and that they can save (e.g. www.acorns.com, www.qapital.com or Bank of America's Keep the Change).

We are going through an amazing time, where technology is changing everything we do and how we do it. I believe, though, that the digital transformation era will not be machines against humans, but more how humans are empowered by technology. Financial advisors and brick-and-mortar branches will not disappear, but tech will absolutely change the way we use them. I am a firm believer that there is an unbreakable relation between money, human behaviour and coaching. So for me, the future of WealthTech has to do with wealth and technology, but most importantly, understanding human behaviour, human interactions and how to coach people to manage their finances better. Whether that will be done in a branch, over FaceTime with an advisor, via an app on your phone or through a voice assistant at home is yet to be seen, but most likely it will be a combination. Only when we understand our relationship with money, expenses, budgeting and saving will we be better positioned to grow wealth in Latam. Technology certainly plays an important role in speeding up the process and shifting our financial behaviour.

Challenges in the Japanese Wealth Management Market – Digital Issuance and Distribution of Japanese Real-Estate Securitized Products

By Shinsuke Nuriya
CIO and CFO, Crowd Realty

Japan has a serious savings problem, caused by the low financial literacy relative to peer countries, and exacerbated by social security programmes as a result of unfavourable population demographics. In order to achieve sufficient levels of savings, individuals will need to invest in potentially higher yielding, unsecured assets outside of bank savings deposits. We believe that real estate both domestically and abroad offers attractive investment opportunities, but that current regulations and investment vehicles present excessive barriers to entry for individuals. Thus, we propose a peer-to-peer real-estate equity crowdfunding marketplace as a WealthTech solution.

Japan's demographic development is a major challenge. Japan's population peaked in 2010 and has gradually declined since then. The government expects that, by 2060, Japan's population will further decrease from its present figure of 127 million to 99 million, and the number of live births per year will be at least halved. Japan's old-age dependency ratio stood at 26.7% in 2015, which is far above the global average of 8.3%, and is expected to increase to 39.9% in 2060. Eventually, a single elderly adult will be taken care of by only 1.3 individuals in the labour-productive age range of 15 to 64.[1] This will lead to serious reductions in public pension funding. According to the Ministry of Health, Labour and Welfare, the public annuity-to-income ratio was 62.7% in 2014, but is expected to drop to 50.9% at most in 2043.[2] In addition, the amount of employee pension declined 2.5% annually from 2003 to 2013, and the trend seems to be continuing. During the same period, the ratio of companies without a retirement benefit system increased from 13.3% to 24.5%.[3] Due to this demographic imbalance, wage security is difficult for the younger generations, and their savings patterns are insufficient to cover future retirement costs. Under these circumstances, Japanese citizens are being urged to reshape their wealth management strategy.

The Japanese wealth management market differs significantly from the global market, particularly in the composition of individual asset holdings and the level of financial literacy. According to the Bank of Japan, at the end of 2016, the balance of Japanese households' total financial assets was JPY 1752 trillion, of which cash and deposits accounted for 52.3%, reflecting the conservative Japanese approach to asset allocation.[4] On the other hand, in the United States and Europe, cash and deposits only accounted for 13.9% and 34.6%, respectively. This trend of concentration in saving deposits has persisted through the nation's deflationary phase. Under the low interest rate environment, successful wealth management requires a shift from passive bank deposit saving towards active equity investment. However, the low financial literacy is a challenge. According to surveys conducted by the Bank of Japan, compared with the United States and major EU countries, the percentage of correct answers given to common true/false questions regarding financial knowledge was 7–9% lower in Japan by all demographic classifications, including gender, age group and income level.[5] While many of the Japanese respondents

---

[1] Cabinet Office, Government of Japan. Aging Society Report, 2017.

[2] Ministry of Health, Labour and Welfare. Fiscal Validation Results, "Current State and Prospect of National Pension Plan and Welfare Pension Insurance", 2014.

[3] Ministry of Health, Labour and Welfare. Investigation Report on Employment Conditions, 2014.

[4] Bank of Japan. Flow of Funds "Overview of Japan, the United States, and the Euro area", 2016.

[5] Bank of Japan. Financial Literacy Survey, 2016.

indicated support for financial education offerings, the proportion of respondents who had participated in financial education programmes was only one-third that in the United States. In addition, according to a poll conducted by the Cabinet Office of Japan, among Japanese citizens over the age of 60, 42.7% of respondents answered that they had done nothing to prepare for their post-retirement years.[6] Therefore, we must reform Japanese individuals' consciousness of wealth management. An innovative wealth management method with ease and high transparency is key to improving individuals' financial literacy.

Japanese Financial and Real-Estate Securitization Markets

The existing financial infrastructure in Japan is dysfunctional. Along with a declining population and increase in underutilized real estate, there are an increasing number of real-estate projects for which existing financial institutions, such as banks, are unlikely to provide loans due to lack of collateral value, low risk tolerance of the institution and low liquidity of the assets. According to NRI, the average age of housing stock in Japan will increase from 22 years in 2013 to 29 years in 2030, and the number of vacant houses will be over 21 million in 2033, with a 30.4% vacant ratio of the total housing stock.[7] Even though there is an increasing number of micro entrepreneurs who run real-estate utilization businesses, they have received insufficient funding. Japan's financial system relies heavily on indirect finance, because of investors' lack of confidence in direct investment, which enables Japanese banks to hold deposits cheaply. Thus, the current financial system is based on centralized traditional finance options provided by banks and the reconstruction of a financial system based on distributed peer-to-peer (P2P finance has been neglected).

The securitization of real estate in Japan is still at an early stage compared with what is seen in developed countries. Out of ca. JPY 2.4 quadrillion of total real-estate assets in Japan, 0.7% have been securitized through public real-estate investment trusts (REITs), or J-REITs.[8] It has been 16 years since the J-REIT market was established; however, the market has experienced no real growth due to contractual limitations on investment targets and the recent hype of the Japanese real-estate market. J-REITs cannot acquire opportunistic assets such as development and renovation assets, as they have to keep a stable income cash flow for dividends. For such reasons, there are limited numbers of J-REITs with operational, yield-producing assets. Also, J-REITs need to invest in major cities and could not be a supplier of risk capital to rural areas. Individual investors in J-REITs tend to focus on dividend yield while placing less importance on principal value or net asset value. As a result, there are an increasing number of J-REITs that offer monthly unsustainable dividends by spending down their original principal. Because internal reserves are not allowed for J-REITs due to strict conduct requirements, J-REITs need to raise funds in capital markets and acquire assets at the same time. However, as J-REITs need to raise funds mainly by public offerings, they raise capital only when the offerings are expected not to dilute their listed investment units, so that they can secure investors' dividends. Thus, fundraising methods for J-REITs are very limited. There needs to be a new capital market for real estate that can replace the J-REIT market and boost securitization of real estate.

WealthTech Provides Solutions for Japan

In recent years, technology has been evolving so quickly that our lifestyle is constantly being upgraded to adapt to new paradigms. A P2P economy is a decentralized model whereby two individuals

---

[6] Cabinet Office, Government of Japan. Aging Society Report, 2017.

[7] Nomura Research Institute. Housing Market in 2030, 2016.

[8] Cabinet Office, Government of Japan. National Economic Accounting, 2017.

interact to buy or sell goods and services directly with each other, without intermediation by a third party. We see this being used by companies like Airbnb and Uber. Often referred to as the sharing economy, there is no centralized control of power, allowing people to more directly profit from their goods and services rather than paying unnecessary middlemen along the way. We believe that the sharing economy model is key to provide a brand new capital market for real-estate securitization in Japan.

An online P2P direct financing marketplace can solve our issues of Japanese wealth management. The new financial scheme can carry out real-estate securitization with ease, quickness and low transaction costs, combined with digital technology such as equity crowdfunding. The new scheme allows individual investors to capitalize on both onshore and offshore real estate in small amounts on a property-by-property basis, whereas so far they are only able to buy hard assets or invest in stocks of public

J-REITs that manage and operate multiple assets. Compared with J-REITs, the new equity crowdfunding investment products have relatively higher yields, higher flexibility of asset allocation (even internationally) and higher levels of information disclosure. On the other hand, it is easier for individuals who need to raise funds to procure funds from P2P financing provided by individuals with flexible standards of credit-scoring and decision-making than to procure funds from traditional financing providers such as banks, who have non-flexible screening standards. In order to provide further liquidity to the market, we need to create a distributed virtual stock exchange for secondary trading with the latest cutting-edge technologies, including blockchain. Therefore, the creation of a Japanese distributed P2P financial system will balance the supply and demand of capital by P2P transactions. This massive paradigm shift in financial infrastructure will improve individuals' asset management options, for a longer and more financially secure life.

How to Unlock WealthTech in Turkey

By Günes Ergun
Managing Consultant, East Management Consulting

Turkey, the 18th largest economy in the world, has been growing steadily, attracting both foreign and local investors while boosting national consumption and wealth. During the last 15 years, the strong GDP growth has been coupled with foreign exchange volatility and slow growth in equity markets. Important wealth gains have been observed, especially through diversification of the business interests of ultra-high-net-worth individuals (UHNWIs),[1] controlling almost 10% of the total wealth in the country. UHNWIs' wealth grew by 18% between 2006 and 2016, while the UHNWI population grew by 2% during the same period. UHNWIs represent 0.002% of Turkey's population, while multi-millionaires make up 0.004% and millionaires 0.07% of the population. Almost half of their wealth is inherited, and increases through business interests. The income inequality in Turkey is represented by its Gini coefficient of 0.4, the highest ratio (biggest gap) in Europe. The political risks and upheaval in 2015/2016 slashed wealth by 20% in 2016, due mainly to devaluation of the Turkish lira.[2]

According to surveys, financial literacy in Turkey is close to the lowest score among European countries, indicating a low level of financial knowledge, behaviour and attitude. Turkey, the fourth largest gold-buying country globally, has an estimated 2200 tonnes of gold "kept under the pillow", worth US$100 billion, equal to 13% of Turkey's economic output in 2015.

---

[1] With net worth of over USD30 million excluding primary residence.

[2] The Wealth Report, Knight Frank Research, 2017. http://www.knightfrank.com/wealthreport.

The Turkish financial sector and banking system have led innovation in products, services and the use of technology worldwide. The level of deployment of technology and innovation in the Turkish banking system is higher than in many Western countries. The accelerated progress in financial technologies has created both opportunities and hurdles for FinTechs to rise in Turkey. The tech-savvy and young population is keen to absorb more technology in their interaction with the financial world, and many banks offer sophisticated digitized services, chatbots and digital payment means to their customers. There's a lot of potential in areas banks cannot reach or cannot service in a profitable way. New models are needed to shift the traditional way of doing business. Innovative financial products can now touch a broader customer pool via technology platforms created by entrepreneurs with problem-solving skill sets.

The wealth which is kept "under the pillow" is usually injected into the economy during a period of crisis. Turkey has gone through a rollercoaster economy during the last few decades, due mainly to social and political turmoil. Now, Turkey is at the crossroads of both political and economic crises once again. The population needs to be reconnected and contributing to the country's wealth, as well as to their own future, instead of being limited by individual protectionism. The financial inclusion and democratization of a broader portion of the Turkish population can be a revolutionary breakthrough during the turmoil. Engaging more people to invest consciously and responsibly will improve financial literacy, boost financial inclusion, energize wealth kept out of the economy and create self-esteem for a larger portion of the population, which can also create wealth. Investors shall be more aware of the risk they bear, and FinTechs are building their business models around this increased investor consciousness. The good news is that the government is willing to enhance financial inclusion and help FinTechs when they approach the regulatory bodies with robust business ideas and transparent models.

To unlock WealthTech, FinTechs and financial institutions need to tap into the intrinsic potential of three customer segments: family-run businesses ("family firms"), high-net-worth individuals (HNWIs) and a broader group of individuals who do not recognize their wealth.

In Turkey, family firms constitute 95% of all businesses. A few family offices, private banks and corporate entities take on the role of managing the wealth of family firms based on their trusted relationships and network. Recently, independent family offices started developing services to manage mostly the savings accounts of their clients. In midterm, we expect that these offices will manage a broader range of wealth – including funds, shares, real estate, art collections and taxation. However, there is a bright white space where technology and new business models can meet to enable wealthy families to prepare better for the future of their second and third generations. The burgeoning family offices and consulting companies try to meet the expectations of their customers by building bridges of trust, leveraging their networks and experience, but not necessarily by demonstrating the measurable outcomes of their financial advice, efficiencies and customer experience. The "cost of services" does not seem to be the primary concern of clients in choosing the right advisor; they are merely biased by the "packaging of the offer". Many family offices and private banks in Turkey fail to define and manage risk, as their vision of global markets and trends remains limited or they do not want to simplify and revamp their product range.

Turkish HNWIs manage their wealth through family offices and private banking services, where the penetration of technology and innovative products is also rare. Due to the political and economic turmoil in Turkey, HNWIs have been looking to diversify their wealth geographically and distribute their assets across borders. As a result, their wealth management costs and efforts increased. They are now more exposed to global markets and risks. Many Turkish HNWIs prefer to move their families abroad for security reasons and better education, but keep the core of their business in Turkey. This reallocation of families and businesses creates both opportunities and challenges in managing wealth; they are chasing for new products, new

services and trusted partners to ease their day-to-day financial operations while travelling across regions and time zones.

Since early 2010, the Turkish economy has benefitted from foreign direct investments (FDIs). FDIs are now outflowing, mainly due to the recovery in mature markets and political risk in the region. This trend will shuffle the way to manage wealth too. The biggest opportunity lies under cover of the "unrecognized wealth" of wealthy individuals (WIs). The line between HNWIs and WIs is blurring, as the definition of wealth is widening. Individuals are willing to value gold, real estate, art collections, pension funds and their retirement, and diversify into new streams of investing with the excess of their income or accrued assets. There are around 30 portfolio management entities in Turkey, around 30% of these being independent and the remaining majority part of banks and financial institutions. The portfolio management firms manage around US$15 billion and the independent firms constitute only 2% of this market. The regulatory bodies aim to boost the market to reach US$45 billion by 2020, and to increase the share of independent portfolio management firms. The financial institutions have to deal with their clumsy legacy systems and heavy human capital, as they are tied to personal interactions between customers and their financial advisors. However, the independent firms, in order to tap into the lion's share of the growth market, need to come up with innovative business models and technology to leverage new ways to recognize and reach WIs.

WealthTech firms will reshape this space. First, wealth management firms shall bring simplified products to match the evolving needs of customers. More and more affluent clients are looking for uncomplicated products and simplified user interfaces to have better visibility over their portfolio and the risk involved with it. Customers are willing to invest their wealth, plan for unfortunate occasions, but also spend wisely. The simplification is not only around the product, but also how the product is delivered. The greater level of service has to be achieved through the speed of access to data, optionality and a better view on risks and returns.

Affluent customers are looking for more intuitive and forward-looking experiences in receiving support and services in their decision-making.

The user experience part is to be built on experience and technology, innovation and creativity. Customers are willing to contact their advisors and check their status anytime and anywhere. With the current breakthrough technologies such as big data analytics, machine learning and robo-advisory, a higher quality of service can be achieved at lower cost.

In addition, wealth management firms need to be connected to the global networks and advise at the global scale. These capabilities have to be built on the backbone of digital technologies, data analytics and genuine interfaces. The customers' needs are more global than ever, and serving these evolving needs can be achieved efficiently through technology networks rather than physical ones.

Finally, companies in the wealth management space have to establish trust and continuity of their business through transparency and sharing of knowledge. Lower-cost services such as digitized customer interfaces and robo-advisory will help especially the WealthTechs to demystify the most sophisticated products in the eyes of their customers, and shine a light on the risks and rewards (and fees and taxation).

In Turkey, the WealthTech space is ready to flourish. Companies will aim to satisfy their customers in investing, valuing, planning and spending with a genuine value-add. As the Turkish economy needs to maintain the growth trend, it is now time to uplift the future onto more prosperous grounds.

What is the Future of WealthTech?

WealthTech Strategies

PSD2 is game changing for retail banking. Banks' monopoly on their customer's account information and payment services will disappear.

FinTechs will empower asset owners with tools that lower costs, offer transparency, enable faster discovery of opportunities and are customized.

The future will be **focused on** the **customers**, the clients, the asset owners and the **platforms** that serve and empower them.

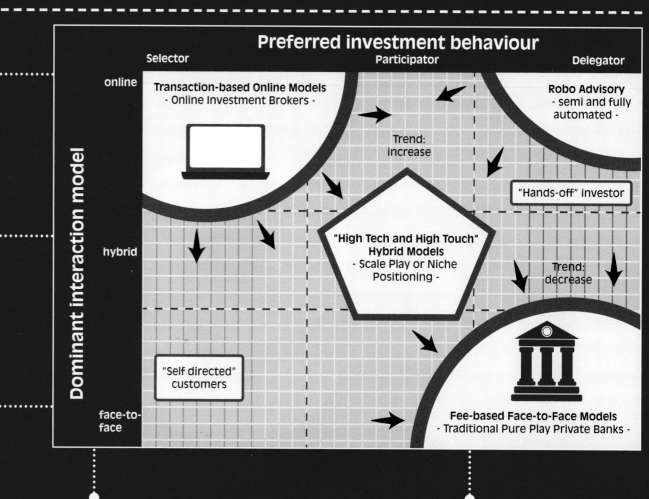

Preferred investment behaviour

Selector   Participator   Delegator

Dominant interaction model

online

Transaction-based Online Models
- Online Investment Brokers -

Robo Advisory
- semi and fully automated -

Trend: increase

"Hands-off" investor

"High Tech and High Touch" Hybrid Models
- Scale Play or Niche Positioning -

hybrid

Trend: decrease

"Self directed" customers

face-to-face

Fee-based Face-to-Face Models
- Traditional Pure Play Private Banks -

Humans will be outperformed by machines in activities related with reasoning based on the analysis of large amounts of information. As a result, finance and wealth management will profoundly change.

Key **Benefits and Applications for AI:**
- Improve advice to customer
- Improve portfolio management
- Autonomous execution
- Decreasing customer churn with behavioural analysis
- Improve sales process

In China Tech Giants are leading FinTech. Will this also happen in the West?

- Ant Financial runs world's largest money-market fund and launched wealth management platform, Ant Fortune.

- Tencent processed more than 46 billion gift transfers during Chinese New Year. On its platform users can buy mutual funds and insurance.

- Reasons for their success: focused on unmet needs, data driven, fast innovators, mastered partnerships and platform models combined with favourable regulators.

- China might provide blueprint for how tech firms in the West can address this market.

Wealth Management in 2058 includes:

- Law of robots including robo-ethics, robo-liability and robo-payroll.

- Transhumanist trading techniques

- Virtual Reality portfolio advice

- Eye Retina Trading

Predictive Analytics

Will anticipate client needs and offer additional products and services

Quantum Computing

Quantum Computing involves the use of composite algorithms and systems that use physics and quantum methods to solve the most complex mathematical problems. It will help asset managers to solve complex client challenges.

The Millennial Opportunity

- Robo-Advisors target millennials who are set to inherit around $30 trillion from their baby boomer parents and grand parents.*

- 60% of millennials distrust financial markets**

* Accenture Report

** CNN Money

BI Intelligence forecasts that Robo-Advisors – investment products that include any element of automation – will manage around $4.6 trillion by 2022.

Wealth Management Canvas

Jobs to be done	Trust Building Channels	Value Proposition	Return Generating Activities	Risk Management Activities

Customer Segments	Legal and Regulatory Delivery	Investment Philosophy	Other Unique Activities	

		Offering	Skills	Resources	Service Providers

Revenue Streams	Pricing Models	Investments	Expenses

Executive Summary

Many industries have already been transformed by digitization. Among the most prominent examples are the media or the music industry. Just as with those, the banking industry deals with information as the primary "good" delivered to customers. Thus, a networked customer equipped with technology is the starting point of all future developments. This leads to a fundamental shift from the providers to the customers – who will benefit from this development, as they will get more banking for less money. But there will also be changes on the provider side, driven by new technologies like cryptocurrencies, blockchain, artificial intelligence, etc. While many are still sceptical about cryptocurrencies, for example, we will soon see new application areas in cross-country trading or central banks issuing their own currencies as digital coins. This leads to new questions regarding security, etc. But does this mean that we can expect a new financial order? Four drivers might spur this development in the future:

- First, the emerging peer-to-peer economy will lead to a fundamental change in how economies work in the future. This peer-to-peer economy is not only characterized by transactions among peers, but also has an increasing impact on the existing digital infrastructures. First examples are AKASHA's peer-to-peer social networking platform or Sharetribe's peer-to-peer service marketplace. They all have in common that they are not built on centralized digital platforms like Google or Facebook.

- Second, from a technical point of view, the internet developed from the "internet of information" to the "internet of services", and is currently taking another step towards the "internet of values". While the first phase covered the standardization and exchange of information with the Hypertext Transfer Protocol (HTTP) and the Hypertext Markup Language (HTML), the second phase focused on standards like the Simple Object Access Protocol (SOAP). The third phase now focuses on standards around blockchain, digital payments and other areas for the exchange of value.

- Third, the development of cryptocurrencies has led to a new possibility to exchange "money" among individuals (peer-to-peer) who do not necessarily know and trust each other. Among the examples are bitcoin or ether. These cryptocurrencies all have the advantage that they provide a standard for exchanging money across country borders in almost real time, without the limitations of the existing financial infrastructures that require currency exchange platforms and banks.

- Fourth, many national regulators started to decrease hurdles for FinTech start-ups, and their solutions might lead to a deregulation of this market. Examples are London, Hong Kong, Singapore and Switzerland. All these countries, for example, introduced so-called regulatory sandboxes, where start-ups can test innovative solutions in a protected area.

All these changes together will lead to new, globally connected cross-industry ecosystems. The question is still open as to whether the large technology companies like Apple, Google, Amazon, etc. will take a big part in this. China for example, with its large technology companies Ant Financial and Tencent as the dominant players, is driving this change to a new scale. This will force both WealthTech start-ups and the incumbents to reposition themselves along the value chain. In addition, regulation will play an important role nationally and globally to enable this new financial system. To do all this, companies, regulators and all other involved stakeholders will need new development "tools". The ideas, frameworks and models presented in this part will support this challenge: "The best way to predict your future is to create it" (Abraham Lincoln).

In summary, this part focuses on how the future of the global investment management industry and WealthTech may look from different angles.

The Networked Client

By Blake Kannady

Vice President – Product Strategy, Director – User Experience,
Envestnet, Inc.

At first light, sensors "wake" the house. The gate camera scans for one minute and subsequently deactivates the motion sensors. Unless I hit snooze, the blinds open at 8:59:58 with my phone that wakes me with a nifty app that was included in my last upgrade. My smart clock gives me a colourful pixilation of the forecast as I adjust my eyes to look out the real window, feet away. I stretch, pop out of bed and meet Alexa in the bathroom. She's got a calendar briefing and then today's financial headlines. I hear the espresso machine finishing as I descend the last stair and speak up loud enough to ask the remote to turn on the TV. Just as I sit down to breakfast, I get a text notification on my tablet – "Payday!" an overnight deposit. "Would you like to transfer your predicted surplus for the month to your Travel budget?"

This scene is not for the latest smart home tech that will allow you to float through life. What we are filming is for a new smart service. That smart service is one I can adopt aside from the other interactions, most of which were simulated. If I am being honest, I love to dream up how things should work, but take my personal application of them with a heaped spoon of cynicism. I generally mistrust sharing online, I am hesitant to deploy devices with "smart capabilities" for fear that they decrease in necessity as they increase vulnerabilities, and I try to be a right-on-time adopter. The service, more specifically, connects notifications and actions to the activity in my financial accounts. It works with a variety of smart devices and places to prompt an action based on another action in another smart device or place. Today, with everything connected – from my refrigerator to my car – this innovation is one of the most impactful for a "networked client". That is how to use my connected devices, my connected providers and my connected places to be informed, to be actionable and to automate things to promote my financial wellbeing.

I think the Internet of Things has become a bit overblown, and I am not alone.[1] We are a bit ahead of ourselves in what we expect from a world that has ubiquitous connectivity, especially concerning interconnectivity. I can have my coffee maker online and for that handshake get some value through information and automation. But does it solve a problem? The coffee maker is smart enough and making a cup at home is the most money I'll save in regards to caffeine. So, what can I do to become a "networked client" and what services can I use to make my money smarter? Large financial institutions are deploying smarter code and pursuing automation as the next wave to drive proprietary profits,[2] and those innovations are starting to filter their way down to the retail market. So, how does a client implement them? Let's focus on what we can do within the networks we are already a part of, and usually for costs we are already incurring.

I have a smart device that I pay for, along with a monthly service fee. I can use this connectivity to make myself smarter, automate things that drive better behaviour and use it to communicate more effectively. A network easily accessed through these devices is that of information. It has never been easier to educate yourself financially. Do you prefer doing this through socialization? Use your social networks and the way those social networks embed themselves with other services to make decisions. Do you like educating yourself and conducting your own analysis? It has never been easier to tap into the vast network of analysts, economists and research that drive our world economy. I can usually do this with a few paid subscriptions or as value I get back for having an account at a wealth management firm. Even more "networked" and cool, if this information is on-demand and can often be surfaced based on what is relevant to me at a particular time.

---

[1] Parks Associates, IoT Strategy: "Smart home cloud platform trends", 20 January 2017.

[2] CBS News, Sunday Morning: "When the robots take over, will there be jobs left for us?", 9 April 2017; WSJ.com, Markets: "BlackRock bets on robots to improve its stock picking", 28 March 2017.

In the pursuit to help shape innovation and learn more about you, many firms provide personal financial wellness apps for free alongside their content. These are smart programs that form a network for you based on your financial transactions, accounts and topics that are important to you. They automatically and smartly glean trends and insights to inform you of your financial behaviour and in doing so make it easier to move money around so that it is in the right place at the right time. Begin using these services by aggregating your accounts. And remember, viewing in one place is not the same as having in one place. Think of the place you choose to do this as your personal financial command centre. You will have an easier time viewing everything in one place, it's easier to establish smart notifications and alerts to notify you of important activity and you are providing a fuller picture of your wealth and subsequent needs to providers that want to serve you. This approach will align your needs and financial firm resources in a much quicker fashion. The more firms can learn about you, the more likely you are to be provided with financial experts and products when you need them. Wealth management is no longer being driven by product; it is being driven by behaviour. Other "networks" you can harness are the various parties vying to have you as a customer. Instagram vs. Snap, Uber vs. Lyft, credit card points vs. frequent flyer miles, Facebook vs. Google, on and on. Each day you are given personalized, contextual opportunities to spend and often, the more you participate in the process the more you receive in return. As these systems integrate with and are adopted by our financial providers, we start to see the "networked client" coming alive in a truly comprehensive way.

In the meantime, financial advice providers can continue to learn a lot from their technology competition[3] – always reducing clicks and using the information they have to reduce my decision-making and data input. If you want me to take action based on a piece of information, serve it up in a pop-up notification on my phone and let me swipe it to interact more. Find ways to connect things to help me save and manage my day-to-day expenses (my monthly budget with my thermostat, for example), and don't improve something that doesn't need it. Help me know when things change, what communications are important and let's interact when something's actionable. If I can text a friend money, I should be able to do the same to fund a new account.

Devices are now an extension of us.[4] The more providers consider what I can use my device for and fit their products, services and interactions within it, the more likely I am to respond positively and repeatedly. Let's use financial planning as an example. A "networked client" wants to participate in the process when and how it is most convenient for her or him. So innovate to achieve that. Make the process collaborative, focus the technology on making me more informed when I need it most and let me interface with professionals in the way I like best. Maybe it's still face to face, but with live video.

What about the vast networks of financial products? Large institutions have figured that this is one of the best networks for automation, so it should follow that a "networked client" would too. Let managed, "smart" (algorithm-driven, factor-based/enhanced, AI-influenced, etc.) portfolios handle your long-term wealth management. If there is a portfolio management team behind it that you can trust and that provides good value, great. If there is a team of experts on sourcing and deploying technology to increase returns, even better. And if you find a way to automate this all together, then you're among an emerging frontier that will likely gain the most. Another area of automation that provides a bevy of apps to choose from are those services that automate your savings. These can do wonders to augment your behaviour and ease your interaction with your money. Does it take forever

---

[3] Accenture 2017 Financial Providers: Transforming Distribution Models for the Evolving Consumer.

[4] Think Advisor, Investment Advisor: "Envestnet's Jud Bergman on the Kasparov Principle: 'Humans plus machines deliver better outcomes' than either alone says the firm's CEO", 3 April 2017.

and cause a fight with your spouse to review your annual credit card summary? Download a smart budget app that categorizes your day-to-day spending and use it to take a more informed look at where you can save throughout the year. Have trouble not spending extra money if it stays in your account? Download a savings app that automatically finds and moves surpluses to designated goals.

A "networked client" is more valuable to those that want them as customers. In the short term, this can happen a lot faster with both sides working towards common use cases. Machines have made me stronger. Considering the way they're designed, deployed and connected can potentially make me wealthier too.

The Investment Managers of the Future are Going to be Millennials

By Jerry Floros
Founder and CEO, MoneyDrome Ltd

"FinTech" has taken the financial industry by storm. It has revolutionized many financial services and products that used to be the exclusive domain of banks and brokerages. The latter have slipped in market share and reputation due to legacy banking and outdated technical infrastructures. And the innovation train has left the station.

New financial technologies like bitcoin (cryptocurrency) and blockchain (distributed ledger) will take some time to reach mainstream adoption. However, common bank transactions such as payments, borrowing, lending foreign exchange transfers and wealth management are already building up momentum and the FCA (UK Financial Conduct Authority) is doing its fair share to make these new financial technologies available to the general public as soon as possible.

For some, FinTech might be bewildering with many new terms, concepts and financial products – such as bitcoin, blockchain, neobank, robo-advisory and Ethereum. The potential for losing market share to start-ups is just one of the reasons why big banks are pouring money into their own technology, as well as start-up ventures.

"Digital disruption has the potential to shrink the role and relevance of today's banks, and simultaneously help them create better, faster, cheaper services that make them an even more essential part of everyday life for institutions and individuals" wrote Julian Skan, Managing Director of Financial Services at Accenture, in a 2015 report. "To make the impact positive, banks are acknowledging that they need to shake themselves out of institutional complacency and recognize that merely navigating waves of regulation and waiting for interest rates to rise won't protect them from obsolescence."[1]

Many of the traditional banks and brokerages have had success with their own innovations, but for the most part it has been "copy and catch-up". It's only when the newcomers and challengers shake up an industry that the incumbents react, either denial at first – FinTech will eventually fade – or simply adopt a "crush the competition" strategy. Neither has worked, as more and more FinTech start-ups are entering the financial industry and disrupting every financial product or service available. This has benefitted retail investors and mass consumers alike, as now the entry barrier to investing and trading has been lowered to allow a greater number of average consumers to invest any surplus funds they may have sitting around in a savings account gathering dust.

With interest rates very low and tending into the negative zone (meaning we will eventually pay to store our savings at the bank), leaving one's savings in a savings account is simply "economic nonsense". However, the biggest challenge for the average consumer is access to wealth managers and financial markets, as well as financial knowledge and experience. Most traditional wealth management firms have a £500,000 minimum deposit requirement and in return they offer their standard fees of "2% + 20%" (2% management fee + 20% performance fee) for the management of your portfolio.

Innovative FinTech "robo-advisory" companies offer the same wealth management services online and have lowered the minimum deposit requirement to £10,000 for a fee structure of a mere 0.75% or less. Countless other "robo-advisors" have

---

[1] https://www.accenture.com/us-en/insight-future-fintech-banking.

sprung up and are offering even lower minimum deposits and fees, as well as "zero-robos" which are offering their services with zero percentage fees (presumably hoping to build up a large customer base and huge transaction volume as a new business model).

Information Overload

In the new era of superfast connectivity and digitization of everything, the biggest beneficiary is the millennial. But at the same time, the millennial is its weakest victim.

This dichotomy can be very easily explained. On the one side, we have the incredible power of knowledge combined with efficiency literally in the palm of our hands – smartphones – and on the other side, we are flooded with information, cascading down on us like a waterfall. The benefits are easy to see, the risk not so.

Having easy and instant access to a universe of knowledge has given the average person an incredible advantage over his "analogue predecessor". If anything, the speed and volume at which information is consumed is simply "mind-boggling" and something we take for granted.

Mobile and Mobility

Throughout history, there have always been times when innovation has unleashed an industrial revolution. The fourth industrial revolution is already taking place and in FinTech, the financial revolution has already started and is taking the financial industry by storm.

What at first appeared to be just a buzzword, FinTech is now fully entrenched in society and millennials are jumping the train from legacy banking. It is not only banking that is being disrupted, it is also the financial industry that is being revolutionized. And the main reasons for this are the mobile and mobility.

For millennials, being without their smartphone or at least connected online through a tablet, TV or laptop is inconceivable. It has reached the point of addiction. Just about everything is done on the smartphone, from checking e-mails and surfing the internet to posting on social media and banking.

This inevitable transition from analogue to digital has returned the decision-making process to the individual, because we are no longer dependent on third parties such as consultants and advisors to give us advice ("disintermediation"). Just about everything can be searched and researched on the internet and almost everything can be ordered online.

According to recent statistics, in 2017 there are an estimated 2.3 billion smartphone users worldwide and this number is expected to rise to 2.9 billion by 2020. It is estimated that by 2020, more than 70% of the world population will be using mobile phones, of which globally 6.1 billion will be smartphones.[2]

The "Ericsson Mobility Report"[3] details the trends and forecasts of the future, including the Internet of Things (IoT) and the impact of ultrafast broadband and 5G networks around the globe.

Network speeds and mobile usage penetration hold the key to technological advancements across the globe, because of network effects – the more that join, the more useful that network becomes. Smartphones have played a key role and will have an even greater impact in the FinTech world, because they will enable the unbanked/underbanked to be served and this financial inclusion will significantly expand the global financial markets.

---

[2] https://www.statista.com/statistics/330695/number-of-smartphone-users-worldwide/.

[3] https://www.ericsson.com/en/mobility-report.

User Experience and Digital Utility

User experience is the single most important aspect of digital disruption. Any website, app or platform that is successful is the result of a carefully designed and crafted user experience. The likes of Uber, Airbnb and Amazon have succeeded beyond their wildest dreams because they have focused strongly on their user experience.

There are five factors that greatly influence user experience:

- Fast – app and platform users value speed above all.
- Fluid – navigating around the user interface must be easy and smooth.
- Frictionless – anything that slows down or causes friction must be removed.
- Seamless – being able to switch seamlessly from one device to another.
- Intuitive – everything must be instinctive, self-explanatory and easy to use.

"Utility" is an economic term introduced by Daniel Bernoulli which refers to the total satisfaction received from consuming a good or service.[4] When all of the above elements are combined into a simple – and at the same time superior – user experience, the result is "digital utility".

Artificial Intelligence, Analytics and Big Data

Because of regulatory compliance, banks and financial institutions hold more data on financial transactions from around the globe than the financial markets themselves. In addition, these same banks and financial institutions store vast amounts of data from the suppliers, vendors, partners, customers and their own internal data and transaction infrastructures. Think Citibank, Goldman Sachs, HSBC, UBS, Credit Suisse, JP Morgan, Morgan Stanley, Blackrock, Barclays, Deutsche Bank… the list goes on and on.

So, what do these big financial companies do with all this data?

Well, they use it for their own best interests and profits. Although most of it is transactional data, most banks and financial institutions consider all their data proprietary. And for good reason too; after all, big data is power and profits.

The disruption and shrinking margins brought about by FinTech newcomers, as well as regulatory compliance, will compel those same banks and financial institutions to gradually start releasing and distributing their data through open APIs and third parties.

> The year 2018 is set to be a game-changing year for retail banking. As the PSD2 (Revised Payment Service Directive) becomes implemented, banks' monopoly on their customer's account information and payment services is about to disappear.
>
> In short, PSD2 enables bank customers, both consumers and businesses, to use third-party providers to manage their finances. In the near future, you may be using Facebook or Google to pay your bills, making P2P transfers and analyse your spending, while still having your money safely placed in your current bank account. Banks, however, are obligated to provide these third-party providers access to their customers' accounts through open APIs (application program interface). This will enable third-parties to build financial services on top of banks' data and infrastructure.[5]

The gradual use of big data will enable the financial industry to become more efficient and at the same time more profitable. It will

---

[4] https://en.wikipedia.org/wiki/Expected_utility_hypothesis.

[5] https://www.evry.com/en/news/articles/psd2-the-directive-that-will-change-banking-as-we-know-it/.

enable all parties involved to analyse and use this data to build better data infrastructures, become more efficient and give third-party developers a platform on which to design and build useful applications.

Digital banks and robo-advisors have led the way in integrating big data and analytics into their platforms, but there is still a long way to go. WealthTech innovators – such as digital investment managers, hybrid trading and blockchain platforms of all sorts – are pushing forward innovative financial products and services that were not even in existence a couple of years back. Innovative trading platforms and apps that incorporate artificial intelligence, machine learning and big data will have the comparative

advantage over their peers, as they will be able to provide a more integrated service to their platform users.

Retail investors will be offered all the tools, information and data that the traditional big banks and brokerages have used for the past several decades in the simplified technological format of an app on a smartphone. Digital disruption in finance will enable millennials to keep more of their financial gains and at the same time be more in control of their own finances.

Artificial intelligence, machine learning and big data analytics are the new frontiers of FinTech, and millennials will be at the forefront of digital disruption in the financial world.

Empowering Asset Owners and the Buy Side

By Dr Efi Pylarinou
Co-Founder, DailyFintech

There is an undisputable shift in the relationship between the sell side and the buy side. The balance of power is no longer overwhelmingly tilted towards Wall Street and the City, which was the case up until the 2007–2008 crisis. Stricter and more demanding regulatory requirements for financial service providers and the acceleration of tech innovations in financial services – FinTech – are the main drivers that have reshaped the rules governing the relationship between the sell side and the buy side.

It used to be that the sell side, with its few players and ever-increasing concentration of power over its clients (i.e. the buy side, which includes asset managers, mutual funds, pension funds, hedge funds, etc.), was acting more like lords. Nowadays, even though the buy side and the sell side continue to need each other, their relationship is rather one in which "The dealer has essentially been demoted from maître d' – deciding where everyone sits and recommending dishes – to a waiter taking orders", as described in a *Bloomberg Markets* article "The Rise of the Buy Side".[1]

As a result of the regulatory changes, the sell side (i.e. the JPMorgans, the Goldmans, etc.) have reduced their balance sheet activities, pooled back from risk-taking and, in several cases, pulled out of market-making activities. At the same time, buy-side firms (i.e. the Blackrocks of the world) have accumulated more inventory of assets and are, in many cases, in more need of the type of tools for analysis and risk management that the sell side customarily provided for them.

The current era is a customer-centric one. This is true not only for the end-user, the individual or otherwise (referred to as retail), but also at the B2B level. The buy side is the customer and the invisible market forces are pushing towards empowering them.

The Sell Side's Reaction to the New Era

Given the new reality imposed on the sell side, there has been ever-increasing pressure to restructure the business units serving buy-side clients that otherwise were significant sources of profitability.

A few of the large bulge bracket firms have chosen to divest their business units of portfolio and risk management analytics. These are businesses with multi-asset capabilities that had been built over years. Barclays, at the end of 2016, sold Point, their risk analytics and index business, to Bloomberg. UBS sold Delta to StatPro, a cloud-based performance and analytics provider for the buy side. Citi has spun off the legendary Yield Book analytics group and is looking to sell or IPO (public offer) this subsidiary. JPMorgan continues to operate and enhance JPMorgan Markets. Credit Suisse also maintains Locus.

The only sell-side company that is acting more like a platform is Goldman Sachs. They had developed an in-house portfolio and risk management system that was clearly ahead of its time 20 years ago:

> Securities Database, also known as SecDB, allows users to test out potential trades and assess the risk of those positions… it was so guarded that chief operating officer Gary Cohn said he wouldn't sell the rights to use the technology for US$1 billion—maybe for $5 billion, the Journal reported.[2]

---

[1] https://www.bloomberg.com/news/features/2016-08-15/the-rise-of-the-buy-side.

[2] http://www.marketwatch.com/story/goldman-sachs-has-started-giving-away-its-most-valuable-software-2016-09-07-71034235.

Deutsche Bank and the likes were salivating in the previous era, to licence such a system. Fast-forward to today and this same sophisticated risk management tool, whose key technology is a relational database (instead of the commonly used sequential databases), is being offered for free to Goldman Sachs' clients. This tool, along with free access to Marquee (software that integrates Goldman Sachs technology for the entire trade cycle) and Simon (a structured products marketplace), are empowering buy-side clients for their needs across the entire life cycle of an investment. Simon is focused on structured products and helps clients design products based on their hedging needs or investment views, instead of spending hours on the phone with sales and trading. Goldman Sachs aims to increase their equity-linked note business and to become a platform for brokers or other distribution channels that have access to a broader buy-side segment.

SecDB is mobile and can capture cross effects and domino effects in a complex portfolio, and calculate real-time, meaningful and more accurate risk metrics. This is the technology that allowed Goldman Sachs to navigate the 2007–2008 crisis in a much better way than other sell-side firms, even though they were actually deeply involved.

Rest-of-Market Positioning in the New Era

Asset owners are either individuals or institutions. Both groups either choose to manage these assets on their own, or choose a buy-side entity to manage their assets (an asset manager, a hedge fund, a pension fund, a mutual fund, etc.).

The buy side remains loyal to the ubiquitous Bloomberg Terminal and many FinTech incubators continue to deter early-stage entrepreneurs from attempting to disrupt that positioning. The Bloomberg portfolio and analytics platform, PORT, is being transformed by offering buy-side clients (that are already Bloomberg Terminal customers) a pay-as-you-go-type app store for their mobile needs and additional FinTech modular services. The Eikon Thomson Reuters offering is also adding value, with a desktop and mobile version, and an app store with improvements in its analytics capabilities and continuous integration of FinTech capabilities.

Several FinTech start-ups are targeting asset owners directly, with an offering that empowers the buy side or do-it-yourself (DIY) asset owners.

Robinhood, a zero-commission equity broker, is an example of eliminating brokerage fees in equities and exchange traded funds (ETFs) (operating in the USA and Australia for now). Robinhood continues to build partnerships that (directly or indirectly) empower the buy side and independent asset owners. For example, a collaboration with the investment research network Closing Bell, which serves independent and buy-side analysts, traders, investors, wealth managers and Wall Street research firms; a partnership with the social trading network StockTwits and the crowdsourced hedge fund platform Quantopian.

Alpha Modus offers bespoke solutions (Mods) that are truly alpha-generating strategies. It is bringing the cognitive capabilities of IBM Watson to financial markets (for now only for US equities) to design customized alpha-generating algorithms tailored to any buy-side investment philosophy. For example, an Equity Tactical Mod, which is a smart beta strategy based on taking positions on the S&P 500 and the Euro Stoxx 50; the Early Look pre-15:45PM EST Imbalance Meter for NYSE-listed stocks, which captures unstructured imbalance information starting at 14:50PM EST through 15:45PM EST each afternoon. The Mod store offers an alternative approach to asset management.

Electronifie and Trumid are one entity as of March 2017, focused on improving trading conditions for corporate bond investors. Their unified platforms aim to improve transparency, price discovery and liquidity in the corporate bond market, in which the buy side holds most of the inventory. Empowering the buy side and corporate bond asset owners is paramount in a fixed-income market which, despite continued strong bond issuance, faces huge liquidity and fragility problems.

Contineo, out of Hong Kong, is creating a community and a platform for wealth mangers and private bankers to access issuers of equity-linked structured products. This is an over-the-counter (OTC) market that is in great need of more transparency, flexible product design and post-trade management. A market that Simon on the Goldman Sachs platform is also serving.

Conclusion

Regulation has changed the relationship of the sell side and the buy side. WealthTech is an unstoppable trend that continues to transform this relationship. This tech-enabled push started from outside Wall Street and the City, from FinTech start-ups, and continues within the digital transformation of sell-side companies (e.g. Goldman Sachs, JPMorgan, etc.).

On the one hand, Goldman Sachs from the sell side is leading in making a bold choice to empower its buy-side clients with its free, sophisticated tools. The longer-term strategic vision is to become a platform (on which value is created) serving the buy side. It remains to be seen whether others who have not divested their portfolio and risk management capabilities (e.g. Morgan Stanley, Deutsche Bank, Credit Suisse, etc.) will follow suit as part of a broader "platformification" transformation that empowers their buy-side clients. In five years' time we probably won't be using the terms sell side and buy side any more. We will be focused on the customers, the clients, the asset owners or gatherers and the platforms that serve and empower them.

On the other hand, and at the same time, FinTechs will continue to empower asset owners with tools that lower costs, offer transparency, enable the faster and better discovery of opportunities, and are customized or contextualized. Services that were only available in the past from the sell side, which led to an imbalanced relationship between the sell side and the buy side, in favour of the former. The next phase or level of empowerment for asset owners will come with the integration of these scattered FinTech tools on platforms.

Last but not least, traditional data and analytics providers like Bloomberg and Thomson Reuters are also transforming their offerings and empowering their clients, by creating app stores and integrating FinTech tools in their mobile platforms.

An Industry Driven by Digital, Data and Artificial Intelligence

By Alpesh Doshi
Managing Partner, CEO, Fintricity

The Old Guard

With the turmoil of 2008, we saw a microscopic lens fall upon the financial services industry. Investment banking and capital markets were primarily the areas scrutinized by the regulators, governments and the general public, and the so-called "casino banking" that took place. The banking industry had never had it so good, with previous deregulation and trading freedoms to invent financial products which benefit both industry and investors.

However, the most likely to suffer in the market, either directly through defunct mortgages or through mutual funds or other collective investment vehicles, were investors. Investors in this context include pension funds, mutual funds, family offices, sovereign wealth funds, high-net-worth individuals (HNWIs) and retail clients.

The asset and wealth management industry was largely seen as a victim, rather than part of the problem. If we look at the performance of asset management over the past 30 years, we have consistently seen the underperformance of active management. With fees considered, a large majority of the funds have not, on average, delivered good performance over their lifetime. Fundamentally, the industry has "no economic justification for being as large and rich" as it is.[1] It has made fund managers and fund management company owners wealthy, but the investors who pay their fees have not had their returns.

Current Market and Innovation

With the emergence of new technologies and business models, the industry is ripe for disruption. However, incumbents do not appear to be concerned, even though they pay lip service to innovation and are purporting to undertake a digital transformation. Clayton Christensen has famously said that it is mostly difficult for incumbents to innovate due to their blind spot for disruption.[2] It is difficult to see for the industry because of the ingrained assumptions, processes and, more than that, arrogance and complacency that permeates senior management. When threats come from innovative companies outside their traditional set of competitors, they find it hard to imagine that the industry will be disrupted. Furthermore, the ability for these businesses to shift their operating and business models because of vested economic interests (and the internal capability to make that transformation) is often lacking.

The Future Will be an Industry That is Digital

Digitization enables easier access to alternative asset classes (e.g. private equity, venture capital, hedge funds) and new asset classes. For example, initial coin offerings (ICOs) have emerged as a new way of investing in companies. These offerings have grown significantly in 2016/2017 and will continue to do so.

There is also a large movement in the traditional asset management industry from active to passive-based investments, and the move has gathered pace. Boston Consulting Group forecast that between 2016 and 2020, passive asset investment such as ETFs (exchange-traded funds) will account for 42% of all

---

[1] Fox, J. (2013) "Just how useless is the asset-management industry?" https://hbr.org/2013/05/just-how-useless-is-the-asset.

[2] Christensen, C. M., Raynor, M. E. and McDonald, R. (2015) "What is disruptive innovation?" https://hbr.org/2015/12/what-is-disruptive-innovation.

investments – up from 10% in 2008 – with a total market size of $71 trillion.[3] In addition to this, a growing interest into robo-advisors and purely digital asset management continues, with companies like Betterment and Wealthfront also growing.

The Coming Shifts

Shifting sentiments, better and more easily accessible investment choices, better access to data/information and transformation of multiple industries to new business models are some of the reasons why the asset and wealth management industry is likely to change. Technology-driven democratization is driving smaller family offices and retail investors to look for alternative ways of investing, with the promise of lower fees, transparency and better returns.

As new asset and wealth managers emerge, they will use digital, data and analytics-driven models to provide scalability, accessibility and transparency, and more liquid and wide-ranging choices to investors. The end-to-end management of investments will be almost completely automated, and decisions will be driven by aggregated data, artificial intelligence (AI) and machine learning models, algorithms and risk models and, finally, the whole stack will be supported by the application of blockchain technology. For investors, this change will offer a multitude of benefits:

- **Transparency** of their entire portfolio, visibility of asset performance, real-time risk calculations and detailed data on their assets.
- **Granular control of assets** using digital channels and real-time adjustment of portfolios.

- **Management,** of active or passive investment strategies, diversification and easier regulatory reporting and analytics.
- **Access to countless** investment opportunities offered by digital channel purchasing and management.

The 21st-Century Asset and Wealth Manager

The digital asset or wealth manager of the 21st century will be driven by machine learning AI, engaged and managed through digital technologies, and will leverage the emerging new economy models.

Emerging new economy models are transforming how investors can reach and invest in businesses, driven by data/AI, transparent, with new risk and investment models. Traditional asset and wealth managers cannot reach those investment opportunities that are emerging.

Marketplace lending and crowdfunding. This model is suited for investors wanting to put their money into marketplaces. Building out new risk, credit and investment models with data-provided marketplaces (and other external, public and proprietary sources) enables individual investments as well as portfolio investments. Active and passive models also exist, again driven by data and leveraging AI and machine learning models for investment.

Blockchain-based ICOs. As new investment routes are emerging through ICOs, investors can invest in those offerings directly. These are potentially high-risk investment types. Numerai, for example, combines new types of AI-driven investment by issuing their own token to investors.[4]

[3] Boston Consulting Group (2016) "BCG Perspectives – Global Asset Management 2016: Doubling Down on Data". https://www.bcgperspectives.com/content/articles/financial-institutions-global-asset-management-2016-doubling-down-on-data/.

[4] Metz, C. (2017) "An AI hedge fund created a new currency to make Wall Street work like open source". https://www.wired.com/2017/02/ai-hedge-fund-created-new-currency-make-wall-street-work-like-open-source/.

New economy companies. With digital transformation on the rise, new economy companies need investment in a different model compared to the traditional asset and wealth management models. For example, Uber drivers who require loans for their cars cannot get them from traditional lenders or investors. With the availability of data and analytics of drivers from these types of companies, new investment models can be created to enable digital investment and management.

Emerging markets investments. As the emerging markets grow and start-ups create new operating models, investors have the opportunity to reach these businesses through digital investment channels where asset managers do not invest directly or can't reach them.

We are also seeing the emergence of new types of hedge funds, driven by machine learning and AI models. Sentient Technologies (which raised $143 million of funding) and Aidyia (a Hong Kong-based hedge fund) are building these funds from the ground up, applying these new models.[5]

New Opportunities and the Future

Investors are now restless. They're not seeing traditional asset managers provide returns or reasonable fees. With liquidity being abundant, investors (family offices, institutional investors, sovereign wealth funds, pension funds, retails investors) are more willing to look for alternative investment opportunities and channels. As the world undergoes a digital transformation, and with the emergence of new businesses, markets and operating models, the time is right for a new way. A new set of asset and wealth managers are coming. They are driving operating models and costs significantly lower than the incumbents. They are transforming investment in traditional listed markets, driven by leveraging machine learning and AI, and they are looking at their own (and market) transformation by leveraging technologies like blockchain to make themselves even more efficient. These managers will move away from stock picking and identify new sources of alpha.

New and emerging start-ups are attacking every aspect of the traditional asset and wealth manager, by focusing on new business models such as marketplace investment models, where the firms don't need to comply with the regulations of traditional asset management firms (because they don't have a fund structure or take investments on their own book). Digital asset management businesses are built differently, by creating a fantastic digital customer experience, automated underwriting and investment processes, agile software development methodologies and transparency built in. They provide end-to-end investment control and management of their investments in real time, and clearly and concisely declare fees, with these fees being significantly lower and not based on a percentage of assets under management (AUM) but fixed charges regardless of portfolio size.

The engine of these companies is driven by collecting, organizing and feeding data into their own machine learning and AI models, and continuously evolving those models, refining them for better underwriting, risk and investment.

The future's bright, and the future of asset management may already be here through the new start-ups. Watch out BlackRock, they're coming!

---

[5] Metz, C. (2016) "The rise of the artificially intelligent hedge fund". https://www.wired.com/2016/01/the-rise-of-the-artificially-intelligent-hedge-fund/.

WealthTech – Taking Private Banking and Wealth Management Digital

By **Dr Daniel Diemers**
Partner Financial Services, PwC Strategy

The Analogue Castle of Wealth Management is Under Siege

In recent years, private banking and wealth management (PBWM) executives have been so busy staying abreast of new regulatory issues and the associated fundamental changes to their business models that most have understandably had little time to explore the latest developments in technology and assess their impact. But while digital has not fundamentally disrupted the PBWM industry yet, it becomes clear that executives around the world are required to make clear choices on where and how they want to play in a digital age. Enter WealthTech, as a specialized form of FinTech. The question of WealthTech is not if it will disrupt PBWM, but when.

Clients Request Tailored Solutions and "Bring Back the Fun"

The urgency comes from clients themselves, who prefer solid brands and long-term relationships, but whose lifestyle becomes increasingly digital beyond financial services. Also, client satisfaction with today's PBWM services is not overly high. In a recent study, only 39% of interviewed high-net-worth individuals (HNWIs) would recommend their current PBWM provider to a friend. With HNWIs above $10 million assets under management (AUM) that rate drops – counter-intuitively – even down to 29%. An alarming statistic indeed in an industry that typically relies heavily on referrals, image and word-of-mouth.[1]

---

[1] PwC (2016) "Strategy & Global Wealth Management Study: Sink or Swim". http://www.strategyand.pwc.com/media/file/Sink-or-swim.pdf.

Survey results showed that affluent, high-net-worth (HNW) and ultra-high-net-worth (UHNW) clients clearly want a provider that matches their needs and lifestyle, and provides a tailored, highly customized user experience. They also request more transparency: on risks, on pricing, on peer choices and on competitors' offerings and benchmarks. It is 2018 not the 1990s, after all. The quality of advice, interestingly, still stands at the heart of a PBWM offering, in line with the most-cited preference around wealth preservation and generation, but clients also want more fun, engagement and entertainment alongside.

Understanding the Relevant Technologies for WealthTech

Talking to many PBWM executives across Europe, the Middle East and Asia, most of them clearly understand the shifting tectonics of their industry. However, basic knowledge about some of the key technologies is usually low to very low. But in order to make the right strategic decisions, a clear understanding of what is coming at you with WealthTech is critical, isn't it? Artificial intelligence (AI) and machine learning (ML), for example, have not been deployed broadly yet across PBWM, but the potential is big. Supporting advisory processes is just one of the many applications, and AI/ML will fundamentally change the way investment products are originated, managed and distributed. Also, AI/ML can transform mid- and back-office processes so that they no longer need (many) people to run them.

Big data and cloud-based services are introducing new ways of managing data within the PBWM industry. But the new PBWM level playing field requires PBWM players who are able to leverage all the data available – internally and externally – to provide the best and most tailored service possible to their clients. And that means managing data well. Cloud-based services are also gradually becoming as common as in other industries. And utilities (e.g. for know-your-customer (KYC), anti-money laundering (AML) and client onboarding, or product data) will further reduce cost-to-serve in an industry under margin pressure.

Cryptocurrencies – still for many a source of scepticism – will soon become just another asset class and foreign currency. As the first providers are launching cryptocurrency-based investment products, the first mutual fund products are coming to the market, with many more to follow. Thus the time is ripe to open up to a new trend in global money and payments, especially as the next generation of clients will definitely be much more open to cryptocurrencies than today's clients. Blockchain, alongside cryptocurrencies, has been one of the most hyped technologies over the past one or two years. It is beyond doubt that blockchain can help rationalize mid- and back-office processes in the PBWM industry, and reduce costs for registries, custody, trading, clearing and settlement. The first applications are already being tested, and blockchain has definitely moved "out of the lab", as a recent survey among 1300 global banking professionals shows.[2]

Another technology to watch is virtual and augmented reality (VR/AR). While still in its infancy 20 years after the first experiments in the 1990s, this is probably one of the most disruptive technologies for PBMW – not in the short term, but over the coming three to five years and beyond. VR/AR will radically change the way we interact with people, computers and the internet. In PBWM this technology will also change the way we advise, how we represent data to our client and how we work internally in the industry.

Barbarians at the Gate? – The Forces of Disruption

Disruption is felt within financial services, no doubt. In the most recent 2017 edition of PwC's global FinTech survey, 80% of respondents felt that their business model was under threat of disruption. Poking a bit deeper, the most prominent fears are (in order of importance): (a) increased margin pressure; (b) loss of

market share to attackers; (c) data protection issues and threat to client privacy; (d) increased customer churn.[3]

With regard to where the disruption will be coming from exactly, the jury is still out. There are three likely camps. Either banks or wealth managers themselves will apply these new technologies in such an innovative way that they will create or adapt their business models for the future. Another source of disruption could be from non-banks, which rapidly innovate and suddenly enter the market with new offerings. Similar patterns have been seen in other industries. As a third group, large tech companies – the Amazons, Alibabas, WeChats, Googles and Facebooks of the world – strategically decide to leverage WealthTech to enter the PBWM arena, where margins are still significantly higher than in other industries.

Act Now: Strategic "Ways to Play" in WealthTech

In the WealthTech future, private banks and wealth managers will have four possible strategies to choose from, within client preferences that range from face-to-face communication to digital only, and from delegators ("manage my wealth") to self-selectors ("I manage my money myself"). These four strategies (traditional face-to-face models, online-only platforms and robo-advisory, and hybrid models, "high-tech/high-touch"), as shown in Figure 1, can be pursued either stand-alone or in combination (likely the choice of large international banks).[4]

For traditional PBWM incumbents, hybrid models are clearly the best strategy going forward, as the traditional face-to-face model can be largely maintained in that approach while new, innovative ways to deploy WealthTech can be chosen. Thus, the business

[2] PwC (2017) "Global Fintech Report". https://www.pwc.com/gx/en/industries/financial-services/assets/pwc-fintech-exec-summary-2017.pdf.

[3] PwC (2017) "Global Fintech Report". https://www.pwc.com/gx/en/industries/financial-services/assets/pwc-fintech-exec-summary-2017.pdf.

[4] PwC (2013) "Strategy & Viewpoint: Taking Wealth Management Digital". http://www.strategyand.pwc.com/reports/taking-wealth-management-digital.

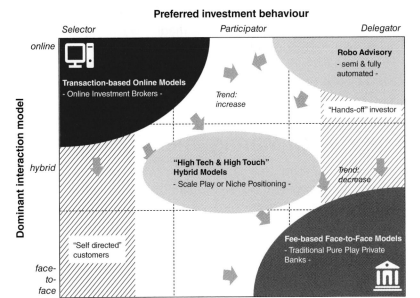

Figure 1: Four strategic choices in WealthTech

The diagram includes the following labels:

Preferred investment behaviour — Selector — Participator — Delegator

Dominant interaction model — online — hybrid — face-to-face

Transaction-based Online Models
- Online Investment Brokers -

Trend: increase

Robo Advisory
- semi & fully automated -

"Hands-off" investor

"High Tech & High Touch" Hybrid Models
- Scale Play or Niche Positioning -

Trend: decrease

"Self directed" customers

Fee-based Face-to-Face Models
- Traditional Pure Play Private Banks -

model needs to remain agile and resilient, and change fluidly as the market and client behaviours evolve.

How to Win in "High-Tech/ High-Touch"?

Easier said than done. In talking to PBWM executives in Europe and the Middle East, many confess that they struggle (primarily internally) to get the organization and strategic direction headed towards a hybrid "high-tech/high-touch" business model. After all, the cultural and technological legacy in PBWM weighs in heavily, while clients, especially in mature markets, are not pushing the envelope on innovative business models. There are a well-documented number of ingredients to a successful and winning recipe: invest, partner, cooperate, co-create with your clients, foster internal innovation, etc. But most importantly: put the right strategy in place and align the culture around it. And if the culture doesn't fit, change it. All the mentioned initiatives will help transform a traditional PBWM culture over time.

While it is hard to predict precisely which technologies will disrupt PBWM and how, it is clear that the industry will be transformed via WealthTech. All the above-mentioned technologies that form part of WealthTech exist and are irreversible (i.e. they will enter PBWM and WealthTech will not just "go away"). We all struggle naturally with the basic understanding that many of these changes are happening on an exponential curve, not in a linear fashion. Just like Moore's law shows a doubling of computer power every two years, the above-mentioned technologies will provide opportunities in three to five years that seem impossible today.

Final Remarks and Outlook

Some open questions remain though. How will regulation of PBWM evolve? The current trend points to higher degrees of regulation, with a specific focus on consumer protection and full transparency of data. The latter point collides with a very traditional theme around PBWM, which is client confidentiality and privacy. Regarding data handling and protection, we currently see two fundamentally different approaches: the "US model" drives full disclosure and an open market for client data, while the "EU model" defends a more citizen-centric "right to own your data" approach. New, innovative PBWM business models – especially cross-border – will depend on the outcome of these two opposing, potentially antagonizing, antitheses.

To summarize, WealthTech is forcing the PBWM industry to rethink models and mindsets. We can sit back and react more or less passively to technological developments, or we can view digital transformation as an opportunity to get closer than ever before to our clients. The choice is ours, and technology can either help along the journey to "high-tech/high-touch", WealthTech-driven business models or become a disruptive force that will transform those too slow to adapt to the new realities.

The Wealth Management Canvas – A Framework for Designing the WealthTech Firm of the Future

By Dr Claude Diderich
Managing Director, Diderich Consulting LLC

Many WealthTech firms are facing challenging times because they have often not fully designed their business model. Understanding how technology can help investment customers satisfy their needs and fulfil their jobs to be done is key for success and to deliver value. The wealth management canvas provides a framework to support WealthTech firms in designing and validating their business models in a holistic way. It relates innovative technologies to the value proposition and allows us to define a sustainable competitive advantage. It is a proven tool for transforming creative WealthTech ideas into viable businesses. It focuses on those aspects that matter most and helps avoid many pitfalls.

Numerous WealthTech firms face challenging times because they only focus on one area in their business model. First, many young technology companies, trying to compete in the wealth management space, implement strategies for delivering value to their customers, relying on differentiation through technological capabilities. They build innovative user experiences (like simplifying client risk profiling or introducing chatbots), automate business processes (like rebalancing portfolios), or try using artificial intelligence algorithms to forecast financial markets. Second, the inclination to assume knowing better what customer needs are than the customers themselves – a weakness found in numerous traditional wealth management business models – is spilling over to start-ups. Believing that investors' sole goal is seeking absolute positive return is a fallacy. The third, and probably most critical, flaw of many WealthTech business models is that they fail to answer the question: "Why would a customer be willing to pay (a premium) for the product or service offered?" This is even truer for those business models where the individual paying for the offering is not identical to the one consuming it. Prominent examples of business models in this category are fund selection platforms, risk profiling systems, or investment reporting tools.

The Wealth Management Canvas

Addressing identified weaknesses of many WealthTech strategies requires the involvement of stakeholders covering different areas of expertise. Success depends on stakeholders understanding each other through speaking a common language. In addition, it is key to ensure that potential blind spots in the business model are identified and fixed early in the design process. To approach these challenges, I adapted and extended the prominent business model canvas, invented by Osterwalder and Pigneur (2010),[1] to the WealthTech industry, focusing on the challenges faced in the age of digitization. This led me to introduce the *Wealth Management Canvas* (WMC) framework shown in Figure 1.

The WMC comprises four main dimensions (one colour per dimension), coinciding with the four *strategy views* introduced by Diderich (2016)[2]:

1. Customer segments and their jobs to be done (see top left four boxes), focusing on

   - identifying customer needs, through applying the jobs to be done theory (Christensen *et al.*, 2016),[3]

---

[1] Osterwalder, A. and Pigneur, Y. (2010). *Business Model Generation.* Hoboken, NJ: John Wiley & Sons.

[2] Diderich, C. (2016). "Initiating the strategy process using design thinking". 36th Strategic Management Society (SMS) Annual International Conference. Berlin, Germany. https://ssrn.com/abstract=2927941.

[3] Christensen, C. M., Hall, T., Dillon, K. and Duncan, D. S. (2016). *Competing Against Luck.* New York: HarperCollins.

Jobs To Be Done

- What jobs are customers trying to get done?
- Which needs do they have?
- What pains are they suffering from?
- What is the value associated to those needs?

Trust Building Channels

- How are new customers identified/acquired?
- How are customers retained?
- How is trust in the value proposition managed?

Value Proposition

- What value is delivered?
- Which jobs to be/needs to be done are addressed?
- How is uncertainty of success managed?
- What happens in the case of failure?

Return Generating Activities

- How is performance generation supported?
- How does return generation relate to the investment philosophy?

Risk Management Activities

- How is risk defined?
- How is risk managed?
- What can go wrong?
- How does risk management relate to the investment philosophy?

Investment Philosophy

- What fundamental beliefs about markets are assumed?
- What underlying theory is relied upon?

Other Unique Activities

- What unique activities (excluding return generation and risk management) are required to deliver the value proposition?
- What activities support the trust building channels?
- How is the offering delivery managed and monitored?
- How is the relationship with services providers managed?
- What key checks and balances are in place to ensure legal and regulatory compliance?

Customer Segments

- Whom is value created for?
- What are their common characteristics/uniqueness?
- Who is deciding on the purchase?
- Who is paying the bill?
- Who is explicitly not considered?

Legal and Regulatory Delivery

- Which legal/regulatory requirements need to be fulfilled?
- What legal delivery structures are used?
- Who is owning which part of the delivery process?
- How are potential conflicts of interest avoided?

Offering

- What are the features?
- What is the relationship between offering and value proposition?
- How are promises made delivered upon?

Skills

- What key skills are required?
- Who provides these skills?
- How is longevity ensured?

Resources (incl. technology)

- What technology is required?
- How many human resources are needed?

Service providers

- Who are the key service providers?
- What is their contribution?

Revenue Streams

- Who is paying?
- How many paying customers are expected per segment?
- What is the price sensitivity of each customer segment?
- How is the willingness to pay of each customer segment characterized?

Pricing Models

- How does the price relate to value?
- How are customers preferring to pay?
- Are revenues one-off or recurring?
- Does the pricing model include contingencies?
- What indicators is price related to?

Investments

- Which upfront investments are required?
- How are investments financed?
- How will investments be amortized?

Expenses

- Which major expenses are incurred?
- What indicators do expenses relate to?
- What is the cost of trust building?
- What potential claims may exist in the case of not delivering the value proposition?

Figure 1: The Wealth Management Canvas

Note: The Wealth Management Canvas is derived work based on the Business Model Canvas from Strategyzer.com and released under Creative Commons Attribution Share Alike 4.0 international license.

- segmenting customers according to their needs, their value perception and their willingness to pay for having their needs satisfied,
- ensuring that customer segments and offerings relate to each other through making the trust-building channel explicit, as well as
- securing legal and regulatory delivery requirements.

2. Offering an associated value proposition (see central column), ensuring that
   - the offering consistently allows delivering the value proposition promised based on a well-defined investment philosophy, and
   - the offering's value proposition matches with customer jobs to be done.

3. Capabilities (see top right 6 boxes), subdivided into

- return generation and risk management activities, as well as other unique activities required to deliver the promised value proposition,
- required skills and resources, including access to specific knowledge and unique technologies, as well as
- key service providers, answering the make or buy decision.

4. Financials (see bottom row), covering

- revenue streams and associated pricing models (Ramanujam and Tacke, 2016)[4], and
- required investments and incurred expenses.

Developing a WealthTech business model using the WMC requires answering questions related to all 17 building blocks shown in Figure 1. Coherence between the building blocks must be ensured. For example, does the value proposition relate to actual jobs customers in the identified segment are looking to get done? Are the investment philosophy and the activities managing return and risk aligned? Consistency throughout the business model description not only supports telling a great story, it also ensures that the business model will work in practice.

Avoiding Pitfalls Through Validation

Before starting to implement a business model designed using the WMC, three questions need to be answered (Brown, 2009)[5]:

- Is the offering desirable from a customer perspective? This can be shown using the WMC by ensuring a link between the value proposition, the offering and the jobs to be done of the targeted customer segment. Avoid averaging out customer segments and be reminded that no one size fits all.
- Can the offering and associated value proposition be delivered? This means ensuring that the applied activities, skills, resources and service providers support the delivery of the offering. Beware of focusing too much on technology and back-testing.
- Is the offering economically viable? Answering this question means ensuring that the expected revenue streams cover the investments and expenses incurred. To assess the willingness to pay, the trust-building channel of the WMC plays a critical role. It ensures that the targeted customers can be acquired and retained.

Designing the Business Model of RoboRebalance

To illustrate how the WMC works, consider designing a hypothetical business model for RoboRebalance, a WealthTech firm. Assume tech-savvy individuals investing their wealth in portfolios of 20 to 30 stocks, exchange-traded funds and mutual funds as customers [customer segment]. Rather than actively managing the holdings, they want to keep portfolio risk constant over time. They are looking for a solution that rebalances their portfolio whenever necessary and minimizes transaction costs. In addition, they are concerned with their privacy [jobs to be done]. To satisfy the customers' needs, RoboRebalance proposes offering a software solution that runs on their computer and interfaces with their bank of choice through application programming interfaces (APIs) [offering]. Using a rebalancing algorithm based on published academic literature, considering bank-specific transaction costs [investment philosophy], the software analyses their portfolios for changes in risk, automatically generates transactions and sends them to the banks for execution if and when needed. Running the software on their computer rather than in the cloud addresses their concerns over privacy [value proposition].

[4] Ramanujam, M. and Tacke, G. (2016). *Monetizing Innovation*. Hoboken, NJ: John Wiley & Sons.

[5] Brown, T. (2009). *Change by Design*. New York: HarperCollins.

RoboRebalance licenses the software, in a joint effort with multiple banks, aiming at a win–win situation (RoboRebalance sells software licences and the banks provide transactions and custody services) [trust-building channel]. The separation of roles and responsibilities is such that RoboRebalance does the transaction calculations and provides them as advice, whereas the bank executes them and ensures custody. RoboRebalance operates solely as a technology provider, not requiring any banking or asset management licences [legal and regulatory delivery].

Moving to the blue capability part of the WMC, performance is defined by the return of the targeted portfolio, net of costs [return-generating activities] and risk as the portfolio's volatility, estimated using implied option volatility and historical correlations [risk-management activities]. Other key activities to consider are handling the API between the bank and the software as well as implementing and supporting the rebalancing algorithm. In addition, managing the relationship with supported banks is important, both on the marketing and on the technology side [other unique activities].

Key skills [skills] required are rebalancing algorithm expertise as well as knowledge around using APIs to communicate with banks [service providers]. Key resources required are data to calculate portfolio characteristics and risk [resources]. When analysing the economic aspects of the designed business model,

RoboRebalance is licensing the software to the customers, charging an annual fee related to the number of securities in the portfolio to be managed [pricing model, revenue streams]. No cash flows are exchanged between RoboRebalance and the banks, avoiding any potential conflicts of interest. Key investments made are in the development of the software system [investment] and expenses are software support, managing the relationship with the supported banks and handling the trust-building channel, as well as sales and marketing [expenses].

Concluding Remarks

The WMC is a simple framework for describing the business model of any WealthTech firm. It ensures that the three key challenges most technology start-ups are confronted with are addressed. It provides a comprehensive approach, avoiding the trap of focusing only on technology and ignoring customer needs. The WMC makes sure that actual customer needs are satisfied by requiring customer jobs to be done to be made explicit and matched with value propositions for which unique activities exist. Finally, relating the revenue stream and pricing model back to the value proposition guarantees that customers are willing to pay for the offering delivered.

Success depends on developing the right offerings for the right customer segments at the right price.

The Ingredients of IKEA's Approach for a Starry Wealth Management – Choose to Change the Competitive Arena in a Mature Sector

By Dr Alessandro Bologna
Investment Advisor, Deutsche Bank S.p.A. – Wealth Management

While waiting for the birth of my first son, I prepared the room that would welcome him. When I had finished putting together a chest of drawers bought at IKEA, I was seized by a mood of satisfaction mixed with pride that led me to wonder: "How is it possible that I am so happy to buy furniture in a box that I need to bring home and in addition build too?" Reflecting on the distinctive features that convinced me to be an IKEA customer, I might mention:

- fair pricing
- the perception of a good level of quality
- simplicity of instructions
- modern and attractive design
- the satisfaction of always being able to successfully complete the task and a wonderful catalogue that allows you to view the result in advance.

I therefore asked myself what ingredients Mr Kamprad used to change the competition within a sector that is highly mature and saturated. We can clearly see an analogy with wealth management: a very mature market with players who have to reinvent themselves in order to remain competitive. In addition, the disruption is coming from other sectors – technological innovation in products, processes and channels, combined with the dissatisfaction of the end customers and the reduction of margins.

In the following paragraphs I will try to identify the ingredients that made it possible for IKEA to move to a different competitive level and apply them to a business model in the wealth management industry.

The proposed approach allows us to move away from the current selling proposition to a new way of service that creates real customer involvement and engagement through contributing to the process of value creation and minimizing, at the same time, the typical cognitive and behavioural mistakes of relationship managers, which often give sub-optimal results.

The model outlined below could be used for a single goal, multiple objectives or a holistic approach, with a focus on the real needs of customers with an adequate time horizon, an educational involvement that explains step by step what and why something is done, with related check points during the life of the relationship. The ingredients replicable from the IKEA business case are as follows.

Stripping Out the Basic Elements

IKEA decomposes single items of furniture into their essential elements. This system allows them to check the quality and consistency of each single element that contributes to the construction of the overall result. In the same way, an advanced approach to wealth management should start from the client's needs, focusing on important goals, each one with the essential characteristics well identified as follows:

1. Time horizon.
2. The financial objective connected to the goal:
   - minimum acceptable
   - optimal target.

3. Available capital:
   - initial capital
   - periodic in/outflows
   - the debt to service the objective.
4. Prioritization among other goals.

The ongoing monitoring will be done through the probability of reaching the goal within the relevant time horizon. The value added of this kind of approach, such as for IKEA, is modularity (i.e. you can use it for a single goal or may implement a holistic approach, considering pension plans, succession, long life cycle and insurance coverage). In addition to all the above mentioned, you can have an upstream optimization between objectives with different time horizons and different grades of priority assigned, thanks to an asset and liability management (similar to that used, for example, by pension funds).

Do It Yourself and Education

Another winning and discriminating element in IKEA's recipe is the DIY mechanism and educational approach, a sort of gamification. This has three main aspects and implications:

1. High level of engagement and satisfaction for the client, who is able to successfully finish the task.
2. Impact on pricing – for IKEA, in terms of cost reduction of logistics, transportation and assembly and for the client, due to less return costs of products.
3. Loyalty, through a process of education and involvement that leads clients to feel they are part of the production process and aware of the constructive logic and quality (experience).

It is possible to achieve the same benefits in wealth management by applying DIY involvement, fulfilment and satisfaction, putting the client at the heart of a goal-based approach. Using a goal-based investment model has the positive collateral effect of minimizing the typical errors identified by behavioural finance, such as overconfidence and unrealistic optimism. This kind of approach confirms the client as the primary actor in the process and enhances the traditional approach twofold. First, the approach anchors each goal to the correct time horizon, minimizing anxiety and temporary volatility. Second, financial literacy and education have to be a focus, helping clients understand different scenarios and their probabilities. Finally, the benefit in terms of pricing is transferred to the client thanks to the platform that allows setting goals based on transparent pricing/fee models. For the wealth manager this means having a process which is extremely scalable, with a grade of customization and support on demand, increasing as a function of complexity (existing modularity in IKEA, from total DIY to a personal assistant who helps you plan your purchases up to transport and assembly).

In terms of education, it would be useful for a goal-based wealth manager to visualize the goal and best practices similarly to the famous IKEA catalogue. This could be implemented through scenario analysis by empirical experiments on specific objectives achieved by other clients.

Pricing

As outlined in the previous points, economies of scale due to automation of the process allow the limiting of costs for clients. In fact, there are only the platform and service to remunerate. Investments are chosen with transparency in terms of maximum efficiency and it becomes immediately clear to the client that his first gain is in the fees saved. When a wealth manager achieves the breakeven point, all additional revenues go straight through to the bottom line because the approach is highly scalable and all the bespoke services are charged to the client on demand.

Quality, Sustainability and Risks

Linked to pricing, there is always the issue of quality and of the optimization of the price/quality ratio. IKEA has strong minimum standards for quality and sustainability. This can be applied to the wealth management model which needs high risk management standards, not only for the market, but also for other risks, providing clients with strong processes of selection and monitoring of counterparties and suppliers (management and continuous monitoring of the operational risk, credit risk, counterparty risk, solvency risk, concentration risk, etc.).

Credibility and Trust

Another key ingredient from IKEA is the credibility and confidence built during decades. The Scandinavian brand has been able to create and maintain these for the long run. Credibility and trust were created not only with the quality of the products, but also with the high level of attention during the post-sales process. In the same way, in a goal-based approach, such credibility is the result of being a partner of clients along the way to correctly set and achieve their goals. Loyalty passes through the fact that this model is not based on selling products or services, but as a partnership along the whole customer life cycle.

Conclusions

This is just a simple example of an innovative model that can be obtained by mixing a series of ingredients of a successful business model within a mature sector. Now try to imagine a traditional financial operator who wants to change their competitive position by combining some of the ingredients mentioned with the experience of a tech giant. In addition, big data and artificial intelligence (AI) can be deployed to set, manage and monitor goals, rather than the ability to manage the customer experience, post-sales and loyalty of a big e-commerce brand. Combining wonderful ingredients (1, IKEA's way of changing the competitive perception) with an innovative business model for wealth management (2, goal-based investment approach) and a disruptive platform, in terms of client experience, channel and use of AI to support decisions (3, tech disruption) it will become possible to deliver a global WealthTech unicorn.

FinTech and the Wealth Management Challenge

By Peter Guy
Editor in Chief, Regulation Asia

Private banking and wealth management are being reshaped by technology. How clients react, and benefit, will determine the future of WealthTech.

Emerging technologies are driving major changes throughout the banking industry. The entire meaning of wealth management and private banking services is being turned upside down by technology that is providing unprecedented access to data, information and advice. This revolution is already affecting how investment decisions are made. And most importantly, the evolving relationship between clients and private banks is changing the future of how money is managed.

The banking industry has also been reshaped by regulatory changes related to new technologies. They have altered competition, services and products in traditional banking activities from payment processing to asset management. Financial regulations are already shifting certain financial services activities from banks to non-banks. This has prompted the emergence of a class of "shadow banks" such as peer-to-peer lenders, and robo-advisors for wealth management. Traditional lines among financial products and services are being crossed and blurred.

Technology has surfaced as an enabler to entry, lowering barriers so new institutions can challenge big banks. Big data analytics and new distribution channels have allowed technology start-ups to disrupt the traditional business of banks. Most of this has occurred in the consumer lending space, but private banking and high-net-worth wealth management segments are also being altered.

The Promise

For the last five years, regulators have benefited from the early phases of FinTech evolution. Regulators and financial institutions have been able to observe a wide array of start-ups to determine which models are realistic and feasible. Accommodative measures – such as allowing FinTech start-ups their own regulatory "sandbox" – have encouraged explosive growth.

FinTech's ultimate promise emerges from its potential to unbundle banking services into their basic functions and re-price them. In wealth management, the new entrants driving this trend include robo-advisors, and incumbent financial institutions complicate change by experimenting and adopting new technologies to build upon their existing business models.

Amid a complex mix of operational expectations and real returns for investors, regulators and financial institutions, FinTech is now entering a more difficult phase. They need to identify, assess and respond to the risks posed by FinTech innovations. How these risks should be mitigated – or technology restricted – is a matter of macroeconomic, technological and regulatory importance.

For example, an inherent contradiction has not yet been resolved in the blockchain proposition. Its most important concept is anonymity among counterparties. However, financial institutions and markets work in a way that requires transparency and party identification for security and regulatory reasons. Compromising this element would reduce blockchain to another form of data stack, making it difficult to fulfil its original promise.

Disintermediation – Always Unpredictable

The disintermediation inflicted by technology has affected banking in unpredictable ways. What is occurring can be described as "modularization of supply".

Increasing digital capability and availability is carrying out more of the business of wealth management. Discretionary management is being encroached by robo-advisors like Mint and Nutmeg. Clients are shifting to these alternatives from existing, traditional providers of private banking services.

A global private banker observed: "The challenge is how to provide bespoke investment advice in a digital environment. The advisory model has been traditionally human-to-human. But, banks are looking at combining artificial intelligence (AI) and robo-advisors."

He predicts: "This would result in a standardised, advisory process without a human involved. In five to 10 years, digitalisation will probably be possible and allow end-to-end profiling and setting of investment goals."

The entire process includes scenario building and portfolio exposure management. It would allow the construction and execution of a portfolio with alerts and management through dashboards. Portfolios can be balanced and risk levels adjusted in a humanistic way, yet without much human involvement.

High-end private banking requires a deep understanding of each individual client's needs and demands, while providing a global set of products. Addressing the tide of uncertain technological change is best done from the client's viewpoint. "The best solutions consider the customer as the starting point for technology solutions", said a private banker. "Clients want relevant information about how we make it work for them as we hold their portfolios. It is not a competition against traditional services, but rather a complement."

Communication with clients is also changing. Innovation is opening differentiated, easy-to-access communication channels, allowing clients to be reached quickly.

Obstacles Facing WealthTech

It is no surprise that FinTech innovation has made relatively more progress in China. The reason is that the country's developing banking system and regulatory framework must deal with a shadow banking sector that serves the world's largest and fastest growing customer base. Western economies and financial systems are saddled with legacy systems that are far more difficult to adapt and coordinate with regulatory requirements. FinTech trends in emerging markets are often able to bypass current technologies and produce greater financial inclusion.

However, FinTech is one of the most regulated sectors of technology. To assess its relative benefits and risks, governments must consider its impact on investor protection, market fairness and integrity, and financial stability – both locally and internationally.

Regulatory planning for FinTech start-ups cannot be confined to local or national disclosure requirements. In his capacity as chairman of the Financial Stability Board, the Bank of England's Mark Carney questioned how and where FinTech might generate risks to financial stability.

In a speech on 25 January 2017 at the Deutsche Bundesbank G20 conference, Carney said:

> In this process, systemic risks will evolve. Changes to customer loyalties could influence the stability of bank funding. New underwriting models could impact credit quality and even macroeconomic dynamics.

> New investing and risk management paradigms could affect market functioning. A host of applications and new infrastructure could reduce costs, probably improve capital efficiency and possibly create new critical economic functions.

FinTech's threat or promise to disintermediate financial services is constrained by regulatory criteria, which require that functions representing traditional banking activities under another description be regulated as such. Therefore, those systemic risks and products related with credit intermediation – including maturity transformation, leverage creation and liquidity mismatch – should be regulated in the same way, regardless of how they are delivered.

Carney questions how technological developments could alter the safety and soundness of existing regulated firms. Macro- and micro-economic, financial and supervisory responses need to be clearly defined for systemically important markets. He asked which FinTech activities would demand more operational oversight as they become systemic.

Fintech and the Next Financial Crisis

Financial crises are cyclical or secular events. Modern national and international financial systems are particularly vulnerable to crises and inherently prone to panics and runs.

FinTech firms and shadow banking could magnify the challenge for regulators trying to stem a financial panic. They may reduce the incentive for individuals and institutions to flee from one another. Any failure to reverse the level of fear may precipitate a wider collapse in the financial system.

But this fragility does not mean they cannot be made safer. Indeed, failure creates the right management incentives and encourages innovation and renewal. Policymakers should instead try to build a system in which an unregulated or poorly regulated shadow banking sector doesn't allow an idiosyncratic event to catalyse a systemic crisis.

How FinTech could play an accelerating and exacerbating role in the next crisis remains an open issue.

Risk of Information Overload

Private banking clients already have unprecedented access to financial data and research reports on smartphones, tablets and desktop devices. How banks deliver, present and interpret all this information throughout the client relationship is important for how a portfolio is structured and managed. Gaining clarity and mutual understanding is a constant struggle, with the avalanche of data available from banks and on the internet.

According to the head of information technology for a European private bank: "Big data is an evolving development. Banks are still struggling to manage the large quantity of in-house data while at the same time complying with secrecy laws and record-keeping regulations."

He points out: "The relationship manager needs to help clients make both technology and investment decisions today. In the beginning of the client–advisor relationship, it is necessary and practical to define how much information the client would like to receive on a day-to-day basis."

He also observed that technology is being pushed and pulled by clients and banks alike: "Big technology changes are being adopted by all demographic segments, not just tech-savvy millennials. They are being driven by their own needs and forces that continually seek improvement. But these changes are enablers, rather than hindrances."

New tools are being used differently, depending on the client. Emerging technologies allow for better monitoring and presentation of risk scenarios. Even then, high-net-worth individuals (HNWIs) generally prefer paper over tablet presentations.

Relationship managers improve communications and frequency of dialogue with their clients in a more meaningful way. They can be better prepared for meetings.

However, the ability to access a world of information with an array of analytical tools doesn't reduce the uncertainty over markets and investment opportunities. According to a strategic management consultant: "People are using lots of different tools these days. But market uncertainty remains. Despite all the information, uncertainty is high so is the need for service."

The consultant pointed out:

> The popularity of robo-advisory indicates that life planning has always been difficult for advisors so robo-advisory algorithms are useful. Digital platforms have proven to be intuitive and cheaper.

> There is lots of data available. The issue is how to capture and sort it out to provide useful advice. Clients need to get more comfortable with the risk and return of their investments relative to their own lifestyles and goals. Actually, more information may not necessarily assist this particular dynamic.

When Tech Generations Collide

Millennials are at the vanguard of how FinTech is redefining financial services and products. However, older and more traditional high-net-worth clients are also redefining private banking.

As millennials age, they will be used to the digital experience, but they may also want to meet with a relationship manager. Like the generation before them, millennials are still choosing banks based on experience and service. But one key difference is that they don't want any information on paper.

One wealth manager remarked: "The ability to serve clients completely through digital channels will become an industry standard. Leading banks will be able to provide product specialties and experts in areas beyond general banking services.

The fluctuations of investing performance affect each client in unique ways that technology cannot cope with.

When a client hits poor returns and makes losses, perhaps loses lots of money, they want to talk to someone. Investment is a mixed bag of results and emotions. Quarterly meetings to talk about the client's portfolio, feelings and goals are part of the portfolio rebalancing process.

One of the most overlooked opportunities in FinTech is finding a way to increase the application of instant messaging to communicate with clients. While it is commonplace elsewhere, banks have been slow to use it for numerous reasons.

One wealth manager said: "It is more effective and popular for reaching clients than email. Although email is a standard corporate platform and a significant and transformative platform for many industries it will slowly fade away. So instant messaging is the most important technological change emerging. However, security and compliance remain key problems."

Whatever changes and surprises arise from all of the new services and platforms being developed and launched, private banking and wealth management clients should benefit from a combination of personal service as well as technology.

Cognitive Decision-Making with "Insights-as-a-Service"

By Paolo Sironi

IBM Industry Academy, IBM

There was a time when financial data was scarce, orders were collected and executed manually, market data was primarily handled on spreadsheets. That world is gone.

There was a time when financial information was channelled through conventional media and could be consumed only by reading newspapers or watching the news. That world is certainly also gone.

In today's digital world, decision-making requires individuals and their financial advisors to digest big data and harvest investment insight behind the news, gathering real-time knowledge about unconventional relationships between prices, corporate deals, market changes, economic interests, political shifts and human behaviours.

As markets change faster than ever, insights-based decision-making needs to be made available to front-line investors in a timely and digestible manner. This requires a Copernican change in investment management operations, opening risk-based architectures to real-time data analytics and allowing front-end digital applications to consume and visualize investment analytics that were previously restricted to the ivory towers of risk departments and trading floors. Luckily, recent FinTech innovation is generating a shift in how technology is architected, providing an opportunity to change how the world interacts with financial technology. As data and information is nowadays very fluid, analytics supporting decision-making should also be agile and flexible to design alternative investment experiences (thus added-value workflows) without loss of consistency. Financial technology to date has been architected around specific workflows driven by specific client requests or idiosyncrasies on how they tackled the problem to solve. The creation of robust financial services platforms, hosting a modular set of FinTech microservices, is the solution to the re-engineering task addressing investment decision-making in the digital age.

Microservices are building blocks to assembling workflows. A complex application can be built by stringing together a collection of individual components, instead of attempting to fine-tune a rigid container. Just like during earthquakes, rigid architectures have no chance to adjust to even small changes in the terrain, and thus become fragile and break. Microservices, instead, are flexible API-driven analytics which can be accessed via cloud-based investment platforms and consumed in a fit-for-purpose modality, granting flexibility to enhance decision-making by calling new calculations, dropping outdated sources, mixing a variety of investment signals as markets and sentiment change. Having deconstructed investment analytics into a set of streamlined microservices, and hosting them on a scalable platform, machine learning (ML) techniques can be deployed to exploit this powerful constellation of data-driven, information-based, "insights-as-a-service". A cognitive process can be layered on top, aiming to tap into the streamlined microservices more easily than a closed-off, opaque software package. This cognitive layer, which consists of ML techniques, is the ultimate game changer, since it augments investors' intelligence based on actionable insights.

How Could This Work in Practice?

Since investment insights can be modelled and tested as scenarios, a set of scenario-based risk management functions can be built as microservices that more easily architect a solution to a particular business problem. Insights-driven scenario generation tools can model a given shift to a particular risk factor. Cognitive computing expands the hard link between risk factors and portfolio holdings. The source of risk is no longer the risk factor itself, but the point in time and short-lived "insights factor" which can be sourced by a machine learning process that links back what happens outside a portfolio to a potential change in investment performance. The risk factor is nothing else but a connector between cognitive insights and final investments. Clearly, as modern data/information systems become ever more complex, digital visualization is key to create enough transparency to act upon given cognitive insights. "Knowledge graphs" are therefore essential to leverage data on companies, their competitors, their key employees, their supply chain, their market of reference and potential contagion from apparently unrelated instances. Natural language processing can break down a news article into its entities, relationships and concepts. Determining their relevance becomes simply a matter of finding a linkage between an article and a knowledge graph.

Cognitive-enabled architectures based on "insights-as-a-service" microservices and scenario analysis have deeper ramifications for the entire industry at large. The complexity can be abstracted away, such that any financial advisor has the ability to address client concerns like "what does this news article mean for my investment portfolio?" or "what exactly am I invested in?" with a single mouse click. This provides clients with real value: the information they need to more confidently make investment decisions. That is, in essence, digitization of knowledge.

Why Knowledge Digitization Will be a Norm in Investment Management

Financial markets have experienced a structural change since the 1950s, when modern portfolio theory (MPT) was initially formulated. Until the financial deregulation of the early 1980s, markets were fairly simple and financial products were fairly simple (the first fixed-income index appeared only in the 1970s), thus MPT provided a tale for a simple world based on mean-variance assumptions. MPT assumes a world of investment symmetries, where one-size-fits-all optimal portfolios could generate unprecedented wealth for American households of different risk profiles. With the 1980s, the Western world entered a more asymmetrical phase: markets became highly volatile and financial products became highly complex (for example, structured finance, subprime notes). This allowed financial institutions significant power to trade the asymmetry of information and develop market views as the main wealth management narrative, which continued until the global financial crisis (GFC). In the aftermath of the GFC, regulation stepped up to impose higher transparency in investment decision-making and reduce the information asymmetry of financial markets. Markets are still very complex, financial products are getting progressively simplified (see the rise of passive investing) and transparency is the new mantra. Broader MPT criticism suggests that optimal portfolios, as professionals have known them for decades, might not truly exist. In a world of higher transparency about risks and costs (thus reduced asymmetry), low interest rates and margin compression, unusual correlations among risk factors, faster than ever propagation of market-sensitive information and the focus of investment managers is shifting towards the generation of real and perceived added value for final clients. That means assisting investors and advisors to optimize their decision-making by providing intuitive insights into the risks and uncertainties of financial markets. The scenario-based contextualization is centred on cognitive dialogues of how news and events can transform into scenarios, and thus potentially impact investment performance. This becomes a powerful attribute to facilitate an engagement mechanism based on better understanding of financial risks, and facilitate the building of sounder decision-making processes based on "insights-as-a-service".

More Banking for Less Money

By Rino Borini
Co-Founder, Finance 2.0

It all started with fully automated stock exchanges. The next step is digital managers (robo-advisors). The winners are the clients. The global financial industry is facing the challenge of having to completely rethink its business models and adapt them to the new digital and mobile reality. This development encompasses new, disruptive peer-to-peer technologies (from computer system to computer system) such as blockchain, which will revolutionize the worldwide financial market infrastructure.

Customers want to benefit from this new simplicity, transparency and flexibility.

Retail banking is already feeling the pressure acutely. But even in the wealth management business and the product lab, asset management, the changes will be fundamental. Technology-based applications enable financial services to be delivered direct to customers. The potential is enormous, and it also makes the middleman superfluous. Customers want to benefit from this new simplicity, transparency and flexibility. They want to have access to their assets around the clock, for information or management purposes, regardless of their location and the device they're using. The interface between customers and banks is being redefined.

Back to the Future

It's nothing new for wealth and asset management to be facing challenges. A whole 20 years ago the Swiss stock exchange launched the world's first fully electronic stock exchange. Physical open outcry trading was made obsolete. Every step in the process, from stock exchange orders to settlement, was completely automated. The next evolutionary step in the democratization of investing was taken by the fund industry.

When the first exchange-traded funds (ETFs) hit the market, the powerful active fund industry didn't even dignify the new competition with a weary smile. Now the ETF industry manages more than 3 trillion US dollars, with double-digit annual percentage growth – rates active funds can only dream of.

Now, so-called robo-advisory platforms allow even greater automation. They (robo-advisors) manage their clients' wealth with the help of algorithms, and offer an unprecedented customer experience. It should be pointed out that the term "robo" is somewhat misleading, because it's still people who are behind the platforms. But first things first.

ETFs Blaze the Trail

Before a client can become a user of a robo-advisor in the first place, their ability to take risks is assessed using an online questionnaire. On the basis of the resulting investor profile, within seconds the algorithm works out a suitable asset allocation. In most cases the foundation of this asset allocation is around half a dozen standard portfolios that are adapted to different risk aptitudes (from conservative and balanced to aggressive). These portfolios are modelled with ETFs. The investor benefits from low fees and a great deal of freedom, since index funds, like shares, can be traded on any stock exchange trading day. These digital managers practice what seasoned investment pros have been preaching for years: managing assets according to stringent criteria, and keeping emotions out of the equation. Many bankers sneer at these digital managers, but what many financial experts don't understand is that the new reality isn't developing on a linear basis, but exponentially.

Thanks to these platforms, investors with a certain minimum amount can invest their assets like the pros. But the (r)evolution has only just begun. Technological advances will enable customers to be analysed better and more accurately, with the help of behavioural economics and gamification approaches.

But that's only one side of the coin. It gets really exciting when you package different scientific and tried-and-tested investment strategies. As soon as a strategy displays a clear set of rules, it can be used as the basis for an algorithm and be integrated into a digital asset management platform.

The cornerstone was laid several decades back by leading economists such as Markowitz, Fama and French. It's only now, thanks to access to real-time market data and steady technological progress, that it's possible to model scientific theories digitally and implement them physically with securities. The way was paved by cost-efficient ETFs.

Pure Democratization

With this development, what you might call Robo Advisory 2.0, implementing things like momentum, risk minimization, size effect and value strategies, is no problem. And that's not all: as soon as you've set up the technology and defined the interfaces, the logical next step is to package client-specific investment strategies. To do so you no longer need the expensive shell of a fund. As we've already mentioned, any rules-based strategy can be digitized. This doesn't necessarily have to happen via ETFs; you can also do it with individual securities, all over the world. This opens up completely new possibilities for customers, and in the future there will be no need for collective vehicles such as funds or ETFs. Between the provider and the client there is a co-engagement, which translates into pure democratization.

Undreamed-of Possibilities

Not yet foreseeable, but by all means realistic, is the fourth stage of development. Thanks to artificial intelligence, it won't be just the interface between robo-advisors and customers that is redefined, but the interfaces to other customers. Say hello to social investing. People can take investment strategies and stock exchange transactions as inspiration for their own portfolios. Or they can replicate the portfolio of other successful investors one-for-one. One criticism often levelled in this connection is the lack of advice. Naturally there are many people who don't want to do without personal advice. And indeed we're already seeing the first signs of hybrid models. Digital or analogue, it doesn't really matter – both routes are possible. Ultimately it's the customer who decides how much they want to do digitally – at lower cost – and what parts of their assets they want to manage with the support of an advisor. The future belongs to hybrid models and completely digital platforms. The big winners among all this progress are the customers, who get more banking at lower cost. But the most important point is this: customers get much more flexibility when it comes to managing their assets.

How AI Will Cause Robo-Advice to Completely Outperform Human Advice

By Michal Rozanski
Founder and CEO, Empirica S.A.

Most financial advisors are in deep denial about robo-advice. They say that they need human interaction in order to understand the nuances of the financial lives of their customers. And their clients value the human touch. They're wrong. Soon robo-advice will be much more efficient than human advice ever was.

In this chapter, we will share the results of our analysis on the most important areas where the application of machine learning will have the greatest impact in taking wealth management to the next level.

What AI Is and Why You Should Care

"Computers can only do what they are programmed to do." Let us explain why this is a huge misconception, which was only valid because of the limited processing power and memory capacity of computers. Most advanced programs which mimic specialized intelligences, known as expert systems, were indeed programmed around a set of rules based on the knowledge of specialists within the problem's domain. There was no real intelligence, there were only programmed rules. But there is another way to program computers which makes them work more similarly to the functions of the human brain. It is based on showing the program examples of how certain problems can be solved and what results are expected. In this way, computers equipped with enough processing power, memory and storage are able to recognize objects in photographs, drive autonomous cars, recognize speech, or analyse any form of information which exhibits patterns.

We are entering the age where humans are outperformed by machines in activities related to reasoning, based on the analysis of large amounts of information. Because of that, finance and wealth management will be profoundly changed during the years to come.

Real Advice – Combining Plans with Execution

A great area for improvement in finance management is the combination of long-term wealth building with the current financial situation of the customer as reflected by his bank account. For robo-advisors, an integration with bank application programming interfaces (APIs) opens the door to an ocean of data which, after analysis, can dramatically improve the accuracy of advice provided to the customer.

By applying machine learning capabilities to a customer's monthly income and expenses data, wealth managers will gain a unique opportunity to combine two perspectives – the long-term financial goals of their customers and their current spending patterns. Additionally, there is the potential for tax, mortgage, loans or credit card costs optimization, as well as using information on spending history to predict future expenditures. By integrating data from social media, robo-advisory systems could detect major changes in one's life situation, job, location, marital status or remuneration. This would allow for automated real-time adjustments in investment strategies on a very fine granular level, which human advisors are simply unable to deliver.

New Powerful Tools in the Portfolio Manager's Arsenal

Hedge funds that are basing their strategies on artificial intelligence (AI) have provided better results over the last five years than the average.[1] What is interesting is that the gap

---

[1] http://www.eurekahedge.com/.

between AI and other strategies has been growing wider over the last two years, as the advancements in machine learning accelerated. The main applications of machine learning techniques in portfolio management can be categorized according to the following areas:

- Making predictions on real-time information from sources such as market data, financial reports, news in different languages and social media.

- Analysis of historical financial data of companies to predict the company cash flow and important financial indicators based on the past performance of similar companies.

- Analysis of management's public statements and activity on social networks in order to track the integrity of their past words, actions and results.

- Help in accurate portfolio diversification by looking for uncorrelated instruments which match requirements of the risk profile.

- Generation of investment strategies parametrized by goals such as expected risk profiles, asset categories and time span, resulting in sets of predictive models which may be applied in order to fulfil the assumptions.

To give an example of machine learning accuracy, the algorithms for sentiment analysis and document classification are already at acceptable levels, well above 90%.

Autonomous Execution

When it comes to the execution of the actual orders behind portfolio allocation and rebalancing strategies, many robo-advisors are automating these processes, passing generated orders to brokerage systems. The next step would be autonomous execution algorithms that take into consideration the changing market situation and learn from incoming data, allowing for increased investment efficiency and reduced costs.

Machine learning can be applied to quantitative strategies like trend following, pattern recognition, mean reversion and momentum, as well as the prediction and optimization of statistical arbitrage, and pairs trading. Additionally, there is a possibility to apply machine learning techniques in (already quite sophisticated) execution algorithms that help execute large orders by dividing them into thousands of smaller transactions without influencing the market, while adjusting their aggressiveness to the market situation.

What's interesting is that algorithms could also be trained to make use of rare events – like market crashes – and properly react in milliseconds, already knowing the patterns of panic behaviour and shortages of liquidity.

Explaining the Markets

If portfolio valuations are provided to customers in real time from robo-advisory systems, explanations of the market situation should also be delivered like this. Every time the customer logs in to the robo-advisor, she should see all the required portfolio information, with a summary of the market information relevant to the content of her portfolio. This process includes the selection of proper articles or reports concerning companies from the investor portfolio, classification and summarization of negative or positive news, and delivering a brief overview.

Additionally, machine learning algorithms can be used to discover which articles are read by customers and present only those types of article that were previously opened and read by the customer.

The result will be not only an increase in customer understanding, but also – by providing engaging content to investors – an increase in their engagement and commitment to portfolio strategy and wealth management services.

Talking with Robots

The ability to deliver precise explanations of the market situation, in combination with conversational interfaces aided by voice recognition technology, will enable robo-advisors to provide financial advice in a natural, conversational way.

Voice recognition is still under development, but it could be the final obstacle on the way to redesigning human–computer interaction. On the other hand, thanks to deep learning, chatbot technology and question-answering systems are getting more reliable than ever. KAI, the chatbot platform of Kasisto, who has been trained in millions of investment and trade interactions, already handles 95% of all customer queries for India's digibank.

Decreasing Customer Churn with Behavioural Analysis

The ability to track all customer actions, analyse them, find common patterns in huge amounts of data, make predictions and offer unique insights for fund managers delivers a powerful business tool not previously available to wealth managers. What if nervousness caused by portfolio results or market situation could be observed in user behaviour within the system? This information, combined with the results of investments and the patterns of behaviour of other investors, can give a wealth manager the possibility to predict customer churn and react in advance (see Figure 1).

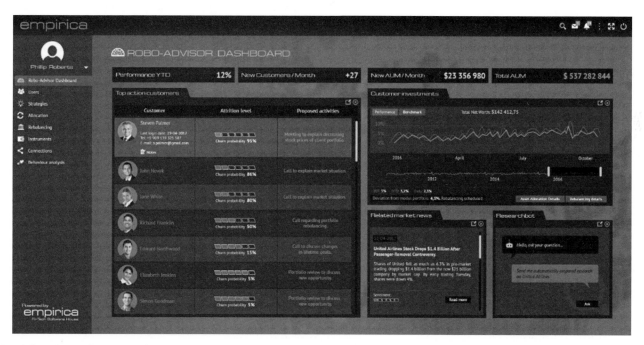

Figure 1: Machine learning applied to customers' churn reduction in a robo-advisory system

Source: http://empirica-software.com

When speaking with wealth management executives using our robo-advisory solutions, they indicate behavioural analysis as one of the most important advancements to their current processes. Customers leave not only when investment results are bad, but also when they are good if there is a fear that the results may not be repeated in the future. Therefore, the timely delivery of advice and explanations of market changes and the current portfolio situation are crucial.

The same model we used to solve the behavioural analysis problem has been proven to predict credit frauds in 93.07% of cases.

Summary

Other areas applying machine learning in the processes supporting wealth management services are:

- Security based on fraud detection, which actively learns to recognize new threats.
- Improving sales processes with recommendations of financial products chosen by similar customers.
- Psychological profiling of customers to better understand their reactions in different investment situations.
- Analysis and navigation of tax nuances.
- Real-estate valuation and advice.

Implementing AI functions (like the ones described in this chapter) in robo-advisory systems will be an important step towards the differentiation of wealth managers in the market. Today's wealth managers' tool set will look completely different in five years. Choosing an open and innovative robo-advisory system that tackles these future challenges is crucial. Equally important will be wealth managers' incorporation of data-analytic processes and the use of this data to help their customers.

Artificial intelligence is poised to transform the wealth management industry. This intelligence will be built on modern software platforms that combine data from different sources, process it and transform it into relevant financial advice. The shift from data-gathering systems to predictive ones that help wealth managers to understand the data has already started. And wealth management is all about understanding the markets and the customers.

Security in the Future of WealthTech

By Bruno Esteves Macedo
FinTech and Digital Banking Speaker, Business Architect, five degrees

The technical advances made in internet-related technologies during the past decades have led to a bold new world and widespread FinTech digital shift. From mobile internet, self-learning artificial intelligence (AI), robotics, big data analytics and self-driving vehicles to the Internet of Things (IoT), we are just at the beginning of a paradigm shift with an increasingly digital, 24-hour connected society. Established financial institutions (FIs) are historically considered as the most resistant industries to disruption by technology. However, they need to look at new technology and partnering solutions if they want to keep up with this new financial society.

The General FinTech Challenge

The exponential growth of FinTech (the industry is expected to manage US$2.2 trillion in assets by 2020) is creating a security concern by pushing commonly offline and time-consuming financial processes to be tucked into online millisecond decisions while managing the same amount of financial assets. FIs are basically trying to transform their traditional businesses into digital-focused, cloud-based and mobile-ready ones, migrating their services to something with a low-capital-cost operation, a focus on data capture, a change from human to algorithms-based service, regulatory arbitrage and a focus on transferring risk management to customers. This is a big change, which usually takes years but now is mostly requested to be performed in months and through outsourcing to speed the process up. This combination of factors naturally raises security discussions and concerns with experts. How prudent are governments and FIs being in this entire process concerning the security issues and risks involved?

This chapter is based on my experience in these last three years of FinTech multinational industry, events and discussions. It seeks mainly to raise the importance and urgency of discussing the security challenges of FinTech towards the visible intentions of governments and FIs to expand and heavily invest in the FinTech industry (while expecting that the newcomers will maintain or even increase safety and prudence). For the scope of this chapter I have chosen four viewpoints that I found present in the majority of conversations: business, technology, human resources and general regulation. It is important to clarify that due to the nature and scope of this chapter, there is no intention to dive deeply into academic or technical financial security details.

The Technology Security Concern

Among FIs, banks have been struggling to research, develop, assimilate and apply new technologies rapidly in response to their underperforming and outdated core banking systems (CBSs) that barely support current key processes. With renewed pressure to tamp down costs and adjust to volatile conditions, FIs currently have little confidence in their CBSs to respond to clients, manage risk and keep up with technology. FinTechs are fuelled by these internal impediments, ambitious entrepreneurs, eager job-creation-seeking governments, innovative technologies and consumer demand, which have been presenting themselves and have been seen as the answer.

Considered a modern-age gold rush, global investment in FinTech already surpasses US$13.8 billion and is paving the way for new and bold organizations that can induce much-needed financial innovation in financial services. Yet strangely, there seems to be little direct discussion about whether the pressure on the FinTech industry has the required response from the perspective of technology security, regarding the near future. Young FinTechs experience thousands of security attacks per year, with a portion of those being serious and successful. However, they are still pressured and requested to widen their range of services and grow rapidly. These young companies (on average less than five years in existence) do not possess the technological knowledge and experience of big e-commerce internet-oriented industry players. Yet, they are requested to deal with huge amounts of personal data and wealth. From another viewpoint, FinTechs typically do not always adhere to the same internal bank information technology (IT) restrictions and tests (if they do, they tend to do it at a later stage, as this implies costs that are usually not supported at the beginning of their projects).

The big security "elephant in the room" question is whether these young technology firms can really handle safely these amounts of personal and sensitive data like the big e-commerce players (e.g. Amazon, Microsoft, Apple) do, when the industry witnesses an ever-increasing number of service channels, business offers and an even higher number of cyber-attacks. For the future it is crucial that we have the best of the e-commerce technology combined with the best of banking security practices as a basis for the future of WealthTech.

The Human Capital Security Risk

A FinTech professional often combines traditional finance, internet technology and financial regulation expertise. Strangely, although empirically banks have some of these professionals in their internal IT departments, it is still uncommon to name these professionals. The result is that currently, HR departments are eagerly looking for FinTech professionals with technological, financial and regulatory skills.

It does not seem to be a problem to find pure technology-based professionals, as software developers are no different in FinTech from other software-based industries. However, to find developers with corporate banking security experience or similar financial knowledge is harder. This can be a challenge for future WealthTech security developments, as every developer with this knowledge gap will require close supervision from someone with the necessary business knowledge. Otherwise, situations like wrong

stochastic or financial models, missing or corrupted financial data, missing or insufficient financial-related privacy and security implementations are more likely to occur.

In parallel with the rise of the FinTech industry over recent years, the traditional financial sector has reduced its headcount as a result of the financial crisis and cost pressures. Big institutions such as Commerzbank, Deutsche Bank, Bank of America and Citibank have taken the lead on reducing their human capital already, or intending to cut down their hiring by several to tens of thousands of people. This provides a perfect human talent transfer to the growing FinTech industry. However, HR managers seem to be presented with a culture clash challenge, as financial professionals who have been highly paid with lots of benefits and a risk-averse culture are often uncomfortable in a start-up environment with an entrepreneurial spirit. Even when successfully hired, they might take some time to adapt and might be hard to retain in young FinTech companies, as the big e-commerce players are always on the lookout for the best talent with the more appealing proposals. Therefore, from a scenario where traditional financial institutions had on their premises large numbers of specialized employees, we are now moving to a new business paradigm that is typically run on the cloud, with a small number of employees with financial and technological experience.

The Regulation Security Risk

FIs' regulation is crucial, especially after the devastating effects of the financial crisis. Regulators act based on a risk approach, so they look more closely at banks and other big FIs than young FinTechs (especially in the early stage of development). Therefore, FinTechs tend to respond to regulatory WealthTech compliance as late as possible, which raises concerns over the security of services and private data.

In the future of WealthTech security, regulatory authorities face the challenge to be flexible enough to allow new WealthTech companies to emerge at lower costs, not to slow down or harm existing and emerging markets, while still be as effective as they are currently. Banks and FIs must also be extremely demanding in their WealthTech outsourcing requirements from FinTechs at every stage, as they are ultimately responsible for complying with all the relevant laws and regulations for their overall service offering, including any products or solutions offered by FinTech partners.

Conclusion

While FinTechs innovate, lower costs, fund new businesses and take risks, the industry is expecting them to be safer and more prudent than before. The result is an enormous amount of financial data sometimes being used by FinTech companies with young professionals who might not have the empirical experience of traditional banks or the technological know-how of big e-commerce players.

The needs of FIs, banks, investors, partners and governments are huge and FinTechs have a unique opportunity to provide solutions. Although there have been an increasing number of security issues and losses within the industry, WealthTech innovation will not slow down. This entails security challenges for the near future, which continue in many cases to be either underestimated, misjudged or ignored. The future of security in WealthTech starts today and must be a top priority for governments, FIs and FinTechs.

How China is Shaping WealthTech and the Future of Financial Services

By Henri Arslanian

FinTech and RegTech Leader, Hong Kong, PwC

Over the past five years, China has emerged as the global leader in B2C FinTech, not only from an innovation perspective but in terms of adoption as well. China's large tech firms and FinTech start-ups have transformed entire industries, from payments to peer-to-peer (P2P) lending. But can China also shape the future of the wealth management industry, capturing the mass affluent segment? And can the Chinese model be exported successfully, with innovation from China reshaping how things are done worldwide?

The Wealth Management Opportunity in China: From HNWIs to the Mass Affluent

China is on track to soon become one of the world's largest markets of high-net-worth individuals (HNWIs). In 2015, China was estimated to have 2 million HNWIs; this is projected to double by 2020. During that period, China's personal investable assets are expected to increase from CNY 113 trillion to CNY 200 trillion (about US$16 trillion to US$29 trillion). Both domestic and global private banks have been trying to capture this opportunity by focusing heavily on both the HNW and ultra-high-net-worth (UHNW) markets.

But increasingly, they have also begun to target the mass affluent segment, the more than 15 million Chinese consumers with investable assets of between US$100,000 and US$1 million. These are the lesser-known winners of China's economic boom, who've climbed into the upper middle class. The World Economic Forum reports that China will see 100 million upper middle class and affluent households by 2020.

As it grows, that customer base wants and needs to be served differently from the traditional private banking model. It is in this area that many of the new entrants, including large tech firms and FinTech start-ups, have been operating.

Numerous robo-advisory offerings have emerged that aim to service these mass affluent customers. These tools can help users navigate their risk preferences and shape their portfolio quickly and efficiently, without the need for a human investment advisor. The number of Chinese consumers using robo-advisory services to manage their investments is expected to reach nearly 80 million by 2021, according to market research firm Statista.[1] That's compared with less than 2 million such users in 2016.

The Chinese Tech Dragons

Large tech firms such as Ant Financial and Tencent have emerged as important players in the financial services ecosystem in China. Ant Financial boasts more than 450 million active users and is partly owned by Alibaba. Ant Financial operates a money-market fund, Yu'e Bao, which has become the largest money-market fund in the world. Its estimated US$165 billion of assets under management comes from just over 260 million users. Ant Financial is expanding aggressively worldwide and acquired MoneyGram for US$1.2 billion in 2017.

Tencent is also expanding rapidly into financial services. With its 700 million + active monthly users, it plays a critical role in the lives of Chinese citizens. For example, Tencent processed more than 46 billion red packet gift transfers during Chinese New Year week in January 2017 – replacing the traditional red envelope normally passed from person to person by hand. On its platforms, users can conveniently buy anything from mutual funds to insurance products. Similarly to Ant Financial, it is expanding globally – most recently with investments in Tesla.

---

[1] https://www.statista.com/outlook/298/117/personal-finance/china#market-transactionValue.

While these large tech firms still focus mainly on the vast retail market, they are increasingly looking at the wealth management space. For example, Ant Financial launched its wealth management platform, Ant Fortune, while Tencent launched Licaitong to offer segmented and personalized financial products to this increasingly growing mass affluent segment.

Established Chinese FinTechs

In addition to the large tech players, many FinTechs have established themselves as dominant players that are increasingly focusing on this mass affluent segment.

For example, Lufax began as a P2P player in 2012, but now offers a suite of financial products aimed at the mass affluent segment. Lufax sells a large number of fixed-income, money-market and mutual funds and insurance products sourced from domestic financial institutions to its 25 million + registered users, who can buy products via mobile phones and online accounts. CreditEase is another example of a FinTech that also began in P2P lending but which has since expanded into wealth management by focusing on the HNW and mass affluent segments. It offers a wide range of products and services for onshore and offshore investment in areas such as fixed income, private equity, capital markets, hedge funds, real estate and insurance, as well as investment immigration and international education.

Why So Successful?

These new players, from the large tech players to the emerging FinTechs, have been successful for a number of reasons.

- **They focus on unmet needs**
  These tech firms have focused on areas where there was a gap in the market. For example, alternative lending offerings originally took off in China as a source of capital for start-ups and small businesses. The traditional state-owned banks

preferred to lend to large, state-owned enterprises, neglecting smaller players and leaving a void that FinTech players stepped in to fill. The same is now arguably happening with the mass affluent segment.

- **They are data-driven and can innovate fast**
  These tech players are not financial services incumbents who just happen to have a good digital channel. They are firms that are data-driven, digital native and mobile first, applying those advantages to the delivery of financial services. This allows them to fully leverage the data they have towards better pricing of risk, evaluation of creditworthiness and product development. It also confers an advantage in user experience design, with delivery mechanisms that provide products in convenient and easy ways.

- **They have mastered partnerships and platform models**
  Instead of themselves becoming financial institutions, these tech firms have often opted for an open ecosystem approach whereby they work with various financial institutions to offer a range of products, providing choice and transparency to their customers. For example, Ant Financial does not see itself as a bank but rather as a financial services provider, a platform that can offer hundreds of different funds for its clients to choose from, as investment opportunities.

- **They understand and master market adoption habits**
  These tech firms have leveraged the digital savviness of Chinese consumers. China leapt into mobile products and services, and its consumers have consistently been seen as being ahead of other countries in the use of new technology. For example, China is estimated to have over 730 million internet users, with 95% of them accessing services through their phones. This has allowed these tech firms to quickly deploy new solutions.

- **They have a favourable regulatory framework**
  In order for innovation to flourish, regulations must not be excessive and regulators may have to be pragmatic and practical. China is often described as a big sandbox, with regulators allowing new technologies to emerge, carefully

monitoring them and intervening only when they need to or when critical mass has been reached. For example, the P2P sector was able to flourish without many regulatory constraints. Regulators intervened only once the industry had grown, putting in place guidelines and legal frameworks to govern its use; the size of loans made through P2P lenders was capped, and lenders were forced to use custodian banks to reduce counterparty risk.

Can the Same Happen in the West?

The big question is always whether large tech players in the West – such as Facebook, Amazon, Google or Uber – could enter the mass affluent wealth management space as their Chinese counterparts have done. Facebook, for example, in addition to its numerous regulatory licences across the USA, obtained its financial services licence from the Central Bank of Ireland in November 2016. While the focus in the short term seems to be on facilitating payments between its 1 billion plus users of Facebook Messenger, could Facebook enter the mass affluent wealth management sector one day?

Amazon is already offering many financial products, but mainly to its merchants in the form of small business loans. Since 2012, Amazon has offered loans ranging from US$1000 to US$600,000, mainly for merchants who want to invest in inventory to sell their wares on Amazon's marketplace. If customers are happy buying all their daily necessities on Amazon, wouldn't they be open to buying investment products as well? And with an ever-increasing number of US households using Amazon's Echo, couldn't they ask Alexa for investment advice?

Is Data the Differentiator?

These large tech firms arguably have as much data on their customers as their Chinese counterparts. The question is whether they will expand further into providing financial services to the mass affluent. For many, this would be seen as a natural expansion of their business. And they would in many cases have an edge compared with traditional wealth management firms. For example, Facebook probably has a better idea not only of the background and education of an individual, but also of his or her life goals, aspirations and upcoming projects; this vastly exceeds what is generally known by incumbent banks. For example, Facebook could offer wealth planning solutions or life insurance products to a new father who announces the birth of his child to his Facebook network.

The same advantages could in theory apply from a compliance and regulatory perspective as well. Tech firms are more likely to have a grasp on the identity and behaviour patterns of their users by triangulating various pieces of data. This may be more accurate than the "know your customer" processes currently in place at traditional banks, which rely on passport photocopies and multiple-page questionnaires.

Conclusion

While the developments taking place in China to capture the mass affluent segment have been quite remarkable, it will be interesting to see if and how these models are replicated in other countries. The large tech firms and FinTech start-ups have an opportunity to capture this mass affluent segment, and what is happening in China may give a blueprint for how tech firms in the West can address this market.

From the Technological to the Financial Singularity – A Journey Without Return to the Future of Finance

By José Manuel de la Chica Rodriguez
CTO Santander Universities, Banco Santander

The first generation of the internet focused on connecting businesses and people, and the second wave centred on social interactions. Now we are entering the third generation, called the "Internet of Convergence" or the "Internet of Value". This internet will be mostly boosted by the confluence of different technological advances that will allow us to design disruptive and complex systems gifted with ubiquity, hyperconnection, decentralization and intelligence.

Throughout this generation many industries, including banking and FinTech, will create new services, products and platforms based on the merging of exponential technologies: machine learning (and especially reinforcement learning), cryptocurrencies and blockchain, mobile phones, the internet of things, quantum computing, virtual reality (VR), augmented reality (AR), APIs, digital identity, decentralized and autonomous networks, cybersecurity and, of course, the data economy.

This new technological environment will lead to big opportunities in the financial industry. One of the most controversial effects, according to the futurists, would be "financial singularity" – an event that would change irreversibly the investment industry within 20 years.

The Artificial Intelligence Super Explosion

Before explaining what financial singularity is, you need to understand an underlying and more general and widespread theory: technological singularity. This concept refers to a hypothetical and crucial event in human evolution when, as a result of the advances in technology and the processing capacities of the new digital processors, for the first time in history, engineers will build artificial intelligence (AI) more intelligent than the average human brain.

This advanced AI could start a chain of self-improvement cycles, with new and more intelligent generations appearing more slowly and at greater cost in the beginning, but faster and faster every time. This revolution would finally generate an artificial superintelligence explosion, with surprising and unpredictable repercussions in our economies and societies.

This possibility would entail a new technological landscape composed of hundreds of independent AIs with varied abilities and purposes that would evolve and learn through data, algorithms and sensors. They could even create other AIs or improve themselves.

This scenario is what Raymond Kurzweil – futurist, scientist and inventor – named the "technological singularity".[1] Kurzweil predicted that this would happen between 2029 and 2045, taking into account the acceleration of the exponential technologies, mainly advances in computing processors.

Nevertheless, the term "singularity" was used before in a non-physics context by John von Neumann and Vernor Vinge. Vinge applied this idea to the unexpected irruption of advanced AI with unknown and unprecedented consequences for humanity.

In the physics community, singularity refers to a very infrequent point in the universe, usually inside a black hole's centre, where

---

[1] Kurzweill, R. (2005). *The Singularity Is Near: When Humans Transcend Biology*. New York: Viking Press.

physical rules are breaking down as a result of its infinite mass and gravity force.

Everything that exists in the vicinity of a black hole is attracted and trapped towards the singularity once it crosses the virtual line, a no-return frontier, known as the "events horizon". Nothing, not even light, can escape from the singularity attraction once it crosses this decisive boundary.

Due to this total darkness, a "singularity" cannot be observed directly. In fact, physicists do not really know what happens inside one. In the same way, futurists and engineers cannot see beyond the technological singularity. We can only suspect and guess about the post-singularity effects, and its impact on global markets and economies.

This is the main meaning for the word "singularity" and its stronger implication on our reality. From a physical, technological or financial perspective, nobody really knows what will happen when the singularity is reached. From that moment in time, the most profitable investments will be made by investors with sufficient advanced technology, data sources and skills at their disposal. As a result, investors without AI tools will lose out, because they cannot compete. A new model of investment competencies and skills will be needed to survive in this new ultra-competitive scenario, highly driven by AI.

On the positive side, this kind of technology will be progressively democratized, even demonetized, and largely used by individual, non-professional investors. A new generation of financial services will be provided by banks and FinTech companies: evolved robo-advisors, personal investment assistants, open-predictions services and platforms, insurance for investors and even crowd-investing fully managed by AIs, many of them offered by technological companies and not by banks.

AI technologies are already being applied within banks and FinTech companies. An increasing number of AI solutions – with a very specific purpose – are emerging to resolve frequent tasks and challenges. Most of them are based on reinforcement learning and particularly in neural networks, probably the most extended approach in the investment use cases today. They are achieving encouraging results in fraud and risk detection, predictions, optimization, investment advice and services personalization and – my favourite – anomalies detection.

In parallel, low-latency/high-frequency trading software is being widely used by professional investors and traders, while commercial robo-advisors and financial bots are already democratizing access to intelligent financial advice. All these AIs usually have at their disposal many valuable datasets, thanks to the rise of the API economy and the expansion of open APIs and open data.

If we take into account the latest advances in cloud services, processing and quantum computing, AIs will soon be able to predict almost in real time, making investment decisions faster and more accurate than any human helped by traditional software tools.

How will a "superintelligence explosion" leveraged by this type of AI, specialized in investments, impact the financial industry? The financial singularity could be the answer.

When AIs Rule the Markets: The Financial Singularity

This concept of "financial singularity" describes a future state where, as a result of the convergence of the most advanced computer technologies – such as big data, machine learning, deep learning, blockchains, ultra-powerful processors, quantum computing (now beginning) and cloud computing – we will be able to predict, with minimal errors, all market behaviours and trends. A decisive point from which investors (humans or machines) could determine prices perfectly for every asset in the world, minimizing their risks and increasing the ratio of their correct decisions. It refers to a time when markets could work almost automatically, governed by technology and, consequently, the chance of achieving outperformance (alpha) will go progressively to zero.[2]

The financial singularity is described by some economists as a theoretical moment in the future when most investment and economic decisions in the world (or even all of them) will be made by superintelligent machines rather than humans, financial organizations or investment experts. If human fallibility is removed from the markets, and asset prices reflect real value, then a utopian period of super-efficient markets will become a reality as a result.

In their book *The Incredible Shrinking Alpha*,[3] Larry E. Swedroe and Andrew L. Berkin pose a decisive question about this environment. Alpha is defined as the outperformance of an investment against a market index: will the alpha opportunity eventually go to zero for every investment strategy in the future?

If not, my question is: could the financial singularity have an equivalent "events horizon", a non-return line defined by minimum possible alphas?

In order to reach the "financial events horizon" – the point with the lowest alphas ever generated by the financial industry and, therefore, the nearest moment to a hypothetical financial singularity in the financial history – we'll have to admit that technology will be required to overcome a critical challenge: AIs are mostly reactive, not proactive agents, and they basically take decisions driven by external events detected or data changes. Could they be transformed into proactive intelligent agents, like human investors?

---

[2] Shiller, R. J. (2015). "What is the financial singularity, and will it ever happen?" https://www.weforum.org/agenda/2015/07/what-is-the-financial-singularity-and-will-it-ever-happen/.

[3] Swedroe, L. E. and Berkin, A. L. (2015). *The Incredible Shrinking Alpha: And What You Can Do to Escape Its Clutches.* Buckingham Strategic Wealth.

To create a truly proactive AI, engineers need to build "strong artificial intelligence" that exhibits behaviours and reactions at least as skilful and flexible as human brains. This is essentially the ultimate step before reaching the technological singularity. So, both singularities are narrowly connected to each other.

AI in Wealth Management

In my opinion, if the financial singularity happens, it will not occur suddenly. Before the entire replacement of human investors by machines, we will experience a coexistence transition, where AIs will make human investors' decisions progressively more and more efficient. AIs will learn from human behaviours using massive data: their mistakes, hits, reactions, decisions and results, merging their data with data from others. Investments will be progressively more competitive and they'll get better returns. Machines will turn into more intelligent agents, training their algorithms and learning continuously from investors, users and markets until definitely becoming capable of substituting us in making super-efficient decisions.

After the coexistence, a second phase – the stage of replacement – might commence, with a progressive and massive substitution, probably not fully, of humans by autonomous AI systems. This period could culminate when machines are able to make their own decisions – even legally and criminally. The AI systems would also show irresponsibilities, bad practices, faults or crimes in the same way than human brokers do.

The Rise of the Financial Events Horizon

I think it will be difficult for us to reach such a state of "financial singularity". Even if a superintelligence explosion happens in the future, it would not imply the emergence of super-efficient markets managed by hyperconnected machines.

The alphas probably never will be equal to zero, because external tensions – forces generated by the markets, which are chaotic, multicultural and with different interests – will be equalized to internal tensions. These internal forces will be generated by all the intelligent machine feedback, one to another, day by day: the decisions taken by one machine will be the input data for another machine, and vice versa. Machines will be continuously learning about the real world and market behaviours, including decisions and actions from other machines, using all the available data and insights coming from multiple sources.

Progressively, the previous chaos in investments will almost disappear but not completely, because not all the possibilities can be analysed and processed by the AIs, even with tons of data and the best algorithms and processors. They will always need more and more data to improve their predictions: the more intelligent competitive machines are, the more intelligent other machines need to be to compete in this extreme scenario. They will finally accomplish a breakeven, a point where most financial decisions will be perfect to a very high degree, but never 100% perfect.

AIs will pursue financial perfection in every decision (selling at the highest price, buying at the lowest price), but this is mathematically impossible in such an extremely complex scenario. And AI is basically mathematics and statistics. We won't ever finally reach this utopian and perfect order, designed and governed by super AIs.

It will be interesting to observe if and when we reach financial singularity, with successful predictions and investment advice offered by autonomous agents and intelligent machines. Maybe soon all of us will believe that reaching the singularity is possible.

Welcoming the 2058 Class of the "Galactic Academy of Wealth Management"

By David Gyori
CEO, Banking Reports Ltd

This is the exact speech of Mr Kelvin Helius – president of the famous "Galactic Academy of Wealth Management" – welcoming the 2058 class of students.

Dear Students, dear distinguished human and robotic scholars of wealth management, let me please warmly welcome you to the famous "Galactic Academy of Wealth Management", the number one school and think-tank of Wealth Management Technology in our beloved galaxy.

Your distinguished class, the class of 2058, is different and highly significant. This is the class starting its ambitious and challenging studies in wealth management exactly 50 years after the beginning of the GCTFS, the Great Crisis of Traditional Financial Services. The fearful GCTFS erupted back on planet Earth in the late year of 2008.

Looking back to 2008, now, 50 years later we have to conclude with a high degree of certainty that that was the point of transformation, the igniting force of the great digital revolution in finance. The 2008 crisis first awakened forces such as FinTech – the thousands of digital start-ups challenging the pre-crisis status quo of long outdated mammoths in all branches of financial services. Later, FinTech evolved into more specific and specialized categories of digital financial services, sub-areas such as WealthTech, InsurTech, RegTech, RiskTech, ComplianceTech, PayTech, IdentityTech, TradeTech and more have emerged. This is how our beautiful discipline of WealthTech was born.

Let me please proudly say that our prestigious institution, your future alma mater, the "Galactic Academy of Wealth Management" is famous for its progressive, precise and highly thoughtful curriculum of WealthTech.

Dear class of 2058, during the forthcoming two years of your intensive studies, your focus of interest and your anchor of activity will revolve around our renowned curriculum of "The 10 Pillars of WealthTech". You will spend long days and months learning, analysing and practising these 10 distinguished disciplines, the 10 pillars of modern WealthTech. Let me therefore please list these 10 pillars – the key building blocks of your years of study – and give brief explanations of them!

Wealth hibernation: As you very well know, about 50% of our population chooses cryo-death,[1] so they hibernate themselves as the end of their life is approaching. We have also had the first successful cases of reanimation, when people with previously incurable diseases have now been unfrozen and treated successfully afterwards. This brought the question of "wealth hibernation and reverse inheritance" into the focus of wealth management firms. You will learn how your future clients will have to be offered a choice between (1) wealth hibernation: while they are hibernated, their wealth is managed on a discretionary basis by long-term robo-algorithms or (2) reverse inheritance: while they are hibernated, their children and grandchildren inherit their wealth, but when they are reanimated, a so-called "reverse inheritance" process has to occur, when the reanimated parent or grandparent takes their fortune back from their children and grandchildren. The first product – wealth hibernation – is a perfect cross-sell product for "reanimation insurance" while the second product – reverse inheritance – has to be complemented by offering insurance for the descendants in case their ancestor is reanimated and takes his or her fortune back.

Ex-forex: As you become world-class wealth managers, it is paramount to understand the past. You will have to learn about currencies. Currencies existed for thousands of years before

---

[1] Cryogenics is the study of what happens to materials at really low temperatures. Cryonics – the technique used to store human bodies at extremely low temperatures with the hope of one day reviving them – is being performed today, but the technology is still in its infancy. Source: https://science.howstuffworks.com/life/genetic/cryonics.htm

they recently went extinct in the 2040s, being replaced by the GalactoDollar. The concept of a galaxy-wide currency is quite a new one. In the past, more than 150 different currencies existed. There were so-called "currency traders", making profits by utilizing the volatility of "forex rates". In the 2040s the GalactoDollar gradually took over and now, as you very well know, this is the sole legal tender in our galaxy. The Galactic Central Bank (GCB) maintains monetary policy, keeping long-term interest rates at around 3%. Before we immerse ourselves too much in current monetary matters, I would like to mention that back in the early 2000s it was not only the over 150 different denominations circulating on planet Earth, but there used also to be "cash". Cash was money printed on paper or minted into metal coins. Dear young students… I know it is very hard to imagine why and how these millions of papers and coins were circulating, but believe me: it all did once exist.

Astrocommodities: As humanity and machines have widened their living beyond planet Earth, new commodities have emerged. Looking at you, my young students, I can very well imagine that you have hardly heard of such exotic things as oil, natural gas, gold, copper or silver. Yet, they used to be at the centre of commodities trading. Our curriculum is modern and so therefore instead of these outdated commodities, you will learn about the new ones such as antimatter, stardust, gamma rays, asteroid soil, comet debris and meteor rock. We will also mention some more advanced neo-commodities, such as black hole extract and interstellar turf.

Law of robots: As I am looking at you, my dear students, it is clear that now over 30% of freshmen at our distinguished academy of wealth management are robots. You very well know that humans and robots are now equally important clients as well as wealth managers, cooperating and competing. The "law of robots" is an absolutely essential discipline. We will learn about such things as co-bots (humans and machines working very closely together), robo-ethics (how and when robots can have their own assets, their own wealth and how robots can handle inheritance among themselves), robo-

liability (when a robo-trader makes a mistake, who is liable and to what extent), robo-payroll (how much a robot should earn, how robo-salaries are set).

Transhumanist trading techniques: Transhumanism – as you very well know – is the physical and mental combination of humans and machines. 50 years ago it would have been unimaginable for people that our brains are now just downloaded to the cloud and so our memories are recorded and stored. One of the progressive trends in wealth management is to combine our downloaded knowledge with robo-algorithms. Transhumanist trading techniques combine the advantages of imprecise, yet highly emotional humans and precise, yet unemotional machines.

Holoconsulting: In 1894 people invented something called the "radio". This was only able to transmit voice. Later, in 1925 they built their first "televisions". These were machines that could transmit two-dimensional black and white pictures. In 1953 came televisions with two-dimensional colour pictures. Why did we have to wait till 2020 for the first really good holoprojectors to appear? I mean, it is so trivial that three-dimensional colour picture and sound have to be transmitted in order for people to be able to efficiently and realistically communicate… anyway. Now that our holoprojectors are transmitting real-life-compatible, lifesize three-dimensional images so easily, it is very important to learn how to holoconsult clients in a polite, yet efficient way. For example, you never project yourself into the house of a client without permission.

The virtual reality portfolio rollercoaster: Clients have always had difficulties understanding the true meaning of volatility – the big ups and downs in asset prices, throughout different asset classes. Therefore, wealth management firms offer the "virtual reality portfolio rollercoaster". You put virtual reality glasses on the client and upload the price performance of an asset or portfolio. The software translates the price history into a rollercoaster ride and plays it on the virtual reality glasses. In this way, the client can really get a tangible feel of the given volatility – the size of ups and downs – and the bumpiness and nature of the price history.

Eye retina trading: Traders used to have so-called "traders' screens". These were multiple physical screens in front of asset traders. This was inconvenient, and they could only have a maximum of five or six screens packed onto their tables. Now, traders work with the "eye retina trading" technique. They put in electric contact lenses – as you know, the electricity comes from their own bodies – and see whatever screen they want in front of them. By blinking and focusing on certain places, they can click and zoom and highlight things.

Comprehensive internet reader robots: Back in the 2010s there were about 2 million news articles published on the internet per day. Now this number is much higher, about 10 million news articles per day. In our galaxy, we are currently using about 600 languages (100 human and 500 machine languages). This is why wealth management firms have developed "comprehensive internet reader robots". These robots read all the news articles published and analyse them, by natural – and machine – language processing, to come up with daily sentiment calculations for each company traded. This daily news sentiment analysis put together provides a sentiment history. The daily sentiment numbers and sentiment histories are beautifully visualized on three-dimensional gauges.

Human biosentiment sensors: For hundreds of years of the stock market, people have been talking about "the sentiment of the market". They could conclude that "the market is nervous", "the market is depressed" or "the market is euphoric". As if the market was a human being. Now we already have the technology to truly measure market sentiment. This is why we put biosensors on every trader and analyst. We measure their blood pressure, their heart beat, their respiration and much more. This data – through an internet of things mechanism – is centralized galaxy-wide and therefore we have a true biologically measured market sentiment aggregation.

Dear class of 2058: as you see from the 10 pillars of our curriculum, we are living in exciting times. Let me please express my happiness and appreciation at seeing you here as the new incoming class of our beloved "Galactic Academy of Wealth Management". Let me please say to you loud and clear: WELCOME! Welcome to the new world of WealthTech!

List of Contributors

All chapters are included in this book, all abstracts can be read online on http://fintechcircle.com/insights/.

Giles Adu
Co-Founder, ClearMacro
www.linkedin.com/in/gilesadu/
www.twitter.com/gilesadu1

See chapter:
Wealth Managers Can Deliver Effective Client Outcomes with a Data-Driven Investment Process

Robert Alcorn, CFA
Founder, Vestor.io
www.linkedin.com/in/robertalcorncfa
www.twitter.com/robalc77

See abstract:
Horses for Courses – Which "Robo" Will Get You Over the Finish Line?

Nicole Anderson
Emerging Technology Innovation and Investment Expert, Managing Partner, REDSAND PARTNERS
www.linkedin.com/in/nicolejmanderson
www.twitter.com/NicoleAnMo

See abstract:
Innovation and Investment – WealthTech a Catalyst for displacement of VC's by Asset Managers?

Guillaume Andreu
Associate Director, Julhiet Sterwen
www.linkedin.com/in/guillaume-andreu-644505
www.twitter.com/andreou

See abstract:
How Artificial Intelligence can be leveraged to enhance decision making

Scott Andrews
CEO and Co-founder, InvestiQuant
www.linkedin.com/in/adendauchess
www.twitter.com/iQPortfolio

See abstract:
Disruption Investing Creates Brand New Asset Class?

Arez Aran
Founder, Panorama Investments
www.linkedin.com/in/arez-aran-93568636
www.twitter.com/Veztup

See abstract:
The Dawn of the Robo-Advisors

Stefan Arn
Head of WM IT and UBS Switzerland IT, UBS Business Solutions AG
www.linkedin.com/in/stefanarn/
www.twitter.com/stefan_arn

See chapter:
Use Cases and Monetization Challenges of Blockchain Applications in Wealth Management

Henri Arslanian
FinTech and RegTech Leader, Hong Kong, PwC
www.linkedin.com/in/regtech
www.twitter.com/HenriArslanian

See chapter:
How China is Shaping WealthTech and the Future of Financial Services

Chris Bartz
CEO and Co-Founder, Elinvar
www.linkedin.com/in/chrisbartz/
www.twitter.com/chbartz

See abstract:
The integrated solution for Wealth Managers: Comprehensive. Digital. Customized.

J.B. Beckett
Author and Founder, New Fund Order
www.linkedin.com/in/JonBeckett/
www.twitter.com/JonSBeckett

See chapter:
Fiduciary Robo-Selection is Possible in a New Fund Order

See abstract:
Have we seen the Tesla of the Fund Market yet?
Digitalisation of Fund Research and Crowd Ratings
Building Critical Mass in Boutiques: A Crowd Solution?
Rethinking Bull, Bear and Media Influence on Investor Behaviour

Richard Beetz
Project Manager, Exicon Mobile
www.linkedin.com/in/richardbeetz/
www.twitter.com/RichardBeetz

See chapter:
Survival of the Fittest – Cyber Resilience

Niall Bellabarba
Director of International, Elinvar.de
www.linkedin.com/niallbellabarba
www.twitter.com/NiallNilo78

See abstract:
Robots for Good

Emilie Bellet
Founder and CEO, Vestpod
www.linkedin.com/in/ebellet/
www.twitter.com/emilieldn

See chapter:
Empowering Women Financially – The Why and the How

Colin Bennett
Head of Digital Distribution, Global, GAM Investments
www.linkedin.com/in/colinbennett
www.twitter.com/colinbenne77

See chapter:
Presentation Technology – Enriching the Client Experience in a Physical and Virtual World

Frank Bertele
Founder and CEO, NETZ
www.linkedin.com/in/frankbertele/
www.twitter.com/netz_uk

See chapter:
No "One Size Fits All" – Personalized Client Service and Social Selling in Wealth Management

See abstract:
NETZ – Bringing business development into the 21st century
Building a High-Powered Business Development Engine for Wealth Managers

Shashidhar Bhat
Ex-Head Digital Banking, EMEA, Citi
www.linkedin.com/in/shashidharbhat
www.twitter.com/shashibhat

See chapter:
Making Digital Advice Personal is as Important as Making Personal Advice Digital

See abstract:
The Future of Wealthtech – a distributor perspective
Reassessing Operations' Role in a Digital Bank

Nick Bilodeau
Head of Marketing, Insurance, American Express, Canada
www.linkedin.com/in/nickbilodeau/
www.twitter.com/FinMktg

See abstract:
Holistic Financial Platforms: The Integration of Wealth Management Across Personal Financial Service

Paula Blazquez
Head of Inno Capital, InnoCells
www.linkedin.com/in/paulablazquez
www.twitter.com/PauBSBS

See abstract:
The Roboadvisor Fever

Jukka Blomberg
Founder and CEO, WealthyTec
www.linkedin.com/in/jukkab
www.twitter.com/JukkaBlomberg

See abstract:
Robos – The Future of Investment Advisory

Mariusz C. Bodek
Digital Transformation Executive, KPMG
www.linkedin.com/in/mariuszbodek/
www.twitter.com/mariuszbodek

See chapter:
Leveraging Corporate Innovation by Opening Banks to External Ecosystems

Dr Alessandro Bologna
Investment Advisor, Deutsche Bank S.p.A. – Wealth Management
www.linkedin.com/in/alessandro-bologna-aaa99a54
www.twitter.com/ale_bologna?s=09

See chapter:
The Ingredients of IKEA's Approach for a Starry Wealth Management – Choose to Change the Competitive Arena in a Mature Sector

David Craig
President, Financial and Risk, Thomson Reuters
www.linkedin.com/in/davidwicraig
www.twitter.com/davidwicraig

See abstract:
The augmented investment management industry

Denisse Cuellar
Fintechs and Startups Partnership Manager, Banco de Credito BCP
www.linkedin.com/in/denissecuellar
www.twitter.com/denissefintech

See abstract:
WealthTech in Latin America – Just the beginning

Yawei Cui
Senior Academic Director, Moodys Analytics
www.linkedin.com/in/cuiyawei
www.twitter.com/CuiYawei

See abstract:
How Do Highly Customizable and Adaptive Robo-Advisors 2.0 Change Wealth Management Landscape?

Neil Darke
Founder and CEO, The Lifehouse.Co
www.linkedin.com/in/neildarke
www.twitter.com/TheLifehouseCo

See abstract:
Beyond Wealth: Financial Wellbeing

José Manuel de la Chica Rodriguez
CTO Santander Universities, Banco Santander
www.linkedin.com/in/delachica/
www.twitter.com/Delachica

See chapter:
From the Technological to the Financial Singularity – A Journey Without Return to the Future of Finance

Dean Demellweek
Senior Digital Transformation Manager, BNP Paribas
www.linkedin.com/in/deandemellweek
www.twitter.com/deandemellweek

See chapter:
How Blockchain Drives Innovation in Asset Management

Xavier De Pauw
CEO, MeDirect Bank
www.linkedin.com/in/xdepauw/
www.twitter.com/XavierDePauw

See chapter:
Launching MeDirect Bank as a Challenger Bank

Charles D'Haussy
Head of FinTech, Invest Hong Kong
www.linkedin.com/in/charlesdhaussy/
www.twitter.com/charlesdhaussy

See chapter:
Welcoming an Artificial Intelligence Robot as a Colleague

Dr Claude Diderich
Managing Director, Diderich Consulting LLC
www.linkedin.com/in/diderich/
www.twitter.com/diderichconsult

See chapter:
The Wealth Management Canvas – A Framework for Designing the WealthTech Firm of the Future

See abstract:
Strategizing about Robo-Advice

Dr Daniel Diemers
Partner Financial Services, PwC Strategy
www.linkedin.com/in/ddiemers/
www.twitter.com/DanielDiemers

See chapter:
WealthTech – Taking Private Banking and Wealth Management Digital

Martin Dienstbier
Technology Transfer Manager, IOCB TTO
www.linkedin.com/in/martin-dienstbier-147bb59/
www.twitter.com/brokerchooser

See abstract:
An individual investor's guide to the online brokerage galaxy

Vladimir Dimitroff
Principal, Synpulse
www.linkedin.com/in/vdimitroff
www.twitter.com/Maistora

See abstract:
Customers Rediscovered
Wealth reimagined
Robots in the next-gen Operating Models

Patrick Donaldson

Head of Market Development, Wealth Management Asia, Thomson Reuters
www.linkedin.com/in/patrickdonaldsontr/
www.twitter.com/GPMDonaldson

See chapter:
The Augmented Investment Management Industry

Alpesh Doshi

Managing Partner, CEO, Fintricity
www.linkedin.com/in/alpeshdoshi
www.twitter.com/alpeshdoshi

See chapter:
An Industry Driven by Digital, Data and Artificial Intelligence

David Dowsett

Global Head of Strategy, Innovation and Emerging Technology, Invesco
www.linkedin.com/in/david-dowsett-a9b6b/
www.twitter.com/GPMDonaldson

See chapter:
Embracing Emerging Technology

Steven Dryall

Principal, Incipient Industries
www.linkedin.com/in/sdryall
www.twitter.com/SDryall

See chapter:
Cryptocurrencies and Blockchain

Jan Enno Einfeld

Head of Investing, Comdirect bank AG
www.linkedin.com/in/jeeinfeld/
www.twitter.com/jeeinfeld

See chapter:
Leveraging Corporate Innovation by Opening Banks to External Ecosystems

Matt Elton

CEO and Co-Founder, FinnoLux
www.linkedin.com/in/mattelton
www.twitter.com/fintech_matt

See abstract:
Digital Transformation of Private Banking

Bill Eng

Co-Founder and CEO, FinChat Technology
www.linkedin.com/in/bill-eng-7a10a0114/
www.twitter.com/finchat_logger

See abstract:
Compliant Social Messaging in Client Advisory

Günes Ergun

Managing Consultant, East Management Consulting
www.linkedin.com/in/g%C3%BCnes-ergun-4a029248/
www.twitter.com/gunesergun

See chapter:
How to Unlock WealthTech in Turkey

Bruno Esteves Macedo

FinTech and Digital Banking Speaker, Business Architect, five degrees
www.linkedin.com/in/armindom
www.twitter.com/armindom

See chapter:
Security in the Future of WealthTech

Mario Facchinetti

Innovation In Real Estate, SwissPropTech
www.linkedin.com/in/m-facchinetti/
www.twitter.com/swissproptech

See abstract:
SwissPropTech

Balazs Faluvegi

CEO, Blueopes Co.
www.linkedin.com/in/faluvegi
www.twitter.com/bf79

See abstract:
Social Responsibility and Impact Calculation – the Inevitable way for robos in the next decade

Catherine Flax

CEO, Pefin
www.linkedin.com/in/catherineflax/
www.twitter.com/CatherineFlax

See chapter:
Personal Financial Intelligence – AI and the Future of Money Management

Jerry Floros
Founder and CEO, MoneyDrome Ltd
www.linkedin.com/in/jerryfloros/
www.twitter.com/Moneydrome

See chapter:
The Investment Managers of the Future are Going to be Millennials

See abstract:
FinTech – The Penny has Dropped
A.I. and Big Data will be key to the success of WealthTech

Sascha Freimueller
Managing Partner and Founder, Dufour Capital AG
www.linkedin.com/in/sascha-freim%C3%BCller-b404ab/
www.twitter.com/s_freimueller

See chapter:
Transforming Banks' Wealth Management to Prosper in a Digital World

Adam French
Founder, Scalable Capital
www.linkedin.com/in/adam-french-2192034a
www.twitter.com/adamjamesfrench

See chapter:
Why I Left Goldman Sachs for FinTech

Dieter Fromm
Founder and CEO, moneymeets.com GmbH
www.linkedin.com/in/dieter-fromm
www.twitter.com/moneymeets_DF

See chapter:
Moneymeets.com – Germany's Leading Personal Finance Management Portal

Daniela Galeote
COO, Wealthinitiative
www.linkedin.com/in/daniela-galeote-4bb90326/
www.twitter.com/Wealth_I

See abstract:
Wealth Management Platforms

Mike Gardner
CEO, Agreement Express
www.linkedin.com/in/mikegardneragreexp
www.twitter.com/mikeagreexp

See abstract:
Building Operational Excellence to Remain Competitive and Client-Centric

Chris Gogol
Founder and CEO, WealthArc
www.linkedin.com/in/krzysztofgogol
www.twitter.com/KrzysGogol

See abstract:
Client-driven digitalisation – unpacking the complexity of wealth management

Kunal Goklany
Director, Operations and Technology, Citi Bank
www.linkedin.com/in/kunal-goklany-613426/

See chapter:
Making Digital Advice Personal is as Important as Making Personal Advice Digital

Yaron Golgher
Co-Founder and CEO, I Know First
www.linkedin.com/in/yaron-golgher-739230/
www.twitter.com/i_Know_First

See chapter:
AI-Powered Wealth Management Products and Investment Vehicles

See abstract:
From Chemistry to the Financial Markets: Finding Order in Chaotic Systems by Applying AI
AI-WealthTech Firms – Shortcut for Industry Giants Vs. Empowerment of Individual Investors

Emmanuel Gonnet
VP Product Management and Development, Univeris
www.linkedin.com/in/emmanuelgonnet/
www.twitter.com/egonnet

See abstract:
Fiduciary Algorithms: Holding Our Algorithms Accountable

Dr Laura Grassi
Assistant Professor, Politecnico di Milano
www.linkedin.com/in/grassilaura/

See abstract:
Incumbents and Robo Advisors in Asset Management: Implications, Digitization, Positioning and Strategies

Kris Grgurevic
Chief Commercial Officer, Niiio Finance Group
www.linkedin.com/in/grgurevic
www.twitter.com/krisg1107

See chapter:
How Gamification Can Attract Consumers to Sign Up

Benjamin Gross

Founder and CEO, Visualize Wealth LLC
www.linkedin.com/in/benjaminmgross/
www.twitter.com/benjaminMgross

See abstract:
The Future of WealthTech

Max Gutbrod

Principal, Baker McKenzie
www.linkedin.com/in/max-gutbrod-2109a210/

See abstract:
Adapting Asset Management to Investment Purpose

Wiwi Gutmannsbauer

COO Asia Pacific and Operating Head Wealth Management Asia Pacific and Head WM Omnichannel Management, UBS
www.linkedin.com/in/wiwi-gutmannsbauer-10439a45/
www.twitter.com/GuwiWiwi

See chapter:
Use Cases and Monetization Challenges of Blockchain Applications in Wealth Management

Peter Guy

Editor in Chief, Regulation Asia
www.linkedin.com/in/peter-guy-a702311/

See chapter:
FinTech and the Wealth Management Challenge

David Gyori

CEO, Banking Reports Ltd
www.linkedin.com/in/davidgyoribankingreports/
www.twitter.com/DavidGyori1

See chapter:
Welcoming the 2058 Class of the "Galactic Academy of Wealth Management"

Sascha Gysel

Head Banking Trends & Innovation, Head e-foresight Think Tank, Swisscom
www.linkedin.com/in/saschagysel/

See abstract:
Everything as a Digital Asset Class

Christian Habich

Consultant, ARKADIA Management Consultants
www.linkedin.com/in/christian-habich-2a3095138/
www.twitter.com/HabichChristian

See chapter:
White Label vs Hybrid Advisory – Robos Strategic Options in a Differentiated Future

Pierre-Jean Hanard

Partner–Startup Advisor, The Startup Platform
www.linkedin.com/in/pjhanard
www.twitter.com/pjhanard

See chapter:
Wealth Management-As-A-Platform – The New Business Architecture with PSD2

See abstract:
Social computing: an opportunity in investment advisory

Meirav Harel

Founder, MHfintechs
www.linkedin.com/in/meirav-harel-mhfintechs
www.twitter.com/meiharel1

See abstract:
7 Tips for Creating Excellence in Investment Trading Websites: Insight from Developing an Investment
Robo-advisors, Algo-trading and AI, VS. Social Trading and Crowd Wisdom: Seemingly opposing development

Martin Hartenstein

Head WM OCM Strategy and Business Transformation, UBS Switzerland
www.linkedin.com/in/martin-hartenstein/
www.twitter.com/MCKHartenstein

See chapter:
Use Cases and Monetization Challenges of Blockchain Applications in Wealth Management

Ralf Heim

Co-CEO, Fincite GmbH
www.linkedin.com/in/ralfheim/
www.twitter.com/RalfHeim

See chapter:
Digital Asset Management in 2020 – Seven Theses

Ryan Held, PhD

Managing Partner and Founder, Dufour Capital AG
www.linkedin.com/in/ryanheld/
www.twitter.com/held_dc

See chapter:
How to Digitalize Wealth Management at Banks

Harald Helnwein
CEO, Novofina
www.linkedin.com/in/Novofina/
www.twitter.com/novofina

See chapter:
Digitizing Wealth Management

See abstract:
WealthTech, first of all, is about people
Once Upon a Time

Tobias Henry
Digital Wealth Lead – Managing Principal, Capco
www.linkedin.com/in/toby-henry-79498b13/
www.twitter.com/tobiashenry

See chapter:
The Hybrid Advice Model

Dr Bolko Hohaus
Founder and CEO, HCP Hohaus Advisory
www.linkedin.com/in/bolko-hohaus-5406219
www.twitter.com/BolkoHo

See abstract:
The Uber Moment of Asset Management Just Ahead

Jasper Humphrey
Ex-Head Technology, Systems, Modules,
swissQuant Group AG
www.linkedin.com/in/jasperhumphrey
www.twitter.com/jasperhumphrey

See chapter:
Challenges of Digitizing Wealth Management Advisory

Laura Irmler
Senior Consultant, ARKADIA Management Consultants GmbH
www.linkedin.com/in/laura-irmler-260095138/
www.twitter.com/laura_irmler

See chapter:
Digital Business Model for Wealth Management Operations as Matchmaker of Generations

Juho Isola
Co-Founder and CEO, TAVIQ Ltd
www.linkedin.com/in/juhoisol/

See abstract:
Digitally enhanced client acquisition process
What is value?

Vaughan Jenkins
Independent Consultant, META Finance
www.linkedin.com/in/vaughan-jenkins-consult/
www.twitter.com/amrfvr

See abstract:
Time Travelling Wealth Customers

Shalini Joshi
Wealth Management Consultant, TCS
www.linkedin.com/in/ShalinJoshi
www.twitter.com/Ishina

See abstract:
Reimagine Advice: Augmenting Human Touch with Digital

Dr Yannis Kalfoglou
AI Strategist, Samsung Electronics
www.linkedin.com/in/ykalfoglou/
www.twitter.com/plakatech'

See chapter:
Embracing Emerging Technology

See abstract:
Automation as a launchpad to the future

Blake Kannady
Vice President – Product Strategy, Director – User Experience, Envestnet, Inc.
www.linkedin.com/in/blakeckannady

See chapter:
The Networked Client

Oren Kaplan
Co-Founder and CEO, SharingAlpha
www.linkedin.com/in/oren-kaplan
www.twitter.com/orenkaplan2

See chapter:
The 100 Trillion Dollar Market Failure

See abstract:
It's time for a fund rating and advisor ranking platform
What do Wealth Managers and Fund Selectors have in common?

James Felton Keith
Chairman, International Personal Data Trade Association
www.linkedin.com/in/jfkii/
www.twitter.com/JFKII

See abstract:
Personal Data as an Asset Class

Gabriella Kindert

Head of Alternative Credit, NN IP
www.linkedin.com/in/kindert/

See chapter:
Key Success Factors in Gaining Market Share and Scale in Alternative Lending

See abstract:
Best practices and key recommendations for incumbent players to nurture innovation

Dirk Klee

Chief Operating Officer Wealth Management and Joint Chief Operating Officer UBS Switzerland AG and Member of the Executive Board UBS Switzerland AG, UBS Business Solutions
www.linkedin.com/in/dirkkleeinnovationarchitect/
www.twitter.com/dirk_klee

See chapter:
Use Cases and Monetization Challenges of Blockchain Applications in Wealth Management

Suhnylla Kler

CEO, SDB Asset Management
www.linkedin.com/in/suhnylla-kler-17312b3/

See chapter:
"To Infinity and Beyond!" – Building WealthTech Applications has Never Been Easier

Desiree Klingler

Senior Consultant, Roland Berger
www.linkedin.com/in/désirée-klingler-50046689/

See abstract:
Robo-advisory: Digital first – Human second?

Matthias Koller

Director, Wealth Management Innovation Lab, UBS Switzerland AG
www.linkedin.com/in/matthiaskoller/
www.twitter.com/matthiaskoller

See abstract:
Future Wealthy Individuals: Who are they? What do they need? Emerging technologies: What matters next?

Anida Krajina

Marketing, Tritra
www.linkedin.com/in/anidakrajina/

See abstract:
AI and behavioral finance collided

Jiri Kram

Customer Experience Solution Architect, Oracle
www.linkedin.com/in/jirikram
www.twitter.com/jiri_kram

See abstract:
Why architecture matters!

Alex Kreger

CEO, UXDA
www.linkedin.com/in/alexkreger/
www.twitter.com/uxdesignagency

See abstract:
WealthTech Future is About Providing a Delightful Financial Experience Creating Wealth Management Platform: If, What and How Considerations

Sandhya Krishnamurthy

CEO and Founder, S2E Consulting LLC
www.linkedin.com/in/sandhyakrishnamurthy
www.twitter.com/S2EConsulting

See abstract:
Creating Wealth Management Platform: If, What and How Considerations Financial Advice when Machines Make Financial Decisions on your Behalf

Andreas Kubli

Head Multichannel Management and Digitization, UBS Switzerland
www.linkedin.com/in/andreas-kubli-4a5445/
www.twitter.com/AndreasKubli

See chapter:
Use Cases and Monetization Challenges of Blockchain Applications in Wealth Management

Thomas Kuhn

Scientific Assistant at the Chair of Negotiation, ETH Zurich
www.linkedin.com/in/thomas-kuhn-a98b38100/

See abstract:
Business Drivers of Wealth Management

Veronika Kuznetsova

Managing Director, SuperCharger Fintech Accelerator
www.linkedin.com/in/veronika-kuznetsova-cfa-58a00136/

See abstract:
We Need An Intelligent Price Comparison Chatbot That Helps Us Invest In What We Believe In

Dominique Lahaix

Founder and CEO, eCairn Inc
www.linkedin.com/in/dlahaix
www.twitter.com/dominiq

See abstract:

Social Selling and Building Trust on Social Platforms

Peter Lancos

CEO, Exate Technology

www.linkedin.com/in/peter-lancos-b51b71ab

See abstract:

Internal Data Controls – Cost or Opportunity?

Dr Veronica Lange

Head of Innovation Group Technology Office,
UBS Business Solutions AG

www.linkedin.com/in/veronica-lange-2b83692/

www.twitter.com/verolange

See chapter:

Use Cases and Monetization Challenges of Blockchain
Applications in Wealth Management

Kamales Lardi

Founder and Managing Partner, Lardi & Partner
Consulting GmbH

www.linkedin.com/in/kamaleslardi/

www.twitter.com/KamLardi

See chapter:

Wealth Management is Dead, Long Live
Wealth Management

Kirsi Larkiala

Board Executive, Corporate and Investment Banking Executive,
Grannenfelt Finance Oy

www.linkedin.com/in/kirsilarkiala

www.twitter.com/kirsikkalar

See abstract:

How Wealthtech will change the rhythm of sales towards corporate
institutional clients?

Mike Lawrenchuk

Owner, 9999337 Canada Inc

www.linkedin.com/in/mike-lawrenchuk-039655123/

See abstract:

Power of the Global Community

David Lee, CAIA, JD

Managing Director, Privé Services Limited

www.linkedin.com/in/davidhyungteklee

www.twitter.com/misterdavidhlee

See abstract:

Three Factors of Driving Digital Advisory

Byron Levin

Director, FST

www.linkedin.com/in/byron-levin-39106a48/

www.twitter.com/FutureStartTech

See abstract:

Block by Block the Chain Keeps Growing
The #FinTech Fairytale
Looking into the future of FinTech rather than merely following the FinTech Illusion
The #FinTech Fairytale

Daniel Liebau

Founder, Lightbulb Capital

www.linkedin.com/in/liebauda/

www.twitter.com/liebauda

See abstract:

Investing in Innovation: Yes! But How?!

Gian Li Yi

Senior Manager, RHB Investment Bank

www.linkedin.com/in/gian-li-yi-193b0a27/

See abstract:

Smart Machine for WealthTech

Clyve Lo-A-Njoe, CISSP

CEO, Blue Arca Cyber Security

www.linkedin.com/in/clyve/

See chapter:

Survival of the Fittest – Cyber Resilience

Nik Lysiuk

Senior Analyst, Compeer Limited

www.linkedin.com/in/niklysiuk

www.twitter.com/compeerlimited

See abstract:

Challenges for the Wealth Sector

Bruno Macedo

Business Architect, Five degrees

www.linkedin.com/in/armindom/

www.twitter.com/armindom

See abstract:

Security in the future of WealthTech

Amlan Mandal

CTO, BankerBay

www.linkedin.com/in/amlanmandal

www.twitter.com/awesomeamlan

See abstract:

A hybrid robo advisory offering

David Newman
Co-Founder, Delio
www.linkedin.com/in/david-newman-3ab2b23b/
twitter.com/deliowealth

See abstract:
Enabling Private Asset Propositions with Technology: Why and How

Iain Niblock
CEO and Co-Founder, Orca Money
www.linkedin.com/in/iain-niblock/
www.twitter.com/orca_money?lang=en

See abstract:
Peer to Peer Lending: Crossing the Adviser Divide

Niclas Nilsson
Founder and CEO, Capnovum
www.linkedin.com/in/cannilsson/
www.twitter.com/cannilsson

See abstract:
Islamic WealthTech

Uday Nimmakayala
CEO and Founder, WealthObjects
www.linkedin.com/in/udayn
www.twitter.com/udaybhaskar_n

See abstract:
Build your own Digital Wealth Platform in One Day

Mike Normansell
PR and Content Manager, Wealthify
www.linkedin.com/in/mike-normansell-mcipr-1300ab18
www.twitter.com/wealthify_com

See abstract:
What's the right amount of 'robo' for investment management?
What does the future hold for robo?

Eloi Noya
Managing Director, LoanBook Capital
www.linkedin.com/in/eloinoya/
www.twitter.com/EloiNoya

See abstract:
The New Asset Class of P2B Lending

Dr Bernardo Nunes
Data Scientist, Growth Tribe Academy
www.linkedin.com/in/bernardofn
www.twitter.com/_bernardofn

See abstract:
Behavioural Solutions for Digital Wealth Management

Shinsuke Nuriya
CIO and CFO, Crowd Realty
www.linkedin.com/in/nurishin/
www.twitter.com/nurishin85

See chapter:
Challenges in the Japanese Wealth Management Market – Digital Issuance and Distribution of Japanese Real-Estate Securitized Products

Emeka Nwonu
Lead Consultant, CrystalPearl Consulting Limited
www.linkedin.com/in/Emeka Nwonu
www.twitter.com/Emeka_Nwonu

See abstract:
The Future of WealthTech is Hinged on Collaboration

Johan Nylander
China Correspondent, Journalist
www.linkedin.com/in/johannylander
www.twitter.com/johannylander

See abstract:
China going cashless thanks to fintech boom

Rodger Oates
Consulting Partner, Tata Consultancy Services
www.linkedin.com/in/rodgeroates
www.twitter.com/rodgeroates

See abstract:
Private Banks are Zombies, They Just Don't Realize it Yet

Stephen Ong
Founding Partner, The Hub Exchange
www.linkedin.com/in/stephenjhong
www.twitter.com/thehubex

See chapter:
Wealth Management – Preparing for a Digital Revolution

Telly Onu
Fintech/Blockchain Advisor, Impact Ecosystem Innovator, Freeman Capital
www.linkedin.com/in/tvonu/

See abstract:
Intergenerational Customer Centricity in Wealth Management

Adam Oskwarek
Advisor, Spindizzy.biz
www.linkedin.com/in/adamoskwarek
www.twitter.com/adamolac

304

See abstract:
Emotions, Building Balance and New Asset Classes

Dr Jochen Papenbrock
CEO and Founder, Firamis
www.linkedin.com/in/jochenpapenbrock/
www.twitter.com/FiramisCompany

See abstract:
Graph-based AI generating new business models in Wealth and Asset Management

Alpesh Patel
CEO and Founder, Alpesh Patel Ventures Limited
www.linkedin.com/in/alpeshbpatel/
www.twitter.com/alpeshbp

See abstract:
Can We Really Change Behaviour?

Richard Peers
Industry Lead Retail, Private, Wealth Banking, Microsoft
www.linkedin.com/in/microsofta2z
www.twitter.com/peerster

See chapter:
Digital Super Powers – The Role of Artificial Intelligence in Wealth Management

Hien Phamthu
CEO, AssetMas
www.linkedin.com/in/hien-pham-thu-2a439143/
www.twitter.com/StombardAlfred

See abstract:
The Educational Wealth-Coin

Hari Pillai
Assistant Vice President, Channel Digital Strategy, Invesco Canada
www.linkedin.com/in/hari-pillai-b-e-mba-pmp-3355a415/
www.twitter.com/hpillai05

See abstract:
The new age of AI enabled investing

Katarina Prozorova
Founder and CEO, Robo-Advisor IIWOII
www.linkedin.com/in/katarina-prozorova-mba-13204691/
www.twitter.com/ikatarinai

See chapter:
How Emerging Technologies Will Change Emerging Markets – Welcome Robo-Advisor X.0!

Andreas Przewloka
Chief Operating Officer and Operating Head WM Europe, UBS Europe SE
www.linkedin.com/in/andreas-przewloka-27a0752/
www.twitter.com/pscherlo

See chapter:
Use Cases and Monetization Challenges of Blockchain Applications in Wealth Management

Alberts Pumpurs
Account Director, Financial UX Design Agency
www.linkedin.com/in/albertspumpurs
www.twitter.com/pumours

See abstract:
Human Psychology and Simplicity are Keys to Design Useful WealthTech

Dr Efi Pylarinou
Co-Founder, DailyFintech
www.linkedin.com/in/efipylarinou/
www.twitter.com/efipm

See chapter:
Empowering Asset Owners and the Buy Side

Giovanni Ravone
Head of Innovation, Rubik Financial
www.linkedin.com/in/giovanniravone
www.twitter.com/gvnrvn

See abstract:
AI and Tech Giants Will Disrupt WealthTech

Paul Resnik
Director Marketing, PanPlus and Co-Founder, FinaMetrica
www.linkedin.com/in/paulresnik/
www.twitter.com/RegulationAsia

See chapter:
How to Give "Sleep-Tight" Robo-Advice

Dr Lipa Roitman
Founder and Partner, I Know First
www.linkedin.com/in/lipa-roitman
www.twitter.com/i_Know_First

See chapter:
AI-Powered Wealth Management Products and Investment Vehicles

Pierre-Alexandre Rousselot
General Manager, KeeSystem
www.linkedin.com/in/pierre-alexandre-rousselot-3b48b951
www.twitter.com/keesystem

See abstract:
*Technologies That Wealth Managers Won't be Able to go Without In 2030
Digitising Wealth Management to increase client satisfaction
and company performance*

Michal Rozanski
Founder and CEO, Empirica S.A.
www.linkedin.com/in/michalrozanski1
www.twitter.com/MichalRoza

See chapter:
How AI Will Cause Robo-Advice to Completely Outperform Human Advice

Georges Ruchti
Senior Business Developer, Hypothekarbank Lenzburg AG
www.linkedin.com/in/georgesruchti
www.twitter.com/hypilenzburg

See abstract:
Another Swiss Revolution

April Rudin
President, The Rudin Group
www.linkedin.com/in/aprilrudin/
www.twitter.com/TheRudinGroup

See chapter:
Becoming Millennial-Minded is Key for WealthTech

Sam Rudnick
AUM Growth Manager, eToro
www.linkedin.com/in/samrudnick/
www.twitter.com/samuelrudnick

See abstract:
Building the Next Generation of Wealth Management

Anni Kristiina Salo
Marketing Communications Manager, FA Solutions
www.linkedin.com/in/annisalo/
www.twitter.com/anniksalo

See chapter:
*Dreaming of a Ledger-Free, Globally Connected Wealth
Management Industry*

Eric Salzmann
Co-Founder, fintechrockers.com
www.linkedin.com/in/salzmann-eric-a7970144/
www.twitter.com/Salz_Er

See abstract:
Social Banking: How to Make Customers Happy

Francisco Santos
CEO, Industrias Metalurgicas Nacionales CA
www.linkedin.com/in/francisco-santos-27438725/
www.twitter.com/franboracay

See abstract:
Translation to Spanish

Peter Sarlin
Co-Founder and Executive Chairman, Silo.AI
www.linkedin.com/in/psarlin
www.twitter.com/pesarlin

See abstract:
News and natural-language processing in wealth management

Joshua Satten
Blockchain Partner- Financial Services, North America, Wipro Limited
www.linkedin.com/in/joshua-q-israel-satten/

See abstract:
*Blockchain in Asset Management: Disrupting and Advancing Business
Architecture by introducing DTL*

Veronica Schaerer
Innovation Strategist & Project Manager, UBS
www.linkedin.com/in/veronicarebecaschaerer

See abstract:
*Banks are not going to die a slow death by a thousand cuts
That's why the future of WealthTech lies in Switzerland*

Sandro Schmid
CEO, AAAccell Ltd
www.linkedin.com/in/sandro-schmid-4508708/de
www.twitter.com/twitter.com/?lang = de

See abstract:
Robo-Advisor 2.0

Patrick Schoeni
Managing Partner, Jud Schöni & Partner AG
www.linkedin.com/in/patrickschoeni
www.twitter.com/schoenpa

See abstract:
*Blockchain Leadership – How a Technology Calls for
Next Generation Leaders*

306

Angelique Schouten
CCO and Global Board Member, Ohpen
www.linkedin.com/in/angeliqueschouten/
www.twitter.com/schoutena

See chapter:
How a Digital Architecture Can Lead to Tangible Business Results

Rob Seidman
Offering Manager, IBM
www.linkedin.com/in/robseidman
www.twitter.com/RobSeidman

See abstract:
The New Paradigm: Insights-as-a-Service

Nikolaus Seitz
Legal Counsel, FinanzInvest Holding Group of Companies
www.linkedin.com/in/nikolausseitz
www.twitter.com/nikolaus_seitz

See abstract:
Gamification of the customer journey in wealth management

Dorian Selz
Co- Founder and CEO, Squirro
www.linkedin.com/in/dse
www.twitter.com/dselz

See abstract:
Turning Data Into a Competitive Advantage For Asset Managers

Tushar Shah
Co-Founder and Director, Centrum Group
www.linkedin.com/in/tushar-shah-50b5421/

See abstract:
The e-property entrepreuner

Nael Shahbaz
Wealth Manager, SAMT AG
www.linkedin.com/in/naelshahbaz
www.twitter.com/NaelShahbaz

See chapter:
WealthTech – Business as Unusual

Monisha Shivdasani
Head of Marketing, Social Beat
www.linkedin.com/in/monashivdasani/
www.twitter.com/monisha2577

See abstract:
Are you curating your wealth management strategy to fit into digital disruption? Bedrock Banking to Rising Rock Stars

Enrica Sighinolfi
Business Manager Wealth Investment Advisory EMEA, Deutsche Bank
www.linkedin.com/in/enricasighinolfi
www.twitter.com/enricasgh

See abstract:
Give me something that I don't have. The Future of WealthTech.

Paolo Sironi
IBM Industry Academy, IBM
www.linkedin.com/in/thepsironi
www.twitter.com/thepsironi

See chapter:
Cognitive Decision-Making with "Insights-as-a-Service"

McKenzie Slaughter
Founder and CEO, Prohaus Group
www.linkedin.com/profile/mckenziemslaughter/
www.twitter.com/prohausvc

See abstract:
Making Self Directed Portfolio Management Social Intergenerational Customer Centricity in Wealth Management

Lex Sokolin
Global Director Fintech Strategy and Partner, Autonomous
www.linkedin.com/in/alexeysokolin
www.twitter.com/LexSokolin

See abstract:
The post-robo world of digital advice in 2025

Dr Jeremy Sosabowski
CEO, AlgoDynamix
www.linkedin.com/in/jeremysosabowski/
www.twitter.com/algodynamix

See chapter:
Financial Forecasting and Portfolio Optimization in the 21st Century

Konstantin Speidel
Program Manager Digital Transformation – Vice President, Allianz Global Investors
www.linkedin.com/in/konstantin-speidel

See chapter:
Just Do It! Using the Buzz Around Innovation to Empower Banks and Asset Managers

Florian Spiegl
Co-Founder and COO, FinFabrik
www.linkedin.com/in/florianspiegl
www.twitter.com/fmspiegl

See abstract:
Technology as an Enabler of Accessible and High-Quality Advice

Peter Stephens

Head of Blockchain and UK Group Innovation, UBS Business Solutions AG UK

www.linkedin.com/in/pestephens/

www.twitter.com/stephepa

See chapter:

Use Cases and Monetization Challenges of Blockchain Applications in Wealth Management

Sarah Stewart

Analyst, Strategic Insight

www.linkedin.com/in/sstewart20

www.twitter.com/sstewart202

See chapter:

The Counter-Intuitive Reality of Robo-Advice Demographics

See abstract:

The Financial Technology Revolution is a Myth

Dr John Stroughair

ex-Partner, Goetzpartners

www.linkedin.com/in/john-stroughair-61366112/

See chapter:

How Gamification Can Attract Consumers to Sign Up

Angela Sun

Global Head of Strategy and Corporate Development, Bloomberg

www.linkedin.com/in/angela-sun-68b6a33/

www.twitter.com/AngelaSunNYC

See chapter:

The Business Case for Gender Equality

Brian Tang

Managing Director, Asia Capital Markets Institute (ACMI)

www.linkedin.com/in/brian-w-tang-7131293/

www.twitter.com/CapMarketsProf

See abstract:

AI and Robo-Advisory – Opportunities and Regulatory Challenges

Rohith Thatchan

Investment Analyst, Bambu Roboadvisory

www.linkedin.com/in/rohiththatchan/

See abstract:

Robo-Advisors: A Gift in Disguise for the Wealth Management Industry

Denis Thomas

Associate Director, KPMG

www.linkedin.com/in/tdenisk

www.twitter.com/tdenisk

See chapter:

Blockchain as a Backbone to Asset and Wealth Creation

Hien Pham Thu

Team Head and Senior Quant Analyst, Deutsche Bank

www.linkedin.com/in/hien-pham-thu-2a439143/

www.twitter.com/StombardAlfred

See abstract:

The Educational Wealth-Coin

Eric Thuillier

Managing Partner, Investivity

www.linkedin.com/in/ethuillier/

www.twitter.com/ThuillierEric

See abstract:

Advancing the Robo-Advisory Proposition for All Clients: Wealthy and Non-Wealthy

Dr Roman Timm

Partner, Dufour Capital AG

www.linkedin.com/in/roman-timm-phd-95a307/

See chapter:

How to Digitalize Wealth Management at Banks

Marc Torrens

CIO, Strands

www.linkedin.com/in/marctorrens/

www.twitter.com/marctorrens

See abstract:

Personalized Wealth Management as the Next Wave of Robo-Advisory

Richard Turrin

Artificial Intelligence, FinTech, WealthTech, and InsurTech Professional, Chief Innovation Officer, Singapore Life

www.linkedin.com/in/turrin/

See abstract:

Wealthtech and AI: You can run but you cannot hide.

Matthias W. Uhl

CIO, FLYNT Bank AG

www.linkedin.com/in/matthias-w-uhl/

See abstract:

Digital Wealth Ecosystems are the Future of WealthTech

Mirko Ulbrich

Founder and Head of the Board, SAMT AG

www. linkedin.com/in/drulbrich

See abstract:

Stock market will change and classic wealth manager will lose Brick and Mortar WealthTech will move online

Index

INDEX